Overview

Contents

Understanding SOAP

Kennard Scribner
Mark C. Stiver

A Division of Macmillan USA
201 West 103rd St., Indianapolis, Indiana, 46290 USA

ACQUISITIONS EDITOR
Sharon Cox

DEVELOPMENT EDITOR
Steve Rowe

MANAGING EDITOR
Charlotte Clapp

PROJECT EDITOR
Paul Schneider

COPY EDITOR
Mary Ellen Stephenson

INDEXER
Kelly Castell

PROOFREADER
Kathy Bidwell

TECHNICAL EDITOR
Matthew Kirkconnell

TEAM COORDINATOR
Meggo Barthlow

MEDIA DEVELOPER
JG Moore

INTERIOR DESIGNER
Aren Howell

COVER DESIGNER
Gary Adair

COPYWRITER
Eric Borgert

PRODUCTION
Stacey Richwine-DeRome

About the Authors

Kennard Scribner started out managing a pizzeria, but when he found out he could make less money and work harder in the Air Force, he immediately signed up and was whisked away to foreign lands, starting with Omaha, Nebraska. (Don't let him fool you; he loved it there.) After earning a commission and several assignments later, Kenn left the Air Force to pursue his hobby of Windows programming as a full-time measure. Now Kenn finds himself teaching COM and implementing COM technology as he journeys around the town helping others get their projects off the ground. Along the way, he started The EnduraSoft Corporation to write and market ActiveX controls, although these days he's spending more time writing words than code! Kenn is the author and coauthor of several books, including *Sams Teach Yourself ATL Programming in 21 Days* and *MFC Unleashed*. You can reach Kenn at kenn@endurasoft.com.

Mark C. Stiver is a consulting software engineer with one of the world's largest supplier of information services for the legal and business industry. He has more than 11 years of experience working on a wide variety of commercial, industrial, and military software development projects. Recently he completed a two-year effort, developing an n-tier, distributed product using XML as the base protocol to integrate Windows desktop, Windows NT Server, and UNIX applications. Currently, he is involved in the design and development of XML-based interfaces for integrating with large-scale systems.

Dedication

To my beautiful wife, Judi, and my wonderful children Aaron and Katie,
as well as to the authors of the SOAP specification.

—Kenn Scribner

I thank God for my beautiful wife, Donna, and my three wonderful children
Brendan, Nicholas, and Sydney. They are the true measure of my life.

—Mark Stiver

Acknowledgments

Whew! There turned out to be a lot more to SOAP than I first had thought! I couldn't have made it through this book without the help of a lot of special people, starting with my wife, Judi, and my kids Aaron and Katie. Their loving kindness while I pecked away at my keyboard helped me many times in the wee hours of the morning. No way could I have completed this material without the awesome help of my partner in crime, Mark Stiver. Mark was a pleasure to work with, as always, and as is usual I learned a lot more from him than I was able to teach, and for all of his hard work and dedication I'd like to offer my heartiest thanks.

I'd also like to thank Mike Culver of Microsoft for jumping in and sending the alpha copies of SOAP SDK. We felt it was important to cover what we could, even though at the time this material was very early in its formative stage. Mark and I know how it is when senior company executives put you under the gun! Thanks, Mike!

No book gets published without the hard work and dedication of a lot of people, and the hardworking folks at Macmillan are especially talented. Sharon Cox, the acquisitions editor, and Steve Rowe, the development editor, made this book a pleasure to write. Their patience exceeded that of Job as they waited for us to complete Chapter 10, which required a significant effort to complete. I'd also like to thank Chris Webb for, well, for being Chris! He loved the idea of a book about SOAP and kindly got us started. I'd like to thank Kirk (Matt "Kirk" Kirkconnell) for wading through the technical aspects of the material…any technical errors that remain belong to Mark and me. (And we apologize in advance if you do find the bugs we inserted into the material!) I'd like to thank Mary Ellen Stephenson for the terrific editing job. She actually makes me sound like I can speak the language. And the wonderful formatting you see was done by Katie Robinson…thanks, Katie! Finally, I'd like to thank the terrific crew in the back office, who tirelessly print the books and get them out to you. Thanks, guys!

Of course, I can't forget to thank the SOAP specification authors, especially Don Box. With any luck, Don, I've added some value to your work. Thanks for such cool technology! Conies all around when next you visit!

Finally, I'd like to thank you, kind reader, for picking this book from the shelf of other good books and shelling out your hard-earned money for a copy. Both Mark and I know how hard you work and how valuable your time is…thank you for taking the time to read this material. If you have questions or comments, definitely drop me a line at kenn@endurasoft.com!

—Kenn Scribner

Well, it's finally done. It's been a long haul and an enormous amount of work, but I'm glad we did it. First and foremost, I have to thank my wife, Donna, for supporting me through this effort. She didn't know what we were getting into, but she stayed strong. I thank my children for making me smile and laugh; they truly make things worthwhile. To my friend Kenn Scribner—he constantly listened to me no matter how insane I became. Kenn is one of the hardest working people I know, and his dedication to everything he does is unmatched. This was a project that I will never forget. Thanks, Kenn.

I also want to thank Mike Culver and Microsoft for their help. It's always fun to see what the next cool thing is to come out of Redmond! My first contact with Macmillan was through Sharon Cox and Steve Rowe. Many months and a roller coaster ride later, I have to say that these are really great people, who were supportive and helpful through the entire process. Thanks to the technical editor, "Kirk," for spending his valuable time to make this book a much better product. Thanks to Mary Ellen Stephenson for her hard work, turning our techno-babble into clear and understandable text. Thanks to Katie Robinson for making it all look great. I want to thank everyone else that has been involved in making this book happen, from the cover design to putting the book on the shelves—many thanks. I want to thank Don Box, David Ehnebuske, Gopal Kakivaya, Andrew Layman, Noah Mendelsohn, Henrik Frystyk Nielsen, Satish Thatte, and Dave Winer for their hard work and commitment to define a protocol that we can all use. A special thanks to Don Box, one of the smartest people I've ever met, who has been instrumental in making SOAP what it is today.

Thanks to Lee Zahn, for his strong technical insight, but more importantly for being a great friend. To Martha Lightner, for being a terrific manager and friend, but mostly for simply listening. To all the people I've worked with over the years, you have taught me a great deal and I am very fortunate for knowing you. Finally, to Chris Weiler, for opening the door to opportunity and creating an environment where we can learn and grow (and even catch a movie now and then).

Let's not forget you, the reader. I sincerely hope that you find this material satisfying and useful. Hopefully by providing this information, we will allow you to get an extra hour of sleep or spend time with your family. Thank you!

—Mark Stiver

Tell Us What You Think!

As the reader of this book, *you* are our most important critic and commentator. We value your opinion and want to know what we're doing right, what we could do better, what areas you'd like to see us publish in, and any other words of wisdom you're willing to pass our way.

You can fax, email, or write me directly to let me know what you did or didn't like about this book—as well as what we can do to make our books stronger.

Please note that I cannot help you with technical problems related to the topic of this book, and that due to the high volume of mail I receive, I might not be able to reply to every message.

When you write, please be sure to include this book's title and author as well as your name and phone or fax number. I will carefully review your comments and share them with the authors and editors who worked on the book.

Fax:	317-581-4770
Email:	adv_prog@mcp.com
Mail:	Brad Jones
	Associate Publisher
	Sams Publishing
	201 West 103rd Street
	Indianapolis, IN 46290 USA

Introduction

In September of 1999, with relatively little marketing fanfare, a new technology was introduced to the world. This draft standard, which specified the use of XML and HTTP as an RPC-like data communication infrastructure, was intended to provide a mechanism for distributing objects over the Internet. Since then, the *SOAP: Simple Object Access Protocol Specification (Version 1.0)* has been ratified (December 10, 1999) and Version 1.1 is now in the midst of heated discussion as people begin to understand this compelling technology as well as its implications. Today, the fanfare is loud indeed.

The basic idea behind SOAP is to use well-formed (eventually valid) XML as a wire protocol, or packet layout language, that can be transported to a remote system, typically using standard HTTP (Version 1.0), although other transport mechanisms are supported (Version 1.1). Ostensibly, this eliminates many of the roadblocks that hinder today's suite of distributed systems to one degree or another. For example, when using HTTP port 80 is commonly opened to allow Internet access through many corporate firewalls, but port 135 (RPC Endpoint Mapper) is typically closed for security reasons. Any RPC-based distributed object technology immediately fails if it tries to access objects behind such a firewall.

SOAP relies on many new XML-based technologies, such as schemas and XML links, and data within the SOAP packet is (recommended to be) strongly typed. Note that some of these technologies involve draft standards, possibly leading you to believe SOAP's stability is questionable in some of these areas. However, all the relevant XML standards appear to be stable enough to incorporate SOAP into your applications without fear of too much change.

Our goal, as the authors, is to bring you SOAP as it exists and to explain why things are the way you find them today as well as how things might change in the foreseeable future. Because SOAP is a specification rather than an implementation, we'll first describe what SOAP is and then provide a means to use SOAP by way of example. In all likelihood, by the time you read this, many compelling implementations will be available, and most, if not all, of them will overshadow our simple example. However, you'll at least have working code that implements the SOAP protocol and helps you understand the difficulties and challenges you face when distributing objects across Internet bounds.

The Internet Distribution Model

SOAP was initially based on HTTP, in Version 1.0 of the specification. This later changed to allow for a wider variety of transport protocols, such as SMTP or messaging protocols in the latest revision of the specification, Version 1.1 (still to be ratified by the IETF). Many contemporary implementations still use HTTP as their base transport protocol. Because SOAP includes HTTP in its lineage (and assuming you also use HTTP in your implementation), it follows the Internet Distribution Model. This model, in a nutshell, states that you fire a request to a remote server and then wait for a response.

> **NOTE**
>
> Much of the remainder of this book will assume the use of HTTP as the base SOAP transport protocol. One reason for this is SOAP was originally designed to be an RPC protocol, and the request-response model HTTP provides dovetails nicely with this original intent. Also, HTTP is still mentioned in the 1.1 version of the specification while other protocols, such as messaging or connection-oriented protocols, are not specifically mentioned. This is not to infer that HTTP is the only protocol that SOAP will support. The book follows this course merely as a practical concern, as it is easy to demonstrate SOAP code using this simple transport protocol (HTTP).

This model, by its very nature, dictates your remote object's design to a great degree. For one thing, you must program stateless objects, as all state information is lost from call to call. (Or, you must provide an additional protocol layer to account for this.) Any meaningful state information must be stored, such as in a database or a cookie, so that further calls can access the stored state and process the information. An example of this would be a counter object.

The Internet Distribution Model also has other ramifications, not the least of which is that you have no callback mechanism. Clients using your object must repeatedly poll your server as they await the object's method completion. When your object completes its processing, it can then fire the resulting information back to the client in the response packet for the particular poll iteration. (Again, you can alleviate this by providing additional plumbing, but the point remains the same—you must do the additional work on your own.)

This distribution model isn't inherently bad, however. It's very scalable and meets the needs of today's high-bandwidth servers. It's also very fault-tolerant, as any object state information is typically saved to a durable resource.

The Goals of SOAP

The original SOAP specification outlines two major design goals (from the 1.0 specification):

> "Provide a standard object invocation protocol built on Internet standards, using HTTP as the transport and XML for data encoding."
>
> "Create an extensible protocol and payload format that can evolve."

The 1.1 specification simply states:

> "A major design goal for SOAP is simplicity and extensibility."

Both specification versions list several additional aspects of distributed object architectures that SOAP avoids completely:

- Distributed garbage collection (orphaned objects)
- Bi-directional HTTP communications (callbacks)
- Pipelined messages or multiple call requests
- Objects-by-reference
- Remote object activation

The areas the specification does not address are left to the individual SOAP implementation's architect to design into a specific implementation. For example, a common (scalable) implementation to manage orphaned objects is to set a timeout period, and if the client makes no method calls by the expiration of the timeout period, the implementation destroys the instance of the object. This is not necessarily the responsibility of the wire-protocol, but it is managed by the remoting architecture as a whole.

SOAP's goal is to solve some challenging real world issues that hinder existing distributed protocols and architectures. While existing protocols do address the items mentioned, and SOAP does not, SOAP addresses areas in which existing protocols fall short, such as scalability and the capability to share disparate yet interoperable (using SOAP) architectures. (This book addresses these issues and more.)

SOAP and HTTP: Protocol

The original version of the SOAP specification is very closely aligned with HTTP, and both versions have you add an HTTP header to describe the object to be activated (presumably for an activate/don't activate decision). However, the original (Version 1.0) authors clearly knew other protocols would be of interest and left several protocol-related details moderately vague. At the time, their goal was to provide an approved specification to allow developers to begin providing SOAP implementations. With the release of the 1.1 specification, the path is clear to add other Internet protocols as transport layers, to include perhaps SMTP and messaging (to be discussed in Chapter 4, "SOAP and Data: Protocol Transports").

The purpose of the protocol, which in SOAP terms is called a *transport*, is to take a chunk of data and move it somewhere. It is up to the transport to locate the remote system and initiate communications. SOAP's role is to provide a mechanism for determining which object is referenced by the SOAP method call and to provide whatever information is required to complete the invocation within the chunk of data. HTTP happens to be the first transport the specification calls into play.

SOAP and XML: Payload

The arrangement of information within the SOAP packet, which is the chunk of data mentioned in the previous section, is to be textual and comply with quite a few XML specifications. The textual nature allows for maximum system compatibility, as all contemporary computer architectures accept text as input. You further can state which character set you're using, such as UTF-8 or UTF-16. (Note that this is done in the protocol header, though.)

But more than that, the text is in XML, which allows you to dictate what data content the text should encapsulate. Using XML schemas and namespaces, you can (and should) apply rigid data types to your remote methods. You can use XML parsers implemented on the individual systems to read your schema and extract the method information, or you can (someday) rely on standard SOAP implementations that will handle this for you.

Who Should Read This Book

This book is aimed at the computer professional interested in learning about the nuts and bolts of the SOAP protocol and what the various aspects of the specification mean with respect to distributed object computing. We, the authors, assume that you are familiar with the concepts involved with distributed objects in general and have a passing knowledge of HTTP and XML. The more you know about these topics the better, and a casual knowledge will do. But you won't learn them from scratch by reading this book. Other books directed toward those technologies will be of more interest to you.

SOAP is architecturally independent, so a given vendor's operating system is not required. SOAP works in MVS (an IBM mainframe operating system) just as well as Linux (a PC-based version of UNIX). As long as you can find a validating XML parser for your operating system, you should be able to implement SOAP. Having said this, most of the examples we will show were written for Windows using a variety of languages, including primarily Visual Basic and Visual C++. This wasn't done to endorse Microsoft or Microsoft products. In fact, although a team that included Microsoft developers wrote the SOAP specification, SOAP tries to be operating system agnostic. Instead, we used Windows simply because we have Windows-based personal computers in our homes, which allowed us to develop the examples more easily. The *concepts* the examples embody are what you should derive from the example code, unless you too happen to be using Windows, in which case you can use the code directly.

But like HTTP and XML, we don't intend to teach you to code for Windows. Instead, we assume that you understand ISAPI filters and IIS. (If you're unfamiliar with them, you'll probably find that the architecture you're using has similar mechanisms.) Always remember that the overall goal is to accept HTTP packets, process the XML payload they contain, and formulate a response. The implementation details are just that—details.

The book is broken into 10 chapters. Chapter 1, "Essential SOAP: A Comparison of SOAP to Existing Distributed Object Technologies," provides you with a more detailed look at SOAP, and then compares several contemporary distributed computing wire-protocols by applying a set of fairly standard distributed systems design criteria. This should give you an idea where SOAP fits into the overall distributed object framework.

Chapter 2, "SOAP and XML: The Foundation of SOAP," takes you through some of the newer features of XML and relates them to the SOAP payload framework. For example, you'll see how namespaces are used to disambiguate XML tags and how schemas are used to describe the remote objects.

Chapter 3, "Distributed Objects and XML: The Road to SOAP," provides a general XML implementation as an example of what people have traditionally done when using XML to transport data from one system to another. The goal here is to show how SOAP adds significant value by first providing a specification, so everyone is interoperable, and by specifying a well-designed architecture that is both flexible and complete.

Chapter 4, "SOAP and Data: Protocol Transports," takes you into the world of the original SOAP transport—HTTP. Here, you see how HTTP's constructs help you ship data from one system to another, monitor and filter incoming SOAP requests, and generally manage SOAP communications. You'll also go beyond HTTP and examine the impacts of using SMTP and other messaging protocols and how layering protocols affects SOAP's operation. You'll also implement some basic SOAP security logic here.

Chapter 5, "SOAP and Data: The XML Payload," shows you the basic layout of the SOAP data packet. You'll see how the object data is arranged within the XML document, what tags are required and what they mean, and how you serialize information into SOAP packets in general.

Chapter 6, "SOAP and Data: Data Types," builds on the information in Chapter 5 when you study the SOAP data types and how SOAP manages various situations. You'll see how simple data types are serialized as well as more complex data types, such as structures and arrays.

Chapter 7, "SOAP and Communications: Invoking Remote Methods," ties Chapter 4 through Chapter 6 together when you reach out to a remote object. Here you will see how SOAP responds to correct method invocations as well as various levels of error.

Chapter 8, "SOAP: BizTalk and the SOAP Toolkit," takes you on a slight tangent when you learn of BizTalk and Web Services. Rather than being a specific technology, BizTalk is more of a source for standardized schemas based on business type, as well as a proposed transport protocol in its own right. At some time in the future, you might witness the marriage of the concepts behind SOAP to the concepts behind BizTalk to create a stronger, more encompassing distributed architecture. Web Services enables you to use SOAP directly from objects you've created in Visual Basic or Visual C++, making SOAP method calls easy and painless. (At least, that's the goal.)

Chapter 9, "The Future of SOAP," looks at some issues the SOAP specification doesn't address, as well as possible future directions. Perhaps none of the predictions will come true, or maybe they all will. They are issues, nonetheless, and directions that contemporary SOAP developers frequently discuss.

Finally, Chapter 10, "Implementing SOAP: The COM Language Binding," brings you to language binding, which is a way of saying that the chapter introduces a SOAP implementation as one way to implement the specification. You'll examine both client- and server-side object code, as well as a sample application that uses the object when you see a real-world SOAP implementation that intercepts Windows Component Object Model method calls and formulates a SOAP request-response scenario.

Essential SOAP: A Comparison of SOAP to Existing Distributed Object Technologies

IN THIS CHAPTER

SOAP: (n): Hydrolysis or saponification of the sodium salt of a long chain of fatty acids.

Not anymore. There is a new SOAP on the block. The Introduction gave you an idea of what SOAP *really* is and why it's necessary. This chapter furthers that introductory discussion by more fully explaining SOAP's purpose, and then by comparing SOAP (as a wire protocol) to the commonly-used distributed object technologies and their wire protocols in use today.

It's important to remember that SOAP is itself a wire protocol rather than an entire distributed object architecture. On the other hand, entire distributed object architectures are designed around their wire protocols for efficiency. Some distributed object technologies concern themselves with security, for example, and carry security information within their data packets. They have mechanisms to efficiently encode the security information to speed the data's consumption on the receiving end.

Also, unlike contemporary distributed object architectures, SOAP makes use of *openly available* technologies that, when combined, specify a wire protocol. This protocol can be used to facilitate highly and ultra-distributed architectures. As you've seen from the introduction, SOAP commonly uses the HTTP protocol to transport XML-encoded serialized method argument data from system to system. This serialized argument data is used on the remote end to execute the client's method call on that system, rather than the client's local system.

This chapter begins by exploring the SOAP wire protocol and why such a protocol makes sense. Then the chapter introduces the wire protocols of other contemporary distributed systems to see how they are incorporated into the overall distributed architecture. This should provide you with a good feel for where SOAP fits in relation to other systems as well as help you better understand the SOAP specification itself.

The Argument for SOAP

After reading the introduction, you might wonder why the SOAP protocol is generating so much interest. After all, it is just another Microsoft XML-based initiative, isn't it?

In truth, SOAP does have roots in Microsoft, as one of the main specification authors works for Microsoft. That said, though, SOAP is a compelling technology in its own right and was honestly developed to be vendor independent. You can see this simply by examining the two fundamental SOAP technologies—HTTP and XML. These two technologies are international standards, and although Microsoft has played a significant role in the development of several of the key XML technologies, XML is nonetheless not under Microsoft's control.

A better way to view SOAP is based upon its technical merit. SOAP is fundamentally the combination of textual information shared via the Internet. The textual information is encoded in an XML format, which has specific rules for encoding and processing. The actual transmission of the XML data is managed by the transport protocol, which is (today) commonly HTTP served by a Web server. The combination of the open XML encoding style and the pervasive HTTP protocol makes SOAP possibly the most interoperable wire protocol yet invented.

If you are using HTTP as your SOAP transport protocol, then SOAP processing is very much aligned with the Internet, which specifies a stateless programming model. That is, object clients request services from a remote entity, which in turn responds with the pertinent information. After the remote entity responds, all state information regarding that invocation is destroyed unless measures are taken to persistently store the state information for later use. Regarding SOAP, rudimentary SOAP servers also follow this basic stateless, request/response scenario. SOAP itself doesn't preclude you from implementing more exotic servers that are capable of state management and decoupled request/response pairs (as with asynchronous callbacks). This makes it easy for scripts as well as more complex applications to implement SOAP.

Heavyweight Versus Lightweight Protocols

You will find a description of several contemporary distributed object technologies in this chapter. Although the purpose of the descriptions is to afford a comparison of SOAP to other wire protocols (and complete architectures, which SOAP does not provide), keep these questions in mind as you read the descriptions:

- How complex is the wire protocol for the given system, and is it an open standard?
- How complex is the given system?
- If you design a distributed application using the given system, what are the development costs associated with the system? For example, is it easier to hire developers who know XML/HTTP or an architecture-specific protocol like IIOP or RMI?
- If you design a distributed application using the given system, what are the administrative costs associated with the system when you ship your application to an arbitrary user?
- Does the selection of a given system bind you to a specific vendor, and, if so, can you easily migrate your application to another vendor?

One argument in favor of the SOAP protocol is that it is a tremendously lightweight protocol. That is, the protocol itself requires two fundamental capabilities:

- The capability to send and receive HTTP (or other) packets
- The capability to process XML

At this time, HTTP is a pervasive technology. One can hardly imagine a business that doesn't handle HTTP data, at least if it interacts with the Internet in any meaningful fashion. At the very least, HTTP processing is well understood and widely implemented.

XML is a very new technology—in fact, many XML specifications are not yet complete, which tells you that current implementations of XML processors will be modified and redistributed as the specifications become full standards. An example of this is the XML schema, generally considered a better way to validate an XML document. XML schema-based validation is not fully implemented in the current crop of validating XML parsers, at least not at the time this was written.

Nonetheless, XML is a compelling technology with a rich document object model that enables you to extract information from within the document with minimal effort. You can encode information within the document without regard to how it could (or should) be presented to a reader. For that, you can implement a document style sheet and convert the raw XML information into another format (currently either a different XML tree or HTML) for presentation. Although this is an exciting capability for many applications, especially Web-based ones, it's perfect for implementing an XML-based wire protocol for calling remote procedures.

Each of these technologies is relatively easy to incorporate into applications and generally requires no (or little) special administrative intervention to use. Products that ship using the SOAP protocol can, in many cases, use existing HTTP servers and XML processors resident on the user's system. (Some modifications to the HTTP server might be required to read the HTTP header and admit/deny the SOAP packet, which will be addressed in the upcoming section "SOAP and Security.") This makes using the SOAP protocol very easy to incorporate into the user's enterprise as well as very easy to administer.

Contrast this to using any of the other contemporary systems mentioned later in the chapter. If you use CORBA, DCOM, or Java RMI, you must install the proper runtime environments, have the users configure their systems to accommodate the distributed infrastructure, and administer the systems in addition to managing your application's particular needs. You will also likely need to reconfigure your firewall(s) to allow the system-specific packets to enter and leave your local network if they are destined for remote servers outside of your local network. In that sense, these distributed architectures are heavyweight systems, making the decision to use them and their protocols an expensive one in many cases.

Advantages and Disadvantages of SOAP

As with any tool, some aspects of using SOAP can be seen as advantages, whereas other aspects can be thought of as disadvantages. How you view SOAP depends entirely on the problem you are trying to solve and what constraints your current design or situation places upon you that limit your solution set.

The lists of advantages and disadvantages shown here are not meant to be comprehensive. Rather, the intention is to introduce you to SOAP-related issues beyond the technical details you'll find within the specification. You'll no doubt add to both of these lists as you become more fluent in the SOAP protocol and its implementations.

Some advantages of using SOAP are

- SOAP is built upon open technologies, rather than vendor-specific technologies, and facilitates true distributed interoperability. No single vendor dominates the SOAP market, at least not at this time.

- The SOAP specification can ultimately consolidate the various HTTP tunneling protocols (IIOP and RMI to name two) into a single specification, making implementations easier and potentially more interoperable. Note (as mentioned in the Introduction) that SOAP typically uses HTTP but does not require its use, at least not with the 1.1 version of the specification.

- SOAP will likely work out-of-the-box in a wide range of user locations that enable HTTP port 80 POST access.

- SOAP encourages loosely-coupled distributed applications.

- Changes to the SOAP infrastructure will likely not affect applications using the protocol, unless significant serialization changes are made to the SOAP specification.

However, there are some aspects of SOAP that you could consider disadvantageous:

- SOAP was initially tied to the HTTP protocol. This mandated a request/response architecture that was not appropriate for all situations. While the latest version of the specification loosens HTTP's grip over the protocol, you'll find many available implementations still use HTTP.

- Assuming true validating XML processors (with full schema support), managing the various schemas on an application-by-application basis will be problematic. Note that this assumes schema-based interface definitions, which are *not* mandated by the SOAP specification. They are an obvious extension, however.

- Given that there are no true validating XML processors (with full schema support), general-case method deserialization must be done by discovery.

- SOAP serializes by value and does not support serialization by reference at this time. Although serialization by value isn't inherently bad, it does mean multiple copies of the object will, over time, contain state information that is not synchronized with other dislocated copies of the same object.

Whether or not the advantages of using SOAP outweigh the disadvantages will likely depend to a great degree upon the requirements levied upon your distributed architecture.

SOAP Myths and Legends

SOAP was designed with a specific purpose in mind, that being to serialize remote method invocations using a readily available serialization protocol over a ubiquitous transport layer. If you reflect upon the requirements levied on distributed object architectures, you'll realize they must implement (at least) these four things:

- A serialization mechanism that converts the method call to a form suitable for transmission over the network
- A transport layer that ships the method data back and forth between the remote systems
- A mechanism that supports object discovery and activation/deactivation
- A suitable security model and implementation to protect both the local and remote systems from intrusion and attack

SOAP, by itself, is the lowest layer of "goo" (to use the word Don Box, SOAP's primary inventor, would probably use) that manages the first two aspects of any distributed object architecture implementation. SOAP specifies how things are to be serialized, using special XML tags and semantics, as well as how the XML information is to be transported, which is currently specified to be HTTP.

SOAP is not meant to replace the *entire* distributed architecture. The distributed architecture is responsible for implementing the remaining two aspects as well as a myriad of others. SOAP, for example, doesn't necessarily need to implement some form of security. Instead, SOAP delivers the data to the remote system and should facilitate, or at least not impede, security checks and balances.

The current SOAP specification suggests using HTTP as the transport protocol, if only because HTTP is the only such protocol mentioned in the specification. (SMTP isn't mentioned, for example.) In any case, SOAP is clearly intended to be used as a remoting protocol, and some transport protocol must be selected. For legacy reasons if for no other, HTTP is still the transport protocol of choice.

Finally, the SOAP specification alludes to the use of schemas to validate remote method calls. It does not *require* this, however. Even so, distributed system architects would be wise to include a schema for each object interface their distributed SOAP-based system will support when validating XML processors with schema support eventually become widely available. At this time, however, there are no validating XML processors with full schema support. Because of this, the possibility that schemas might be used should be designed into the system for easy integration at a later time.

Comparing Distributed Object Technologies

Let's examine the wire protocols of other contemporary remoting architectures. This is interesting because it shows you just how strong SOAP is in comparison. After providing a rudimentary definition for some remote architecture design considerations, this section will describe three contemporary wire protocols with respect to their design considerations, and then will examine SOAP in particular.

Design Considerations

Arguably there are many design facets you should consider when choosing a remoting architecture. However, for discussion purposes, the following list is used in this section:

- Scalability
- Performance
- Activation
- State management
- Garbage collection
- Security

The wire protocols are not necessarily responsible for each and every design facet of the entire remoting architecture. They don't all implement security, for example. However, each protocol provides some level of support for some or all these design facets. Some protocols transmit security information as an integral part of their data packets, whereas others rely upon external systems to assure a secure connection. Each of these design considerations is discussed to attempt to apply the same definition to all the wire protocols, beginning with scalability.

Scalability

Scalability refers to the remoting architecture's capability to deal with greater numbers of concurrent clients. Dealing with 5, or even 500 simultaneous clients is one thing. Dealing with 10,000 or 25,000 is another thing entirely. Servers have limited resources—processor throughput, memory, disk space, connection bandwidth, and so on. Bloated wire protocols require more processing time, memory, and bandwidth. More efficient object wire representations can be processed more quickly while consuming fewer resources. Of course, the wire protocol is but a part of the overall architecture, which in its entirety might be more or less scalable (connection-oriented versus connectionless, stateful versus stateless, and so on). Even so, the wire protocol clearly plays a part in the overall scalability of the given system.

Performance

Wire protocols themselves don't perform, but the architectures into which the protocols are integrated do. How well the wire protocol supports better overall system performance is of critical concern to enterprise architects. Some protocols facilitate increased server performance by implementing an efficient protocol, which is more easily processed than others are. Some protocols include everything necessary to process the remote invocation, requiring a single round-trip to gather the relevant information. Other systems might require multiple round-trips because of limitations or design features implemented within their wire protocols. Security concerns, for example, often force additional round-trips to resolve the credentials of a potential client, thus decreasing the overall system performance in favor of a more secure architecture.

Activation

If the architecture is object-based, the wire protocols don't actually activate the remote object in question—their encompassing architectures manage that task. How well the wire protocol supports activation is important, however, because it increases the overall system performance if the underpinnings of activation are included within the protocol.

State Management

Some systems require connection-based communications between client and server. This implies a myriad of system state management requirements to be implemented, reducing system scalability. Other systems are connectionless by nature, but this imposes increased system state management responsibility when dealing with related method invocations. If any state information is to be shared between method calls, the systems must persist the information for later recall and use. The wire protocols themselves give you a fair idea of how connection oriented the overall system is.

Garbage Collection

Garbage collection refers to reclaiming system resources consumed by orphaned clients and servers. If a client successfully activates a remote object and then subsequently loses the connection, both the client and server are orphaned. If one of the systems crashed outright, then the orphaned object doesn't represent a problem for that system. The computer will be rebooted and the system's integrity restored. However, some wire protocols support mechanisms for clients and servers to determine the status of the remote entity, enabling the remoting architecture to deal with orphans. This usually involves terminating the orphaned object and reclaiming the system resources.

Security

Some wire protocols incorporate security information to facilitate the remote object's or system's determination regarding the client's security credentials and to enable or disallow the remote invocation. This potentially increases the size of a given protocol's packet and requires additional processing overhead. However, this is not necessarily a high price to pay for a more secure architecture. Other wire protocols relegate security processing to external mechanisms, allowing the protocol itself to be more processing efficient.

Given these rudimentary design considerations, let's examine several current remoting architectures and wire protocols. With this information in mind, you should be able to see how SOAP fits into the overall remoting picture and to make a more informed decision regarding the distributed architecture you choose.

CORBA

The overall CORBA remoting architecture is shown in Figure 1.1.

FIGURE 1.1

The CORBA remoting architecture.

In Figure 1.1, you see the client requesting the services of a remote object using the CORBA infrastructure. The client is compiled and statically linked to its *stub* (called a *proxy* when actually activated). It can search the Interface Repository to dynamically invoke a remote object. When the client wants to invoke the remote object, it first calls the object's binding method, which causes the CORBA runtime to determine precisely where the object resides and forces the server to activate the object. Upon notification from the object that it has completed its initialization, the server will return an object reference to the client. The client can then invoke remote methods as it sees fit. You'll see some of the details in the following sections, beginning with "CORBA and Scalability."

GIOP—The CORBA Wire Protocol

Of interest to this discussion is the general purpose CORBA wire protocol, known as GIOP, or General Inter-ORB Protocol. The TCP/IP specialization of GIOP is called IIOP, for Internet Inter-ORB Protocol. GIOP specifies the basic wire protocol, whereas IIOP maps that protocol to TCP/IP.

GIOP specifies a series of messages that inter-operating ORBs can pass between themselves to generally deal with object location and use. (The client's local ORB, upon locating the remote object, passes the client an object reference it will use to invoke the remote object's methods directly.) The message type is stored in the GIOP header, which contains information common to all message types. Such information includes the size of the message, the GIOP version in use, the byte ordering, and an enumerated value indicating the message type. The data contained within the message body must be properly aligned, but the overall format is not specified and is therefore vendor or implementation specific. You can see this arrangement in Figure 1.2. Data is sent in Common Data Representation format, which is to say the receiver is required to perform any necessary byte swapping.

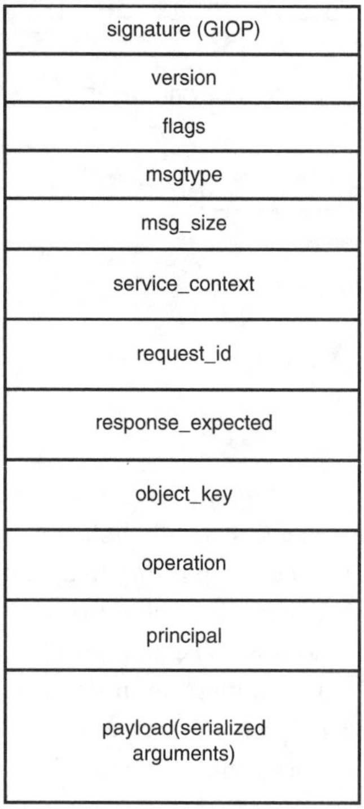

signature (GIOP)
version
flags
msgtype
msg_size
service_context
request_id
response_expected
object_key
operation
principal
payload(serialized arguments)

FIGURE 1.2
The GIOP packet layout.

The lack of a specified message arrangement led to the IIOP specification, which in addition to mapping the GIOP message to TCP/IP, led to the creation of the Interoperable Object Reference (IOR) specification. The IOR is an endpoint, an IP address and port, that is mapped to an object reference within an ORB.

CORBA and Scalability

Because CORBA implements a stateful programming model (at least implicitly), it is not as scalable as a stateless architecture. CORBA does provide a mechanism for tailoring the desired server scalability depending upon your needs. This is accomplished through the proper selection of the process activation mode (PAM). This is also related to CORBA's object activation model.

The default activation mode is usually *Shared Activation*, which uses multiple threads within a single process to manage object requests instead of multiple processes. Process threads require fewer resources per instance than actual processes, which is where the resource savings apply in this case. Conserved resources lead directly to increased scalability.

CORBA and Performance

After an object reference has been obtained, CORBA allows direct client-server interaction. Once you have determined where the object resides (from your ORB), CORBA steps out of the picture.

CORBA and Activation

CORBA relies upon its wire protocol for activation when it issues the *LocateRequest* message to the ORB. If the object location can be determined, the ORB passes the request to the specific object's Object Adapter, which can activate the object in one of four formats, called *policies*. One policy, the *Persistent Server Policy*, states the object is continuously active. Other policies involve true activation from scratch and will require the Object Adapter to access the Implementation Repository to obtain activation parameters. One such policy is the *Shared Server Policy*, which is related to CORBA's concept of shared activation; this leads to increased scalability.

Note in Figure 1.2 that the ORB and Object Adapter reside on the server computer. The Implementation Repository can reside on other remote systems. Thus, invocation might take several network round-trips to accomplish.

CORBA and State Management

Because all CORBA 2.0 implementations are required to implement IIOP as well as GIOP, they are by nature connection oriented. This allows individual object implementations to maintain state data between method calls.

CORBA and Garbage Collection

Neither GIOP nor IIOP support garbage collection intrinsically. CORBA itself manages object reference by reference counting, but the ORB manages each object reference rather than the object itself or the client. CORBA as a technology has no concept of distributed memory management, and any garbage collection mechanism is therefore vendor specific (reducing ORB interoperability).

CORBA and Security

CORBA's main security mechanism is the use of Secure Sockets Layer, or SSL. SSL essentially implements secure TCP/IP through encryption. However, there is a secure Inter-ORB protocol, SECIOP that provides a secure layer between GIOP/IIOP and the ORB. There is no intrinsic CORBA facility for authentication, authorization, or identity (the capability to impersonate another user on the remote system).

DCOM and DCE RPC

DCOM is arguably the most complex remoting architecture discussed in this chapter. It is also the least scalable, although it does manage security concerns well. The DCOM architecture is shown in Figure 1.3.

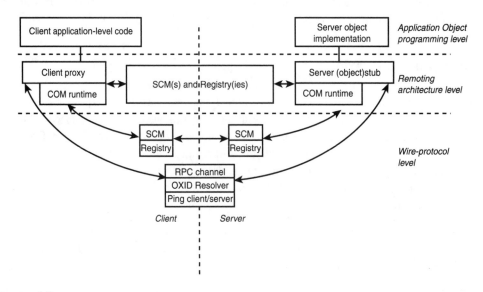

FIGURE 1.3
The DCOM remoting architecture.

In Figure 1.3, the client requests the creation of a remote object, which results in the client receiving an interface to a local proxy. The local Service Control Manager (SCM, pronounced *scum*) takes the remote system information that the client presented when the proxy was created (or reads it from the system Registry database) and contacts the SCM on the remote computer. The remote SCM activates the remote object and passes back the remote object's class object reference to the local system. This reference is given to the object's proxy, which the client then uses to create instances of the remote object. At this point, the client deals directly with the remote object, through its proxy, using a very DCE RCP-like wire protocol with certain extensions.

ORPC—DCOM's Wire-Protocol

Figure 1.4 shows you the layout of the Object Remote Procedure Call (ORPC) packet, which DCOM passes between remote object instances and their client(s).

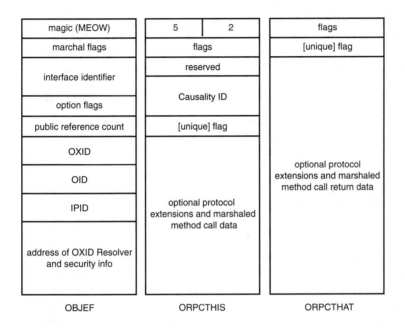

magic (MEOW)	5	2	flags
marchal flags	flags		[unique] flag
interface identifier	reserved		
	Causality ID		
option flags			
public reference count	[unique] flag		
OXID			optional protocol extensions and marshaled method call return data
OID			
IPID	optional protocol extensions and marshaled method call data		
address of OXID Resolver and security info			
OBJEF	ORPCTHIS		ORPCTHAT

FIGURE 1.4
The DCOM ORPC packet layout.

DCOM uses three very different packets for invoking remote methods (actually there are more, but these are the most interesting for this discussion). After some DCE RPC negotiations and security administration, the client system eventually requests that the remote object be activated (or accessed if already active). The remote system's response is encoded within the OBJREF packet, which identifies the particular instance of the remote object. The client squirrels this information away for later use. For example, the client is provided a unique object identifier (OID) as well as what could be considered an ID to thread context information (OXID) and a pointer to a particular running object's interface (IPID). The client will require this information later when using the object.

With the remote object's information in hand, the client invokes an object method using the ORPCTHIS packet (Figure 1.4). In Figure 1.4, you see the marshaled (serialized) method arguments placed within the packet along with the DCOM version (5.2), various flags, and the causality ID. The causality ID represents an invocation within a given logical thread of execution that can span remote systems. (*Causality* is used to enforce synchronization and to avert deadlocks in remote calls.) The server executes the method and eventually responds with an ORPCTHAT packet, which you also see in Figure 1.4.

DCOM and Scalability

DCOM is generally not considered widely scalable because of its garbage collection architecture and connection overhead. To be sure that all the participants in a remote method invocation remain online and active during the method call, all the clients involved in the call are required to send ping messages to the servers at two-minute intervals. You can change the interval, and even omit the garbage collection entirely, but this hampers DCOM's normal operational behavior and is generally not recommended. Regarding scalability, as the number of clients and servers grows for a given causality, the ping transmission requirements also increase. Ten, or even 100, clients and objects work well in this case, but the system falls well short when trying to serve (as an example) 1 million clients.

DCOM and Performance

DCOM requires several round-trips to activate and use the remote object. After you have the OBJREF information, however, DCOM allows direct object access. Obtaining the OBJREF information requires three round-trips, to include passing security information between client and object. The number of round-trips increases if the object requires activation.

DCOM and Activation

DCOM provides the SCM for activation purposes, and object activation is typically a two-step process. First, the client obtains a reference to the remote object's class object through its local SCM from the remote SCM. Using the class object reference, the client creates one or more instances of the remote object, through its proxy, with no further help from the SCM.

DCOM and State Management

Part of the reason DCOM is so complex is that it was designed to enable object location transparency. That is, the DCOM architects didn't want object clients to know whether the object was activated and used locally or remotely. The result of this is such that DCOM is very much driven by system state information, as evidenced by the pinging mechanism mentioned earlier. Although this does provide relatively seamless object invocation and use from the client's perspective, clients are free to maintain any state information they require (or desire). This makes the move to a more stateless model very difficult without rewriting both the clients and objects to a significant degree. Further, interfaces that were not originally designed for remote use often pose significant difficulties, such as user-interface–related interfaces or iteration interfaces. DCOM truly cannot be used without regard to the particular interface in question, although it does work (quite well) in many cases.

DCOM and Garbage Collection

When the remote object's system recognizes a connection break because of a lost ping, the object's system waits for two additional timeout periods (a total of six minutes). After this time, if the client system has not sent a ping notification, the server system destroys the remote object and reclaims the server's resources.

DCOM and Security

DCOM is very security oriented, although you are free to select the degree to which your communications should be secured. You can transmit information in clear text (least secure), encrypt both the message header and method call data (most secure), or select a variety of other alternatives that fit between the two extremes. DCOM also enforces the concepts of *authentication* (you are who you say you are), *authorization* (you can do what you say you can do), and *identity* (the server can impersonate another entity on your behalf when using the remote object). Although this slows the overall system performance somewhat, this security awareness is heartening if you require a more secure architecture.

Java RMI

Java's Remote Method Invocation (RMI) remoting architecture is depicted in Figure 1.5.

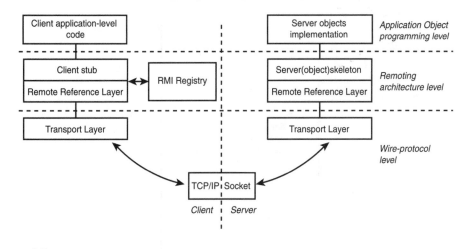

FIGURE 1.5

The Java RMI remoting architecture.

In Figure 1.5, the Java client begins the remote invocation by requesting the object's remote location from the RMI Registry (itself an RMI object, which must be implemented using a well-known network location). With the remote object's location in hand, RMI downloads a stub that the client can use to invoke the remote object methods. RMI is unique in that the stub can be downloaded over the network from the remote system. Other remoting architectures require the stub (or proxy, in DCOM's case) to reside locally prior to invocation.

JRMP—The Java RMI Wire-Protocol

As you can see in Figure 1.6, JRMP is a relatively simple protocol that consists of five main payload messages as well as five additional messages for multiplexed flow control. JRMP packets consist of a header followed by one or more messages. The header contains the ASCII codes for the characters "JRMI", the protocol version, and the sub-protocol to be used. There are three sub-protocols you can select: SingleOpProtocol, StreamProtocol, and MultiplexProtocol. *SingleOpProtocol* indicates a single message follows the header, enabling the connection to be immediately closed. *StreamProtocol* and *MultiplexProtocol* indicate one or more messages follow the header and the connection can remain open. MultiplexProtocol is used when multiplexing calls from both client and server on a single socket to conserve resources.

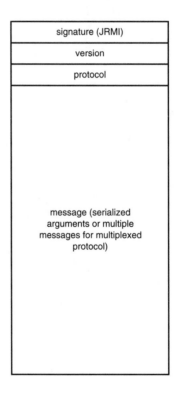

FIGURE 1.6

The JRMP packet layout.

The information contained within the JRMP packet follows the Object Serialization protocol (instead of CDR or NDR) and is specific to Java. Remote object information is passed by value, rather than by reference.

RMI is also capable of tunneling, which is to say that it can also be transported over HTTP. This allows for a much broader expanse of clients and servers.

RMI and Scalability

RMI itself is relatively scalable, but you still must deal with the RMI Registry. If the RMI Registry is limited to a single server, RMI's scalability could be more limited than if multiple Registry servers were used. Also, the StreamProtocol and MultiplexProtocol protocols are stateful and connection oriented, further degrading RMI's overall scalability. RMI's capability to tunnel using HTTP is a major advantage to using RMI in a highly distributed environment. Note this mode forces you to use SingleOpProtocol, which matches HTTP's own stateless model.

RMI and Performance

RMI employs a remote object database in much the same way that CORBA uses the ORB or DCOM uses the SCM/Registry. Clients must access the (potentially) remote RMI Registry to locate specific remote objects. After receiving the remote object's network address, the client can begin the activation process. Scripted Java applets, such as those that run within a browser, can also use RMI. In this case, RMI will convert the JRMP response packet to HTTP at a cost of increased processing time. Overall, however, RMI is very performance minded—it was developed to support Java specifically, rather than generic objects created from any given language. This allowed the protocol designers to optimize the protocol for performance within the Java framework.

RMI and Activation

RMI employs a lazy activation protocol that enables the client to activate specific server instances. After the client has selected the relevant server and object, RMI opens a connection to the remote system (a return connection can also be attempted, depending upon the sub-protocol) and the remote RMI daemon activates the remote object. At that time, any required remotely held Java classes are sent to the client (including the stub, if necessary), and the objects begin inter-operating.

RMI and State Management

Two of the three JRMP sub-protocols are connection oriented and therefore maintain state. However, you do have a connectionless alternative sub-protocol you can use to program a stateless architecture, so RMI is quite flexible in that regard. It is up to you to choose which model to implement within your own systems.

RMI and Garbage Collection

Java RMI has a strong garbage collection architecture, which makes sense considering Java's native concept of garbage collection. Like CORBA and DCOM, RMI implements distributed reference counting to maintain instances of remote objects. When a client obtains a reference to a remote object, the object is considered *leased*, and the client must periodically renew the lease for the server to consider the client/server connection alive and healthy.

RMI and Security

Java itself is very security conscious, so it probably isn't too surprising to find RMI is also security aware. Java applets using RMI are subject to the normal applet security restrictions. Java applications using RMI can elect to use the RMI Security Manager if one has been defined. The Security Manager then enables dynamic class loading and other features of RMI if the proper credentials have been established. If no Security Manager has been defined, RMI will still operate but will disable dynamic class downloading.

SOAP

Unlike the previous distributed object architectures, SOAP is merely a wire protocol. To truly compare SOAP with these other architectures, you would need to implement the SOAP protocol as part of a distributed architecture of its own (or replace an existing architecture's wire protocol with SOAP). Even so, SOAP offers many advantages, even as a wire protocol.

Figure 1.7 shows you the SOAP packet layout.

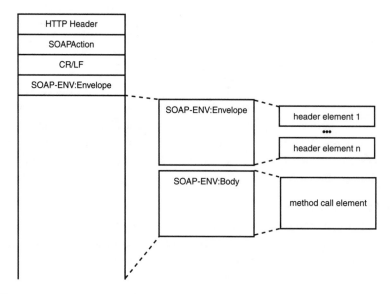

FIGURE 1.7

The SOAP packet layout.

From Figure 1.7 you can see that the SOAP payload is encapsulated within the SOAP envelope (which is itself part of the HTTP payload, assuming you're using HTTP as your transport protocol). The SOAP envelope, in turn, consists of the SOAP header and body. The SOAP header is optional, but, if present, must immediately follow the opening envelope (root) XML tag. If it exists, you'll likely find one or more header elements that provide meta-information regarding the method call. This meta-information could be nearly anything, although the SOAP specification uses the inclusion of a transaction ID as a specific example. The SOAP body contains the serialized method arguments. The remote method name is to be used to name the method call's XML element, and it must immediately follow the SOAP body opening XML tag.

The data is serialized in XML using a combination of XML elements and attributes. Even though SOAP specifies XML, which is text based, you can still identify arguments by reference and create structures and unions just as you would using a binary protocol.

SOAP and Scalability

SOAP commonly uses the HTTP protocol and is therefore very scalable in its native form. It is arguably the most scalable protocol investigated in this chapter, especially if the (stateless) HTTP request/response model is maintained.

SOAP and Performance

As a wire protocol, SOAP performance is somewhat degraded by the requirement to extract the SOAP envelope from the transport packet and parse the contained XML information. (Other wire protocols don't use XML, or even text, allowing for optimized information extraction.) The XML processor must be loaded, activated, and fed the XML information. Then the method call argument information must be discovered (assuming the lack of an interface/method schema that would identify the relevant information beforehand). This might not be a trivial undertaking as XML processors grow to support more XML features (and therefore require more system resources to operate). However, SOAP is quite interoperable, which perhaps mitigates the XML processing if you consider the other protocol conversions you must undertake to connect disparate computer architectures.

SOAP and Activation

Because SOAP is merely a wire protocol, it doesn't provide an activation mechanism. This is not an omission but rather a deliberate act to relegate object activation requirements to the distributed object architecture that implements the SOAP protocol.

SOAP and State Management

SOAP is inherently stateless if it uses HTTP as its foundational transport. HTTP is connectionless and dictates a request/response architecture. As with some Internet applications, you can save object state between method invocations, but this is outside the scope of the SOAP protocol itself no matter what transport protocol you select.

SOAP and Garbage Collection

SOAP itself makes no attempt to manage orphaned objects or support remote garbage collection. In fact, the specification explicitly states that this is not addressed by SOAP. SOAP, as a protocol, cannot manage all aspects of the distributed object architecture. A distributed object architecture that implements the SOAP protocol would also need to implement the mechanics of garbage collection (timeouts, pings, and so on).

SOAP and Security

Because SOAP is a wire protocol, SOAP does not implement security. However, SOAP can use the HTTP protocol, allowing you to potentially employ application-level security coupled with secure sockets or HTTPS. SOAP also mandates the use of the SOAPAction HTTP header field, which allows your firewall (or equivalent technology) to filter SOAP method invocations or deny SOAP processing entirely. Your firewall would examine the SOAPAction header and filter the SOAP packet based upon the object name, the particular method (remotable or not), or a combination of the two.

Summary

SOAP is a compelling and innovative use of available technologies that are not tied to a specific vendor. SOAP's purpose is to specify a wire protocol that can be used to facilitate highly and ultra-distributed architectures. To that end, SOAP uses a transport protocol, typically HTTP, to transport XML-encoded serialized method argument data from system to system. The serialized argument data can be used on the remote end to reconstitute the client's method invocation for object processing and response.

SOAP specifies a very lightweight protocol from an administrative and use perspective. Users of SOAP-based applications need only be able to (typically) process HTTP requests and parse XML data. These requirements are relatively easy to manage, especially when compared with the requirements levied by other contemporary distributed processing architectures.

As with any technology, using SOAP comes with advantages and disadvantages, depending upon your particular viewpoint. Some solid SOAP advantages include

- A vendor-agnostic technology base and wide remote system interoperability
- The encouragement of loosely coupled applications
- Relative application protection, should the SOAP specification change

SOAP will also likely work on a user's system with few system modifications.

SOAP disadvantages include

- General-case object deserialization must be done by discovery because there is no good way to describe the serialization pattern (it might change with schema acceptance)
- SOAP serializes by value rather than by reference, causing a dislocated object's state to differ. (Although in some cases, passing by value is an advantage rather than a disadvantage.)

Also remember that SOAP is a wire protocol rather than a complete distributed object architecture. Although SOAP attempts to provide conduits for supporting many aspects of distributed computing, it cannot actually implement all those aspects as many fall outside the scope of the wire protocol's intended use. SOAP also suggests using the HTTP protocol only—other protocols, however, are not precluded by the specification. SOAP does provide for schema interface validation, even though current XML processing technology does not yet offer this capability.

And finally, when comparing SOAP as a wire protocol to other contemporary wire protocols, SOAP fares well in most areas. It might take more time to process the SOAP packet than other protocols, simply because the XML information must be parsed. On the other hand, the SOAP protocol is very scalable and relatively efficient. It is flexible for growth because of native XML properties. Also, don't forget that SOAP doesn't *require* an object system be layered on top of it. Just like standard RPC mechanisms, some programming languages don't use objects and simply want to execute a remote method. SOAP allows for this usage pattern naturally.

SOAP and XML: The Foundation of SOAP

IN THIS CHAPTER

Communicating information is at the crux of systems development. This has become increasingly more apparent since the birth of the Internet. XML and the peripheral technologies surrounding it, such as XML Namespaces, XML Schemas, and so on, are enabling developers to provide greater flexibility in the systems that they build. This chapter discusses why there is so much appeal to using XML and how XML technologies are fundamental to the overall goals of SOAP.

XML's Appeal

Several techniques have been used over the years to communicate information, and many of them are still used in contemporary architectures. These techniques include proprietary approaches, spatial and referential schemes, and finally (and most importantly) structured data. Understanding how we arrived at XML provides insight as to why we need SOAP.

Proprietary Formats

Let's assume that two systems could agree on a predefined format, such that when one system transmits information according to this format, the second system will be able to understand the message content. For example, take the serialization process of an object-oriented system. Objects in the system can be persisted to a file for future use. However, this is typically executed in a particular order and, therefore, to de-serialize the objects, you must follow the exact same order.

When considering the serialized file approach, there is no room for mistakes. Any deviation from the file format specification will result in failure—or worse, incorrect data. You can observe this when working with word processors. Regardless of the vendor that you choose, your word processor documents will normally be saved in that vendor's proprietary format. The only way that a word processor can read files created by another vendor's word processor is by understanding the format specification. Typically this is not an exact science, so results are less than perfect. As new versions of word processors are released, the problem is compounded. As new features and functions are added, formats need to change. It becomes necessary for vendors to support the new format, the old format, and other vendor's formats. This is tedious and error prone.

Although establishing interfaces is necessary in any reliable system, the main goal is to provide interfaces that can grow with time without severely impacting existing applications.

When considering SOAP, the main goal is to provide open interfaces for moving data between systems. A proprietary system, by nature, can not and will not do this.

Spatial and Referential Schemes

Other forms of data sharing still require the definition of very distinct interfaces, however, the use of spatial and referential mechanisms enable developers to cleverly organize data such that formats are open and flexible. Given a particular stream of data, identifiers are used to specify that particular information immediately follows or references data in another location. This provides greater expandability, and minimizes the overhead necessary to describe the contents of the package.

One example of this mechanism is a layered approach, similar to the TCP/IP packet structure. At the TCP layer, data is divided into TCP segments that consist of *source* and *destination ports*, a *sequence number*, a *code bits* field, a *data* field, and others. The *code bits* field describes the type and purpose of the segment, and the *data* field varies in content, based on these *code bits*. Below the TCP layer is the IP datagram layer, which acts as the basic unit of transfer in the TCP/IP model. It contains *source* and *destination IP addresses, version, protocol, time-to-live*, and so on. All IP software is required to read the *version* to determine the format of incoming IP datagrams. The IP software can then accept or reject the datagram, based on whether or not it supports that version.

Solutions such as this are prevalent in many network systems and provide some degree of structure, average support for expansion, and reasonably compact data streams. However, the negative aspects include size limitations, data streams that are difficult to debug, and new formats that are adopted rather slowly.

Once again, SOAP cannot flourish in this environment. SOAP was founded upon extensible data streams that are easy to read and write, and formats that can change at will without negatively impacting applications.

Structured Data Scheme

With the advent of the Internet, structured data is becoming the de facto standard for communication. Structured data is generally more readable, easier to manage, and fairly simple to work with in a programmatic sense. Structured data is built using a *markup language* to describe the contents of the data in a hierarchical structure. The history of markup dates back to editing hand-written word on paper, but instead of circles and lines drawn around the text, today's markup comes in the form of *tags* surrounding data. The data contained within the *start tag* and *end tag* is called the *value*, and is similar to the hand-written word on paper. Together, the start tag, end tag, and value make up an *element*.

Consider the following example showing an element consisting of the start tag, <Tag>, and the end tag, </Tag>, with the value of 123:

```
<Tag>123</Tag>
```

When this principle is applied to the Internet, for example through the use of Hypertext Markup Language (HTML), it's easy to apply structure to data:

```
<B>Display this text in BOLD</B>
```

In this case, the HTML tags `<B>` and `</B>` are used to denote that `Display this text in BOLD` should be formatted with a bold font. A Web browser interprets this information such that it can graphically render text and images.

The grandfather of current markup languages is the Standard Generalized Markup Language (ISO 8879), or SGML. In its normal form SGML is extremely extensible, but very complex. It is actually better suited for creating other markup languages, such as HTML (an implementation of SGML), for more specific uses. This is how Extensible Markup Language, or XML, was proposed.

XML was created as a subset of SGML designed to give data *meaning* as opposed to HTML, which provides presentation information. XML retained many of the properties of SGML, but is smaller and defines extensions for the Web that SGML doesn't address. To capture the true essence of why XML was created, one only needs to read the XML specification. The creators of XML focused on 10 major design goals as summarized in the following:

- XML shall be straightforwardly usable over the Internet.
- XML shall support a wide variety of applications.
- XML shall be compatible with SGML.
- It shall be easy to write programs which process XML documents.
- The number of optional features in XML is to be kept to the absolute minimum, ideally zero.
- XML documents should be human-legible and reasonably clear.
- The XML design should be prepared quickly.
- The design of XML shall be formal and concise.
- XML documents shall be easy to create.
- Terseness in XML markup is of minimal importance.

Not only do these goals apply to XML; the majority of these goals are also at the heart of what SOAP is trying to accomplish.

Essential XML

SOAP's power is centered on the intrinsic behavior of XML and related XML technologies. In order for you to fully appreciate SOAP and its capabilities, you *must* have a strong foundation in XML. It is beyond the scope of this book to teach you the basics of XML. However, it would be unreasonable to assume that you understand all the emerging technologies associated with XML, because several of these are still undergoing development. Therefore, this section will briefly review XML to provide the basis for discussion of the newer aspects of XML.

Documents, Elements, and Attributes

An *XML document* is really just a collection of data, consisting of both *physical structure* and *logical structure*. Physically, the document consists of textual information. It contains *entities* that can reference other entities, which are elsewhere in memory, on a hard disk, or more importantly on the Web. The *logical structure* of an XML document includes processing instructions, declarations, comments, and elements. XML documents contain ordinary UNICODE text (as specified by ISO/IEC 10646) that represent markup, or *character data*.

The general form of an XML document looks something like this:

```
<?xml version="1.0" ?>
<Car Year="2000">
    <Name>Corvette</Name>
    <Color>Red</Color>
    <Engine HorsePower="345">5.7 Liter V8 SFI</Engine>
    <Transmission Type="manual">6-speed</Transmission>
</Car>
```

You are immediately aware that this is an XML document due to the *XML declaration* at the top, specifying that this document conforms to XML version 1.0. In this example, `<Car>` is the *root element* or *document element* of this XML document; `<Name>` is just one of the *child elements* contained within `<Car>`; and `Year` is an *attribute* of the `<Car>` element.

Any text document is considered a *well-formed* XML document if it conforms to the constraints set forth in the XML specification. For example, one very important constraint is the limitation to one and only one root element in a document. An XML document is considered *valid* if it is well-formed, has an associated Document Type Definition (DTD), and complies with this definition. These terms describe the overall quality of an XML document. Be aware that an XML document can be well-formed but not valid; however, it cannot be valid if it is not well-formed.

It is common to find *processing instructions* embedded within the document, but they are not considered part of the document's content. They are used to communicate information to application-level code without changing the meaning of the XML document's content.

The following notation denotes the syntax of *processing instructions*:

```
<?target declaration ?>
```

The processing instruction contains a target followed by one or more instructions, where the target name specifies the application in which the processing instruction is applied to. A common target name found in XML documents is the reserved target *xml*. This enables the XML document to communicate instructions to XML parsers. The most common (but optional) processing instruction used in XML documents is the XML declaration as previously discussed.

> **NOTE**
>
> SOAP v1.1 does not allow a Document Type Declaration or Processing Instructions.

Recall that an *element* consists of a *start tag*, *end tag,* and *value*. Rather than going to the trouble of using a start and an end tag when you have no value to include, you can combine the tags to form an *empty-element tag*:

```
<Car>
    <Name>Corvette</Name>
    <ConvertibleTop />
</Car>
```

> **CAUTION**
>
> Since XML markup—such as elements and attributes—are sensitive to case and white-space, caution should be used when naming them.

A parent element can contain an infinite number of child elements, and the same child element can appear multiple times under its parent element (as siblings):

```
<Car>
    <Name>Corvette</Name>
    <Name>Speedy</Name>
    <Color>Red</Color>
    <!-- ...etc... -->
</Car>
```

Also, the same element name can appear under different parent elements. In this case, the element <Name> appears under the <Car> element as well as the <SoundSystem> element:

```
<Car>
    <Name>Corvette</Name>
    <SoundSystem>
        <Name>Bose</Name>
    </SoundSystem>
</Car>
```

You are not allowed to overlap tags within an XML document. The following document would *not* be considered a well-formed XML document because the `<Color>` element starts before the `<Name>` element ends:

```
<Car>
    <Color>3721-<Name>Red</Color>Corvette</Name>
</Car>
```

This example is trying to specify that the color of the car is `3721-Red` and the name of the car is `RedCorvette`. However, this does not meet the XML specification constraints. Instead, it should be rewritten as follows:

```
<Car>
    <Color>3721-Red</Color><Name>RedCorvette</Name>
</Car>
```

Elements can be embedded within values of other elements:

```
<Car>
    <Name>Corvette</Name>
    <Base>MSRP<Price>39,475</Price>with options</Base>
</Car>
```

In this case, the `<Price>` element was embedded between the first part of the `MSRP` value, and the last part of the `with options` value.

Attributes provide more specific information about a particular element. Choosing between using an attribute or an element can sometimes be a difficult process. In a lot of cases, either form will work. One approach is to use attributes to denote element classifications based on the problem domain. Another aspect to using attributes deals with ease of access to data. If you want to obtain the car's color every time you encounter a `Car` element, then `Color` may be a good candidate for an attribute.

> **NOTE**
>
> The SOAP working draft uses attributes in a variety of ways. In particular, the `id` and `href` attributes are used for unique identifiers and references, respectively.

One big advantage that SOAP buys you is that it forces proper structuring of request data (and response data when applicable). This is extremely important when performing SOAP serialization. Incorrectly building the XML structure will cause the document to not be well-formed, and therefore to fail XML parsers.

The following is an example of a SOAP request, or in the most basic sense, an XML document:

```
<SOAP-ENV:Envelope
        xmlns:SOAP-ENV="http://schemas.xmlsoap.org/soap/envelope/"
        SOAP-ENV:encodingStyle="http://schemas.xmlsoap.org/soap/encoding/">
    <SOAP-ENV:Body>
        <m:Add xmlns:m="Some-URI">
            <Param1>3</Param1>
            <Param2>4</Param2>
        </m:Add>
    </SOAP-ENV:Body>
</SOAP-ENV:Envelope>
```

Although the specific details of the XML are not important for this discussion, notice the use of the processing instruction, elements, and attributes to construct a well-formed XML document.

Entity References and Character Data (CDATA)

It is not uncommon for the contents of an XML element to contain characters that are used for XML markup, such as <, >, ", and so on. XML makes a distinction between data that should be parsed and data that should not be parsed; it uses the terminology *parsed character data* and *character data,* respectively. Consider the following XML where the <Car> element contains data that should not be parsed:

```
<Car Year="2000 "The New Millennium"">
    <Name>Corvette</Name>
</Car>
```

The additional quotes in "The New Millennium" corrupt the syntax of the <Car> element, therefore the parser cannot interpret the Year attribute. Proper use of *entity references* allows you to instruct parsers to treat data as character data by using an alias notation that is treated as markup. The preceding example should be changed to:

```
<Car Year="2000 &quot;The New Millennium&quot;">
    <Name>Corvette</Name>
</Car>
```

Here, the quotes have been replaced by their entity reference and will now be correctly parsed. When the parser encounters " it makes the appropriate replacement of the markup with the actual character data. XML provides several predefined entity references for ampersand (&), less-than (<), greater-than (>), quote ("), and apostrophe ('). You can also define your own entity references based on the character set defined in your XML document, for example

```
<!ENTITY copy "&#169;">
```

In this case, the copy entity reference is used to represent the copyright symbol, which happens to be character 169 in the associated character set.

CDATA is an alternate form of markup that is better for larger quantities of text to be explicitly described as character data, as shown here:

```
<Car Year="2000">
    <Name>Corvette</Name>
    <Description><![CDATA["I bet it's fast!"]]></Description>
</Car>
```

Rather than using entity references for each individual character, you can specify that an entire block of text should be treated as character data. Be aware that CDATA sections *cannot* be nested within one another.

2

**SOAP AND XML:
THE FOUNDATION
OF SOAP**

> **NOTE**
>
> You cannot use CDATA sections within attribute values. You are strictly limited to entity references when faced with this situation.

As you build your own SOAP serializers and de-serializers, be aware that you must *cleanse* your data before building the SOAP packets. This means that you are responsible for *inspecting* the data for special characters that will interfere with the parser's interpretation of the markup, and applying the appropriate substitutions. Using entity references and CDATA sections allows you to manipulate the data stream to ensure that a well-formed document is created. The following example shows how you might use CDATA in your SOAP payload:

```
<SOAP-ENV:Envelope
        xmlns:SOAP-ENV="http://schemas.xmlsoap.org/soap/envelope/"
        SOAP-ENV:encodingStyle="http://schemas.xmlsoap.org/soap/encoding/">
    <SOAP-ENV:Body>
        <m:LogMessage xmlns:m="Some-URI">
            <Message><![CDATA[File:'somefile.cpp' line:<122>]]></Message>
        </m:LogMessage>
    </SOAP-ENV:Body>
</SOAP-ENV:Envelope>
```

In this example, the text `File:'somefile.cpp' line:<122>` is treated as normal character data without interfering with the XML parser.

Parsers: The DOM and SAX

Applications that have been developed to parse XML documents are typically called *XML processors* or *parsers*. There are two basic types of parsers, *validating* and *non-validating*. Validating parsers have the capability to enforce rules against the XML document, an important aspect of processing SOAP packets.

There are currently two popular Application Programming Interfaces (APIs) available for parsing an XML document: the Document Object Model (DOM) and the Simple API for XML (SAX). The main difference between the two models comes down to the amount of memory required by each, in order to parse the document. The DOM requires the entire XML document to be loaded into memory for processing, whereas SAX is an *event-driven* system that is more efficient for extremely large XML documents.

The Document Object Model

The fact is, an XML document can be represented as a tree, therefore the DOM provides a simple way to represent a tree-like object model. As you can see in Figure 2.1, an XML document consists of a *document* object containing a single *node* object. This *node* object uses a *node list* to reference one or more *child nodes*.

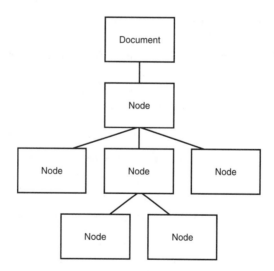

FIGURE 2.1
The Document Object Model.

Each XML element can be considered as a *node*, with the root element acting as the top node in the tree. The DOM presents nodes as the fundamental type of all objects in the model.

The next example shows you how to use the Microsoft XML DOM in a Visual Basic application. Microsoft's DOM is located in MSXML.DLL and is implemented using COM interfaces.

In order for Visual Basic to apply the *Intellisense* feature that auto-expands object interface methods, you must load the DOM library into your project. To do this, from the menu select Project, References and enable the *Microsoft XML 1.0* (or greater) reference (see Figure 2.2). Click OK.

> **NOTE**
>
> If you return to the References menu after you've selected the *Microsoft XML 1.0* library, you should notice that it has been renamed as *Microsoft XML, version 2.0* (or greater).

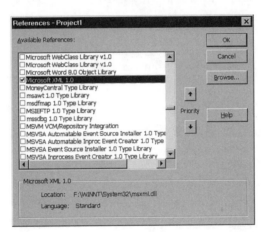

FIGURE 2.2
The Visual Basic References menu.

Now, consider the following XML:

```
<Car>
    <Name>Corvette</Name>
    <Year>2000</Year>
    <Color>Red</Color>
    <ConvertibleTop />
</Car>
```

The code for this example is shown in Listing 2.1. In the first line of the listing, you see how the *DOM Document* is created. The variables declared afterwards are used to reference specific nodes within the DOM document. The XML document is loaded into the DOM using the `loadXML` method. In this case, the XML document is loaded as a string—rather than as an input file—for simplicity purposes. The DOM provides access to the `documentElement`, and this is stored in `rootnode`. You are not required to establish this reference, but it does make the programming syntax slightly more readable as you develop your code. Again, a reference to the nodelist is created to simplify the code by using the `nodelist` variable. The last portion of the code iterates through the root node's children and displays the value of each node.

> **NOTE**
>
> When using the May 2000 technology preview release of the Microsoft XML parser, you will need to use the MSXML2 library, rather than the MSXML library, shown in Listing 2.1.

LISTING 2.1   Using Microsoft's DOM from Visual Basic

```
Dim dom As New MSXML.DOMDocument
Dim rootnode As MSXML.IXMLDOMNode
Dim node As MSXML.IXMLDOMNode
Dim nodelist As MSXML.IXMLDOMNodeList

dom.loadXML ("<Car><Name>Corvette</Name>" + _
            "<Year>2000</Year><Color>Red</Color>" + _
            "<ConvertibleTop /></Car>")
Set rootnode = dom.documentElement
Set nodelist = rootnode.childNodes

For Each node In nodelist
    MsgBox node.nodeName + ": " + node.Text
Next
```

As you run this example, notice how each node name and value are displayed in a message box. The *empty-value element* `<ConvertibleTop />` only shows the node name, however.

There are five important objects or interfaces to Microsoft's DOM, three of which you've already seen in Listing 2.1: `XMLDOMDocument`, `XMLDOMNode`, and `XMLDOMNodeList`.

DOMDocument is the highest level object that represents the XML document as a whole; it enables you to access the *document element* at the top of the XML tree. The document level also enables you to work with style sheets and transformations as described in the "Style

Sheets and Transformations" section later in this chapter. The following code fragments show examples of using the DOMDocument object:

```
dom.async = True          'Enable asynchronous loads
dom.Load "filename.xml"    'Load XML from a file
dom.loadXML "<Car></Car>"  'Load XML from a string
dom.transformNode ssObj    'Transform using a style sheet
dom.validateOnParse = True 'Enable validation of the document
```

> **NOTE**
>
> Microsoft's XML parser (as well as other parsers) allows you to enable or disable validation for your XML document. Be aware that validation takes place when the XML document is being loaded.

Now that you have an idea of how the DOMDocument works, let's move on to the DOM node. XMLDOMNode is the primary object of the DOM. From an object-oriented inheritance point of view, all objects are derived from the node. Types of nodes include the document, elements, attributes, and so on. The node object supports several useful methods as shown in the following example code:

```
Set node = dom.documentElement    'Reference to document element
node.Text = "some text"           'Populate node with text
MsgBox node.nodeName              'Display the node name
if node.hasChildNodes then        'Test for children
```

There are several objects that provide specialized versions of the node object. These include the element object, comment object, and others.

As its name implies, the XMLDOMNodeList is simply an indexed collection of node objects. The node list is automatically updated as changes are made to the nodes contained within. The following shows the two node list methods that are normally used:

```
nlen = nodelist.length     'Get the number of nodes in the list
Set node = nodelist.item(0) 'Reference the first node in list
```

The two other important objects or interfaces, to Microsoft's DOM are XMLDOMNamedNodeMap and XMLDOMParseError. The XMLDOMNamedNodeMap object allows you to work with nodes as a named collection of objects, rather than as an indexed collection. In the following example, the Year attribute is retrieved from the document element and its value is displayed:

```
Set NNM = dom.documentElement.Attributes 'Get attribute named node map
Set YearNode = NNM.getNamedItem("Year")  'Retrieve the named node
MsgBox YearNode.text                      'Display the node contents
```

The XMLDOMParseError object provides detailed information about the most recent parse error encountered. It provides an error code and description as well as positional information referencing the location of the error within the document. The following example displays error information if the XML document cannot be loaded:

```
If (dom.Load(FilePath) = False) Then
    MsgBox dom.parseError.errorCode
    MsgBox dom.parseError.reason
    MsgBox dom.parseError.filepos
End If
```

You should understand that parse errors are only used to notify you of errors encountered while loading the XML document into the DOM; they are not going to provide information concerning navigational errors, such as iterating past the end of a *node list* or requesting an invalid *attribute* name.

The five objects just described are the most common in Microsoft's DOM implementation. However, there are many other objects, as shown in Table 2.1, which you may need as you develop your SOAP systems.

TABLE 2.1   Other DOM Objects

Object Name	Description
XMLDOMAttribute	Attribute object
XMLDOMCDATASection	CDATA object
XMLDOMCharacterData	Text manipulation
XMLDOMComment	Comment (that is, `<!-- Comment -->`)
XMLDOMDocumentFragment	Portion of a document's tree
XMLDOMDocumentType	Document type declaration data
XMLDOMElement	Element object
XMLDOMEntity	Entity (parsed or unparsed)
XMLDOMEntityReference	Entity reference (if available)
XMLDOMImplementation	Mechanism for testing DOM support
XMLDOMNotation	Notation found in DTD or Schema
XMLDOMProcessingInstruction	Processing instruction
XMLDOMText	Text of element or attribute

You can find more information about Microsoft's DOM by going to Microsoft's XML Web site:

`http://msdn.microsoft.com/xml/default.asp`

Keep in mind, that although Microsoft's implementation is fairly common, many other vendors have published free versions of their own DOM implementation.

Before you decide to use the DOM, you should know about another model that provides a faster, more efficient scheme for processing XML documents. This model is called SAX.

SAX

The Simple API for XML (SAX) is a low-level, *event-driven* or *event-based* system which operates in a fashion similar to a Graphical User Interface (GUI). For instance, when a start tag is encountered during parsing, an event can be triggered which executes your *event handler* or callback function to handle the event. One benefit of this method is that it requires much less memory and resources than the DOM does because SAX doesn't store the document in memory. This can be extremely useful when dealing with very large XML documents. Another advantage to using the SAX callback functionality is that you can implement your own data structures for internally storing the document. Therefore, you don't have to make a copy of the parser's tree structure into one of your own structure, as you would have done with the DOM.

In the following sample code fragments, you will see some of the available event handlers, using the Apache.org parser. The following is a slightly modified version of the examples provided with the Apache.org parser. Here, the SAXHandlers class in the class header file encapsulates the event handlers for both document and error events.

```
#include <sax/HandlerBase.hpp>
class AttributeList;

class SAXHandlers : public HandlerBase
{
public:
    SAXHandlers();
    ~SAXHandlers();

    // Document handlers
    void startElement(const XMLCh* const name, AttributeList& attributes);
    void characters(const XMLCh* const chars, const unsigned int length);
    void ignorableWhitespace(const XMLCh* const chars, const unsigned int
length);
    void resetDocument();

    // Error handlers
    void warning(const SAXParseException& exception);
    void error(const SAXParseException& exception);
    void fatalError(const SAXParseException& exception);
};
```

Using this class, the `handler` object is registered for both document events and error events:

```
// Initialize the parser
XMLPlatformUtils::Initialize();

// Create the parser
SAXParser parser;

// Create and register the handler
SAXHandlers handler;
parser.setDocumentHandler(&handler);
parser.setErrorHandler(&handler);

// Parse the document
parser.parse(InputFile);
```

As this code executes the `parse` method, events are triggered to the `handler` object, enabling the application to perform application-specific work for the registered events. For example, the `startElement` method will be called each time the parser encounters the start tag of an element.

Many parsers support SAX, so if you prefer event-driven systems, this may be a reasonable choice for you. Since SOAP serializers and deserializers need to operate quickly, it is within reason to state that a SAX implementation would be better for SOAP.

Choosing a Parser

Your decision on which parser to use should be based on your environment and the application you are developing. Since the focus of this book is on SOAP, it is recommended that you use a mainstream parser that is well supported. With so many new XML drafts being published, mainstream parsers will generally accommodate new functionality very quickly.

Refer to Appendix B, "Resources," for more information about where you can obtain various XML processors.

URIs and XML Namespaces

URI, or Uniform Resource Identifier, is a generic term used to denote some particular entity or object in the Web world using a string representation. This is the most fundamental addressing scheme of the Web. The URI provides the capability for an element name (or attribute name) to be unique, such that the element name doesn't conflict with other element names. The rest of this section reviews the characteristics of URIs and namespaces, and describes how they relate in SOAP.

URLs and URNs

Different types of Web resources require different forms of URIs. Uniform Resource Locators (URLs) and Uniform Resource Names (URNs) are both forms of a URI (see Figure 2.3). Each has its own syntax, designed to fulfill a purpose.

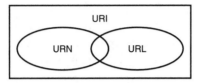

FIGURE 2.3
The relationship between URIs, URNs, and URLs.

Uniform Resource Locators (URLs) are a form of URI used to *locate* a particular resource in the Web world. Basic URL syntax (see RFC1738) is dependent on the *scheme* to which it applies, but follows this format:

```
<scheme>:<scheme-specific syntax>
```

One form of an URL is used to specify a web page located on a web server, similar to

```
http://www.mcp.com:80/some_directory/webpage.html
```

By changing just one of the values in this URL, you are specifying a completely different location, resource, or both on the Web.

Uniform Resource Names (URNs) are another form of URI that provide *persistence* as well as *location-independence*. In a nutshell, an URN uniquely describes some resource that will *always* be available. The following is an example of an URN:

```
urn:some-urn:someinterface.1
```

The exact syntax of URNs is denoted in RFC2141 but the following is a summary:

```
urn:<Namespace Identifier>:<Namespace Specific String>
```

1. Start with the text "urn:" (uppercase or lowercase).
2. The *Namespace Identifier* consists of letters, numbers, and hyphens (uppercase or lowercase).
3. The *Namespace Specific String* consists of letters, numbers, parentheses, commas, periods, hyphens, and other such characters (uppercase or lowercase).

There are efforts underway to provide Internet protocols for resolving URNs. This would work similarly to the way DNS (or another name service) resolves hostnames.

XML Namespaces

In C++, developers use namespaces to uniquely identify their code in order to avoid name conflicts when compiling programs with someone else's code. The same principle applies to XML namespaces. With everyone declaring their own XML element names and attributes, you can expect ambiguous results when trying to combine this data. For example, one system may use the <Title> element when describing a book, while another system may also use <Title> to describe automobile ownership. As long as data from the two systems are never related, everything is fine. However if the data ever converges, there is no way to distinguish between the two meanings. In other words, you may want to think twice before investing in that Internet startup company that sells books about Corvette owners.

An *XML namespace*, as identified by a URI reference, qualifies element and attribute names within an XML document. This not only avoids name collisions, but it also enables *vocabularies* to be re-used. You can think of a vocabulary as a published set of element and attribute names common to a particular user domain.

The following example contains XML that has no associated namespace:

```
<Product>
    <ProductName Type="1">Widget</ProductName>
</Product>
```

In order to reference a namespace, you must first declare one by creating a *namespace declaration* using the form:

```
xmlns:<Namespace Prefix> = <URI>
```

In the namespace declaration, you specify a *namespace prefix* and the URI of the namespace. When the prefix is attached to the local names of elements and attributes, the elements and attributes then become associated with the correct namespace, as follows:

```
<pns:Product xmlns:pns="http://www.mcp.com/prodns">
    <pns:ProductName pns:Type="1">Widget</pns:ProductName>
</pns:Product>
```

In this case, pns is defined to be the *prefix* and is used to associate Product, ProductName, and Type with the http://www.mcp.com/prodns URI. In reality, the URI doesn't necessarily point to anything—its purpose is to make the namespace unique.

XML namespaces also provide the concept of a *default namespace* (denoted in XML as xmlns). This allows you to establish a namespace for an element and all its children, thus avoiding the need to use a prefix on each element name.

> **NOTE**
>
> Default namespaces do not apply to attribute names. Instead, attributes must be explicitly prefixed to a desired namespace.

Initially, an XML document has no assigned default namespace, so any elements that are not qualified with a prefix will be locally scoped.

Now consider the following example:

```
<pns:Product xmlns:pns="http://www.mcp.com/prodns">
    <pns:ProductName pns:Type="1">Widget</pns:ProductName>
    <ProductLoc xmlns="http://www.mcp.com/prodlocns">
        <Building>310</Building>
        <Floor>2</Floor>
        <Room>118</Room>
    </ProductLoc>
    <Cost>495.00</Cost>
</pns:Product>
```

Here, the pns prefix is created to reference a product URI. This same prefix is used to qualify the Product and ProductName elements. Within the ProductLoc element, a default namespace is created, which references a completely different URI than the pns prefix. All elements contained within the ProductLoc element are scoped to the default namespace and therefore require no prefix. However, since Cost is not contained by the ProductLoc element and it doesn't have a prefix, it is locally scoped to the document.

Although SOAP does not require namespaces, you will find them an invaluable part of your SOAP development. Consider the following XML namespaces used in a SOAP call:

```
<SOAP-ENV:Envelope
        xmlns:SOAP-ENV="http://schemas.xmlsoap.org/soap/envelope/"
        SOAP-ENV:encodingStyle="http://schemas.xmlsoap.org/soap/encoding/">
    <SOAP-ENV:Body>
        <m:Print xmlns:m="http://www.mcp.com/calc">
            <Message>Hello World!</Message>
        </m:Print>
    </SOAP-ENV:Body>
</SOAP-ENV:Envelope>
```

In this case, XML defines two namespace prefixes, SOAP-ENV and m, to differentiate between SOAP-specific names and the interface method names. Do not be overly concerned with the syntax of the SOAP packet; at this point it is more important for you to understand how namespaces are applied than for you to understand the specifics of this SOAP call.

XML Schema

Early in the development of SOAP, its creators began constructing a language that could be used to describe the SOAP protocol. This description language was built with XML and was designed to be a programming-language neutral way to define interfaces, types, and more. Component Description Language, or CDL, supported primitive and user-defined data types including aliases, interface inheritance, arrays, and structures. In some ways CDL resembled the syntax found in various flavors of the Interface Definition Language (IDL) used in CORBA and COM/DCOM.

In the spirit of reusing other Internet technology, SOAP's creators chose to abandon the idea of creating yet another language, and to follow the XML Schema initiative. The XML Schema working draft was already addressing many of the same issues that CDL was addressing, but in a generic way.

Be aware that SOAP *does not require* the use of XML Schemas, so nothing prevents you from writing SOAP code while waiting on XML Schemas to be adopted.

This section will introduce schemas from the perspective of using them for general XML documents, followed by a detailed description of schemas and their use with SOAP.

Understanding XML Schemas

Many times as you develop XML documents, you'll need to place constraints on the way data is represented in the document. This may be a particular order that elements should follow, or possibly validating a particular element's datatype. In order to place constraints on data, you must build Document Type Definitions (DTDs) or XML Schemas to provide data about the data, also known as *metadata*. Although DTDs are beneficial to many XML applications, they do not have the characteristics necessary for describing constructs such as inheritance or complex datatypes. To overcome these limitations, a working group was formed to produce XML Schemas based on an original draft from Microsoft. The XML Schema draft is divided into two parts. The first part, *XML Schema Part 1: Structures,* proposes a way to structure and constrain document content. The second part, *XML Schema Part 2: Data Types,* provides a way to describe both primitive and complex datatypes within a document.

> **NOTE**
>
> Since the XML Schema working draft is still being revised, you should consider it incomplete and subject to change. However, it appears that the feature-function has stabilized and only inconsistencies and clarifications will be addressed in subsequent releases.

The draft establishes a means by which the XML Schema language describes the structure and content of XML documents. A desirable feature of XML Schemas is the fact that they are represented in XML, so standard XML parsers can be used to *navigate* them.

At this point you are already familiar with XML and many of the terms used to identify the concepts behind XML. The XML Schema draft defines several new terms that help describe the semantics of using and understanding schemas.

Instances and Schema

An *XML instance document* refers to the document element—including the elements, attributes, and content contained within the document—that conforms to an XML Schema. In the more general sense, an instance may refer to any element (including its attributes and content) that conforms to an XML Schema. An instance that conforms to a schema is considered to be *schema-valid*.

Schemas can be independent XML documents or they can be embedded inside other XML with references to the schema. Schemas take the form of

```
<schema>
    <!-- type definitions, element declarations, etc. -->
</schema>
```

Definitions and Declarations

A great advantage of schemas is that they allow you to create simple or complex *types* for applying classifications to elements. As in most programming languages this practice is called *type definition.* An example of this is as follows:

```
<schema>
    <type name="Person">
        <element name="FirstName" type="string" />
        <attribute name="Age" type="integer" />
    </type>
</schema>
```

The preceding example also shows an *element declaration* (for the element <FirstName>) and an *attribute declaration* (for the attribute Age) that are local to a particular type.

Beyond participating in the type definition, elements may also be declared as top-level elements of a particular type, as shown in the following example where BaseballPlayer is a type of Person:

```
<schema>
    <!-- ...Type definition... -->

    <element name="BaseballPlayer" type="Person" />
</schema>
```

Attributes, however, can only be of simple types as defined in *XML Schema Part 2: Data Types*, such as string, boolean, and float.

Symbol Space

Similar to the concept of a namespace, a *symbol space* is a way to partition the names of *schema components* (type definitions, element declarations, attribute declarations, and so on) such that they do not conflict with each other.

Each name must be unique within a single symbol space but can exist within multiple independent symbol spaces. This allows the same name to be used across different types and potentially to have various meanings.

Every type definition has its own symbol spaces, one for local elements and one for attributes. In this case, the same name can be used for both an element name and an attribute name without ambiguity.

Top-level (or global) elements also have their own symbol space, allowing the same name to be used in other symbol spaces.

Target Namespace

Since element and attribute declarations are used to validate instances, it is necessary for them to match the namespace characteristic of a particular instance. This implies that declarations have an association with a *target namespace URI* or *no namespace* at all, depending on whether the instance has a qualified name or not. You can also infer that each symbol space must follow this rule since each element and attribute is contained within a symbol space. In order for a schema to specify a target namespace, it must use the targetNamespace attribute as follows:

```
<schema targetNamespace="SomeNamespaceURI">
    <element name="ElementInNS" type="string" />
    <type name="TypeInNS">
        <element name="LocalElementInNS" type="integer" />
        <attribute name="LocalAttrInNS" type="string" />
    </type>
</schema>
```

As you can see, all global and local elements are associated with SomeNamespaceURI. Lack of the targetNamespace attribute designates that no namespace is associated.

NOTE

The term *NCName* refers to a name that is not qualified by an XML namespace.

> **NOTE**
>
> The term *QName* refers to a name that may or may not be qualified by an XML namespace.

Data Types and Schema Constraints

Data types consist of a *value space*, *lexical space*, and *facets*. The value space is the data type's permitted set of values, and can have various properties associated with it. A set of valid literals for a data type makes up the lexical space of that data type. Finally, a facet is a single dimension of a concept that allows you to distinguish between different data types. There are two kinds of *facets* used to describe datatypes, *fundamental* and *constraining*.

Fundamental facets allow you to describe the order, bounds, cardinality, exactness, and numeric properties of a given data type's value space.

Constraining facets allow you to describe the constraints on a data type's value space. Possible constraints include minimum and maximum lengths, pattern matching, upper and lower bounds, and enumeration of valid values.

The following is the fragment of a *simple type* definition:

```
<datatype name="HourType" source="integer">
    <minInclusive value="1" />
    <maxInclusive value="12" />
</datatype>
```

In this case, HourType is defined to be of the built-in integer data type, and additionally constrained to values between 1 and 12. This new type can then be used in other type definitions as in the following Hour attribute:

```
<element name="Time">
    <attribute name="Hour" type="HourType" />
    <attribute name="Minute" type="MinuteType" />
</element>
```

The instance for this type may look something like this:

```
<Time Hour="7" Minute="30" />
```

A *complex type* definition with constraints is also shown:

```
<type name="Sphere">
    <element name="Radius">
        <datatype source="decimal">
            <minInclusive value="0" />
```

```
        </datatype>
    </element>
    <element name="Color" type="string" />
</type>
```

This type can be represented by an instance as follows:

```
<Sphere>
    <Radius>23.4</Radius>
    <Color>Blue</Color>
</Sphere>
```

NOTE

The type attribute can be used on elements and attributes when a simple data type or pre-defined data type is referenced. In the case where you want to use facets to constrain the data type, you must use the datatype element as previously shown.

---

minOccurs and maxOccurs

Elements and attributes allow you to specify the minimum and maximum number of times they may appear in the instance. The following example shows how you can force an attribute to appear one and only one time:

```
<element name="Book">
    <attribute name="Author" type="A" minOccurs="1" maxOccurs="1" />
    <attribute name="Title" type="T" minOccurs="1" maxOccurs="1" />
</element>
```

The maxOccurs attribute can also be set to "*" to denote that the element or attribute can appear *many* times. You can also prevent a value from appearing by setting the maxOccurs attribute equal to "0".

Element Content Model

The element content model provides a means for constraining the content of elements. Elements can have *no constraints*, be constrained to have *no content*, or be allowed to contain other elements and text (that is, have *mixed* content), according to further rules. These rules describe a *rich content model* that allows for such things as elements, groups of elements, and *wildcards*.

Wildcards allow you to define the acceptable ambiguity for element content. This means that you can specify that *any* type of element can appear or just an element from a particular namespace can appear. For example

```
<element name="AcceptableCars">
    <type content="mixed">
```

```
        <any namespace="urn:Corvette" minOccurs="1" maxOccurs="*" />
        <any namespace="urn:Porsche" minOccurs="0" maxOccurs="*" />
    </type>
</element>
```

Elements declared *nullable* (that is, `nullable="true"`) can also appear in an instance with the `xsi:null="true"` attribute to designate that the element contains a *null* value, rather than *empty* content. The `xsi:null` attribute comes from the XML Schema instance namespace.

NOTE

The xsi namespace prefix should reference the XML Schema instance `http://www.w3.org/1999/XMLSchema/instance`.

Deriving Type Definitions

Similar to the way that object-oriented programming languages work, schemas allow you to derive types from other types in a controlled way. When defining a new type, you may choose to *extend* or *restrict* the other type definition.

When extending another type definition, you can introduce additional elements and attributes, as shown in the following example:

```
<type name="Book">
    <element name="Title" type="string" />
    <element name="Author" type="string" />
</type>

<type name="ElectronicBook" source="Book" derivedBy="extension">
    <element name="URL" type="string" />
</type>
```

Consider the following restricted type definition where the attribute is fixed:

```
<type name="Ball">
    <element name="Radius" type="decimal" />
    <attribute name="Color" type="string" />
</type>

<type name="RedBall" source="Ball" derivedBy="restriction">
    <restrictions>
        <attribute name="Color" fixed="red" />
    </restrictions>
</type>
```

There are times when an instance wishes to explicitly indicate its type. To do this, the instance can use the XML Schema instance namespace definition of xsi:type as follows:

```
<Car xsi:type="SportsCar">
    <Driver>Me</Driver>
</Car>
```

XML Schemas also support the concept of *abstract types*, which cannot be used directly in an instance via xsi:type. Rather, an abstract type is only available for other type definitions to derive from it. In contrast, you can declare a type definition as final to prohibit other type definitions from deriving from it at all. Finally, a type definition may be declared as exact such that derived types cannot be used in its place.

Ultimately, XML Schemas defines a *ur-type* to be a generic base type that all simple and complex types are derived from, in the event that they do not explicitly identify a source type.

Although this was not an exhaustive coverage of schemas, you have been exposed to many new abstract concepts, all of which in some way relate to how SOAP uses XML to serialize data.

An XML Schema Example

To experience how validation works with schemas, it is beneficial to look at an example of such a case. This section provides a simple example of how Microsoft's XML parser implements *XML-Data*, an older version of the XML Schema draft.

To use XML-Data, you must reference the Microsoft schema urn:schemas-microsoft-com:xml-data from the namespace attribute in your schema definition. By referencing XML-Data, you are telling the Microsoft XML parser how to resolve the data types used within your schema. Take for example the following two files, SCHEMA.XML and TEST.XML, which demonstrate schema usage in Listings 2.2 and 2.3, respectively.

LISTING 2.2 SCHEMA.XML File Contents

```
<Schema xmlns="urn:schemas-microsoft-com:xml-data"
    ➥xmlns:dt="urn:schemas-microsoft-com:datatypes">
    <ElementType name="StudentName" dt:type="string" />
    <ElementType name="GradePointAvg" dt:type="float" />
</Schema>
```

LISTING 2.3 TEST.XML File Contents

```
<TestElement xmlns:myns="x-schema:schema.xml">
    <myns:StudentName>John Doe</myns:StudentName>
    <myns:GradePointAvg>3.5a</myns:GradePointAvg>
</TestElement>
```

As you look at the SCHEMA.XML file in Listing 2.2, you will notice that schemas-microsoft-com:xmldata becomes the default namespace. The schema also defines a dt namespace prefix that is used to reference data types as defined by Microsoft's schema. Each ElementType uses the name attribute to specify an element name used in the TEST.XML document. In this case, the StudentName element requires a value of type string, and GradePointAvg requires a value of type float.

Now look at the TEST.XML file in Listing 2.3. This contains a root element with two children. The root element defines a new namespace prefix called myns, which references the x-schema: schema located in the SCHEMA.XML file. Notice how the StudentName and GradePointAvg elements are scoped to myns. If this had not been done, the elements would not have an associated namespace and therefore would have been exempt from the schema's rules.

If you look closely, you should notice that the files would generate an error when validated by the Microsoft XML parser. This is due to the GradePointAvg value of 3.5a failing the schema validation rules, which require a value of type float. If you change this value to just 3.5, everything will validate as you would expect.

SOAP and Schemas

So how will SOAP use schemas? The answer is, as a serialization tool. Remember that SOAP specifies a way for clients to construct XML documents from method calls and for servers to ultimately parse these documents such that server code gets executed.

To do this well, SOAP implementations must provide a flexible yet concise way to serialize the data into the document. Schemas can be used to describe the method and its arguments. Consider the following SOAP schema for the AddIntegers method:

```
<schema>
    <type name="AddIntegersType"
            xmlns="http://www.w3.org/1999/XMLSchema"
            targetNamespace="Some-URI">
        <element name="AParam" type="integer" />
        <element name="BParam" type="integer" />
    </type>
    <element name="AddIntegers" type="AddIntegersType" />
</schema>
```

In this example, the AddIntegers type is contained within the urn:AddIntegersNamespace namespace, and defines the method parameters AParam and BParam, which are both integer values. With the AddIntegers type defined, the AddIntegers element can then be defined of that type, so that the element can be used in an instance document as follows:

```
<SOAP-ENV:Envelope
        xmlns:SOAP-ENV="http://schemas.xmlsoap.org/soap/envelope/"
```

2

**SOAP AND XML:
THE FOUNDATION
OF SOAP**

```
        SOAP-ENV:encodingStyle="http://schemas.xmlsoap.org/soap/encoding/">
    <SOAP-ENV:Body>
        <m:AddIntegers xsi:type="AddIntegersType" xmlns:m="Some-URI">
            <AParam>7</AParam>
            <BParam>9</BParam>
        </m:AddIntegers>
    </SOAP-ENV:Body>
</SOAP-ENV:Envelope>
```

Very soon, schemas will play a key role in building SOAP implementations; therefore, you should expect the SOAP Working Draft to further integrate schema technology. You can already see the quick migration towards schemas by comparing the differences between SOAP v1.0 and v1.1.

However, rather than waiting for schemas to be fully defined and implemented in parsers, you can start building SOAP solutions now. Although it requires a little more effort on your part, it will only take a short time to develop a simple system. And when you see your first method execute against a remote server, possibly on the other side of a firewall, you will forever be indoctrinated in SOAP.

Style Sheets and Transformations

In Web development, Extensible Style Language (XSL) can be used to transform XML documents into HTML for rendering text and images in a Web browser. XSL Transformation (XSLT) provides similar functionality, but with a goal of transforming one form of XML into another form of XML. XSLT should have an enormous impact on the XML industry, because as developers learn and build better ways to structure XML data, there will be times when they want to transform old structures into new structures. For example, the next section will show how XSLT can be used to transform SOAP v0.9 payloads into SOAP v1.1 payloads. Not only can you transform different versions of SOAP payloads, but other XML protocols (such as XML-RPC as discussed in Chapter 3, "Distributed Objects and XML: The Road to SOAP") can be transformed into SOAP payloads, and vice versa.

Although this section will not provide an exhaustive look at XSLT, it will introduce you to the basic constructs used to build XSLT style sheets.

The XSLT Vocabulary and Templates

An XSL *template* allows you to define rules consisting of patterns that are matched to content within the XML document, as well as behavior associated with each match. Consider the following XML based on the September 1999 SOAP draft:

```
<SerializedStream>
    <Body>
```

```
        <Add>
            <a>1</a>
            <b>2</b>
        </Add>
    </Body>
</SerializedStream>
```

Notice that the outdated SOAP `SerializedStream` element name should be transformed into the newer `Envelope` element name. In order for you to apply this change using XSLT, you must build a style sheet as seen in Listing 2.4.

LISTING 2.4 XSL Transformation Style Sheet

```
<xsl:stylesheet xmlns:xsl="http://www.w3.org/TR/WD-xsl">
    <xsl:template match="/">
        <xsl:apply-templates />
    </xsl:template>

    <xsl:template match="*|@*|comment()|pi()|text()">
        <xsl:copy>
            <xsl:apply-templates select="*|@*|comment()|pi()|text()" />
        </xsl:copy>
    </xsl:template>

    <xsl:template match="text()">
        <xsl:value-of />
    </xsl:template>

    <xsl:template match="SerializedStream">
        <Envelope>
            <xsl:apply-templates />
        </Envelope>
    </xsl:template>

</xsl:stylesheet>
```

Styles should be listed in the style sheet starting with generic rules at the top and migrating to specific rules towards the bottom. Consider the style sheet in Listing 2.4, with the most specific rule being

```
<xsl:template match="SerializedStream">
    <Envelope>
        <xsl:apply-templates />
    </Envelope>
</xsl:template>
```

2

SOAP AND XML:
THE FOUNDATION
OF SOAP

This rule states that a `<SerializedStream>` start tag should first be converted into the `<Envelope>` tag, its contents processed by the style sheet, and finally the end tag replaced by `</Envelope>`.

The next rule simply carries forward the `value-of` any text in the document:

```
<xsl:template match="text()">
    <xsl:value-of />
</xsl:template>
```

When the next template is applied, all elements (`*`), attributes (`@*`), comments, processing instructions, and text will be copied, and the style sheet will be applied to their content:

```
<xsl:template match="*|@*|comment()|pi()|text()">
    <xsl:copy>
        <xsl:apply-templates select="*|@*|comment()|pi()|text()" />
    </xsl:copy>
</xsl:template>
```

The last template denotes that the style sheet starts at the root node of the XML document:

```
<xsl:template match="/">
    <xsl:apply-templates />
</xsl:template>
```

Overall, this style sheet copies all elements, attributes, comments, processing instructions, and element values to the output, with the exception of the `<SerializedStream>` element. Instead of being copied, this element is transformed into the `<Envelope>` element. The following is the final output:

```
<Envelope>
    <Body>
        <Add>
            <a>1</a>
            <b>2</b>
        </Add>
    </Body>
</Envelope>
```

When considering the simple XML document in this example, it seems that the style sheet is somewhat overkill. But in the case of more complex structures, the XSL language provides a robust mechanism for you to transform XML into just about anything you like.

XLink, XPointer, and XPath

Several advantages to HTML are its capability to provide links to other web pages and reference locations within other documents. The XLink, XPointer, and XPath technologies allow you to provide similar functionality with XML, with several added benefits. At the time of this writing, both XLink and XPointer were still in draft form, but XPath has been endorsed as a recommendation. Therefore, you should inspect the most recent version of your parser to ensure it supports these features. The current version of SOAP does not require the use of XLink, XPointer, or XPath, however many of the features provided by these technologies should prove beneficial to SOAP once they've been adopted by the general population of parsers. This section will provide a quick overview and ultimately discuss how this trio may apply to SOAP implementations.

XLink

In HTML, a link generally points to a particular document somewhere in the Web world. Unfortunately, this is a one-way XML street that doesn't inherently provide a mechanism for getting back to the original document. XLink provides a way for resources to be linked in a multidirectional fashion as well as the standard one-way link. The following is an example of using the XLink feature similar to how a link behaves in HTML:

```
<BillMLink xmlns:xlink="http://www.w3.org/XML/XLink/0.9"
    xlink:type="simple" xlink:href="http://www.mcp.com"
    xlink:role="movie" xlink:title="Carl"
    xlink:show="replace" xlink:actuate="user">
        Caddy Shack
</BillMLink>
```

This form is called a *simple link* as described by the `type` attribute, and can only link to a single resource denoted by `href`. The application parsing the XML can use the `role` attribute for application-specific data about the link, and the `title` attribute for displaying information to the user. The last two attributes, `show` and `actuate`, are used to determine the behavior of the link and who must initiate the link, respectively. In this case, `show="replace"` instructs the application to open this link within the same *context* (in browser terms, this means the same window). Whereas, `actuate="user"` specifies that the user must initiate the link rather than the application linking automatically.

An alternate form of an XLink is called the *extended link* and it allows *multiple* resources to be connected as follows:

```
<BillMLinks xmlns:xlink="http://www.w3.org/XML/XLink/0.9"
    xlink:type="extended" xlink:role="movie"
    xlink:title="Bills Movies" xlink:showdefault="replace"
    xlink:actuatedefault="user">
    <BMLink xlink:href="caddyshack.htm">Caddy Shack</BMLink>
    <BMLink xlink:href="groundhog.htm">Groundhogs Day</BMLink>
</BillMLinks>
```

This form of link provides a way for you to specify multiple child elements, each with an independent `href`. One minor difference is that the behavioral attributes are now implied by default values, as denoted by `actuatedefault` and `showdefault`.

One last differentiation that should be made is that of *inline links* versus *out-of-line links*. Inline links are those links that directly reference a particular resource, whereas out-of-line links can reference external content that ultimately references the desired resource. Take for example, an investor who is trying to call her financial advisor. The *inline* way for her to do this is to call the advisor's phone number directly. But what happens if the advisor's number changes? Or worse, what happens if the advisor has skipped town with the investor's money? The *out-of-line* approach is for the investor to call the investment company's phone directory service, which can redirect the call appropriately. In the case of a changed phone number, it can redirect the call to the new number. However, if the investor is sitting in Bermuda with millions, the call can be redirected to the Investment Manager.

With regards to SOAP, it uses the `href` as defined by XLink to reference the unique identifier (the `id` attribute) of an encoded element. This is particularly interesting when serializing data into SOAP packets. In the case where you have several parameters that reference the exact same data, it is more efficient to serialize the data once and reference the single element from the other occurrences as well as maintaining identity relationships across calls.

XPointer

XPointer is used as a fragment identifier that provides syntax for addressing particular portions of an XML document. It extends the XPath language insomuch as it addresses key limitations with XPath. In particular, XPointer allows you to address points, nodes, and ranges within a document without restriction. The following is an example of an XPointer fragment that would be contained in a URI-reference:

```
Input.xml#xpointer(id("top") to id("bottom"))
```

In this case, the XPointer selects a range from an element with an attribute ID of `top`, to an element with an attribute ID of `bottom`.

While XPointer is not directly listed as part of the SOAP working draft, it is referenced by the XLink working draft as a form of linking to locations within an XML document, and thus may provide more efficient SOAP packet structures.

XPath

XPath is a regular expression-like language used by XPointer and XSL Transformations to address parts of an XML document. In particular, an XPath expression describes an object that can be a boolean, number, string, or an unordered collection of unique nodes. The actual syntax allows you to address child nodes, attributes, descendants, and more. The following is an example of an XPath expression:

```
child::Body[position()=3]
```

In this case, the expression references the third Body child element of the current context.

It is recommended that you refer to the XPath Recommendation document for the specific constructs and syntax. However, XPath is not required by SOAP, but may be used by SOAP through the use of the XML linking technologies.

Summary

SOAP is really nothing more than XML documents, conforming to a particular specification, allowing the exchange of messages in a distributed system. The most appealing aspect of SOAP is its capability to capitalize on XML to build distributed systems in an extensible way. Although many of the newer technologies surrounding XML have not achieved the recommendation status, most are fundamentally stable and provide a basis for building better SOAP implementations.

Distributed Objects and XML: The Road to SOAP

IN THIS CHAPTER

"If all you have is a hammer, everything looks like a nail." —Baruch's Observation

Since the advent of XML, developers have been trying to apply it to almost every aspect of computing imaginable. Sometimes XML makes sense for a particular application and sometimes it doesn't. In the case of distributed architectures, however, XML offers the promise of inter-operability without regard to platform, programming language, or component runtime environment.

This chapter will explain why developers seem to be migrating to XML for a distributed protocol. It will also provide an *ad hoc* approach to implementing a distributed system using XML, including reasons why it has become important to select a standard XML protocol such as SOAP. You will also see how a reasonable *ad hoc* approach is not far from SOAP, and that with a few minor modifications it becomes much more flexible and ultimately standardized. The best way to recognize the benefits of using SOAP is to understand how the specification addresses distributed computing using XML technologies; therefore the last part of this chapter provides an overview of the SOAP specification v1.1.

Using XML in Distributed Systems

One of the most prevalent distributed systems in use today involves a Web browser and HTTP server. What could be better than a client application that can render forms and graphics through the use of a simple stream of text called HTML?

This concept has carried us into a new realm of development where server-side text can control client-side behavior, and vice versa. XML simply takes this design to an all-new level by adding structure and context to the streams of text. The question then becomes, how do you best use XML to improve the capabilities of distributed applications?

When considering other protocols, historically the approach has been to provide a way to execute remote functionality. Regardless of whether you're making raw RPC calls or building objects on top of a component runtime, it's still just a matter of serializing function calls.

XML on HTTP gives developers the ability to develop extensible applications quickly and easily on nearly any platform they want. XML is easy to write, easy to read, easy to change, and easy to manage. You are not required to use component runtimes, garbage collection, security, or other extensions. You simply have a flexible means for system communication. Yet, if you choose to apply extensions such as security or garbage collection, they are absolutely permitted and supported by this infrastructure.

Because these systems have become so prevalent, it is important to see how a simple approach might be taken. The next section focuses on an XML and HTTP solution that does not conform to any particular specification. The tagging scheme has been chosen to fit the needs of the particular application, which is a common scenario found in many distributed solutions built upon XML.

An *Ad Hoc* XML Approach

The following example describes an order fulfillment application built to communicate with a Web server via *ad hoc* XML. Assume the application server supports the following interface:

```
OrderNum = OrderItem(PartNumber, Quantity, CustomerID)
```

In this case, a single method or function must be serialized in a way that the Web server can interpret the method and its parameters appropriately.

To properly construct the XML for this method call, a single root node is chosen in which the document element is named Fulfillment to encapsulate the method and its parameters.

The next step is to describe the method signature. The logical choice is to use the method name as an element name and to embed method parameter elements as children of the method.

The resulting request syntax looks like this:

```
<?xml version="1.0"?>
<Fulfillment>
    <OrderItem>
        <PartNumber>WIDGET101</PartNumber>
        <Quantity>4</Quantity>
        <CustomerID>C00316</CustomerID>
    </OrderItem>
</Fulfillment>
```

Listing 3.1 shows the Visual Basic proxy function that the client uses to serialize the method parameters.

LISTING 3.1   PROXY.BAS—Orders Serialization Function

```
'This function acts as a proxy for the remote call
Function OrderItem(PartNumber As String, Quantity As Integer, _
                   CustomerID As String) As Long

Dim reqdom As New msxml.DOMDocument
Dim reqstring As String
Dim inetctl As New XMLHTTPRequest

'Build request DOM
reqstring = "<?xml version='1.0'?><FulFillment><OrderItem>"
reqstring = reqstring + "<PartNumber>" + PartNumber + "</PartNumber>"
reqstring = reqstring + "<Quantity>" + Str(Quantity) + "</Quantity>"
reqstring = reqstring + "<CustomerID>" + CustomerID + "</CustomerID>"
reqstring = reqstring + "</OrderItem></FulFillment>"
reqdom.loadXML (reqstring)
```

continues

3

DISTRIBUTED
OBJECTS AND
XML

LISTING 3.1 Continued

```
'Build a temporary file for displaying the request message
'in a browser window
Dim reqfile As String
reqfile = "C:\_OrdersSample_req.xml"
reqdom.save reqfile
Form1.WebBrowser1.Navigate2 reqfile
Do While Form1.WebBrowser1.readyState < READYSTATE_COMPLETE
    DoEvents
Loop
Kill reqfile

'Make the call
Dim inet As New msxml.XMLHTTPRequest

Dim post As String
Dim url As String
post = "POST"
url = "http://localhost/orders.asp"
inet.open post, url

inet.send reqdom.xml
Do While inet.readyState < READYSTATE_COMPLETE
    DoEvents
Loop

'Load response into DOM
Dim respdom As New msxml.DOMDocument
respdom.loadXML inet.responseText

'Save response to a temporary file for displaying the
'response in a browser window
Dim respfile As String
respfile = "C:\_OrdersSample_resp.xml"
respdom.save respfile
Form1.WebBrowser2.Navigate2 respfile
Do While Form1.WebBrowser2.readyState < READYSTATE_COMPLETE
    DoEvents
Loop
Kill respfile

'Return the order number
OrderItem = respdom.documentElement. _
        getElementsByTagName("OrderNumber")(0).nodeTypedValue

End Function
```

The request is packaged into the body of an HTTP request and POSTed to the endpoint (that is, URL) on the server. In this case, the application posts to the ORDERS.ASP script. This server-side script analyzes the request information and executes the necessary operations to complete the transaction. The ORDERS.ASP script is shown in Listing 3.2.

LISTING 3.2   ORDERS.ASP Script

```
<%@ LANGUAGE=VBScript %>

<%
Dim r
Dim val
dim xmlDoc
set xmlDoc = Server.CreateObject("Microsoft.FreeThreadedXMLDOM")
if (xmlDoc is Nothing) then
    set xmlDoc = nothing
    Response.Write Err.description
End if

xmlDoc.load Request
if (Err.Number <> 0) then
    set xmlDoc = Nothing
    Response.Write Err.description
End if

dim xmlResp
set xmlResp = Server.CreateObject("Microsoft.FreeThreadedXMLDOM")
if (Err.Number <> 0) then
    set xmlResp = Nothing
    Response.Write Err.description
End if

dim resp
dim docelement
dim elementlist

set docelement = xmlDoc.documentElement
set elementlist = docelement.getElementsByTagName("Quantity")

dim ordernum
ordernum = elementlist(0).nodeTypedValue

'Create fake order number
'This is where real work should be done
ordernum = cstr(cint(ordernum)*1234)
```

3

DISTRIBUTED OBJECTS AND XML

continues

LISTING 3.2 Continued

```
if (Err.Number <> 0) then
    set xmlResp = Nothing
    Response.Write Err.description
End if

resp = "<?xml version='1.0'?> + _
        <Fulfillment><OrderItemResponse><OrderNumber>"
resp = resp + ordernum
resp = resp + "</OrderNumber></OrderItemResponse></Fulfillment>"
xmlResp.loadXML(resp)
if (Err.Number <> 0) then
    set xmlResp = Nothing
    Response.Write Err.description
End if

Response.write xmlResp.xml

%>
```

In order for the Web server to return an order number back to the client, a response message must be provided as follows:

```
<?xml version="1.0"?>
<Fulfillment>
    <OrderItemResponse>
        <OrderNumber>567890</OrderNumber>
    </OrderItemResponse>
</Fulfillment>
```

Here, <OrderItemResponse> is used to encapsulate the return value for the OrderItem() method.

In the situation where the server cannot process the request, an error can be returned as in the following:

```
<?xml version="1.0"?>
<Fulfillment>
    <Error>
        <Description>Out of memory</Description>
    </Error>
</Fulfillment>
```

When the client receives the response, it can locate the return value and resume normal processing just as it would for any other synchronous RPC mechanism.

Nothing about this system is hard to understand or implement, which is a big reason why developers are drawn to this type of implementation. However, several issues surface with such a simple design; these are covered in the next section.

A Generic Approach

Even though the preceding example is sufficient for the simple needs of the fulfillment application, the implementation becomes more difficult to manage as the scope of the application increases.

The current serialization is performed by a proxy function specifically designed to serialize the OrderItem() method. As new methods are introduced, new proxies must be built to properly serialize these methods. In turn, server-side parsers must be implemented for each corresponding proxy. This becomes a laborious task for large systems or when system interfaces change.

A better way is to build generic serializers that can use type information to properly encode the XML payload of the request. This also suggests that generic server-side parsers are a better solution for discovering the intention of the request. Combined, these provide a reusable infrastructure that can be applied to any application. Therefore, the <Fulfillment> element should be named to reflect the more generic purpose of encapsulating the body of the method, as seen in Listing 3.3.

Listing 3.3   The Body Element

```xml
<?xml version="1.0"?>
<Body>
    <OrderItem>
        <PartNumber>WIDGET101</PartNumber>
        <Quantity>4</Quantity>
        <CustomerID>C00316</CustomerID>
    </OrderItem>
</Body>
```

Now the problem becomes distinguishing between multiple interfaces that share a common method name. This is a perfect opportunity to use XML namespaces to specify the interface of the method, as seen in Listing 3.4.

3

DISTRIBUTED OBJECTS AND XML

LISTING 3.4 Using XML Namespaces to Distinguish Interfaces

```xml
<?xml version="1.0"?>
<Body>
    <OrderItem xmlns="OrdersInterface">
        <PartNumber>WIDGET101</PartNumber>
        <Quantity>4</Quantity>
        <CustomerID>C00316</CustomerID>
    </OrderItem>
</Body>
```

With this, you have enough information for the server to execute the correct method on the correct interface, and, in turn, the response can be constructed in a similar manner, as shown in Listing 3.5.

LISTING 3.5 The Server Response

```xml
<?xml version="1.0"?>
<Body>
    <OrderItemResponse xmlns="OrdersInterface">
        <OrderNumber>567890</OrderNumber>
    </OrderItemResponse>
</Body>
```

If an error occurs in the infrastructure, a fault can be returned as follows:

```xml
<?xml version="1.0"?>
<Body>
    <Fault>
        <!-- Fault information -->
    </Fault>
</Body>
```

In many situations you will find the need to include extended information with a remote procedure call. Such information includes security, debugging, causality, or transactional processing, as might be required at component runtime.

One option is to have the root element contain both the additional call context and the method element, as demonstrated in Listing 3.6.

LISTING 3.6 Including Extended Information

```xml
<?xml version="1.0"?>
<Body>
    <CallContext>
        <!-- Extended Info -->
```

```
    </CallContext>
    <OrderItem xmlns="OrdersInterface">
        <PartNumber>WIDGET101</PartNumber>
        <Quantity>4</Quantity>
        <CustomerID>C00316</CustomerID>
    </OrderItem>
</Body>
```

Unfortunately, this complicates the process of finding the method within the body of the request. It also forces the component runtime to parse more of the payload than necessary.

An alternative is to repackage the information in a similar way to how HTTP packages its requests. By using the concept of a header and a body, any infrastructure concerned with just the call context can easily extract pertinent fields from the header alone. To build well-formed XML, the header and body elements must then be encapsulated by a higher order element, in this case the <Envelope> element shown in Listing 3.7.

LISTING 3.7   Using a Header and Body

```
<?xml version="1.0"?>
<Envelope>
    <Header>
        <!-- Extended Info -->
    </Header>
    <Body>
        <OrderItem xmlns="OrdersInterface">
            <PartNumber>WIDGET101</PartNumber>
            <Quantity>4</Quantity>
            <CustomerID>C00316</CustomerID>
        </OrderItem>
    </Body>
</Envelope>
```

This serialization pattern provides a great deal of flexibility for the simple OrderItem() example. However, the more interesting concern is to see how it will behave for more complex data types and encoding optimizations.

Complex Serialization

Simple data types, as seen in the fulfillment system example, are easy to serialize within the method element. Each parameter can be represented by a single element containing the value of the parameter.

Compound data types require additional care during serialization; consider the following schema type:

```
<schema>
    <type name="ComplexOrder">
        <element name="PartNumber" type="string" />
        <element name="Quantity" type="integer" />
        <element name="CustomerID" type="string" />
    </type>
</schema>
```

This same type can be represented in Visual Basic and C++ as follows:

```
'Visual Basic Type
Private Type ComplexOrder
    PartNumber As String
    Quantity As Integer
    CustomerID As String
End Type


// C++ Structure
struct ComplexOrder
{
    std::string PartNumber;
    int         Quantity;
    std::string CustomerID;
};
```

Now consider this type when used as a method parameter:

```
Dim OrderInfo as ComplexOrder
OrderNum = OrderItem(OrderInfo)
```

The serialization code can represent the structure as embedded elements under the OrderInfo parameter element, with the request looking something like Listing 3.8.

LISTING 3.8 Serializing a Structure

```
<?xml version="1.0"?>
<Envelope>
    <Body>
        <OrderItem xmlns="OrdersInterface">
            <OrderInfo>
                <PartNumber>WIDGET101</PartNumber>
                <Quantity>4</Quantity>
                <CustomerID>C00316</CustomerID>
            </OrderInfo>
```

```
      </OrderItem>
    </Body>
</Envelope>
```

Modern day remoting architectures evaluate methods such that parameter data referenced multiple times will have its value serialized only once. For instance, consider the following method:

```
RegisterCustomer(CustomerID, ShippingAddress, BillingAddress)
```

Although the `ShippingAddress` and `BillingAddress` may contain the exact same information, as shown in Listing 3.9, this does not mean that they share the same identity. In this case, assuming the two parameters did share the same identity, they could be represented by the diagram in Figure 3.1.

LISTING 3.9 Shipping and Billing Address Structures

```
<ShippingAddress>
    <Street>123 Maple St.</Street>
    <City>Orlando</City>
    <State>FL</State>
    <ZipCode>12345</ZipCode>
</ShippingAddress>

<BillingAddress>
    <Street>123 Maple St.</Street>
    <City>Orlando</City>
    <State>FL</State>
    <ZipCode>12345</ZipCode>
</BillingAddress>
```

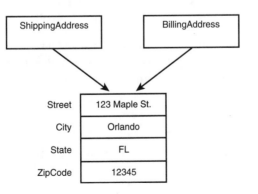

FIGURE 3.1

Multiple references with identity relationship.

3

DISTRIBUTED OBJECTS AND XML

Then the method could be serialized in a way that conserves space and more importantly preserves the identity of the parameters. In other words, it guarantees that the server can represent the data in the same way as it was represented on the client. The end result looks like Listing 3.10.

LISTING 3.10   Serializing Parameters with the Same Identity

```
<?xml version="1.0"?>
<Envelope>
    <Body>
        <OrderItem xmlns="OrdersInterface">
            <CustomerID>C00316</CustomerID>
            <ShippingAddress href="#address1" />
            <BillingAddress href="#address1" />
        </OrderItem>
        <Address id="address1">
            <Street>123 Maple St.</Street>
            <City>Orlando</City>
            <State>FL</State>
            <ZipCode>12345</ZipCode>
        </Address>
    </Body>
</Envelope>
```

Here, <Address> has become a direct descendant of the <Body> element, thus becoming independent from the method element.

Realizing SOAP

After inspecting the changes that were made to the *ad hoc* solution over the last section, you might have realized that this new serialization pattern is basically SOAP for HTTP.

The only remaining changes that should be made are to add the appropriate namespace qualifiers to <Envelope>, <Body>, and so on. Listing 3.11 shows how the preceding XML can be rewritten according to the SOAP specification.

LISTING 3.11   Valid SOAP XML

```
<?xml version="1.0"?>
<SOAP:Envelope xmlns:SOAP="urn:schemas-xmlsoap-org:soap.v1">
    <SOAP:Body>
        <OrderItem xmlns="OrdersInterface">
            <CustomerID>C00316</CustomerID>
            <ShippingAddress SOAP:href="#address1" />
```

```
                <BillingAddress SOAP:href="#address1" />
        </OrderItem>
        <Address SOAP:id="address1">
            <Street>123 Maple St.</Street>
            <City>Orlando</City>
            <State>FL</State>
            <ZipCode>12345</ZipCode>
        </Address>
    </SOAP:Body>
</SOAP:Envelope>
```

As you can see, SOAP on HTTP was derived from a very natural progression. It's not to say that this is the only way to formulate an XML remote procedure call, but it is certainly a simple and yet efficient mechanism for doing so.

The Need for Standardization

Rather than implement a serialization pattern that fits one particular need, it seems reasonable that a standard wire protocol built upon a common set of practices will provide a higher level of inter-operability.

As you've already seen in the last section, even the simplest of *ad hoc* implementations can be transformed into a more powerful and flexible protocol with only minor modifications.

In recent years, several protocols emerged to provide an RPC serialization format using XML. This section provides a description of the major XML RPC efforts that have been underway over the last few years. By understanding the basic principles behind these protocols, you will have a better understanding why there needs to be a standard protocol.

XML-RPC

The XML-RPC protocol defines a way for RPC requests and responses to be serialized into XML documents and sent across an HTTP connection. XML-RPC takes a simple approach to constructing a parameter list for a given method call. Each parameter includes an element describing the parameter type as well as the actual element content, as seen in Listing 3.12.

In this case, the <methodCall> element encapsulates the entire XML-RPC payload, similar to the SOAP <Envelope> element. One major difference between SOAP and XML-RPC is that XML-RPC uses a <methodName> element with the method name RegisterVoter as an element value; SOAP however uses the method name as the name of the element as in <RegisterVoter>. Finally, parameters in XML-RPC are encoded with type information elements such as <string>, which is contrary to SOAP which allows the use of XML Schemas to describe data types.

LISTING 3.12   XML-RPC Example

```
<?xml version="1.0"?>
<methodCall>
    <methodName>RegisterVoter</methodName>
    <params>
        <param>
            <value><string>Joe Voter</string></value>
        </param>
    </params>
</methodCall>
```

Although XML-RPC provides a flexible syntax that is very easy to implement, when compared to the SOAP specification, SOAP is nearly as simple and yet provides a greater level of extensibility for object-oriented systems.

XMOP

XML Metadata Object Persistence, or XMOP, is another effort that was designed to enable inter-operation between object technologies such as COM, Java, and so on by using XML in a similar manner as SOAP. Initially, XMOP used the Simple Object Definition Language (SODL) to serialize objects in XML, which is similar to the way IDL works in DCE RPC. However, just recently the XMOP effort began using the SOAP protocol, which should improve the chances for XMOP to be adopted on a larger scale.

More information can be found on XMOP in Appendix B, "Resources."

ebXML

Electronic Business XML, or ebXML, is yet another effort geared towards building a standard mechanism for business to share information using XML. ebXML uses a messaging approach to share XML documents between disparate business systems. Although there are several parallels between ebXML and SOAP, their scopes are quite different.

One aspect of ebXML is to define a messaging transport that enables clients to request *services* of a particular *Party*. In this case, a Party can be a company, organization, or system that can service a request on behalf of a client.

The following is a list of the requirements that the ebXML transport aims to meet:

- Envelope and headers for messages/documents
- Reliable messaging and error handling
- Message routing
- Security

- Audit trails
- Quality of service
- Platform independence
- Restart and recovery

To support this level of capabilities is a daunting task that may take several years to fully specify. Although the SOAP protocol does not specifically address these issues, many, if not all of these issues could be addressed by using the extensibility built into the SOAP framework.

The question then becomes, should SOAP natively support these features or should they be extensions that developers can include only when desired? Unfortunately this is not an easy question to answer, and different crowds have differing ideals.

SOAP

Neither XML-RPC nor XMOP have gained wide acceptance in the industry, and ebXML is still in its infancy. However, with the exception of ebXML's extensive list of requirements, it's clear that SOAP subsumes their capabilities and has already captured the attention of a large audience of developers.

In September 1999, the original SOAP specification v0.9 was proposed by a team consisting of Don Box from DevelopMentor; Gopal Kavivaya, Andrew Layman, and Satish Thatte from Microsoft; and Dave Winer from Userland Software.

Version 0.9 of SOAP was a great first attempt at trying to describe a protocol that would meet the majority of developers' needs. Eventually its shortcomings and problems were identified, and in November 1999 they were addressed in the v1.0 specification.

Finally, in April 2000, SOAP v1.1 was released with some minor modifications that simplify the specification and provide more modularity for protocols other than HTTP.

Regardless of whether the standard is SOAP, some derivation of SOAP, or possibly a new protocol, it's important for developers to build systems that can inter-operate without regard for platform or programming language.

XML is the most important step to making this happen, and it appears that the development community at large has agreed upon this fact. Unfortunately, developers are now having to face the battle of the XML protocols. Some protocols like XML-RPC are extremely simple and address the bare necessities, but leave little room for extensibility. Other protocols, like what's being developed for ebXML, are large and all-inclusive, which takes a long time to complete thus making them useless for current development efforts. SOAP seems to fit somewhere in the middle. It's a fairly simple protocol to understand, it provides good extensibility, and most importantly, SOAP is available now.

As is the case with most new technologies, it's important for developers to begin using a technology even when it may not be exactly what everyone wants. As time goes on and developers gain experience with the technology, it can be extended and enhanced to meet more of these needs. This basic principle has been proven by existing standards such as FTP, TCP/IP, XML, and so on. The reason they become standards is because developers prefer to use them; and developer preference is usually gained through exposure and experience.

The SOAP architects recognized the need for a simple, yet extensible framework that can become the standard XML RPC protocol of choice. Their intention was not to state that SOAP v1.0 was everything it should be, rather they designed a protocol that could be implemented quickly and effortlessly, and has the capability to grow as developer needs change. In SOAP v1.1, the SOAP authors decoupled SOAP from the HTTP protocol so that SOAP can be treated as a one-way messaging system that can also behave as an RPC or request/response protocol. To fully appreciate the benefits and simplicity that SOAP offers, you must experience the SOAP specification first hand. The following section provides an overview of the SOAP specification and the concepts it describes.

The SOAP Specification v1.1

The complete SOAP specification has been provided for you in Appendix A, "The SOAP 1.1 Specification," and should prove to be an invaluable tool as you develop SOAP implementations. Although the SOAP specification is fairly easy to read and understand, there are several esoteric details that might be overlooked. The following provides definitions for the SOAP terminology used in the specification, as well as an overview of SOAP v1.1.

Frequently Used Terminology

Table 3.1 defines several terms that are frequently used in the SOAP v1.1 specification. It is imperative that you fully understand their meaning in order to grasp the intentions of the document.

TABLE 3.1   SOAP Terminology

Term	Definition
Simple Type	A type that has no named parts, for example, integer, string, and so on.
Compound Type	A type that has named parts that uniquely describe particular content within the type, for example, the C `struct`, the C++ `class`, arrays, and so on.
Accessor	The name of a method parameter or a named part within a compound element.

Term	Definition
Independent Element	An element that appears at the top level of a serialization. The goal of an independent element is to represent instances of types.
Embedded Element	Any element that is not an independent element. Embedded elements represent accessors.
Single-reference	An element that can only be referenced by one accessor.
Multi-reference	An element that can be referenced by more than one accessor.

The remaining portion of this section will provide an overview of the SOAP v1.1 specification.

An Overview of the SOAP v1.1 Specification

This book's Introduction lays the groundwork for why SOAP should be considered a viable option for distributed computing. The SOAP specification clearly establishes its role as a protocol for defining a messaging system as well as remote procedure calls. Although the *O* in SOAP stands for *Object*, nothing in the specification suggests that the intention of SOAP is to provide any sort of object or component runtime. To the contrary, SOAP makes no attempt to define mechanisms for object invocation, garbage collection, and so on. SOAP does, however, provide the necessary mechanisms for building object-oriented systems on top of its infrastructure.

HTTP as a Base Transport

Version 1.0 of the specification mandated HTTP as its base transport, but version 1.1 has decoupled SOAP from HTTP to allow SOAP to be used in a messaging paradigm. This leaves the door wide open for a variety of other transports to carry SOAP, such as FTP, SMTP, and others.

Regardless of the transport, there is always some underlying work that must be done to invoke a method on a server. For SOAP as an RPC mechanism, this means constructing a valid HTTP request message.

By default, clients should start by using the POST method; only in the case where this fails with an HTTP status of *405 Method Not Allowed* should they attempt the request using M-POST. With the existing Web infrastructure, POST seems to be the reasonable choice at this point and time.

Although it is slightly easier to construct and parse the header fields for a POST than for an M-POST, conforming to M-POST can force clients to provide more detail about the client's request. Consider the examples of POST versus M-POST in Listing 3.13.

LISTING 3.13 POST Versus M-POST

```
POST /Script.pl HTTP/1.1
Host: www.mcp.com
Accept: text/*
Content-type: text/xml
Content-length: nnnn
SOAPAction: the-method-uri#DoSomething


M-POST /Script.pl HTTP/1.1
Host: www.mcp.com
Accept: text/*
Content-type: text/xml
Content-length: nnnn
Man: "urn:schemas-xmlsoap-org:soap.v1"; ns=01
01-SOAPAction: the-method-uri#DoSomething
```

> **NOTE**
>
> The original SOAP specification v0.9 originally forced M-POST calls to occur before POST calls, thus forcing clients to provide more detail with the first request.
>
> In SOAP v1.0, the specification called for POST calls to occur before M-POST, due to the limited adoption of M-POST.

SOAP recommends that a SOAPAction header field be provided with each SOAP request, such that the server can gather call information without having to parse the entire SOAP payload. At this point, SOAPAction is optional, and clients only have to use it when mandated by the server. However, it is expected that many of you will want to include SOAPAction in your SOAP implementations, so your server can know the intention of the request message.

Using XML in SOAP

One of the simplest aspects of SOAP is that it only requires calls to conform to proper XML syntax. No other XML technologies are required to make SOAP work, although XML Namespaces and XML Schemas make SOAP development much easier.

SOAP recommends the use of namespaces because they provide a mechanism to scope elements and attributes to various contexts. The specification states that clients are able to dictate whether or not namespaces are to be used in a conversation with the server. On the other hand, servers are responsible for ensuring that clients that use namespaces use them correctly. Servers also have the option to process requests that do not contain namespaces or, at a minimum, to respond with a fault.

The namespace `'urn:schemas-xmlsoap-org:soap.v1'` is the proposed namespace value for SOAP. This value is simply an URN that should be used to qualify SOAP element and attribute names and does not necessarily reflect any particular resource on the Internet.

SOAP also uses the `id`/`href` attribute pairs to distinguish between unique entities within the SOAP payload. This is necessary for providing multi-reference elements in the request and response payloads, such that you serialize the element once and reference it as many times as necessary.

Method Invocation

To execute a SOAP method call, the SOAP payload must be constructed with a `<SOAP:Envelope>` root element containing an optional `<SOAP:Header>` element and a mandatory `<SOAP:Body>` element.

The `<SOAP:Header>` element is used to encapsulate extended information about the call. The `<SOAP:Body>` element contains the actual method call (as its first child element) and the associated method parameters as either embedded or independent elements.

Figure 3.2 shows the basic structure of a SOAP payload.

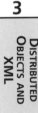

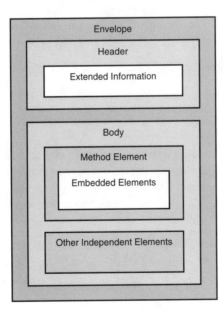

Figure 3.2

The basic SOAP payload structure.

Listing 3.14 shows the basic SOAP structure in use.

LISTING 3.14 Basic SOAP Structure

```
<SOAP-ENV:Envelope
      xmlns:SOAP-ENV="http://schemas.xmlsoap.org/soap/envelope/"
      SOAP-ENV:encodingStyle="http://schemas.xmlsoap.org/soap/encoding/">
   <SOAP-ENV:Header>
      <r:RequestNumber xmlns:r="Request-URI">
         2
      </r:RequestNumber>
   </SOAP-ENV:Header>
   <SOAP-ENV:Body>
      <m:GetTemperature xmlns:m="Thermostat-URI">
         <City>Orlando</City>
         <State>FL</State>
      </m:GetTemperature>
   </SOAP-ENV:Body>
</SOAP-ENV:Envelope>
```

Here, the header contains a namespace-qualified element called RequestNumber that keeps track of the number of times this request has been made.

The body contains a namespace-qualified method name GetTemperature that contains the city and state parameters.

NOTE

By qualifying the method name, you are implicitly qualifying its embedded elements so they do not require a namespace prefix.

Method Response

When a method call has been requested, the server has several options. It can return an HTTP error code or a SOAP fault containing a SOAP/application error, or it can return the results of the method execution. Both the fault and the method results use the standard SOAP payload syntax (that is, <Envelope>, <Body>, and so on).

A SOAP fault consists of four elements—a *faultcode*, *faultstring*, *runcode*, and an optional *detail* element, as shown in Listing 3.15.

LISTING 3.15   SOAP Fault

```
<SOAP-ENV:Envelope
        xmlns:SOAP-ENV="http://schemas.xmlsoap.org/soap/envelope/"
        SOAP-ENV:encodingStyle="http://schemas.xmlsoap.org/soap/encoding/">
    <SOAP-ENV:Body>
        <SOAP-ENV:Fault>
            <faultcode>300</faultcode>
            <faultstring>Invalid Request</faultstring>
            <runcode>1</runcode>
        </SOAP-ENV:Fault>
    </SOAP-ENV:Body>
</SOAP-ENV:Envelope>
```

> **NOTE**
>
> Just as with the `<m:GetTemperature>` element shown in Listing 3.14, the `<SOAP-ENV:Fault>` element does not require its embedded elements to be explicitly qualified because it is an instance of a type.

Any application fault details that need to be included with the fault must be properly typed and qualified using the `<detail>` element as shown in Listing 3.16.

LISTING 3.16   Application Fault Details

```
<SOAP-ENV:Fault>
    <faultcode>300</faultcode>
    <faultstring>Invalid Request</faultstring>
    <runcode>1</runcode>
    <detail xmlns:e="GetTemperatureErr-URI"
            xmlns:xsi="http://www.w3.org/1999/XMLSchema-instance"
            xsi:type="e:GetTemperatureFault">
        <number>5575910</number>
        <description>Sensor Failure</description>
        <file>GetTemperatureClass.cpp</file>
        <line>481</line>
    </detail>
</SOAP-ENV:Fault>
```

Notice that the `<detail>` element uses the XML Schema instance `xsi:type` attribute to denote its content type, `e:GetTemperatureFault`, which is also namespace qualified.

Constructing detailed faults in this way allows the client to fully interpret the application fault when necessary.

3

DISTRIBUTED
OBJECTS AND
XML

Representation of Types in the Payload

One of the most difficult aspects of SOAP to understand is the way types are represented in the payload. It's hard to anticipate the many ways parameters can or should be serialized.

SOAP has the capability to serialize any combination of simple and compound types as supported in modern-day programming languages. This is mostly because of SOAP's inclusion of the XML Schema work that is underway to define a standard mechanism for constructing metadata.

SOAP uses the concept of an accessor as the means to acquire a named value in the payload. Named values include parameters as well as the named parts of a compound type.

There are two kinds of values in a SOAP payload. The first kind is called a *single-reference value* and can only be referenced by one accessor. Consider the following XML fragment:

```
<Car>Corvette</Car>
<Automobile>Corvette</Automobile>
```

In this case, both the `<Car>` element and the `<Automobile>` element contain their own unique `Corvette` values. This means that each `Corvette` value has only been referenced by its surrounding element (that is, accessor) and no other.

The second kind of value in a SOAP payload is called a *multi-reference value* and can be referenced by one or more accessors. Let's examine a similar XML fragment that uses multi-reference values:

```
<Car href="#somecar" />
<Automobile id="somecar">Corvette</Automobile>
```

In this example, `Corvette` is referenced by two accessors, the `Car` accessor and the `Automobile` accessor; thus, it is considered a multi-reference value.

The purpose for distinguishing between single-reference and multi-reference values helps to deal with identity issues of serializing (that is, marshaling) data across the wire. For instance, if two method parameters reference the same value, in some cases you will want the XML to reflect this identity and in other cases you won't. Chapter 6, "SOAP and Data: Data Types," provides an in-depth look at identity and serialization techniques.

SOAP also distinguishes between elements that are independent and elements that are embedded. *Independent elements* are at the highest level of serialization, such as elements contained within SOAP-ENV:Body, and represent instances of types. The name of the independent element is typically the name of the type that it represents. Consider the following XML:

```
<SOAP-ENV:Envelope
        xmlns:SOAP="http://schemas.xmlsoap.org/soap/envelope/"
        SOAP-ENV:encodingStyle="http://schemas.xmlsoap.org/soap/encoding/">
```

```
<SOAP-ENV:Body>
    <m:MyMethod xmlns:m="Method-URI">
        <Car href="#somecar" />
    </m:MyMethod>
    <Automobile id="somecar">Corvette</Automobile>
</SOAP-ENV:Body>
</SOAP-ENV:Envelope>
```

In this example, since by definition `<SOAP-ENV:Body>` is an element that can stand alone, any direct descendants of `<SOAP-ENV:Body>` are considered independent elements. In this case, `<m:MyMethod>` is an independent element that describes the method and `<Automobile>` is an independent element describing an `Automobile` type.

Embedded elements are anything that's not considered an independent element, and they represent accessors. The name of the embedded element is the same as the name of the accessor that it represents. Referring to the last example, the `<Car>` element is an embedded element and accessor since the `<m:MyMethod>` element is an independent element that is at the highest level of the serialization.

The SOAP specification provides a set of rules that define how the preceding constructs should be used to serialize data. It also addresses the more specific procedures that should be followed when serializing particular types such as arrays and strings.

Serialization will be discussed in greater detail in Chapters 5, "SOAP and Data: The XML Payload," and 6, "SOAP and Data: Data Types." However, the basics discussed in this chapter will go a long way to helping you understand how SOAP works.

Summary

This chapter described some of the motivations behind the movement towards XML in a distributed application community. Rather than having new *ad hoc* implementations emerge on a daily basis, it seems viable that SOAP could be adopted as the protocol of choice for its simplicity and extensibility.

A ten-thousand-foot view of the SOAP specification was provided with definitions of the new terminology it introduces. Envelopes contain headers and bodies, bodies contain independent elements that represent types, and independent elements contain embedded elements that represent accessors. Overall, SOAP accounts for everything needed to build a distributed application infrastructure on top of XML.

3

DISTRIBUTED OBJECTS AND XML

SOAP and Data: Protocol Transports

IN THIS CHAPTER

For systems to communicate in today's world, they must agree on common protocols. When considering the Internet, several protocols have emerged to become widely adopted. The OSI Model represents the layered network environment where distributed systems can thrive without being tightly coupled to any particular network environment. This layered approach has enabled developers to introduce new communication protocols to serve various needs. Protocols that are easy to use and that can be applied to a wide spectrum of problem domains have a much better chance of being adopted than those that are complex and overly specialized. This has definitely been true for protocols such as TCP/IP and HTTP, and serves as the basis for discussion in this chapter.

The chapter also presents a detailed look at the HTTP protocol and how it applies to the current working draft of SOAP. Other alternatives to HTTP for transmitting SOAP payloads are considered, such as messaging protocols. Finally, in line with the OSI Model, the chapter introduces the possibilities of layering other protocols on top of SOAP for extensibility purposes.

SOAP and HTTP

When considering SOAP, version 1.0 of the specification defined an XML-based protocol that can travel in HTTP requests and responses. Although version 1.1 of the SOAP specification placed less emphasis on HTTP, there is still a great deal of commercial interest in using HTTP to move SOAP payloads. Because the current Internet infrastructure is heavily based on HTTP as a standardized method of communications, it only makes sense for SOAP to exploit this feature. One of the most compelling reasons for approaching distributed systems this way is to quickly gain support from the Internet community. Nothing about HTTP is platform specific, which makes it an obvious candidate for bridging the gap between disparate systems. Because of this, inter-operability is only bounded by the limitations of current day standards. As new standards in XML and other Internet technology surface, better and faster inter-operability should emerge.

> **NOTE**
>
> SOAP v1.0 relied on HTTP 1.0 as its transport protocol, but SOAP 1.1 doesn't specify any particular version of HTTP. However, SOAP can perform much better with HTTP 1.1 because it provides multiple transactions per connection and greater security capabilities with the HTTP Extension Framework.

The mass quantities of interconnected systems on the Internet are due, in part, to the simplicity of the HTTP protocol. Although text-based protocols do not achieve the same performance as binary protocols, they do allow a wider variety of system platforms to participate in Internet conversations. Based on the reaction of the Internet community over the last 10 years, this trade-off appears to be acceptable. The overall simplicity and compatibility of using text-based protocols is a major motivating factor behind SOAP.

Another aspect of interconnecting systems—one that most developers prefer to ignore because of its complexity—is security. In general, most systems reside behind a firewall or proxy in order to protect the internal network from mischievous attacks. This poses a serious problem for interconnecting non-trivial systems through traditional transports such as DCE-RPC, because the endpoint ports these protocols require for communication are administratively blocked by the firewall. As a human readable protocol, HTTP makes it very easy for humans to visually inspect HTTP traffic and firewalls to quickly gather relevant content within incoming requests. Although the SOAP working draft does not directly address security, it does provide an opening for firewalls (or the equivalent) to assume the responsibility of monitoring SOAP traffic. Security will be discussed further as the specifics of HTTP are presented throughout the rest of this chapter.

Request and Response Model

Most developers are familiar with the typical client/server model of the Internet. In general, the client connects to a server, asks for a unique resource, and, if possible, the server on the other end provides the requested information. After the server has responded, it discards all *state* concerning the transaction, closes the connection, and reverts back to listening for new connections. Conversations are kept short, simple, and to the point. This low-overhead approach provides a very scalable environment for servers to share information with many different clients.

Traditionally, servers don't usually disconnect clients after a single transaction. Re-establishing connections becomes extremely expensive, in terms of system resources, when clients attempt to request multiple resources in a very short period of time. Therefore, HTTP 1.1 provides a *Keep-Alive* feature that enables clients to remain connected to the server so that more than one request can be made. However, the server still discards the state information after each transaction in order to preserve the behavior of the model.

Because SOAP can reside on HTTP, it inherits the behavior of the underlying protocol architecture, and therefore becomes a very scalable protocol as well.

The SOAP request/response method operates in a very similar way to HTTP. When a client makes an HTTP request, the server attempts to service the request and can respond in one of two ways. It can either respond successfully by returning the requested information, or it can respond with an error (or, in SOAP terms, a fault) notifying the client of the particular reason why the request couldn't be serviced. SOAP operates on the same principle, with very similar constructs.

Let's take a closer look at the HTTP protocol to see how SOAP can leverage its capabilities.

HTTP Methods, Headers, and Bodies

HTTP supports several ways to request information via a *request header*. It does so by using *methods,* or *verbs,* to describe its intention to the server, and *header fields* for including *name-value* pairs of request data. When the server responds, it generates a response message, consisting of a *response header* that includes a *status line*, as well as *header fields* for including *name-value* pairs of response data. Together, methods and headers provide an extensible framework that is both simple and succinct.

The GET Method

The GET method is the most commonly used HTTP request. This method provides the server with the necessary information to identify a particular resource, so it can locate the data and send it to the client. The following is a simplified example of such a request:

```
GET /default.htm HTTP/1.1
Accept: text/*
User-Agent: Mozilla/4.0+(compatible;+MSIE+5.0;+Windows+NT;+DigExt)
Host: www.mcp.com:8080
{CR}{LF}
```

The first line, called the *method field*, consists of three space-delimited text fields. The first field provides the request method, the second field identifies the resource that the client is interested in, and the third field specifies the version of HTTP that the client supports.

The Accept field provides a MIME type that specifies the types of data the client can accept. In this case, the client is willing to accept any form of text content as denoted by text/*.

The User-Agent field provides information about the client software that is making this request. This enables the server to alter the content based on the type of client making the call.

The Host field contains the name of the server being requested followed by an optional port number (defaulting to port 80). This information comes in very handy when requests are made through proxy servers.

Finally, the last line of the request must be terminated by a *{CR}{LF}* pair to denote the end of the transmission.

After the server has received the request, it attempts to locate the resource and send the data back to the client. If successful, a response might look something like this:

```
HTTP/1.1 200 OK
Content-type: text/html
{CR}{LF}
<html><head><title>My default.htm page</title></head>
<body>
```

```
    <b>HTTP is good</b>
</body>
</html>
```

The first line in the response is called the *status line* and consists of three space-delimited text fields. The first field is the HTTP version supported by the server, followed by a status code and an explanation or status string.

The `Content-type` field indicates the MIME type of the data content being transmitted to the client. In the case of HTML, this is `text/html`, but in the case of SOAP the `Content-type` is `text/xml`.

> **NOTE**
>
> In the original SOAP working draft (dated September 1999), the specification called for the `Content-Type` field to be populated with `text/xml-SOAP`. Because there is no real difference between the XML used in SOAP and other forms of XML, this customization was dropped for the standard `text/xml` type.

In the case of the preceding example, the actual content is separated from the response header by a `{CR}{LF}` pair. Also, there is no length specified in this response, so the client is required to continuously read the data stream until the server terminates the connection. It is important to note that, when using Keep-Alive connections, servers *must* provide a `Content-length`, otherwise the client would not know when to stop reading the data stream because the server would never terminate the connection.

> **TIP**
>
> Keep-Alive connections are extremely valuable for displaying Web pages because of the large quantity of resources typically requested. However, in the case of SOAP, although the SOAP working draft doesn't discuss Keep-Alive connections, you should choose carefully when deciding to support them in your SOAP servers. Because a well-designed interface for a distributed system should not expect frequent consecutive calls from the same client, it can be beneficial for you to close the connection after each transaction. To do this, you send `Connection: Close` in the request header.

4

PROTOCOL
TRANSPORTS

Although there are many other fields in the request and response headers that have not been mentioned, describing these fields in detail will not provide any significant aid in understanding SOAP. To learn more about these fields, you should refer to the HTTP specification (see Appendix B, "Resources") for details.

Now consider the situation where the server is unable to locate the requested resource. In this case, the server must respond with an appropriate error message that notifies the client of the particular problem, such as

```
HTTP/1.1 404 Object Not Found
Content-type: text/html
{CR}{LF}
<html><head><title>HTTP 404 Not Found</title></head>
<body>
    <h1>HTTP/1.1 404 File not found</h1>
</body>
</html>
```

The GET method supports transmitting data to the server above and beyond the fields that have already been discussed. In particular, the URL can contain a *query string* that consists of delimited name-value pairs, which communicate application-specific data to the server. The following is a sample URL and query string as they exist in the request header:

```
GET /default.pl?search=Lumber+Yard&user=Danny HTTP/1.1
Accept: text/*
User-Agent: Mozilla/4.0+(compatible;+MSIE+5.0;+Windows+NT;+DigExt)
Host: www.mcp.com
{CR}{LF}
```

As you can see, the search name contains the value Lumber+Yard, and the user is Danny. The server can easily parse the URL to retrieve these fields and behave accordingly.

This mechanism is extremely useful for simple HTTP requests, but as requests get more complicated, the query string becomes more difficult to manage. If any special characters are submitted on the query string, they will require special formatting to adhere to the HTTP specification. The specification dictates that special characters be encoded using their equivalent ASCII hex value, as shown in the next request header fragment:

```
GET /default.pl?search=Lots%20of%20spaces HTTP/1.1
```

In this case, the spaces between Lots of spaces are translated into %20 (their hex equivalent) to conform to the HTTP specification header requirements. In order for your software to use this parameter, you must reverse the translation process for all special characters. The bottom line is, URLs are simply not practical for transmitting large quantities of data and this poses a problem for SOAP.

SOAP and the POST Method

A better way for transmitting data is by using the HTTP POST method, which transmits the request content in the *body* of the HTTP request message, rather than on the URL, as shown in the following example:

```
POST /default.pl HTTP/1.1
Connection: Keep-Alive
User-Agent: Mozilla/4.0+(compatible;+MSIE+5.0;+Windows+NT;+DigExt)
Host: www.mcp.com
Accept: text/*
Content-type: text/xml
Content-length: nnnn
{CR}{LF}
<ContentBody>This is the body of my POSTing</ContentBody>
```

This form of request enables the data content to be easily processed without the need for character conversions or concerns of size limitations.

This is the direction taken by the inventors of SOAP. The SOAP working draft requires the use of the POST method (and M-POST method, as described in the next section) to submit SOAP calls to the server. SOAP calls are serialized into XML documents and placed in the message body of the HTTP request as follows:

```
POST /PartServer.pl HTTP/1.1
Host: www.mcp.com
Accept: text/*
Content-type: text/xml
Content-length: nnnn
SOAPAction: the-method-uri#FindPart
{CR}{LF}
<SOAP-ENV:Envelope
        xmlns:SOAP-ENV="http://schemas.xmlsoap.org/soap/envelope/"
        SOAP-ENV:encodingStyle="http://schemas.xmlsoap.org/soap/encoding/">
    <SOAP-ENV:Body>
        <m:FindPart xmlns:m="the-method-uri">
            <PartNo>12345</PartNo>
            <GroupID>7</GroupID>
        </m:FindPart>
    </SOAP-ENV:Body>
</SOAP-ENV:Envelope>
```

The specifics of the message body will be discussed in Chapter 5, "SOAP and Data: The XML Payload," but the HTTP headers require further inspection here.

You should notice that the SOAPAction field has been added to the HTTP header for SOAP-specific purposes. This mandatory field is used to provide information about the intent of the SOAP payload (typically a method call), so that firewalls (or the equivalent) can preprocess the HTTP headers to ensure the call is authorized to proceed. This is a reasonable approach because most system administrators enforce stringent rules on Internet traffic coming through their firewalls, and firewalls are not required to parse the SOAP payload to monitor traffic.

4

If the HTTP header meets the firewall's requirements, then the SOAP call can be forwarded to the appropriate server, where the contents of SOAPAction are matched against the associated method name and namespace URI within the payload. Referring to the example, the-method-uri#FindPart can be broken down into the method name—FindPart—and the URI—the-method-uri. These are compared to the element <m:FindPart xmlns:m="the-method-uri"> to ensure that they do, in fact, match. If either the URI or the method name does not match, the server must return a fault. By performing this check, you are guaranteeing that your SOAP server executes the exact same method approved by the firewall.

In the case where SOAPAction exists but does not meet the firewall's requirements, the firewall will return an HTTP error code. This enables the firewall to impose restrictions on the valid methods that can be executed.

If a SOAPAction value is not present at all, the firewall has the option of returning an HTTP error code or forwarding the call to the server for processing.

So when should you use the SOAPAction field? Considering how easy it is to include it in the request header and the benefits of doing so, the answer is likely *all of the time*. Besides the security ramifications, you might also find it valuable to use SOAPAction for routing method calls to different servers. If this information does not exist in the HTTP header, your SOAP router must parse the message body for details about the method call before routing the request or simply reject the call. This overhead will be much more costly than any performance savings gained from dropping this field.

Assuming that the SOAP call in the preceding example adheres to the HTTP requirements, and that the SOAP server is able to process the request either successfully or as a fault, then the following HTTP response is sent to the client:

```
HTTP/1.1 200 OK
Content-type: text/xml
Content-length: nnnn
{CR}{LF}
<SOAP-ENV:Envelope
       xmlns:SOAP-ENV="http://schemas.xmlsoap.org/soap/envelope/"
       SOAP-ENV:encodingStyle="http://schemas.xmlsoap.org/soap/encoding/">
   <SOAP-ENV:Body>
       <!-- The method response or fault -->
   </SOAP-ENV:Body>
</SOAP-ENV:Envelope>
```

The specifics of the method response or fault will be discussed in Chapter 7, "SOAP and Communications: Invoking Remote Methods." Regardless of the success of the method call, the HTTP response should be HTTP/1.1 200 OK; this tells the client that the fault was with the method call, not the communications layer. The client can then inspect the HTTP message body for more information.

Now that you understand how HTTP is used to communicate SOAP calls using the POST method, consider the M-POST extension that SOAP allows.

SOAP and the M-POST Method

Per the SOAP v1.0 specification, clients must first use the POST method to attempt a SOAP call. If this request fails with an HTTP status of *510 Not Extended*, then the client can reciprocate by using the M-POST method. However, SOAP v1.1 no longer mandates a policy and leaves it up to the SOAP implementation.

The M-POST method comes from the HTTP Extension Framework working draft. This method denotes a *mandatory* request and requires that additional HTTP header fields be included in the request. Once again, this enables firewalls and the like to enforce constraints on the way SOAP calls are processed.

As the new HTTP Extension Framework is slowly adopted, it might become necessary for SOAP clients to support this protocol. Servers or firewalls that want to enforce the use of M-POST can simply deny standard POST requests by using the *510 Not Extended* error.

When the M-POST method is used, mandatory header fields must be included to guarantee a valid HTTP request. The following is an example of a SOAP call using M-POST:

```
M-POST /PartServer.pl HTTP/1.1
Host: www.mcp.com
Accept: text/*
Content-type: text/xml
Content-length: nnnn
Man: "http://schemas.xmlsoap.org/soap/envelope/"; ns=01
01-SOAPAction: the-method-uri#FindPart
{CR}{LF}
<SOAP-ENV:Envelope
       xmlns:SOAP-ENV="http://schemas.xmlsoap.org/soap/envelope/"
       SOAP-ENV:encodingStyle="http://schemas.xmlsoap.org/soap/encoding/">
   <SOAP-ENV:Body>
       <m:FindPart xmlns:m="the-method-uri">
           <PartNo>12345</PartNo>
           <GroupID>7</GroupID>
       </m:FindPart>
   </SOAP-ENV:Body>
</SOAP-ENV:Envelope>
```

Here, the Man field describes a mandatory end-to-end *extension declaration*, which maps the *header-prefix* 01 to the http://schemas.xmlsoap.org/soap/envelope/ namespace. This header-prefix is included with each SOAP-specific header field, as in this case of 01-SOAPAction. This enables firewalls and servers to force clients to include the mandatory fields with their requests. In turn, the firewall or server must respond with the appropriate extension response header field Ext as follows:

```
HTTP/1.1 200 OK
Ext:
Cache-Control: no-cache="Ext"
...etc...
```

In this example, the server sends the *extension acknowledgement* and denotes that the Ext field should not be cached.

Although the HTTP Extension Framework provides a greater means for monitoring SOAP requests, it will be some time before it is fully adopted on the Internet. The original SOAP working draft published in September 1999 mandated that M-POST must be used *first*. If the server responded with an HTTP error *501 Not Implemented* or *510 Not Extended*, then you were required to follow up with a normal POST. Fortunately, the creators of SOAP realized that the additional round-trip under existing conditions would somewhat hinder SOAP's capability to be adopted, so they reversed the order of the calls in SOAP v1.0, and ultimately left it unspecified in SOAP v1.1.

TIP

As you develop your SOAP infrastructure, keep in mind that you might encounter SOAP servers that require the M-POST extensions. In this situation, you might want to temporarily cache this fact for subsequent calls to this particular server, thus avoiding additional round-trips.

You might want to refer to the HTTP specification as well as the HTTP Extension Framework draft to become more familiar with the implications of each protocol. However, what you have just learned is sufficient for developing a SOAP implementation.

Now that you understand how the HTTP request and response messages work with SOAP, you might want to monitor HTTP traffic as you debug your SOAP systems. The next section describes one way to implement such an application.

Monitoring SOAP Traffic

When developing distributed systems, it can be difficult to debug problems in the data stream because of the binary transport mechanisms typically employed. In the case of SOAP, this is not a problem because of its readability on the wire. An obvious solution is to provide a mechanism for *dumping* the HTTP data as it moves between the client and server.

Although there are several Web servers publicly available, Microsoft's IIS server provides a simple interface for intercepting HTTP traffic, and sets the stage for the following example. The example is a simple ISAPI filter that can be installed under the IIS Web server to monitor SOAP traffic.

If you are an IIS user, this gives you a starting point for building a more robust debugging tool if you so desire. If you are using Apache or another type of Web server, you can take the basic idea and construct a similar tool.

XFilter

The XFilter utility was written with Visual C++ and provides a base class for other ISAPI filters to build upon. The basic principle behind ISAPI is to enable you to splice your own code in between various phases of IIS as it processes HTTP requests and responses. To do this, you must provide a DLL with two known entry points, called `HttpFilterProc` and `GetFilterVersion`.

LISTING 4.1   DLLEXPORTS.CPP—ISAPI DLL Entry Points

```
#include "stdafx.h"
#include "FilterBase.h"

extern FilterBase* g_pFilter;

extern "C" DWORD WINAPI
HttpFilterProc(HTTP_FILTER_CONTEXT* pfc,
               DWORD dwNotificationType,
               LPVOID pvNotification)
{
    return g_pFilter->HttpFilterProc(pfc,
                                     dwNotificationType,
                                     pvNotification);
}

extern "C" BOOL WINAPI
GetFilterVersion(HTTP_FILTER_VERSION* pVer)
{
    return g_pFilter->GetFilterVersion(pVer);
}
```

4

PROTOCOL
TRANSPORTS

Consider the code in Listing 4.1. When IIS first attempts to load a filter, it calls the `GetFilterVersion` function. Upon receiving this call, the filter must register for other events or notifications it wants to receive. The filter also provides IIS with version information and a description of the filter.

Assuming `GetFilterVersion` succeeds, IIS begins forwarding all registered notifications to the filter for processing. Each event triggers a call to the `HttpFilterProc` function, passing in the *notification type*, a *filter context*, and a pointer to a notification data structure specific to that particular notification type.

> **NOTE**
>
> A *filter context* provides information to the filter that IIS maintains for the current HTTP transaction. This also includes callback methods for retrieving data, allocating memory within IIS, adjusting response headers, and more.

As you can see from Listing 4.1, the entry points for XFilter delegate all calls to a singleton filter object as described in the `FILTERBASE.H` and `FILTERBASE.CPP` files found in the accompanying source code. The code fragment in Listing 4.2 shows how this base class dispatches events to class methods.

LISTING 4.2   FILTERBASE.CPP—HttpFilterProc Implementation

```
DWORD FilterBase::HttpFilterProc(
                            HTTP_FILTER_CONTEXT *pfc,
                            DWORD dwNotificationType,
                            LPVOID pvNotif)
{
    DWORD rc = SF_STATUS_REQ_NEXT_NOTIFICATION;

    // Dispatch the event as necessary
    try
    {
        switch (dwNotificationType)
        {
        case SF_NOTIFY_ACCESS_DENIED:
            rc = OnAccessDenied(pfc,
                    (HTTP_FILTER_ACCESS_DENIED *)pvNotif);
            break;

        case SF_NOTIFY_AUTHENTICATION:
            rc = OnAuthentication(pfc,
```

```
                    (HTTP_FILTER_AUTHENT *)pvNotif);
        break;

    case SF_NOTIFY_END_OF_NET_SESSION:
        rc = OnEndOfNetSession(pfc);
        break;

    case SF_NOTIFY_END_OF_REQUEST:
        rc = OnEndOfRequest(pfc);
        break;

    case SF_NOTIFY_LOG:
        rc = OnLog(pfc,
                (HTTP_FILTER_LOG *) pvNotif);
        break;

    case SF_NOTIFY_NONSECURE_PORT:
        rc = OnNonSecurePort(pfc);
        break;

    case SF_NOTIFY_PREPROC_HEADERS:
        rc = OnPreprocHeaders(pfc,
                (HTTP_FILTER_PREPROC_HEADERS*)pvNotif);
        break;

    case SF_NOTIFY_READ_RAW_DATA:
        rc = OnReadRawData(pfc,
                (HTTP_FILTER_RAW_DATA *)pvNotif);
        break;

    case SF_NOTIFY_SECURE_PORT:
        rc = OnSecurePort(pfc);
        break;

    case SF_NOTIFY_SEND_RAW_DATA:
        rc = OnSendRawData(pfc,
                (HTTP_FILTER_RAW_DATA *)pvNotif);
        break;

    case SF_NOTIFY_URL_MAP:
        rc = OnUrlMap(pfc,
                (HTTP_FILTER_URL_MAP *)pvNotif);
        break;
    }
}
```

4

**PROTOCOL
TRANSPORTS**

continues

LISTING 4.2 Continued

```
    catch (...)
    {
        rc = SF_STATUS_REQ_NEXT_NOTIFICATION;
    }

    return rc;
}
```

You should also be aware that `FilterBase` is an abstract base class, forcing derived classes to implement the pure virtual `FilterBase::GetFilterVersion` method.

The derived class `XFilter`, is responsible for overloading the `FilterBase` methods that it is interested in, as well as providing the `GetFilterVersion` method for registering with IIS. Listing 4.3 shows the `XFilter` implementation of `GetFilterVersion`. This version of `XFilter` only registers for the `SF_NOTIFY_READ_RAW_DATA` event, which occurs when a client requests information from the Web server.

LISTING 4.3 `XFilter.cpp`—`GetFilterVersion` Method

```
BOOL XFilter::GetFilterVersion(HTTP_FILTER_VERSION *pVer)
{
    pVer->dwFlags = SF_NOTIFY_ORDER_DEFAULT |
                    SF_NOTIFY_READ_RAW_DATA;

    // Setup the filter version and description
    pVer->dwFilterVersion = HTTP_FILTER_REVISION;
    _tcscpy(pVer->lpszFilterDesc, _T("XFilter"));

    return TRUE;
}
```

Each time a client makes an HTTP request against the Web server, IIS calls the DLL entry points, which ultimately get dispatched to the `OnReadRawData` method as implemented by the `XFilter` class and shown in Listing 4.4. This method opens an output stream and dumps the contents of the *raw data* structure. This content is *exactly* what IIS received prior to any processing, which means the HTTP header and body are included in this buffer.

LISTING 4.4 `XFILTER.CPP`—`OnReadRawData` Method

```
DWORD XFilter::OnReadRawData(HTTP_FILTER_CONTEXT *pfc,
                             HTTP_FILTER_RAW_DATA *pfrd)
{
    try
    {
```

```
    // Has this request already been processed?
    if (pfc->pFilterContext == static_cast<PVOID>(this))
        return SF_STATUS_REQ_NEXT_NOTIFICATION;

    // Open the output file
    ofstream pstrm;
    pstrm.open(XFILTER_FILE, ios::out | ios::app);

    // Create a buffer for storing the data stream
    DWORD dwSize = HEADERBUFSIZE;
    CHAR* thebuf = new CHAR[dwSize];

    // Copy the data into the buffer
    memcpy(thebuf, pfrd->pvInData, pfrd->cbInBuffer);
    thebuf[pfrd->cbInBuffer] = 0;

    // Write the buffer to the file
    pstrm << thebuf;

    delete [] thebuf;

    // Flush the data and close the stream
    pstrm.flush();
    pstrm.close();

    // Use the filter context to denote we've already been here
    pfc->pFilterContext = static_cast<PVOID>(this);
}
catch(...)
{
    LogError("Caught exception in OnReadRawData()");
}

// Pass this request on to the next Filter in the chain
return SF_STATUS_REQ_NEXT_NOTIFICATION;
}
```

NOTE

Because of the overhead of processing every HTTP request and response, it is not a good idea to use a filter of this sort for anything but development purposes.

Other notifications you should be interested in are SF_NOTIFY_SEND_RAW_DATA and
SF_NOTIFY_PREPROC_HEADERS. SF_NOTIFY_SEND_RAW_DATA enables you to monitor responses
sent from the server to the client. The SF_NOTIFY_PREPROC_HEADERS notification is sent after
the raw data has been read from the client and parsed into separate header fields, but just prior
to acting on the request.

One caveat exists with this implementation. In reality, the SF_NOTIFY_READ_RAW_DATA notification occurs multiple times during a single request (refer to Microsoft's ISAPI documentation
for a complete explanation). Because of this, the OnReadRawData method will be called several
times, resulting in the same request data being dumped more than once. To correct this, you
need to use the filter context pointer pFilterContext to identify requests that are still in
progress. This example uses the object's identity (that is, the (this) pointer) to facilitate this
process. Each new request provides a *clean* pFilterContext pointer that can be used to determine if the request has already been processed.

Installing XFilter

In order to install an ISAPI filter under IIS, you must launch the *Internet Service Manager*
application. Normally you can install different filters for each Web site hosted by your IIS
server. However, filters that need access to SF_NOTIFY_READ_RAW_DATA and
SF_NOTIFY_SEND_RAW_DATA must be installed under the *Master Properties* of the IIS server,
and therefore these filters will apply to *all* hosted sites.

From within the Internet Service Manager, select the Properties of the host computer as shown
in Figure 4.1.

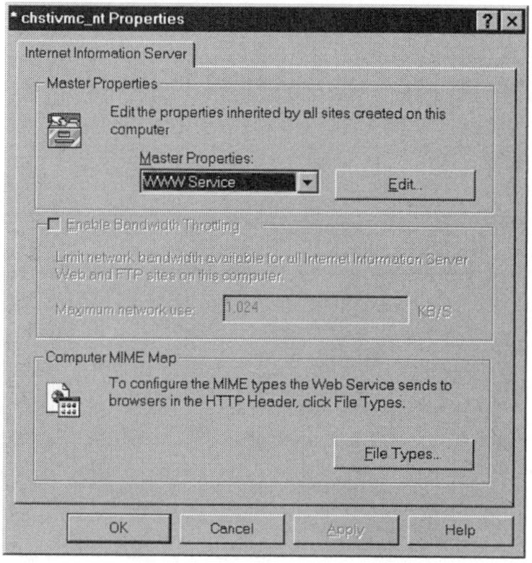

FIGURE 4.1
The Host Computer Properties dialog box.

Here, you choose to edit the master properties of the *WWW Service*. Under the *ISAPI Filters* tab, shown in Figure 4.2, you can add new filters to your server by providing a path to the filter DLL.

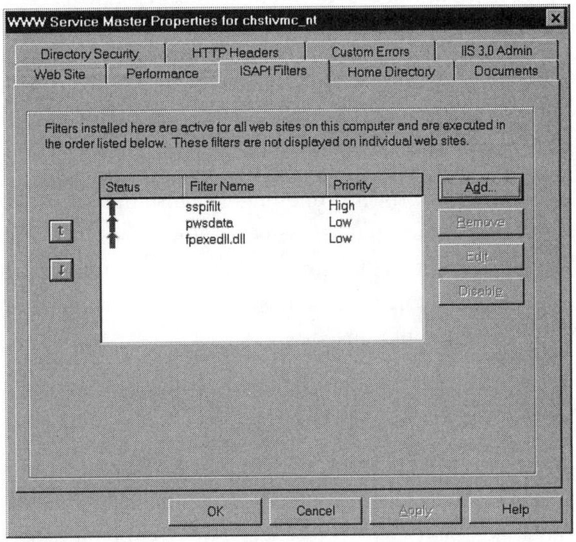

FIGURE 4.2
The WWW Service Master Properties dialog box.

After you have added the filter to your server, you might need to reboot the system so the changes are correctly applied.

To disable the filter, simply remove it from this list.

Bi-Directional HTTP

A common practice in software development involves the use of the asynchronous *callback* mechanism. Occasionally a client might want to send a request to the server and continue processing. Meanwhile, the server executes the call to completion and then notifies the client that the work has been done. When notified, the client can retrieve the results and begin using this data. This is also very useful when clients want to register for notification of various types of events that might occur on the server.

Although this is a widely used technique, it doesn't fit very well into the current Internet paradigm. Usually clients do not run an HTTP server, so the SOAP server has no way to call back to the client. Another problem is the probability that the client sits behind a firewall or proxy that will not allow incoming requests to be directed at the client, even if the client is running an HTTP server.

One way to *simulate* a callback is by having the client launch a new thread that executes a second call to the server and waits, or *blocks,* for the original call to finish execution. When complete, the SOAP server responds to the pending call, thereby indirectly notifying the client. This is not a very feasible approach and defeats the scalability goals of HTTP servers by requiring the second outstanding call to hold a connection.

A second approach might be to provide a centralized client-side SOAP server that can dispatch callbacks to various clients. This too has several drawbacks that make it less than desirable; most importantly, clients cannot be expected to host such a server.

Ultimately, there is no good answer for this dilemma because this is just how HTTP was designed, in order to provide a robust and secure communications link. Rather than trying to change this pattern, it seems acceptable to simply code to this paradigm. However, because the SOAP v1.1 specification has decoupled SOAP from HTTP, mechanisms like callbacks can be implemented more easily on different transports.

SOAP and Other Protocols

The current SOAP working draft focuses on SOAP as an XML protocol for serializing data, without regard for any particular transport protocol. There is no reason why SOAP payloads cannot travel across other existing transport protocols, or possibly new ones. As long as a protocol can move text from one system to another, it can talk SOAP!

There are many protocols in existence today, but the most widely used protocols on the Internet include HTTP, FTP, and SMTP. You already know the scoop on HTTP, so let's consider the other two options.

FTP

Although FTP is just a protocol for transmitting files, when you think about it, that's a large part of what HTTP servers do as well. There isn't much difference between packaging a SOAP call into a data file, transmitting the file to another server via FTP, and then having a SOAP server parse the document to execute a remote method. The results can be placed in a secondary file that is ultimately transmitted back to the client.

Nothing about this is difficult to understand, and it could certainly be implemented. Unfortunately, FTP servers do not typically provide an extensible way for your code to execute upon incoming file transfers, which is an important feature needed to easily inject your SOAP infrastructure into a server.

In reality, HTTP servers are more prevalent and provide better functionality for this type of communication, but there is no reason why FTP couldn't facilitate this type of architecture.

SMTP and Message Queues

A more interesting alternative is a *messaging transport* provided by SMTP servers and messsage queue systems. Messaging systems provide an asynchronous way for clients to communicate with servers. Greater scalability is realized by decoupling the client and server so that client requests are queued and serviced at the will of the server. This keeps connection times extremely low and enables clients to continue processing while the server is formulating a response. Servers also have the capability to more easily distribute load across many systems if the need arises. However, this comes with a drawback, because messaging systems sacrifice performance for asynchronous communication.

More specific to SMTP, it is also reasonable to assume that clients who send messages to a server can also receive messages from a server. This type of bi-directional communication resolves the *callback* issue previously discussed.

SMTP servers that run the equivalent of *sendmail* (a UNIX scripting engine used in email systems), also have the capability to preprocess messages before they are dispatched to the recipient. Assuming that SOAP message headers were provided in a similar manner as HTTP headers are provided, SOAP calls could be routed and authenticated as needed.

Message queue systems offer similar benefits to SMTP servers, but lack the global adoption that SMTP has experienced. Although message queues will probably not become the *de facto* standard for SOAP, they should prove useful as a cross-platform transport in a controlled environment.

Since SOAP v1.1 now views typical SOAP transactions as one-way messages, the message queue architecture may take a stronger hold as a more commonly adopted public protocol.

Layering Protocols for SOAP

You just learned about how messaging systems could be used to carry SOAP payloads. Another interesting view of the SOAP world involves SOAP payloads carrying other protocols.

Consider the possibility of using SOAP and SMTP as the transport for a message queue system. Rather than encoding calls in a proprietary format, they would be encoded into SOAP payloads. In this case, you retain the asynchronous properties associated with SMTP, you get almost immediate acceptance through firewalls, and you have SOAP as a common protocol for disparate systems.

Summary

This chapter focused on the topics surrounding HTTP and how it applies to SOAP. HTTP is currently one of the proposed base transports for SOAP, and provides the typical request and response communications model prominent in the Web world. SOAP mandates the use of POST or M-POST to transfer XML content from the client to the server, and, by using HTTP headers, enables firewalls and proxies to monitor SOAP traffic. By using the stateless and connection-less model of HTTP, SOAP servers are able to provide a highly scalable application to clients, but require special attention when designing interfaces.

SOAP and Data: The XML Payload

IN THIS CHAPTER

As you know from Chapter 1, "Essential SOAP: A Comparison of SOAP to Existing Distributed Object Technologies," SOAP encapsulates the object state or method information in an XML format to be transmitted over the network, typically using the HTTP protocol. In this chapter you'll begin to see how the information the object needs to share is stored in an XML format and how that format should appear if it is to comply with the SOAP specification.

The data your object shares will be stored within the SOAP *envelope*, which is the XML document element, or root XML tag. The envelope will contain two or more child tags, to include the *header* (optional) and the *body* (required) as well as additional elements you design. Your object's serializing code must take the information your object would normally share on its local call stack and format it into XML. On the remote end, the remote object's deserializing XML processor will read the XML information and call the remote object on your behalf using that information, assuming there is no other error such as incorrect method parameters or data types.

> **NOTE**
>
> While reading this chapter, you must keep in mind two factors that, at the time of this writing, affect the use of SOAP. First, XML schemas are still a work in progress, and no commercial XML processor exists that can actually read a schema and apply it to the XML document. Second, SOAP specifies a wire-protocol, which is a subset of an entire remoting architecture.
>
> The effect of the first factor is that you can assume future XML processors will validate an XML document against an XML schema, and all the benefits of using schemas will be in place (inheritance, subclassing, and so on). This chapter was written with this in mind.
>
> The second factor means that SOAP itself has no remote object activation responsibility. In fact, the specification authors expressly indicated activation was *not* a part of the SOAP protocol. That is the responsibility of the remoting architecture as a whole, with SOAP playing but a part. However, this chapter was written with the assumption that such architectures would deal with SOAP packet creation/interpretation and ultimately invoke the remote object's services on behalf of the remote client.

This chapter begins with a discussion of the serialization process to show you how the XML conversion is accomplished (and why). It then moves on to discuss the critical segments of the SOAP XML payload: the envelope, the header, and the body elements.

Serializing Information

In an academic sense, it's often easy to envision totally self-contained objects. Students often implement objects designed to support a single function, such as an object to compute compound interest or implement the *Sieve of Eratosthenes*. (The *Sieve of Eratosthenes* is an algorithm for computing prime numbers.) In real-world computing, however, such self-contained objects are a bit more rare, as objects frequently rely upon other (external) objects for additional processing capability. For example, the word processor used to write these words would format the text for hardcopy printing, but it would not actually print the material. Instead, the word processor would invoke an operating system method (using the operating system as a local object) to actually print the text to one of the configured printers.

In this case, the word processor needs to transfer the formatted information to the print object so that the print object can then, in turn, transmit the data to the printer so it can produce the actual printed page. The question becomes "How is this information transfer performed?"

The truth is the implementation varies from operating system to operating system. For the sake of this discussion, imagine one of three implementations that depends upon the locality of the external object:

- Intra-process
- Inter-process
- Remote-process

If the two objects exist in the same process (often virtual) address space and can share a call stack, their implementation is considered *intra-process*. In the case of the word processor, it can complete a system-defined data structure and pass a pointer to the data structure on the call stack as it invokes the print object's printing method (see Figure 5.1).

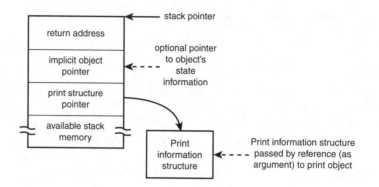

FIGURE 5.1

Object method invocation through an intra-process call stack.

Different object-based systems implement call stacks in slightly different forms, but the essential concept of accessing argument data through a stack is a common implementation. In this case, imagine the call stack contains a return address (to where the processor should return control after the print object's method has completed its task), an implicit object pointer, and a pointer to a system-specific print information data structure. The return address and pointer to the print information structure are fairly obvious. The implicit object pointer may not be so obvious. Some object-oriented languages support an implicit pointer to more effectively facilitate object-oriented features and functions. A good example is the C++ and Java `this` pointer. The underlying purpose of the implicit object pointer is to access called object state information.

In any case, the word processor completes the print information structure and then passes a reference to the structure as an argument to the print object through a print object method. The call stack is created and the print object accesses the argument information, which is the pointer to the print information structure. Since both objects reside in the same process (or virtual) address space, the pointer to the print object is valid and has meaning to both objects. The stack itself acts as a shared memory region, and both objects agreed beforehand as to how the information on the stack should be arranged (arguments stored left to right or right to left, who cleans the stack, and so on).

Now imagine the word processor resides in one process while the print object resides in another process, perhaps one created with special access permissions and security constraints. Their implementation would be an example of *inter-process* object invocation. In this scenario, nearly all contemporary operating systems will put the two objects into separate virtual address spaces. Merely passing a pointer between the address spaces will not suffice because a pointer created in one address space is completely invalid in another. The pointer could just as well be considered a random number. Yet in order for the objects to interact, the word processor must still create some sort of call stack to activate the print object.

Different operating systems will deal with this situation in various ways. Some will construct a pointer to shared memory. The operating system will then map this pointer within the address space of each process. By some internal mechanism, the operating system will create for the word processor a simulated call stack that will allow the print object to retrieve the print information as if the word processor was within the same address space. Other operating systems may queue the method invocation in a system-level message queue after first extracting the print information from the word processor's address space. But no matter how any given operating system handles inter-process object method invocation, the arguments passed between the address spaces must be normalized. That is, pointers to data must be dereferenced and the data collected and packaged in such a fashion that the external object's virtual address space can interpret and use the data. Often, this process is called *marshalling,* or *serialization.*

After the normalized arguments are shipped to the external object's address space, they are often un*marshall*ed or de-serialized to recreate a call stack that is valid in that object's address space. The external object can then access the data from the other object as if they were both intra-process. Any returned information follows a similar path when that data is transferred back to the original calling object. You can see this visually in Figure 5.2.

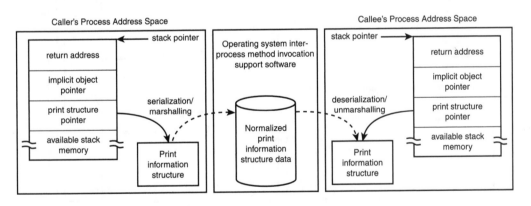

FIGURE 5.2
Object method invocation through inter-process communication.

Remote-process object invocation adds additional complexities involved with transmitting the information from one computer to another. The serialization mechanism is often similar to that of inter-process information transfer. In the remote case, however, an additional layer of software manages the networking aspects of the method call. That is, the remoting software becomes responsible for locating the remote machine, sending the data to the remote machine, and managing errors and broken connections as well as other network-related issues. The remoting software manages (or enforces) security and is typically charged with object activation responsibilities if the object isn't already executing on the remote computer.

Assuming the serialized data is successfully transmitted to the remote computer, deserialization and inter-process communication software local to that machine often take over and invoke the given object's method. If any information is to be returned, the reverse process applies and the results are serialized and shipped back to the original object, as you would expect. You can see this situation in action in Figure 5.3.

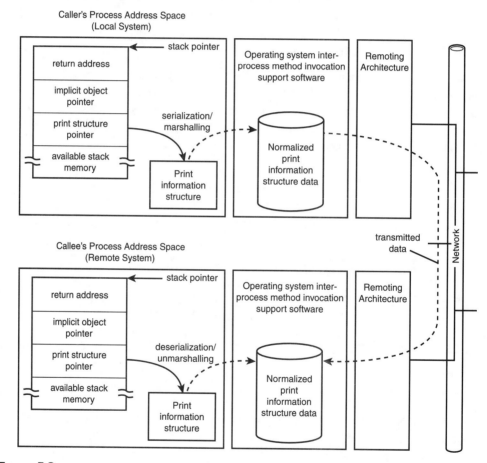

FIGURE 5.3

Object method invocation through remote-process communication.

Directed Data Flow

You will often see the direction of the data flow indicated as the objects are designed and implemented. That is, data may flow unidirectionally from one object to the other, or the data may flow from one object, be somehow manipulated by the second object, and then be returned to the first object.

Information being transmitted to a remote object is referred to in the SOAP specification as [in] data. In fact, all information is relative to the remote object, so in this case, the data comes *into* the remote object. Information that the remote object computes to be unidirectionally transmitted back to the originating object is referred to as [out] data. If the originating object sends information to the remote object and the remote object returns information using the same argument, that data is referred to as [in, out] data. The square brackets, [], are part of the syntax of the Interface Description Language both CORBA and DCOM use. Presumably, the syntax was kept in the SOAP specification for brevity.

Serialization and SOAP

Figure 5.3 has been recreated in Figure 5.4 to show you which parts of the remote object method invocation pertain to SOAP specifically (at least when using HTTP). SOAP itself, as mentioned in Chapter 1, is a specification. You can now see the SOAP specification tells you that, instead of serializing your object's call stack into a proprietary or architecture-specific serialization format, you instead serialize your object's call stack to an XML document. The document is then transmitted to the remote system using the transport protocol (commonly HTTP). If you have a SOAP inter-process communication layer for your particular object architecture, you should be able to communicate with objects created (and used) in other object architectures that previously were unavailable to you because of significant differences in object argument serialization, assuming they also implement the SOAP protocol.

The remainder of this chapter discusses the details involved in serializing object method invocation using SOAP and precisely what the XML format of the arguments must be to comply with the SOAP specification.

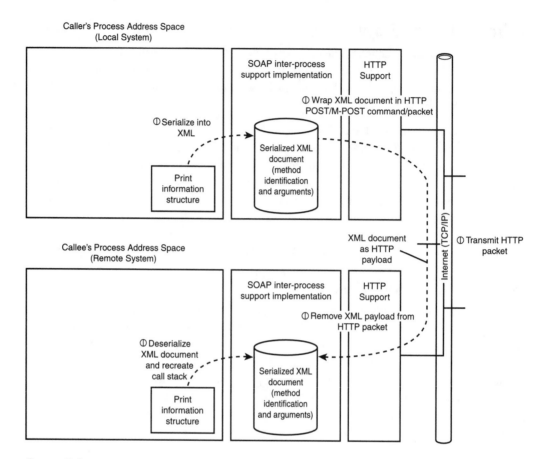

FIGURE 5.4
Object method invocation using SOAP.

A Closer Look at the SOAP Envelope

You examined in some detail the HTTP headers SOAP uses when it employs HTTP as its transport in Chapter 4, "SOAP and Data: Protocol Transports." The XML payload immediately follows the protocol header (again, typically the HTTP header) and begins with the standard root XML element. Note that no XML processing instruction is required, such as the typical `<? xml version="1.0" ?>`. In SOAP's case, the root XML element is referred to as the *envelope*.

The SOAP specification indicates the envelope element as shown in Listing 5.1 (note the `SOAP-ENV` namespace).

LISTING 5.1   Nominal SOAP XML Data Layout

```
<SOAP-ENV:Envelope>
    <SOAP-ENV:Header>
        <!-- The SOAP header element is optional... -->
    </SOAP-ENV:Header>

    <SOAP-ENV:Body>
        <!-- Serialized object information... -->
    </SOAP-ENV:Body>

....<!-- Optional sub-elements... -->
</SOAP-ENV:Envelope>
```

The SOAP envelope, header, and body are collectively known as the *SOAP message*. The specification also lists the following rules concerning the use of the envelope element tag:

- The global attribute SOAP-ENV:encodingStyle may appear on this (or any) element; if it does, it is scoped to that element.
- The envelope element may contain additional namespace declarations.
- The envelope element may contain additional attributes, but they must be qualified by a namespace.
- The envelope may contain additional sub-elements so long as they are qualified by a namespace and follow the body element.

Let's break these rules down a bit and look at them more closely, starting with the encoding style.

The SOAP-ENV:encodingStyle Attribute

The SOAP specification affords you the flexibility to serialize data in ways that are currently unspecified or that may be changes to the current SOAP methodology. That is, an advantage to using an XML schema is that you can apply additional rules to the interpretation of the data within the XML document. Moreover, schemas allow for inheritance, such that you can base a new schema on the SOAP schema while applying additional constraint or specialization within your own SOAP packets.

If you provide such a schema, your customized SOAP processing architecture should interpret the value indicated by the SOAP-ENV:encodingStyle attribute as an additional rule for deserializing the SOAP packet. The most common use for this is to provide alternate serialization algorithms or to further constrain the existing serialization rules. If the

`SOAP-ENV:encodingStyle` attribute is missing, the SOAP architecture should assume the SOAP schema itself is to be applied to the payload and therefore process the SOAP packet more generically.

The default value for the `SOAP-ENV:encodingStyle` is *http://schemas.xmlsoap.org/soap/encoding/*. You might decide to further tailor this schema or provide a schema or schemas of your own. This example shows you the default encoding attribute's use:

`SOAP-ENV:encodingStyle="http://schemas.xmlsoap.org/soap/encoding/"`

For example, imagine you are interested in stacking several method invocations in a single SOAP packet. The SOAP specification mentions only a single method invocation/response pair per instance, but if you know apriori that many method invocations will be transmitted to a given server, you could optimize your SOAP packet data and incorporate multiple method invocations within the *same* packet. As it stands today, SOAP has no concept of stacked method calls. (In fact, it specifically tries not to address this topic, otherwise known as *boxcarring*.)

Consider the example SOAP packet shown in Listing 5.2.

LISTING 5.2 Modified SOAP XML Data Layout Using Alternative Encoding Style

```
<BCAR:Envelope
    xmlns:SOAP-ENV="http://schemas.xmlsoap.org/soap/envelope/"
    xmlns:BCAR="urn:schemas-myurl-com:boxcar"
    SOAP-ENV:encodingStyle="urn:schemas-myurl-com:boxcar" />

    <!-- The boxcar schema tells the SOAP processor that
        the nominal SOAP encoding has been changed. In this
        case, multiple SOAP body/header elements can be
        included within the single SOAP envelope element
        (rather than define a new element in lieu of the
        SOAP envelope). Normally, this packet would cause
        the SOAP processor to return a fault (SOAP status
        300, Invalid Request) because it doesn't follow
        (precisely) the SOAP specification. -->

    <BCAR:Method

        <SOAP-ENV:Envelope>
            <SOAP-ENV:Header>
                <BCAR:EndPoint>
                    http://soap.myurl.com/objects:object1
                <BCAR:EndPoint/>
                <BCAR:CallID>
                    12345
                <BCAR:CallID/>
            <SOAP-ENV:Header/>
```

```
        <SOAP-ENV:Body xmlns:OBJ1="urn:schemas-myurl-com:object1">
            <OBJ1:SomeMethod>

                <OBJ1:CurPrice>$34.65</OBJ1:CurPrice>
            </OBJ1:SomeMethod>
        </SOAP-ENV:Body>
      </SOAP-ENV:Envelope>
  </BCAR:Method>
  <BCAR:Method>

      <SOAP-ENV:Envelope>
        <SOAP-ENV:Header>
            <BCAR:EndPoint>
                http://soap.myurl.com/objects:object2
            <BCAR:EndPoint/>
            <BCAR:CallID>
                23456
            <BCAR:CallID/>
        <SOAP-ENV:Header/>
        <SOAP-ENV:Body xmlns:OBJ2="urn:schemas-myurl-com:object2">
            <OBJ2:AnotherMethod>

                <OBJ2:NumRequested>6</OBJ2:NumRequested>
                <OBJ2:Desc>Left-handed smoke shifters</OBJ2:Desc>
            </OBJ2:AnotherMethod>
        </SOAP-ENV:Body>
      </SOAP-ENV:Envelope>
  </BCAR:Method>
  <BCAR:Method>

      <SOAP-ENV:Envelope>
        <SOAP-ENV:Header>
            <BCAR:EndPoint>
                http://soap.myurl.com/objects:object3
            <BCAR:EndPoint/>
            <BCAR:CallID>
                34567
            <BCAR:CallID/>
        <SOAP-ENV:Header/>
        <SOAP-ENV:Body xmlns:OBJ3="urn:schemas-myurl-com:object3">
            <OBJ3:FinalMethod>

                <OBJ3:InitShutdown>1</OBJ3:InitShutdown>
            </OBJ3:FinalMethod>
        </SOAP-ENV:Body>
      </SOAP-ENV:Envelope>
  </BCAR:Method>
</BCAR:Envelope>
```

In this case, the normal SOAP processing has been modified. (It does not follow the format you saw in Listing 5.1.). Here you see the additional `<BCAR:Method />` element which encapsulates the individual SOAP method invocations for the `SomeMethod()`, `AnotherMethod()`, and `FinalMethod()` methods. The boxcar's schema should identify the additional boxcar elements (delineated by `<BCAR:Method>`) to allow the envelope element to contain multiple method invocations. The individual methods are then serialized according to normal SOAP rules.

This is but a single (contrived) example—you have total control over your object's serialization algorithm(s) and can adjust the packet layout to suit your needs. The key lies with the `SOAP-ENV:encodingStyle` attribute that tells your SOAP processor of the modifications to the traditional SOAP packet. If the (remote) SOAP processor is aware of the different encoding style (because it was created in such a manner), it can process the additional information accordingly. If not, the remote SOAP processor has little option but to return a fault, indicating it didn't understand the packet and could therefore not process the request.

Envelope Namespace Declarations

Namespaces are related to the encoding style in that you can apply additional schema control to the interpretation of the XML payload data by providing a schema of your own to the SOAP processor. In this case, the namespace is no different than any XML namespace and is used in the same manner. For example, assume you have a schema that specifies a new data type. You can scope the use of the data type to the entire SOAP XML document in this manner:

```
<SOAP-ENV:Envelope
    xmlns:SOAP-ENV="http://schemas.xmlsoap.org/soap/envelope/"
    xmlns:SDT="urn:schemas-myurl-com:mysoapdatatypes"
    SOAP-ENV:encodingStyle="http://schemas.xmlsoap.org/soap/encoding/">
    ...
    <!-- SOAP data serialized here... -->
    <!-- Use "SDT" namespace where appropriate... -->
    ...
</SOAP-ENV:Envelope>
```

You also saw an example of an additional namespace in Listing 5.2. As with the encoding style attribute, you can scope the namespace to lower-level elements if that better suits your needs.

The basic SOAP packed is defined by the envelope schema, the XML which you'll find at `http://schemas.xmlsoap.org/soap/envelope/` (also shown in Listing 5.3).

LISTING 5.3   SOAP Envelope Schema

```
<?xml version="1.0" ?>
<!-- XML Schema for SOAP v 1.1 Envelope
-->
<!--
    Copyright 2000 DevelopMentor, International Business Machines
    ➥Corporation, Lotus Development Corporation, Microsoft,
    ➥UserLand Software

-->
<schema xmlns="http://www.w3.org/1999/XMLSchema"
  xmlns:tns="http://schemas.xmlsoap.org/soap/envelope/"
  targetNamespace="http://schemas.xmlsoap.org/soap/envelope/">
    <!-- SOAP envelope, header and body
    -->
    <element name="Envelope" type="tns:Envelope" />
    <complexType name="Envelope">
        <element ref="tns:Header" minOccurs="0" />
        <element ref="tns:Body" minOccurs="1" />
        <any minOccurs="0" maxOccurs="*" />
        <anyAttribute />
    </complexType>
    <element name="Header" type="tns:Header" />
    <complexType name="Header">
        <any minOccurs="0" maxOccurs="*" />
        <anyAttribute />
    </complexType>
    <element name="Body" type="tns:Body" />
    <complexType name="Body">
        <any minOccurs="0" maxOccurs="*" />
        <anyAttribute />
    </complexType>
    <!--
        Global Attributes.  The following attributes are intended
        to be usable via qualified attribute names on any complex
        type referencing them.

    -->
    <attribute name="mustUnderstand" default="0">
        <simpleType base="boolean">
        <pattern value="0|1" />
        </simpleType>
    </attribute>
    <attribute name="actor" type="uri-reference" />
```

continues

LISTING 5.3 Continued

```
<!--

        'encodingStyle' indicates any canonicalization conventions
        followed in the contents of the containing element.  For
        example, the value 'http://schemas.xmlsoap.org/soap/encoding/'
        indicates the pattern described in SOAP specification.

    -->
    <simpleType name="encodingStyle" base="uri-reference"
      ➥derivedBy="list" />
    <attributeGroup name="encodingStyle">
        <attribute name="encodingStyle" type="tns:encodingStyle" />
    </attributeGroup>
    <!-- SOAP fault reporting structure
    -->
    <complexType name="Fault" final="extension">
        <element name="faultcode" type="qname" />
        <element name="faultstring" type="string" />
        <element name="faultactor" type="uri-reference"
            ➥minOccurs="0" />
        <element name="detail" type="tns:detail" minOccurs="0" />
    </complexType>
    <complexType name="detail">
        <any minOccurs="0" maxOccurs="*" />
        <anyAttribute />
    </complexType>
</schema>
```

In Listing 5.3, you can see the layout of the SOAP envelope defined to be an optional header element:

```
<element ref="tns:Header" minOccurs="0" />
```

combined with a single body element:

```
<element ref="tns:Body" minOccurs="1" />
```

The schema then specifies the global SOAP attributes, one of which you've seen (SOAP-ENV:encodingStyle), as well as the SOAP fault structure. (You'll see more of this in Chapter 7, "SOAP and Communications: Invoking Remote Methods.") There is also another SOAP namespace you may see:

```
xmlns=SOAP-ENC:"http://schemas.xmlsoap.org/soap/encoding/"
```

This is used in Chapter 6, "SOAP and Data: Data Types," where you'll see how arrays and structures are serialized.

Additional Envelope Attributes

Although you won't see an example of this in the SOAP specification, SOAP allows you to define and use auxiliary attributes within the envelope tag. (You do see this in the SOAP envelope schema, however, where the envelope is defined with the <anyAttribute /> tag.) If you're interested in qualifying the envelope element, perhaps to specify the number of SOAP sub-packets in a boxcarred implementation (to reuse the previous example), you can do so. However, you must also qualify the attribute using an XML namespace.

Again using boxcarring as an example, examine the sample SOAP XML payload document you find in Listing 5.4.

LISTING 5.4   SOAP Envelope Element with Additional Attribute

```
<BCAR:Envelope
    xmlns:SOAP-ENV="http://schemas.xmlsoap.org/soap/envelope/"
    xmlns:BCAR="urn:schemas-myurl-com:boxcar"
    SOAP-ENV:encodingStyle="urn:schemas-myurl-com:boxcar"
    BCAR:numMethods="3">
    ...
    <!-- Other XML data as in Listing 5.2 -->
    ...
</BCAR:Envelope>
```

You can see the added attribute in the envelope definition in Listing 5.4. In this case, the SOAP boxcar schema specified in the <SOAP-ENV:Envelope> element would again provide a mechanism to record multiple SOAP packets within a wrapper envelope. The attribute the schema implements, numMethods, could then be used to tell the deserialization code how many serialized methods to expect within the envelope.

> **NOTE**
>
> As a matter of XML coding style, you can create XML documents that contain fewer elements with more attributes or more elements with fewer attributes.
>
> The advantage to the former style is you have more information at the element level when parsing the XML document. That is, you don't need to parse more elements to garner more information as the attributes are parsed with the element. Their values are known at that time.
>
> A disadvantage in using attributes is that you can't insert parsable XML code into the attribute value. The attribute value is taken literally. As it happens, this is the main advantage of adding elements instead of attributes. Elements are parsable, and extensible, which is why the authors of the SOAP specification favor this approach over the more attribute-based style.

Envelope Versioning

The specification mentions envelope versioning, and that the traditional major/minor version number scheme is not used. Instead, the URI for the envelope namespace is used instead (`http://schemas.xmlsoap.org/soap/envelope/`). An envelope that does not use this schema (presumably an envelope that does use the standard SOAP encoding schema at `http://schemas.xmlsoap.org/soap/encoding/`) should cause the server to return a version mismatch error.

However, you should note that this is according to the SOAP 1.1 specification, and you may wish to support SOAP packets serialized according to the 1.0 specification. In the case of SOAP version 1.0, the URI for the SOAP namespace (not SOAP-ENV) was `urn:schemas-xmlsoap-org:soap.v1`. If you receive a SOAP packet identified by this URI, you may, instead, wish to provide SOAP 1.0 support rather than return the version mismatch error outright.

Envelope Sub-Elements

The SOAP specification indicates two envelope sub-elements may be present (as you saw in Listing 5.1). The first is an optional header element, to be discussed in the next section. The other is a required body element that will ultimately contain the serialized information to be (or that was) transmitted between the objects.

You can, however, add new sub-elements to the envelope in addition to the header and the body. For example, imagine you want to recreate the DCOM causality functionality, which means you'll need to inject causality information into the remote object invocation. In that case, when you parse the XML payload and discover another invocation using the same causality, you could step in and prevent a possible deadlock condition by servicing the request. (Normally, you would block while waiting for your current method's processing to finish.) The notion of causality, and the XML required to support it, is not dictated by the SOAP specification. Many distributed systems support this concept in some fashion, though. If you want to combine SOAP and causality, specifying an additional envelope sub-element is one way to transmit the causality identifier between objects.

> **NOTE**
>
> This is an example of some information that could be encoded within an additional envelope sub-element. This is not to say adding additional information in this manner is the best or optimum way to do so. The SOAP header is designed for this purpose, as you'll see. However, nothing precludes you from adding additional sub-elements if you so desire, and causality was used merely as a basis for the example.

To do this you could create a new schema that specifies the layout of the causality element. Then, include the namespace declaration within the envelope element tag, as shown in Listing 5.5.

LISTING 5.5   Additional SOAP Envelope Elements

```
<SOAP-ENV:Envelope>

    <SOAP-ENV:Header />

    <SOAP-ENV:Body>
        <!-- Serialized information here... -->
    </SOAP-ENV:Body>

    <!-- Causality ID represents some temporally unique value
         Its data type (integer) would be specified in its
         schema... -->
    <CID:CausalityID
        xmlns:CID="urn:schemas-myurl-com:causalityid">
        1234
    </CID:CausalityID>
</SOAP-ENV:Envelope>
```

The additional causality schema is shown in Listing 5.5—`urn:schemas-myurl-com:` `causalityid`. The causality schema would provide the additional element rules regarding the causality. However, your SOAP processing architecture would need to look for the causality in this case as the causality element is not a part of the SOAP specification. SOAP processors that blindly followed the SOAP specification would ignore this element.

Scoping, Independent, and Embedded Elements

Listing 5.5 also shows the two pre-defined SOAP scoping elements, the SOAP header and the SOAP body. When the SOAP specification discusses various XML elements, it refers to them as *independent*, or *embedded*. It's important to understand the distinctions among these element types because SOAP interprets each differently.

Within the header and body elements you will typically find at least one independent element and zero or more embedded elements. An independent element is an element (or elements) one level deeper than the scoping element. As you'll see, the method element must follow the `SOAP-ENV:Body` tag, so the method element is considered an independent element. Sibling nodes of the method element are also independent elements. All other XML elements are embedded elements, which is to say they're contained within independent elements. You'll also revisit this in Chapter 6. To continue with the previous example, another way to support the notion of causality, without modifying the SOAP processing architecture to accommodate non-standard SOAP packets, is to incorporate the causality element into the SOAP header element. Let's address the header element now.

A Closer Look at the SOAP Header

The SOAP specification allows you to insert an optional payload header element, with which you can tailor your remote method call (the specification uses a transaction identifier as an example). This allows you to pass implicit call information that is not actually part of the method call itself. (The method may or may not be used transactionally, for instance.) This is also where you, as a third party, would place any additional external (out-of-band) information that modifies the SOAP request (a concept usually referred to as *hooking*). The following rules apply when using the header element:

- The header element is optional, but, if it is used, it must be the first element to follow the root (the opening envelope XML tag).
- The header element must adhere to the SOAP specification unless the header is specifically modified by the `SOAP-ENV:encodingStyle` attribute.
- Header sub-elements are always namespace-qualified.
- The header may contain the `SOAP-ENV:mustUnderstand` attribute (value of 0 or 1).

With the exception of the encoding style rule, let's take a closer look at these rules and what they mean. The encoding style affects the header element in the same fashion it affected the envelope element.

Header Element Location

If you include a header element, you *must* place it immediately after the envelope tag (or other root element tag, if you've subclassed the SOAP schema). The header is optional because you may or may not have additional infrastructural information to pass to the remote system. For example, an object may be used transactionally in one instant and non-transactionally in the next. In the former case, you could include the transaction ID in the header. In the latter case, you would omit the header entirely as you have no additional (implicit) information to provide.

Header Sub-Elements

Returning to the notion of causality, to provide an additional example in lieu of the transaction ID shown in the SOAP specification, you could include a causality ID within the SOAP header instead of specifying an additional envelope sub-element. Consider Listing 5.6.

LISTING 5.6   The SOAP Header Element with Causality ID

```
<SOAP-ENV:Envelope
    xmlns:SOAP-ENV="http://schemas.xmlsoap.org/soap/envelope/">

    <SOAP-ENV:Header>
        <!-- Causality ID represents some temporally unique value. -->
```

```
    <CID:CausalityID
        xmlns:CID="urn:schemas-myurl-com:causalityid"
        SOAP-ENV:root="1">
        1234
    </CID:CausalityID>
  </SOAP-ENV:Header>

  <SOAP-ENV:Body>
      <!-- Serialized information here... -->
  </SOAP-ENV:Body>

</SOAP-ENV:Envelope>
```

As you see from Listing 5.6, the causality ID schema is included within the `CID:CausalityID` tag and is used to identify the `CID` namespace. Then, the `CID:CausalityID` sub-element specifies the causality ID in effect for this method invocation. Note the causality identifier's XML element is qualified by the `CID` namespace, according to the SOAP specification. (Independent elements must be namespace-qualified.)

NOTE

You can define common elements within the header that can be referred to from the body. This is for efficiency. The body can refer back to the header, but the header itself must be self-contained. You cannot reference external elements from the header. This allows implementations interested in parsing the header to garner all the header information without having to parse the body contents. Conversely, parsers interpreting the body are assumed to have interpreted the header, so accessing header information is allowed. For example, this is correct SOAP XML encoding:

```
<SOAP-ENV:Header>
    <ns1:DataGram xmlns:ns1="http://www.myurl.com/datagram">
        <ns1:Datum id="SomethingImportant">
            <!-- Define something... -->
        </ns1:Datum>
    <ns1:DataGram>
</SOAP-ENV:Header>
<SOAP-ENV:Body>
    <ns1:Method1 xmlns:ns1="http://www.myurl.com/datagram">
        <ns1:Arg1 href="#SomethingImportant">123</ns1:Arg1>
    <ns1:Method1>
<SOAP-ENV:Body>
```

It is not legal in SOAP to turn this example around and reference body information from the header element.

The Header Element and Its SOAP-ENV:mustUnderstand Attribute

The concepts of transactions and causality are critical to the success of the remote method call. However, if for some reason the remote SOAP processor is unable to handle the transactional or causality information, you most likely don't want the remote server to issue the method call to the object. The object's response would likely be meaningless. SOAP provides an attribute you can apply to your header elements that tells the SOAP processor to reject the SOAP request if the header element is unknown (to the SOAP processor) or contains information other than expected. This is the purpose of the SOAP-ENV:mustUnderstand attribute.

Listing 5.6 has been modified slightly to produce Listing 5.7. In Listing 5.6, the method call specified in the SOAP packet would be processed regardless of the causality, which could potentially destroy intermediate state information and result in erroneous data being returned to the client. With the addition of the SOAP-ENV:mustUnderstand attribute, the SOAP processor must acknowledge the method's causality and be capable of dealing with potential deadlocks.

LISTING 5.7   The SOAP Header Element with Causality ID Revisited

```
<SOAP-ENV:Envelope
    xmlns:SOAP-ENV=" http://schemas.xmlsoap.org/soap/envelope/">

    <SOAP-ENV:Header>
        <!-- Causality ID represents some temporally unique value. -->
        <CID:CausalityID
            xmlns:CID="urn:schemas-myurl-com:causalityid"
            SOAP-ENV:root="1"
            SOAP-ENV:mustUnderstand="1">
            1234
        </CID:CausalityID>
    </SOAP-ENV:Header>

    <SOAP-ENV:Body>
        <!-- Serialized information here... -->
    </SOAP-ENV:Body>

</SOAP-ENV:Envelope>
```

You can see the SOAP-ENV:mustUnderstand attribute applied to the causality (header) element in Listing 5.7. If this attribute is present, the remote SOAP server needs to understand the header element and be capable of processing the element's information. If not, the server must return a SOAP fault to the caller.

> **NOTE**
>
> If the remote SOAP processor does not understand the causality element, it should return the SOAP fault `SOAP-ENV:MustUnderstand` (an enumerated value).

The Header Element and its `SOAP-ENV:root` Attribute

To understand this attribute, forget SOAP for the moment and think about XML in general. If you have an XML node with sibling nodes, can you tell by inspection if any of the nodes are more important than, or has special meaning as compared to, the others? In general, you cannot. You must provide some means to distinguish "important" nodes from the other sibling nodes.

The example used in the SOAP discussion group, where this attribute was first mentioned, is that of a linked list. If you were to encode a linked list as XML elements, you would most likely create an element for each node in the linked list and add it as a sibling node to the other linked list nodes. You would then indicate the nodal link relationships in some manner (perhaps using the XPointer syntax as SOAP does, `href=""`/`id=""`).

But, which node is the head of the list? For this you would probably create a new attribute and anoint the head node with this attribute. This is precisely what the `SOAP-ENV:root` attribute accomplishes. This attribute may be used in any independent SOAP element to indicate that node is the head of a graph and is considered special when compared to the remaining sibling independent elements. It is most useful in the header to indicate the a particular independent header node stands out and merits special attention as compared to other header nodes, not having this attribute. Any special attention the node merits is entirely up to you and your SOAP processing architecture.

A Closer Look at the SOAP Body

The SOAP body element is where the guts of your remote method call are serialized. For example, here you'll find the method name and its serialized arguments and values. The body element is also where the remote method's response information will be serialized, whether the response is a valid return value or a SOAP fault of some kind.

The SOAP specification indicates three types of body elements:

- Call (remote method invocation packet)
- Response (remote method return information)
- Fault (SOAP error packet)

The rules for processing the SOAP body depend upon the type of body in question. In all cases the body element is identified by the `SOAP-ENV:Body` tag pair.

The Call Body Element

In the case of a Call body, the first child element is named according to the method name. The embedded elements contained within the method element represent the serialized arguments, with each argument named according to the method signature.

For example, consider the `CalcPmt()` method, which has the following method signature:

```
float CalcPmt(float fPrinciple, float fInterest, int iPeriod)
```

`CalcPmt()` accepts three arguments, `fPrinciple`, `fInterest`, and `iPeriod`, and it returns a floating point value. Then, imagine you called the remote version of the `CalcPmt()` method using SOAP to serialize the data:

```
// $175000 at 8% per annum for 30 years...
float fPayment = CalcPmt(175000.00,0.0066,360)
```

The resulting SOAP HTTP packet would appear as shown in Listing 5.8.

LISTING 5.8 Serialized `CalcPmt()` Call SOAP Packet

```
<SOAP-ENV:Envelope
    xmlns:xsi="http://www.w3.org/1999/XMLSchema/instance"
    xmlns:SOAP-ENV=" http://schemas.xmlsoap.org/soap/envelope/">
    <SOAP-ENV:Body xmlns:pmtcalc="urn:schemas-myurl-com:pmtcalc">
        <pmtcalc:CalcPmt>
            < fPrinciple xsi:type="float">175000.00</ fPrinciple>
            < fInterest xsi:type="float">0.0066</ fInterest>
            < iPeriod xsi:type="int">360</ iPeriod>
        </pmtcalc:CalcPmt>
    </SOAP-ENV:Body>
</SOAP-ENV:Envelope>
```

The arguments are contained within the method's (independent) element (`<pmtcalc:CalcPmt />`), and the element tags are named according to the method signature. If you don't know the method argument names (their textual representation), it's customary to name the argument elements __paramXXX, where XXX represents the ordinal value of the argument as it appears in the method's argument list. This (suggested) format comes from an earlier version of the SOAP specification.

The method argument elements are children of the method element, which represents the method name found in the method signature, `CalcPmt()`. Note the method element is namespace-qualified and is the first child element of the SOAP body element. The method argument elements do not require namespace qualification. It is assumed they are identified by the enclosing method element's namespace.

The Response Body Element

With the CalcPmt() information serialized into the SOAP message, you can now ship the message to the remote system (a URL, assuming HTTP) for processing. The remote host will invoke the CalcPmt() method, crunch some numbers, and return the resulting floating point value. This information will be serialized in a SOAP Response packet that would appear, as shown in Listing 5.9, assuming no error.

LISTING 5.9   Serialized CalcPmt() Response SOAP Packet

```
HTTP/1.1 200 OK
Content-Type: text/xml
Content-Length: nnnn

<SOAP-ENV:Envelope
    xmlns:SOAP-ENV=" http://schemas.xmlsoap.org/soap/envelope/">
    <SOAP-ENV:Body xmlns:pmtcalc="urn:schemas-myurl-com:pmtcalc">
        <pmtcalc:CalcPmtResponse>
            <return>1284.09</return>
        </pmtcalc:CalcPmtResponse>
    </SOAP-ENV:Body>
</SOAP-ENV:Envelope>
```

The rules for serializing the method response are similar to those for encoding the call. The returned values are encoded as you would encode a structure. The method name (namespace-qualified) follows the SOAP body element tag. Note *Response* has been concatenated to the method name. (This is by convention—the name of the element is immaterial according to the specification.) The method's return value is serialized within the <return></return> tag pair as the response's first accessor value. (Again, the element name is immaterial.) Had CalcPmt() included [out] or [in,out] parameters, the resulting values would be embedded within the method response element as well using the same naming rules as for the Call packet.

The ordering of the return arguments is important. The method's return value is always the first embedded element (the first child of the method response element), followed by the returned parameter values in the order they are arranged in the method's signature. You'll revisit method invocation in Chapter 7.

The Fault Body Element

Had there been an error, SOAP will do different things depending upon the error. If the host is unreachable, for example, you should receive an HTTP timeout error. But assuming the host was accessible, SOAP itself could have problems deserializing the packet, calling the remote method, or might not understand a required header element. You'll see this in much greater detail in Chapter 7.

For now, though, imagine that the remote host was able to interpret the SOAP Call packet but somehow was unable to process the request (perhaps the object threw an arithmetical exception and returned an error code). In that case, the HTTP header would indicate a successful round-trip. The SOAP body, however, would include the SOAP fault element, rather than the method response element, as shown in Listing 5.10.

LISTING 5.10   Serialized `CalcPmt()` Fault SOAP Packet

```
HTTP/1.1 200 OK
Content-Type: text/xml
Content-Length: nnnn

<SOAP-ENV:Envelope
    xmlns:SOAP-ENV=" http://schemas.xmlsoap.org/soap/envelope/">
    <SOAP-ENV:Body>
        <SOAP-ENV:Fault>
            <faultcode>SOAP-ENV:Server</faultcode>
            <faultstring>
                Internal Application Error
            </faultstring>
            <detail xmlns:pmtcalc="urn:schemas-myurl-com:pmtcalc">
                <pmtcalc:ErrorMsg>
                    Arithmetic Overflow
                </pmtcalc:ErrorMsg>
                <pmtcalc:ErrorCode>
                    534
                </pmtcalc:ErrorCode>
            </detail>
        </SOAP-ENV:Fault>
    </SOAP-ENV:Body>
</SOAP-ENV:Envelope>
```

The details of the SOAP fault packet will be more fully discussed in Chapter 7. For now, it's important to note the `SOAP-ENV:Fault` tag immediately follows the `SOAP-ENV:Body` tag.

Encoding Method Parameters

You'll find more detail regarding arguments and argument data types Chapter 6. As it happens, though, certain types of argument elements are commonly stored following the method element (which is itself the first independent element following the body element tag). For example, the members of a linked list would be found following the method element.

Assume that you have a linked list, with each node representing a data structure such as this:

```
typedef struct tagPartNode {
    struct tagNode* pNext;
    int iPartNum;
    int iNumInStock;
} PARTNODE;
```

Then imagine you have three parts stored in your linked list, which is visually depicted in Figure 5.5.

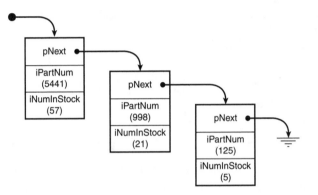

FIGURE 5.5

A linked list of PartNode structures.

Now suppose you wanted to send this linked list to a remote server to be processed, perhaps to indicate parts availability:

```
int AvailableParts( PARTNODE* pHead )
```

In this case, you're sending a pointer to the lead list item (part number 5441, in this case) and you expect the serialization code to chase the remaining linked list items by their respective pNext pointers until you run out of list items. The corresponding SOAP packet for the AvailableParts() method is shown in Listing 5.11.

LISTING 5.11   Serialized AvailableParts() Call SOAP Packet

```
<SOAP-ENV:Envelope
    xmlns:xsi="http://www.w3.org/1999/XMLSchema/instance"
    xmlns:SOAP-ENV=" http://schemas.xmlsoap.org/soap/envelope/">
    <SOAP-ENV:Body xmlns:partcnt="urn:schemas-myurl-com:partcnt">
        <partcnt:AvailablePart>
            <pHead href="#part001"/>
```

continues

LISTING 5.11 Continued

```
        </partcnt:AvailablePart>
        <partcnt:PARTNODE id="part001" SOAP-ENV:root="1">
            <pNext href="#part002"/>
            <iPartNum xsi:type="int">5441</iPartNum>
            <iNumInStock xsi:type="int">57</iNumInStock>
        </partcnt:PARTNODE>
        <partcnt:PARTNODE id="part002">
            <pNext href="#part003"/>
            <iPartNum xsi:type="int">998</iPartNum>
            <iNumInStock xsi:type="int">21</iNumInStock>
        </partcnt:PARTNODE>
        <partcnt:PARTNODE id="part003">
            <pNext xsi:null="1" />
            <iPartNum xsi:type="int">125</iPartNum>
            <iNumInStock xsi:type="int">5</iNumInStock>
        </partcnt:PARTNODE>
    </SOAP-ENV:Body>
</SOAP-ENV:Envelope>
```

The head of the linked list is indicated by the SOAP-ENV:root attribute, where it is passed into the remote method from within the SOAP body element. Note there is no associated value with the method argument, however. Instead, the SOAP applies its href attribute and provides a link to another XML element that follows the method element. In this case, the link indicates the first linked list node is stored as the element with the part001 identifier (note its data type is of PARTNODE, which presumably was declared within the urn:schemas-myurl-com:partcnt schema). .

The part001 element uses the same mechanism to indicate the second linked list node is stored within the part002 element, and so on. Within the node elements themselves, you can see SOAP will store the linked list's next node pointer, the part number, and the number of parts in stock. It is up to the SOAP serialization code to correctly follow the node pointers and record their instance data within the serialized packet.

The linked list provides an example of what the SOAP specification calls a *multi-reference accessor*. Multi-reference accessors serialize their data in this manner. (*Single-reference accessors*, which the previous examples in this chapter have all used, serialize their data inline.) Chapter 6 is dedicated to the SOAP data types in general, and it provides many more details regarding accessors and accessor reference. The important concept to understand at this point is that SOAP will add elements to the envelope as required to support multiple-reference accessor serialization.

Summary

Serialization, or *marshall*ing, is the process of converting a local call stack to a wire representation for transmission to a method outside of the caller's process (or virtual) address space. SOAP specifies a wire protocol that (commonly) uses HTTP as the transport and XML as the data formatting language.

The XML data is encapsulated within the envelope, which represents the root element of the serialized XML data. The envelope will always contain a body element and may contain a header element as well as other ancillary elements. You can, if you wish, add attributes to the envelope element and redefine how the data is serialized (using a modified SOAP algorithm or something completely different).

The (optional) SOAP header element is used to contain implicit instance meta-information, such as transactional IDs, causality information, security context, and so on. If you include the header element within the SOAP packet, it must immediately follow the envelope tag. Any sub-elements you include within the header must be namespace-qualified.

The SOAP body element contains the serialized method information, the results of the method call, or fault information. If the SOAP packet is to be de-serialized for execution, the method name must be used to denote the method element, and that tag must immediately follow the SOAP body tag. The serialized method arguments are recorded inside the method element.

Additional envelope elements follow the body element, and though you can define your own data elements (perhaps to hook the method call), SOAP will serialize multiple-reference arguments in individual data elements here. Common multiple-reference elements include linked list nodes, sparse array data, compound data types that include pointers to other compound data types, and so on.

Now that you have seen the basic layout of the SOAP packet, it's time to take a closer look at the data types SOAP processes and how those types are serialized.

SOAP and Data: Data Types

IN THIS CHAPTER

One can argue that many aspects of SOAP are critical to its capability to work as an RPC protocol (if you accept the fact that SOAP was originally designed to act as an RPC protocol). But if there is at least one critical aspect aside from the transport mechanism, it would have to be the manner in which SOAP, or any RPC protocol, serializes the method call stack and represents the information as that data is transported across the wire. Assuming the method parameters are not patently invalidated when deserialized (bytes reversed and so on), the protocol must faithfully present the call stack and the argument data.

Platform-specific solutions are a bit easier to visualize. If you're sending data only from one known system to another, you needn't worry about the general case. You code your protocol into your application, debug, test, and use it until you are required to replace some or all of the application.

Providing a solution for the general case is much more difficult. In this case, the call stack can be completely arbitrary. You will certainly know the general stack layout, but the number and types of the method arguments will, without a doubt, vary. You must be able to handle all situations if you are interested in writing a general-purpose protocol.

Perhaps some day XML processors will mature as the XML Schema standard is approved and implemented. Then, you can imagine an IDL compiler that would reduce your object's IDL interface definitions to schema form, which ultimately would tell the SOAP serializer what to expect when it serializes the object's method call stack. Today, at least at the time this was written, two things hinder this vision. First, SOAP doesn't mandate the use of schemas. Although SOAP doesn't preclude XML Schema validation, neither does it specify that an interface schema must be present. Second, XML processing technology as it is currently implemented doesn't adequately validate XML when using a schema. You can use a DTD, but the DTD language doesn't provide for data typing to the degree necessary to implement SOAP.

Even so, the SOAP specification does address how arguments should be serialized. It talks about simple data types, such as integers and strings, and it provides direction for serializing more complex data, such as structures and arrays. Let's begin with XML data type encoding, and then move to the SOAP-specific argument serialization requirements.

Encoding Data Types in XML

XML is very flexible when it comes to encoding data types. The XML Schema language, XML-Data, provides you with a rudimentary set of data types, such as strings, integers, general-case numbers, dates, and so on. This information is typically acceptable for basic XML document element definition.

In general, the data types you will encode in XML come from the XML Schema (xsd) specification you can find at http://www.w3.org/1999/XMLSchema. When you see xsd, as a namespace in XML, it refers to allowable data types as specified in the schema. xsi, on the other hand, refers to instance data types and is used in XML documents resulting from a given schema. The xsd type attribute used in a schema is directly related to the xsi data type used in a particular XML document that uses the given schema for validation. The namespace identifier for xsi is usually http://www.w3.org/1999/XMLSchema/instance.

> **NOTE**
>
> At one time, there was a bug in the SOAP specification regarding the use of xsd versus xsi (Version 1.0). The specification used the xsd namespace throughout when it should have used xsi, as all SOAP packets will be instance information, rather than schemas. This was corrected in Version 1.1 of the specification.

SOAP not only mandates the use of XML, however—it further *constrains* how the XML argument data is to be encoded. Not just any arbitrary format will do. Instead, the information must be encoded to conform to the SOAP specification to enable disparate SOAP implementations to deserialize the argument data.

Encoding Data Types in SOAP

To fully understand SOAP's data encoding specification, you must first understand the language SOAP uses to describe the encoding. The SOAP specification uses several terms you should understand, for example.

In SOAP, argument data is encoded either as a *simple type* or a *compound type*. Simple types include the basic argument data types, such as integers and floating point values. Compound types represent more complex data structures, such as unions, and arrays.

If a simple type or a component of a compound type is explicitly named, that particular XML element (which represents an argument variable) is considered an *accessor*. Not all simple types and pieces of compound types require names, so not all argument data will be considered accessors. The reason the specification makes this important distinction is that you can have *single-reference* accessors and *multi-reference* accessors.

Single-Reference Accessors

If a particular piece of information is referenced only once within the SOAP packet, it is considered single reference. Consider the integer value in this example:

```
void SomeMethod([in] int iData);
...
SomeMethod(26);
```

The resulting SOAP encoding will look like Listing 6.1.

LISTING 6.1   SOAP Single-Reference Serialization

```
<SOAP-ENV:Body xmlns:m="urn:www.my-url.com">
    <m:SomeMethod>
        <iData>26</iData>
    </m:SomeMethod>
</SOAP-ENV:Body>
```

In this case, the argument data was passed by value (26), and no other method argument refers to the value (in this case, there is only a single method argument).

Another related single-reference issue is that of *identity*. (The concept of identity comes into play in the next section on multi-reference accessors.) If you pass argument data by value, you should find the value(s) encoded inline. This is simply more efficient. The given value has no need to be identified when deserialized, so none is identified to speed the XML parsing process.

On the other hand, if you are passing in data by identity (by reference instead of by value), you must follow this alternative way to encode the method arguments:

```
void SomeMethodEx([in, out] int* piData); // IDL
...
int i = 26;
SomeMethodEx(&i);
```

In this case, the SOAP serialization code needs to encode the fact the integer value is passed by reference instead of by value. Presumably, the remote method will use the original value and place an output value in the same variable (the purpose of [in, out] arguments). The resulting SOAP encoding for this is shown in Listing 6.2.

LISTING 6.2   Nominal Reference Serialization

```
<SOAP-ENV:Body xmlns:m="urn:www.my-url.com">
    <m:SomeMethodEx>
        <piData href="#arg"/>
    </m:SomeMethodEx>
    <m:piData id="arg" xsi:type="int">
        26
    </m:piData>
</SOAP-ENV:Body>
```

In this case, the argument(s) are serialized in their proper location. The difference between this example and the previous one is the data referred to is actually stored outside the method element. The fact that the data is [in, out] forces the relocation of the referenced information. If it were just [in] data, you could still serialize it as an embedded element within the method's argument element because the remote method merely requires the value. It does not need to know that the value was passed in by reference.

The semantics involved with this method follow those of Java, which is to pass by reference, instead of passing by value. In many cases, this is more efficient from a call stack perspective, at least when structures are involved. It will be less efficient from a SOAP perspective, however, because more of the SOAP packet must be parsed and understood before the actual argument values can be extracted and used. The SOAP encoding you see in Listing 6.2 is also how multi-reference arguments are serialized.

Multi-Reference Accessors

Single-reference accessors represent named XML elements (argument data) that have only one reference in the call stack. That is, if you pass an [in] integer value that no other argument variable makes reference to, then you have a single-reference accessor.

On the other hand, if more than one method argument is bound to the particular piece of information, then you have a multi-reference accessor. Information that is accessed by different method arguments must be encoded in the SOAP packet such that all of the argument references have access to the XML data's scope. If the data were encoded within an embedded element (a child node of a particular method argument), then other method arguments would not be able to make use of that information. (Data embedded within one argument element is considered outside the scope of the other argument elements.)

If data is to be accessed from several different method arguments, the data must be contained within a sibling XML node (or nodes) to the (independent) method element to satisfy XML scoping rules.

The SOAP specification describes multi-reference accessors as independent elements containing the id attribute, which implies a corresponding href reference. The fact that there is one or more references to this particular piece of information makes this value multi-reference. This is also why you'll find the data in its own independent element (as mentioned previously, to allow you to access the data without breaking XML scoping rules).

To illustrate another point, that of identity, examine this code:

```
void SomeOtherMethod([in] int* piData1, [in, out] int* piData2); // IDL
...
int i = 26;
SomeOtherMethod(&i,&i);
```

You would expect the integer data to be encoded as multi-reference for two reasons. First, the data is passed by reference in both arguments. Second, the specific invocation passes into the method a pointer to the *same* variable. (It is referenced by two method arguments.) But also note there is an identity issue here. The serialized XML must somehow convey the fact that the two pointers are, in fact, pointing to the same memory location. The serialized information is shown in Listing 6.3.

LISTING 6.3 Nominal Multi-Reference Serialization with Preserved Argument Identity

```
<SOAP-ENV:Body xmlns:m="urn:www.my-url.com">
    <m:SomeOtherMethod>
        <piData1 href="#arg"/>
        <piData2 href="#arg"/>
    </m:SomeOtherMethod>
    <m:piData id="arg" xsi:type="int">
        26
    </m:piData>
</SOAP-ENV:Body>
```

The trick is to use the href attribute to link the second argument to the same information as the first argument. Had the two arguments referenced different integer pointer variables, you would have seen two different values serialized after the method element.

Essentially, whenever you read "multi-reference", think XPointer and href/id, and expect to see the information serialized outside of the method argument element. (Refer to Chapter 2, "SOAP and XML: The Foundation of SOAP," to review XPointer.) If you read "single-reference", you should expect to see the argument value serialized inline in the embedded argument element.

NDR Pointer Types

In NDR (Network Data Representation, or a "writer makes right" encoding protocol—see Chapter 1, "Essential SOAP: A Comparison of SOAP to Existing Distributed Object Technologies"), pointers to information take on one of three meanings (see Table 6.1). A pointer can be a [ptr], which is the traditional pointer. It can be [unique], which constrains the pointer. Or it can be [ref], which is a pure reference pointer with even more constraints applied. These pointer semantics enable optimizations to serialization code if the pointer type is known a priori.

Table 6.1 provides you the NDR pointer types and their semantics.

TABLE 6.1 NDR Pointer Types

Type	Semantics
[ptr]	Pointer can be NULL, and identity is preserved.
[unique]	Pointer can be NULL, and identity is lost.
[ref]	Pointer cannot be NULL, and identity is lost.

The pointer type has a direct bearing on how SOAP will serialize data marked by a pointer.

Data types using the [ptr] semantics must be multi-reference (use the href/id attributes and serialize the data after the method element). Moreover, in serializing code you must take great care to make sure all pointers keep their proper identity. Two or more incoming pointers that actually refer to the same memory must be serialized such that this fact is maintained when the data is deserialized. NULL pointers will use the xsi:null="1" attribute to indicate they are, in fact, NULL pointers.

[unique] pointers are marked as such to indicate identity is not necessary. (You do this as the method's architect for optimization purposes.) If the serialization code is told beforehand that none of the incoming pointers will point to the same data, it can skip the (expensive) pointer runtime checking. Note that [unique] pointers can also be NULL.

Finally, the most restrictive pointer type, but the easiest to serialize, is the [ref] pointer type. This pointer type literally means *pass-by-reference*, as in this C++ example:

```
void RefData(const string& str);
```

In this case, a pointer to the string data will be placed in the call stack (for efficiency). The SOAP serialization code may use this information to place the value of the string within the method argument element (that is, embed it as single-reference, rather than serialize it as multi-reference data).

The inclusion of the pointer type in the method's IDL code serves as a hint to the serializer, allowing it to both optimize the data for efficient wire transfer and to skip otherwise expensive runtime checks. There is no requirement that you use these hints, at least according to the SOAP specification, so without further guidance, you must assume all pointers are of [ptr] type.

Basic SOAP Data Types

The basic SOAP data types include the simple data types you would expect: single-reference values, multi-reference values, byte arrays (arrays with no external references), strings, and enumerations. Basic data types can be serialized inline within the method element (embedded inside the SOAP body element) or by reference for optimization.

The rules for evaluating basic data types come either from the SOAP specification or from the XML Schema (draft) standard. Where there is a duplication, the SOAP specification takes precedence (strings and arrays). A discussion of the basic SOAP data types appears in the following sections.

Simple Data Types

The SOAP simple data types are defined in the *XML Schema, Part 2: Data types* (draft) standard (http://www.w3.org/TR/1999/WD-xmlschema-2-19991105/) under "Built-in Data types." Table 6.2 lists the primitive data types you'll find there, as well as their meanings.

TABLE 6.2   SOAP Simple Data Types (Primitive)

Data Type	*Meaning*
string	XML character strings (SOAP constrained)
boolean	True or false
real	Real number value (floating point)
timeInstant	Single-string encoding of a data/time combination
timeDuration	Single-string encoding of a year, month, day, and time combination
recurringInstant	An instant of time with a recurring timeDuration
binary	A blob of binary data (can also be hex or base64)
uri	Universal Resource Locator (RFC 2396)
language	Natural language identifiers (RFC 1766)

The simple data types you see in Table 6.2 are intrinsic to XML. However, there is a set of generated (or derived) data types that is allowed (most are ultimately defined by the XML specification itself). The generated data types are listed in Table 6.3.

TABLE 6.3   SOAP Simple Data Types (Generated)

Data Type	*Meaning*
NMTOKEN	XML name token attribute type
NMTOKENS	Collection of XML name token attribute types
Name	XML name
NCName	Non-colonized XML name
ID	XML ID attribute type
IDREF	XML IDREF attribute type
ENTITY	XML ENTITY attribute type
ENTITIES	Collection of XML ENTITY attribute types
NOTATION	XML NOTATION attribute type
decimal	Real values restricted to those with exact fractional parts

Data Type	Meaning
integer	Integer value, negative infinity to infinity
non-negative integer	Integer value, zero to infinity
positive integer	Integer value, one to infinity
non-positive integer	Integer value, negative infinity to zero
negative integer	Integer value, negative infinity to one
date	A timeDuration that starts at midnight of a specified day and lasts 24 hours
time	A recurringInstant that recurs every day

Tables 6.2 and 6.3 tell you that a SOAP implementation must serialize method arguments according to one of many specifications, depending upon the precise data type. Some data types are intuitive, such as string and integer values. Others, such as the IDREF, might not be as intuitive at first glance but are (or might be) commonly used by concrete SOAP implementations.

As an example, assume the following method is to be serialized:

```
datetime OffsetDate(datetime originalDate, time timeOffset);
```

The OffsetDate() method accepts both a datetime and a time value, in a system-specific format, and then returns the resulting datetime value when the time offset is added to the input date. If you started with Tuesday, February 1, 2000, 2:05p.m. (EST) as the date and added three hours and fifteen minutes, you would expect the result to be Tuesday, February 1, 2000, 5:20p.m. (EST). No matter how any individual system represents these values internally, both actually represent simple SOAP data types. The datetime argument represents the timeInstant data type, whereas the time argument maps directly to the SOAP time data type. In this case, the SOAP serialization code will produce this XML encoding (or something equivalent) as the request shown in Listing 6.4.

LISTING 6.4   SOAP Simple (Single-Reference) Data Type Serialization

```
<SOAP-ENV:Body>
    <m:OffsetDate xmlns:m="www.my-url.com">
        <originalDate>2000-02-01T14:05:00-05:00</originalDate>
        <timeOffset>3:15:00</timeOffset>
    </m:OffsetDate>
</SOAP-ENV:Body>
```

Here you can see Tuesday, February 1, 2000, 2:05p.m. (EST) was encoded to be `2000-02-01T14:05:00-05:00`, which is the correct format according to the XML specification. The time offset (`3:15:00`) is a bit more self-explanatory.

Assuming the remainder of the SOAP request was completed properly and the remote method executed, you will find the `datetime` return value in a SOAP response packet similar to the following:

```
<SOAP-ENV:Body>
    <m:OffsetDateResponse xmlns:m="www.my-url.com">
        <return>2000-02-01T17:20:00-05:00</return>
....</m:OffsetDateResponse>
</SOAP-ENV:Body>
```

Byte Arrays

The SOAP specification recommends byte arrays be encoded as opaque MIME Base64 elements because Base64 encoding uses character substitution to remove characters some protocols consider special. A nice feature is that the characters are the same, whether you're using ASCII or EBCDIC. Other encoding techniques, such as UUENCODE, either are non-standard, or the resulting characters have specific meanings to certain protocols.

Base64 Encoding

The technique for Base64 encoding is described in RFC 2045, *Multipurpose Internet Mail Extensions (MIME) Part One: Format of Internet Message Bodies*. Essentially, 24-bit groupings are converted from a binary format to a textual format using the *Base64 alphabet*. The Base64 alphabet provides 64 6-bit values that replace the 4 6-bit sub-groupings contained within the 24-bit grouping, encoded from left to right. Table 6.4 provides you with the Base64 alphabet.

TABLE 6.4 Base64 Alphabet Encoding Values

6-Bit Value	Substitution Value
0–25	'A'–'Z'
26–51	'a'–'z'
52–61	'0'–'9'
62	'+'
63	'/'
(pad)	'='

6

For example, if you have the byte sequence 0x3209AC9B, you first convert the bytes to 24-bit groups (after converting to binary):

Group 1: 001100 (leftmost bit group)

Group 2: 100000

Group 3: 100110

Group 4: 101100

Group 5: 100110

Group 6: 110000 (Last 4 bits are zero-padding.)

Then convert the groups to their decimal equivalent:

Group 1: 12

Group 2: 32

Group 3: 38

Group 4: 44

Group 5: 38

Group 6: 48

With the converted values in hand, you then substitute the equivalent Base64 alphabet value for each grouping:

Group 1: 'M'

Group 2: 'g'

Group 3: 'm'

Group 4: 's'

Group 5: 'm'

Group 6: 'w'

So the raw Base64 encoding for 0x3209AC9B would be (so far) "Mgmsmw".

In this case, the input value required 4-bits of padding because the original value was 32 bits, which is not divisible by 6. There wasn't an integral number of 6-bit groups. If this is the case, you simply pad with zero bits to create an integral number of 6-bit groups.

The problem lies with decoding if you had to pad the original, un-encoded value. If no padding was required (the original binary value was divisible by groupings of 6 bits), then you have no more Base64 encoding to do. However, if the remainder was 8 bits, as it was for this example, you then add two '=' characters to the end of the string. If the remainder of the original value left 16 bits, you append only a single '='. On the other end, if when you're decoding you find a single '=' or a double '=' trailing the string, you know to ignore the final (padded) bits (8 and 16 bits, respectively). For this example, the final Base64 encoded value for `0x3209AC9B` would be "Mgmsmw==".

The typical use for Base64 encoding is to transmit electronic mail, where there exists a maximum line length of 76 characters. The SOAP specification explicitly states there is no such limitation necessary for SOAP processing, so you will not need to break the resulting Base64 string at 76 character intervals.

To decode, you reverse the process. For example, the SOAP specification provides this example:

```
<picture xsi:type="SOAP-ENC:base64">
    aG93IG5vDyBicm73biBjb3cNCg==
</picture>
```

To decode this, convert the textual values to 6-bit groupings (there will be 26 of them because you exclude the trailing '=' characters), and then substitute the appropriate binary value for each grouping. With each grouping now in binary, collect the bits into 8-bit groups and remove the appropriate padding (the final 8 bits, in this case). The original value contained in the SOAP specification then becomes (in hex):

```
68 6F 77 20
6E 6F 77 20
62 72 6F 77
6E 20 63 6F
77 0D 0A
```

Clearly, the specification authors were having a little fun when they added this, because, if you then convert the byte array to ASCII, the message reads *how now brown cow<CR><LF>*.

As a side issue, note that the byte array was encoded with the `xsi` type of `SOAP-ENC:base64`. This is a data type specific to SOAP that is defined in the SOAP encoding schema you'll find at `http://schemas.xmlsoap.org/soap/encoding/`. You'll see this again when you see how general-case arrays are encoded in the upcoming section, "Arrays."

From an efficiency standpoint alone, encoding in Base64 makes little sense. After all, *how now brown cow<CR><LF>* consumes 19 bytes as ASCII, yet the Base64 encoding requires 28 bytes to represent the same byte array. This might not seem like much for such a short byte array, but a larger byte array can increase in size by a proportional amount:

(28 bytes / 19 bytes) × 100 = 147%

The Base64-encoded array is roughly 47% *larger* than the original array (RFC 2045 states that statistically the encoding growth will average about 33%).

SOAP and Data: Data Types

CHAPTER 6

147

6

SOAP AND
DATA: DATA
TYPES

The benefit of Base64 encoding is there are no resulting <CR>, <LF>, '.', or '-' characters that firewalls or other software or protocols might find significant and therefore modify or otherwise molest (such as SMTP, for which this encoding was designed).

SOAP Encoding

After you have the byte array in the Base64-encoded form, you then use it as if it were multi-reference. That is, the information is recorded outside the method element and is accessed by XPointer syntax, as seen in Listing 6.5.

LISTING 6.5   SOAP Byte Array Serialization

```
<SOAP-ENV:Body xmlns:m="www.my-url.com">
    <m:method>
        <rgsBytes href="#arg1"/>
    </m:method>
    <m:rgsBytes id="arg1" xsi:type="SOAP-ENC:base64">
        aG93IG5vdyBicm93biBjb3cNCg==
    </m:rgsBytes>
</SOAP-ENV:Body>
```

The byte array is serialized as a simple, multi-reference accessor, so the array data follows the method element as you would expect. The difference between this encoding and a generic multi-reference accessor lies with the addition of the xsi:type attribute, which indicates the byte array is Base64 encoded. Your other choice for encoding is xsi:hex. Note the serialization of byte arrays need not follow the naming array convention established in the SOAP specification (discussed in the later section "Compound SOAP Data Types").

Large Block Data Transfers

A question naturally arises regarding large block data transfers. If you have a large block of data, should you encode it using Base64 and then transport it using SOAP? The answer is, *it depends*. Generally, Base64 increases the size of the encoded data packet by 33%, so a 1MB block of binary data will become 1.3MB. Whether or not this is acceptable depends upon your particular architecture. If it is acceptable, then by all means encode the binary data and wrap it in a SOAP packet.

If you do not want to encode the data in Base64, perhaps because of the increase in size, or if you do not want to bloat your SOAP packet with a huge binary element, then you must explore alternatives for transporting the data. One common choice is to transport an URL in the SOAP packet that represents an endpoint to obtain the data itself, perhaps via telnet, FTP, or HTTP. After the receiving system processes the URL, it can obtain the data through the alternative transport.

Transporting XML Data

Another good question to ask is what to do in the case raw XML information is to be transported from within a method call (as an argument, perhaps as the contents of a string). In this case, your options depend upon whether you are able to validate the SOAP packets or not. If you are able to use valid XML (that is, you have a schema and your XML processor can validate the XML document against the schema), then you can indicate the given string value is CDATA (unparsed character data). The XML processor will leave the information untouched.

On the other hand, XML processors at the time of this writing are (unfortunately) not able to validate XML documents using general-purpose schemas. In this case, encoding the XML string as a byte array in Base64 appears to be the best alternative, taking into consideration the conditions mentioned in the previous section.

Strings: The Multi-Reference Simple Type

Strings in SOAP are considered a multi-reference simple type, which is to say they are serialized in much the same way arrays of bytes are stored. Either embedded method argument elements that access the string can do so through XPointer syntax, or the string can be stored inline for optimization if it truly is single-reference.

Consider this example:

```
boolean CompareLength([in, ptr] char* s1, [in, ptr]char* s2); // IDL
...
char* s = "Hello, World!";
bSameLength = CompareLength(s,s);
```

In this case, the string *Hello, World!* is passed into the CompareLength() method, presumably to see if the two input strings are of the same length. A blind SOAP encoding is shown in Listing 6.6.

LISTING 6.6   SOAP String Serialization

```
<SOAP-ENV:Body xmlns:m="www.my-url.com">
    <m:CompareLength>
        <s1 href="#str1"/>
        <s2 href="#str2"/>
    </m:CompareLength>
    <m:s1      id="str1"  xsi:type="xsi:string">
        Hello, World!
    </m:s1>
    <m:s2      id="str2"  xsi:type="xsi:string">
        Hello, World!
    </m:s2>
</SOAP-ENV:Body>
```

SOAP and Data: Data Types

CHAPTER 6

149

6

SOAP AND
DATA: DATA
TYPES

The string contents are serialized following the method element, as you would expect. The data types are of xsi:string, although you may also use SOAP-ENC:string. (The type indication here may also be omitted altogether if the underlying schema dictates the type for you.)

However, if the SOAP serialization code uncovered the fact the string was indeed the very same string, you would instead serialize the string's reference shown in Listing 6.7 to preserve the argument's identity.

LISTING 6.7   SOAP String Serialization with Preserved Identity

```
<SOAP-ENV:Body xmlns:m="www.my-url.com">
    <m:CompareLength>
        <s1 href="#str1"/>
        <s2 href="#str1"/>
    </m:CompareLength>
    <m:s  id="str1"  xsi:type="xsi:string">
        Hello, World!
    </m:s>
</SOAP-ENV:Body>
```

Finally, you have the option of encoding the strings inline, if you know a priori they are [in] parameters and [unique] (and therefore constant without regard to duplication). This SOAP encoding is shown in Listing 6.8.

LISTING 6.8   Optimized SOAP String Serialization

```
<SOAP-ENV:Body xmlns:m="www.my-url.com">
    <m:CompareLength>
        <s1>
            Hello, World!
        </s1>
         <s2>
            Hello, World!
        </s2>
    </m:CompareLength>
</SOAP-ENV:Body>
```

Of course, encoding strings in this manner affects your ability to implement the previous optimization should it apply, but, nonetheless, it represents legal SOAP encoding.

Enumerations

Enumerated method arguments are simply encoded using the particular enumerated value. For example, consider this code:

```
enum DayOfWeek { Sunday = 0, Monday, Tuesday, Wednesday,
                 Thursday, Friday, Saturday } DayOfWeek;
boolean IsToday([in] DayOfWeek day); // checks day of week against system time
...
bTodayIsWednesday = IsToday(Wednesday);
```

Normally, the value Wednesday is stored in memory as the integer value 3. (Sunday is 0, Monday is 1, and so on.) However, the SOAP serialization code will encode Wednesday in the SOAP packet as shown in Listing 6.9.

LISTING 6.9   SOAP Enumeration Serialization

```
<SOAP-ENV:Body xmlns:m="www.my-url.com">
    <m:IsToday>
        <day>
            Wednesday
        </day>
    </m:IsToday>
</SOAP-ENV:Body>
```

The enumerated value is serialized as its textual representation (Wednesday) rather than its integer placeholder (3), even though the value 3 is what will be pushed onto the method call stack. It is up to the SOAP serialization code to determine an enumerated value was passed and correctly interpret (and convert) the enumeration as the value is serialized. Although the example shows an enumerated value passed as a method argument, the same holds true for enumerated values stored as structure elements.

Compound SOAP Data Types

SOAP transcends the set of simple data types by allowing you to encode various compound data types, which include structures, generic compound data types, and arrays. The SOAP specification defines a structure as a collection of named members:

> "A 'struct' is a compound value in which accessor name is the only distinction among member values, and no accessor has the same name as any other."

If the collection of members is unnamed and instead referenced by an ordinal position, the collection is called an *array*. The *generic compound data type* is defined to be a particular instance of the struct in which the members are named and typed at the time of execution.

An example of this would be runtime database scheme determination. The information returned from the database would consist of table data (*records*) whose format was not previously known to the caller (*generic*).

Structures

Structures are serialized as multi-reference accessors, which is to say they are referenced in the method element but their data is serialized in (independent) elements following the method element. The members of the struct can be embedded or referenced externally. Imagine this example:

```
struct tag_AutoInfo
{
    string Make;
    string Model;
    int Year;
    string Tag;
} AutoInfo;
int PendingCitations([in] AutoInfo autoinfo); // IDL
...
AutoInfo ai;
ai.Make = "Chevrolet";
ai.Model = "Corvette"
ai.Year = 1999;
ai.Tag = "MEGA HP";
iNumTickets = PendingCitations(ai);
```

The `AutoInfo` structure contains 4 elements—the car's make, model, build (model) year, and its license plate information. When the completed (filled-in) structure is passed into a method, the structure's information will need to be interpreted and encoded for transmission.

The SOAP serialization code for this method invocation is shown in 6.10.

LISTING 6.10   SOAP Structure Serialization

```
<SOAP-ENV:Body xmlns:m="urn:www.my-url.com">
    <m:PendingCitations>
        <autoinfo href="#arg1"/>
    </m:PendingCitations>
    <m:AutoInfo id="arg1">
        <Make href="#s1"/>
        <Model href="#s2"/>
        <Year xsi:type="xsi:integer">1999</Year>
        <Tag href="#s3"/>
```

continues

LISTING 6.10 Continued

```
    </m:AutoInfo>
    <m:Make id="s1">Chevrolet</m:Make>
    <m:Model id="s2">Corvette</m:Model>
    <m:Tag id="s3">MEGA HP</m:Tag>
</SOAP-ENV:Body>
```

In this case, the AutoInfo structure contains three reference members and a single embedded member (the year). The referenced members are strings and are stored in the usual manner for string information (XPointer links embedded within the containing element).

The embedded member, the year value, has the additional requirement that its instance data type must be inserted into the element tag. In this case, the car's year data type attribute is encoded as xsi:type="xsi:integer".

Linked Structures

Linked structures, such as linked lists and trees, present a different challenge to encode. In this case, not all nodes in the graph are equal—there must be a root node of some kind. Originally, the SOAP specification didn't address this situation when there was a SOAP element (body or header) that contained many independent elements. In that case, you could not tell which independent element represented the root of the graph.

Revisiting the example from the previous chapter, imagine you have this linked list node structure:

```
typedef struct tagPartNode {
    struct tagNode* pNext;
    int iPartNum;
    int iNumInStock;
} PartNode;
```

Then assume you pass a linked list to this remote method:

```
int AvailableParts([in] PartNode* pHead ); // IDL
```

The SOAP serializer must look for each node in the linked list and serialize it as you see in Listing 6.11. .

LISTING 6.11 Nominal SOAP XML Linked List Serialization

```
<SOAP-ENV:Body xmlns:m="urn:www.my-url.com">
    <m:AvailableParts>
        <m:pHead href="#node001"/>
    </m:AvailableParts>
    <m:PartNode id="node001" SOAP-ENV:root="1">
        <pNext href="#node002"/>
```

```
        <iPartNum>5441</iPartNum>
        <iNumInStock>57</iNumInStock>
    </m:PartNode>
    <m:PartNode id="node002">
        <pNext href="#node003"/>
        <iPartNum>998</iPartNum>
        <iNumInStock>21</iNumInStock>
    </m:PartNode >
    <m:PartNode id="node003">
        <pNext xsi:null="1" />
        <iPartNum>125</iPartNum>
        <iNumInStock>5</iNumInStock>
    </m:PartNode>
</SOAP-ENV:Body>
```

The linked list's head (root node) is indicated with the SOAP-ENV:root attribute, the same
attribute you saw in the previous chapter. Other linked structures, such as trees, queues, and
general graphs, will be serialized in a similar fashion. As with linked lists, the other data type's
information will follow the method element and make reference to internal nodes in a similar
manner.

Generic Compound Types

Under certain circumstances, the serialization code might not know beforehand precisely what
data is to be returned from a given method call. One such circumstance, for example, involves
the dynamic query of a database for a given table scheme. You first query the database to
determine what a given table looks like (rows, columns, data types, and so on), and then you
decide what data to query for, specifically based upon your previous discovery.

The table information that is returned from the database upon the completion of the first query
is an example of a *generic compound type* (also known as a *generic record* in the 1.0 version
of the specification). The remote serialization code will be required to package the results in a
legal SOAP format, but, happily, the format is identical to the struct format. The members of
the generic compound type will have element names identical to their respective structure
names and will be either referenced or embedded. Embedded members may have their type
indicated by the xsi:type="{type}" attribute, but this is not required.

An issue that does arise is the duplication of member names within a given scope. In a sense,
this is like mixing a structure with an embedded array. Here is an example provided by the
SOAP specification:

```
<xyz:PurchaseOrder>
    <CustomerName>Henry Ford</CustomerName>
    <ShipTo>
        <Street>5th Ave</Street>
```

```
            <City>New York</City>
            <State>NY</State>
            <Zip>10010</Zip>
        </ShipTo>
        <PurchaseLineItems>
            <Order>
                <Product>Apple</Product>
                <Price>1.56</Price>
            </Order>
            <Order>
                <Product>Peach</Product>
                <Price>1.48</Price>
            </Order>
        </PurchaseLineItems>
    </xyz:PurchaseOrder>
```

In this case, the `<Order/>` elements you see within the `<PurchaseLineItems/>` element have the same accessor tag (the element name), so their order is significant even though they may not have been serialized in such a manner because they actually came from an array. This is not considered an error according to the specification, and your SOAP processing code will need to be able to handle this condition if you expect to process generic compound types.

Arrays

Arrays are serialized in the same fashion as compound data types in that they are referenced in the method element but encoded as trailing data within the SOAP body element. Unlike with normal compound types, there are some element-naming issues that might need to be addressed, and there is a SOAP-specific XML data type (as with Base64 encoded byte arrays).

If the array contains single-reference data, the data is serialized inline in an array element. That is, given this sample code:

```
int ShipData(int[] iDataArray);
...
int iData[5] = {0,1,2,3,4};
iError = ShipData(iData);
```

The resulting SOAP serialization will look like Listing 6.13.

LISTING 6.13   Nominal SOAP Single-Reference Array Serialization

```
<SOAP-ENV:Body xmlns:m="urn:www.my-url.com">
    <m:ShipData>
        <m:iDataArray href="#array"/>
    </m:ShipData>
    <m:iData id="array"  SOAP-ENC:arrayType="xsi:int[5]" >
```

SOAP and Data: Data Types

CHAPTER 6

155

6

SOAP AND
DATA: DATA
TYPES

```
            <int>0</int>
            <int>1</int>
            <int>2</int>
            <int>3</int>
            <int>4</int>
        </m:iData>
</SOAP-ENV:Body>
```

The array is referenced in the method's independent element using the href/id combination you're familiar with at this point. The array information itself, simple integers, is stored as embedded elements contained within the <m:iData/> element. The naming of the array data element is interesting in this case, because it assumes the array is described in a schema:

```
<element name="iData" type="SOAP-ENC:Array">
```

The element's type must either be, or have been, derived from SOAP-ENC:Array. Had there not been a schema, the encoding would not use the variable name (iData, in this case) but would instead use the SOAP array data type directly. That is, the array encoding would then become

```
<SOAP-ENC:Array id="array" SOAP-ENC:arrayType="xsi:int[5]">
    <SOAP-ENC:int>0</SOAP-ENC:int>
    <SOAP-ENC:int>1</SOAP-ENC:int>
    <SOAP-ENC:int>2</SOAP-ENC:int>
    <SOAP-ENC:int>3</SOAP-ENC:int>
    <SOAP-ENC:int>4</SOAP-ENC:int>
</SOAP-ENC:Array>
```

The use of SOAP-ENC:int for the array element data is optional because you could also use xsi:int (or even int, if you assume the default namespace).

However, had the array data been a compound type that was accessed assuming the [ptr] IDL attribute (array elements could be NULL, and could point to the same information), the serialization would differ yet again.

For example, consider an array of (revised) parts information structures from the linked list example in the previous "Linked Structures" section:

```
typedef struct tagPartElement {
    int iPartNum;
    int iNumInStock;
} PartElement, *PPartElement;
```

Instead of passing a linked list into the AvailableParts() method, you now pass an array (note you also pass the sizing information):

```
int AvailablePartsEx([in] long iNumElements,
                     [in, size_is(iNumElements)] PartElement[] peArray); // idl
```

Then assume you invoke the method in this fashion:

```
PartElement peData[3] = {{5441,57},
                         {998,21},
                         {125,5}};
iParts = AvailablePartsEx(3,peData);
```

The SOAP serialization will appear as shown in Listing 6.14.

LISTING 6.14   SOAP Multi-Reference Array Serialization

```
<SOAP-ENV:Body xmlns:m="urn:www.my-url.com">
    <m:AvailablePartsEx>
        <iNumElements>3</iNumElements>
        < peArray href="#elements"/>
    </m:AvailablePartsEx>
    <m:peData id="elements"
      SOAP-ENC:arrayType="m:PartElement[3]">
        <m:PartElement>
            <iPartNum>5441</iPartNum>
            <iNumInStock>57</iNumInStock>
        </m:PartElement>
        <m:PartElement>
            <iPartNum>998</iPartNum>
            <iNumInStock>21</iNumInStock>
        </m:PartElement>
        <m:PartElement>
            <iPartNum>125</iPartNum>
            <iNumInStock>5</iNumInStock>
        </m:PartElement>
    </m:peData>
</SOAP-ENC:Body>
```

As you can see, the method serialization in Listing 6.14 is the same as for Listing 6.13, taking into consideration the differences in the array types and the method name. The real difference is the array elements are referenced in Listing 6.14, using id/href, rather than embedded as they were in Listing 6.13. Because of this multi-reference access, the array elements are contained within an array (XML) element. The tag for this array element again reflects the variable (peData), which leads you to believe the element is derived from SOAP-ENC:Array by way of a schema.

Sparse Arrays

In some cases, the entire array need not be transmitted. This is especially true for the sparse array, which is an array with very large bounds but with very little data in relationship to its bounds. Actually, for SOAP's encoding purposes, the sparse array can be any array that contains fewer elements than its capacity in relatively random locations.

In this case, you specify the array bounds as you normally would. The array element data, however, is serialized only where there is an element present in the array. And at that time, the array element is provided a positional attribute to enable the SOAP deserializer to properly place the value in the correct array element upon deserialization.

For example, consider this example:

```
int PartsInBin(PartElement*[] ppeData);
...
PartElement* pPartsArray[100000] = {NULL};
pPartsArray[12] = new PartElement(5441,57);
pPartsArray[221] = new PartElement(998,21);
iParts = PartsInBin(pPartsArray);
```

In this case, the SOAP serializer will produce code similar to Listing 6.15.

LISTING 6.15 SOAP Sparse Array Serialization

```
<SOAP-ENV:Body xmlns:m="urn:www.my-url.com">
    <m:PartsInBin>
        <m:ppeArray href="#elements"/>
    </m:PartsInBin>
    <m:pPartsArray id="elements"
      SOAP-ENC:arrayType="m:PPartElement[100000]">
        <m:PPartElement SOAP-ENC:position="[12]">
            <iPartNum>5441</iPartNum>
            <iNumInStock>57</iNumInStock>
        </m:PPartElement>
        <m:PPartElement SOAP-ENC:position="[221]">
            <iPartNum>998</iPartNum>
            <iNumInStock>21</iNumInStock>
        </m:PPartElement>
    </m:pPartsArray>
</SOAP-ENV:Body>
```

As you can see from Listing 6.15, only the two relevant array elements were transported. It would clearly be wasteful to needlessly transport the entire array, so the two pertinent elements were transported instead. The SOAP deserialization code will fill the remaining elements with NULL (in this case) or zero in the case of numerical arrays.

Partially Transmitted Arrays

Another optimization you can make is to serialize contiguous elements if the array is not completely filled. In this case, SOAP will specify the starting offset (element) that contains valid data and will serialize the remaining valid elements.

For example, examine this modification to the previous example:

```
PartElement* pPartsArray[100000] = {NULL};
pPartsArray[12] = new PartElement(5441,57);
pPartsArray[13] = new PartElement(998,21);
iParts = PartsInBin(pPartsArray);
```

Because the array elements are contiguous, the resulting SOAP encoding will look more like the encoding shown in Listing 6.16.

LISTING 6.16   SOAP Partially Transmitted Array Serialization

```
<SOAP-ENV:Body xmlns:m="urn:www.my-url.com">
    <m:PartsInBin>
        <m:ppeArray href="#elements"/>
    </m:PartsInBin>
    <m:pPartsArray id="elements"
      SOAP-ENC:arrayType="m:PPartElement[100000]">
        <m:PPartElement SOAP-ENC:offset="[12]">
            <iPartNum>5441</iPartNum>
            <iNumInStock>57</iNumInStock>
        </m:PPartElement>
        <m:PPartElement>
            <iPartNum>998</iPartNum>
            <iNumInStock>21</iNumInStock>
        </m:PPartElement>
    </m:pPartsArray>
</SOAP-ENV:Body>
```

You see the first difference in the array element encoding, where the offset is specified (array element 13, offset 12). If the offset is omitted, the element is assumed to be element zero (the first element). The second difference from Listing 6.15 is shown in the next element's data encoding (array element 14), where there is no special attribute at all. The element is assumed to follow the previous element in the array because the elements are contiguous.

Jagged Arrays

There is a special case of array transmission known as the *jagged array*, which is an array with elements that are themselves arrays. In this case, there can be no serialization by value (no embedded data). All the elements, both for the outer and the inner arrays, must be independent elements.

SOAP and Data: Data Types

CHAPTER 6

159

6

SOAP AND
DATA: DATA
TYPES

To show this, consider this example:

```c
typedef struct tagPartsBin {
    PartElement[10] peInStock;
    PartElement[10] peJIT; // just in time parts
} PartsBin, *PPartsBin;

void SetPartsInBin(PartsBin[] pbData);
...
PartsBin pbData[35];
PbData[7].peInStock[0].iPartNum = 5441;
PbData[7].peInStock[0].iNumInStock = 57;
PbData[7].peInStock[1].iPartNum = 998;
PbData[7].peInStock[1].iNumInStock = 21;
PbData[7].peJIT[0].iPartNum = 125;
PbData[7].peJIT[0].iNumInStock = 5; // req'd number...
SetPartsInBin(pbData);
```

In this case, the SOAP serialization will appear as you see in Listing 6.17.

LISTING 6.17   SOAP Jagged Array Serialization

```xml
<SOAP-ENV:Body xmlns:m="urn:www.my-url.com">
    <m:SetPartsInBin>
        <m:pbData href="#elements"/>
    </m:SetPartsInBin>
    <m:pbData id="elements"
      SOAP-ENC:arrayType="m:PartsBin[35]">
        <m:PartsBin SOAP-ENC:offset="[7]">
            <peInStock href="#array-0"/>
            <peJIT href="#array-1"/>
        </m:PartsBin>
    </m:pbData>
    <m:peInStock id="array-0"
      SOAP-ENC:arrayType="m:PartElement[10]">
        <m:PartElement>
            <iPartNum>5441</iPartNum>
            <iNumInStock>57</iNumInStock>
        </m:PartElement>
        <m:PartElement>
            <iPartNum>998</iPartNum>
            <iNumInStock>21</iNumInStock>
        </m:PartElement>
    </m:peInStock>
<m:peJIT id="array-1"
```

continues

LISTING 6.17   Continued

```
        SOAP-ENC:arrayType="m:PartElement[10]">
          <m:PartElement>
              <iPartNum>125</iPartNum>
              <iNumInStock>5</iNumInStock>
          </m:PartElement>
      </m:peJIT>
</SOAP-ENV:Body>
```

The original array is referenced in the method element:

```
<m:SetPartsInBin>
    <m:pbData href="#elements"/>
</m:SetPartsInBin>
```

which tells the SOAP deserializer the array elements are stored in embedded PartsBin elements:

```
<m:pbData id="elements"
  SOAP-ENC:arrayType="m:PartsBin[35]">
    <m:PartsBin SOAP-ENC:offset="[7]">
        <peInStock href="#array-0"/>
        <peJIT href="#array-1"/>
    </m:PartsBin>
</m:pbData>
```

The array contains 35 elements, only one element of which is populated. (This is an example of a partially transmitted array with an offset of 7.) The array elements themselves are (partially transmitted) arrays:

```
<m:peInStock id="array-0"
  SOAP-ENC:arrayType="m:PartElement[10]">
    (Array data)
</m:peInStock>
```

and

```
<m:peJIT id="array-1"
  SOAP-ENC:arrayType="m:PartElement[10]">
    (Array data)
</m:peJIT>
```

In this case, the method argument was a compound type (PartsBin), which was itself composed of another compound type (PartElement).

SOAP and Data: Data Types

CHAPTER 6

161

6

SOAP AND
DATA: DATA
TYPES

This next example, however, brings up an interesting naming convention. In this case, assume you have an array of arrays of strings:

```
typedef StringArray string[3];
StringArray a[2][] = {{"r1c1","r1c2","r1c3"},
                       {"r2c1","r2c2",""}};
```

The resulting SOAP serialization will appear as shown in Listing 6.18.

LISTING 6.18   SOAP Array of Arrays Serialization

```
<SOAP-ENV:Body xmlns:m="urn:www.my-url.com">
    <m:method>
        <m:arg href="#array"/>
    </m:method>
    <m:a id="array"
      SOAP-ENC:arrayType="xsi:string[][2]">
        <SOAP-ENC:Array href="#array-1"/>
        <SOAP-ENC:Array href="#array-2"/>
    </m:a>
    <SOAP-ENC:Array id="array-1"
      SOAP-ENC:arrayType="xsi:string[3]">
        <xsi:string>r1c1</xsi:string>
        <xsi:string>r1c2</xsi:string>
        <xsi:string>r1c3</xsi:string>
    </SOAP-ENC:Array>
    <SOAP-ENC:Array id="array-2"
      SOAP-ENC:arrayType="xsi:string[3]">
        <xsi:string>r2c1</xsi:string>
        <xsi:string>r2c2</xsi:string>
    </SOAP-ENC:Array>
</SOAP-ENV:Body>
```

Note the inner arrays are serialized as SOAP-ENC:Array elements, whereas the containing array is serialized as m:a.

Multi-Dimensional Arrays

The SOAP specification provides an example of a multi-dimensional array of strings as well. Consider this example:

```
string a[2][] = {{"r1c1","r1c2","r1c3"},
                 {"r2c1","r2c2","r2c3"}};
```

Assuming this array of strings was serialized, the resulting SOAP encoding will look like the XML data shown in Listing 6.19. Note this array is serialized in a row-major format. Although the specification doesn't address this particular issue, row-major encoding either can be inferred from the specification as the preferred format, or can be addressed with your own schema.

LISTING 6.19 SOAP Multi-Dimensional Array Serialization

```
<SOAP-ENV:Body xmlns:m="urn:www.my-url.com">
    <m:method>
        <m:arg href="#array"/>
    </m:method>
    <SOAP-ENC:Array id="array"
      SOAP:arrayType="xsi:string[2][3]">
        <xsi:string>r1c1</xsi:string>
        <xsi:string>r1c2</xsi:string>
        <xsi:string>r1c3</xsi:string>
        <xsi:string>r2c1</xsi:string>
        <xsi:string>r2c2</xsi:string>
        <xsi:string>r2c2</xsi:string>
    </SOAP-ENC:Array>
</SOAP-ENV:Body>
```

Default Values

Aside from simple data transfer tasks, SOAP can be viewed as an XML-based RPC layer responsible for relaying a given method's call stack from a local system to a remote system (clearly the specification intended this use). As such, SOAP by itself does not specify default values. That is the responsibility of the objects in question. Therefore, the default values associated with a given method invocation are method/object-dependent.

SOAP does provide a mechanism for efficiently *transporting* default values, however. If a given method identifies a default value for a given argument, SOAP relays this information by *omitting* the argument from the SOAP packet.

SOAP makes no assumptions regarding what the default value indicates. Perhaps the omission of a referenced value means a NULL pointer was passed into the method. Or, a Boolean argument's default is serialized (which is to say nothing is emitted to the SOAP packet) that tells the remote object the argument was false. The responsibility for interpreting the default value lies with the objects and methods in question, not with SOAP.

Consider this example:

```
// Month: January is 0, February is 1, and so on
// DayOfMonth: 1-31 inclusive
int GetJulianDate(int iYear, int iMonth = 0, int iDayOfMonth = 1);
```

SOAP and Data: Data Types

CHAPTER 6

163

6

SOAP AND
DATA: DATA
TYPES

```
...
iJulianDate = GetJulianDate(2000,2); // DayOfMonth defaulted
```

The local system's SOAP serialization code will recognize the omission of the `iDayOfMonth` value as the acceptance of the default value, which is the first day of the month. The resulting SOAP packet will look like the information shown in Listing 6.20.

LISTING 6.20   SOAP Default Value Serialization

```
<SOAP-ENV:Body xmlns:m="www.my-url.com">
    <m:GetJulianDate>
        <iYear>2000</iYear>
        <iMonth>2</iMonth>
    </m:GetJulianDate>
</SOAP-ENV:Body>
```

The remote object's serialization code, upon recognizing that the `iDayOfMonth` information was omitted from the SOAP request packet, will re-create the call stack or invoke the method itself with the appropriate default information inserted (the first day of the month, in this case).

Polymorphic Accessors

Some languages and operating systems allow for *polymorphic accessors*. That is, the accessor can be used as if it were one of several data types, depending upon how you accessed or used it. An example of this is the Win32 variant data type used in scripting situations. (Most compiled languages deal exclusively with type *invariant* data types.)

In Win32, the variant is really an example of a discriminated union, in which the union contains a value that declares the data type of the union's content. Consider the following sample discriminated union:

```
enum DataType { Boolean = 0, Integer Float, Double, };
union tag_MyVariant
{
    // Discriminator
    DataType dt;
    // Anonymous union with variant contents:
    union
    {
        boolean bData;
        int iData;
        float fData;
        double dData;
    };
} MyVariant;
```

Because the variant is declared as a union (discriminated or otherwise), you might expect SOAP to encode a reference to the variant as it would for any compound data type (as a multi-reference accessor). In the variant's particular case, where the variant is used as a single-reference, SOAP offers a shorthand notation. For example, imagine this situation:

```
boolean IsHotToday(MyVariant varCurrTemp);
...
MyVariant v;
v.dt = Float;
v.fData = 34.3; // degrees F
bIsHot = IsHotToday(v);
```

SOAP will serialize this using the shorthand notation for variant (polymorphically accessible) data, which is to indicate its instance data type as an attribute to the method's argument element, as shown in Listing 6.21.

LISTING 6.21   *SOAP Polymorphic Accessor Serialization*

```
<SOAP-ENV:Body xmlns:m="www.my-url.com">
    <m:IsHotToday>
        <varCurrTemp xsi:type="SOAP-ENC:float">
            34.3
        </varCurrTemp>
    </m:IsHotToday>
</SOAP-ENV:Body>
```

Note the `xsi:type="SOAP-ENC:float"`, where the data type attribute holds the encoded discriminator (`floating point`), rather than the actual data type, which was of `MyVariant` type.

Summary

This chapter presents the SOAP data types and how SOAP will serialize method argument information given certain conditions. SOAP recognizes two basic data types, simple and compound. The simple data types come directly from the XML specification. Compound data types are groupings of accessors, such as the structure, or an array.

Accessors can be single-reference or multi-reference. Single-reference accessors are literally accessed once within the method call and are (will be) considered constant input values. Multi-reference accessors, on the other hand, can be accessed more than once and are serialized following the method element.

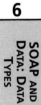

When serializing multi-reference accessors, it is important to keep the argument's identity information. If the multiple references actually refer to the same value, then the information will be serialized once with all `href` links pointing to the single value. This provides the SOAP deserializer with critical information—the data might change, and all references will be accessing the changing data as a single entity.

Chapter 7, "SOAP and Communications: Invoking Remote Methods," uses the information presented here to further explore the SOAP method call, as well as possible response scenarios. There you'll see the remaining pieces of SOAP prior to actually implementing SOAP serialization.

SOAP and Communications: Invoking Remote Methods

IN THIS CHAPTER

Chapter 6, "SOAP and Data: Data Types," put the finishing touches on building valid SOAP payloads. After the SOAP payload has been properly constructed, the next step is to deliver it to the appropriate endpoint. The focus will be on using SOAP as an RPC protocol rather than as a simple messaging protocol.

This chapter brings the conceptual SOAP discussions to a close by examining the needs of an ORPC protocol and how these needs must be met in SOAP implementations. Topics such as wire representation, exception handling, and state management will be discussed. An existing ORPC protocol, specifically DCOM, will be examined and ultimately compared against SOAP. DCOM has been chosen for this discussion because it is a widely adopted ORPC protocol that was derived from DCE RPC. Although DCOM is not an extremely scalable architecture (in Internet terms), it provides a reasonably transparent framework with the necessary security, garbage collection, and object activation features necessary for a robust component architecture.

Finally, the chapter covers the various ways that responses can be formulated and returned to the client, including successful execution and faults.

Remote Procedure Call (RPC)

The concept of a remote procedure call is nearly two decades old, and has carried forward through the years with fairly minor changes. Originally known as the *client/server model*, it was designed as a request/response protocol that mimics procedural programming languages.

To understand how RPC came about, you need to understand the motivation behind distributed systems. Without going into a full dissertation on the history of the Internet, several of the major achievements should be noted.

One major achievement was getting independent computer systems to communicate basic information. Initially, the networks had very limited bandwidth, were error prone, and could not span long distances.

The next goal was to address the deficiencies of networks to improve their overall performance and stability. Protocols such as TCP/IP, IPX, and NetBIOS emerged to gain momentum in mainstream computer networking. Network engineers from research groups and companies such as Cisco improved network reliability and greatly increased the distances that can separate systems.

After faster and more reliable networks were in place, developers began looking for ways to distribute processing loads across multiple systems. Initially, developers found themselves building the networking code directly into their applications. In other words, a program was responsible for opening a connection to another machine, transmitting the appropriate data for processing, and retrieving the results off the wire.

Regardless of how well these systems were built, it quickly became apparent that the networking functionality should not reside within the application itself. Rather, it made sense to layer the application on top of a networking infrastructure that provided transparent interaction with the network, as if the application were simply calling a procedure on the same machine.

A side benefit of this approach was that it simplified the task of building distributed systems. Transparency enabled developers to first build systems that executed locally; when the application appeared to operate as designed, the developers could start distributing functionality across multiple machines with very little coding.

In programming language terms, an RPC maps very well to a C/C++ function call, the idea being that a caller pushes parameters onto the call stack, transfers execution control to the function, and waits for the function to complete its work. In turn, the function pops the parameters off the stack, executes some functionality, pushes the result onto the stack, and returns control to the caller. The caller then retrieves the result and continues with its remaining execution.

Figure 7.1 shows how the logical thread of execution is transferred from machine A to machine B in order to execute the foo() function. First, the foo() call on machine A is serialized and transferred to machine B. Second, the parameters to the foo() method are deserialized and executed on machine B. Finally, the return value is serialized and sent back to machine A for deserialization and the remaining processing.

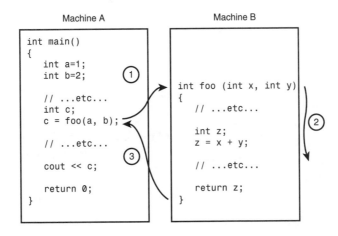

FIGURE 7.1
RPC logical thread of execution.

Once again notice that RPC is based on the request/response model because this is the easiest way to manage concurrency in an application.

This is not to say that RPC is without its complexities. Rather, a new set of problems emerge, such as

- How do you identify a remote endpoint?
- How do you represent data on the wire?
- How do you design interfaces for network bandwidth?
- How do you pass references to data?
- How do you handle exceptions?

With these questions in mind, the following sections will address how to handle these problems.

Remote Endpoints

The first step in engaging another machine in a network conversation is to open a connection to that machine. In the TCP/IP paradigm, this is done through the use of IP addresses and port numbers.

Clients are responsible for determining either the IP address or hostname of the server they want to connect to, as well as the port number associated with the interface they are interested in.

The server, on the other hand, is responsible for ensuring that server applications register with the DCOM *endpoint mapper* so that any incoming requests for a particular interface can be dynamically redirected to the appropriate application interface port. When the server application receives the request, it can then execute the appropriate procedure in the specified interface.

> **NOTE**
>
> The *endpoint mapper* is a DCOM-specific implementation that accomplishes this functionality by simply maintaining a table of interface-to-port pairs.
>
> Other component systems have similar mechanisms such as the Object Request Broker (ORB) in CORBA.

When the client has an open connection with the actual server application, it no longer needs to communicate through the endpoint mapper.

With an open connection established, the client must somehow transmit information so that the server understands the wire representation and can interpret the data content.

Wire Representation of Data

In locally executed programs, data is placed on the stack so that the procedure that has been called can retrieve its parameters. This is a simple process because the caller and the procedure have agreed upon a well-understood ordering of the parameters and have predetermined knowledge of the parameter sizes. This well-understood contract was established at compile time and remains intact for the life of the binary executable.

For remote procedure calls, a contract cannot be enforced so easily. In order to transmit, or *marshal,* parameters across the wire, care must be taken to ensure the data can be properly interpreted at the other end of the wire. To do this, Sun Microsystems introduced eXternal Data Representation (XDR). XDR uses *big endian* order (most significant byte at the lowest memory address) to represent the data on the wire. Because big endian order is the standard for Sun hardware, this guaranteed an optimized wire protocol for Sun platforms. However, both DCOM and DCE RPC use the Network Data Representation (NDR), which enables the marshalling code to write the data in the calling machine's native byte order with some additional information indicating the representation that was actually used. The receiver is responsible for translating this representation into its native byte order before processing the data.

In the DCE RPC (and DCOM) model, the Interface Definition Language (IDL) is used to properly designate how application-specific RPC calls should be represented on the wire. Listing 7.1 shows an example of an RPC interface defined with IDL.

LISTING 7.1   Interface Definition Language

```
[uuid(BCB31762-F16F-11d3-AB76-888888888888)]
interface myinterface {
    void withdraw_money([in]      uuid_t* AccountID,
                        [in, out] long*   Amount,
                        [out]     long*   TransactionNumber);
}
```

In this example, the AccountID and requested Amount are passed to the withdraw_money() procedure. Assuming that the requested Amount was more than the existing account balance, withdraw_money() would return the actual Amount withdrawn as well as the TransactionNumber. In this way, only the [in] and [in, out] parameters are transmitted to the remote procedure. And only the [out] and [in, out] parameters are returned to the caller.

The completed IDL is then compiled into a proxy/stub that is responsible for binding the application code to the networking code.

Whether you are defining remote interfaces in IDL or some other way, you need to be cognizant of your design decisions and the effect they have on the performance of the interface and ultimately your system.

7

SOAP AND
COMMUNICATIONS

Interface Design for Networks

Although transparency is nice for hiding the details of an RPC from the client application, RPC cannot be so transparent to the developer. Any time that a local procedure call must leave its current thread of execution, some delay can be expected because of context switches, memory paging, or other similar reasons. When a call must leave the confines of the client machine to execute code on the server machine, large delays can be expected because of network congestion, system errors, or simply slow transmission rates. Because of this, developers need to be aware of the implications of poorly designed remote system interfaces.

A common example of a poorly designed remote interface is the situation in which a client must iterate through items in a list that is served by a remote machine. Each request for an item involves one or more round-trips to the remote machine, which is very slow and costly. Figure 7.2 illustrates typical round-trips.

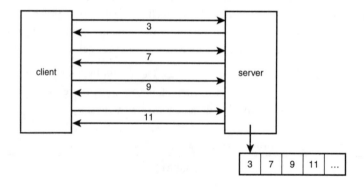

FIGURE 7.2

A remote interface with excessive round-trips.

To avoid such mistakes, it's important to evaluate remote interfaces during the design phase of system development. When building your interfaces, you need to find a balance between round-trips and payload size. One rule of thumb is to optimize the system so that it works best for typical use rather than pathological situations. Figure 7.3 shows the same client/server example, but using a larger payload to communicate the same information.

When properly designed, an interface should be easy to use and should meet the client's needs in an optimal way. One form of optimization used in non-distributed programming is to pass references as procedure parameters.

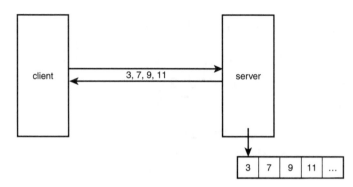

FIGURE 7.3

A remote interface with a larger payload.

Passing References

When a caller decides to execute a procedure, the caller is responsible for pushing the procedure parameters onto the stack just prior to transferring control to the procedure. The caller has two options for passing parameters—the first is to pass parameter values, and the second is to pass references to the parameter values. The difference being that for large quantities of data, it is cheaper to pass the address of a large structure, rather than all the values contained within the structure.

Another reason for parameters to be passed by reference is to enable the procedure to modify the contents of the parameter. This approach is common in various programming languages, even in interpreted languages in which the developer is exempt from handing address pointers.

When running in the same process, any references passed from the caller to the local procedure are considered valid because both the caller and the procedure share the same address space, as shown in Figure 7.4. In this case, `pa` and `pfoo` both reference the exact same address location; any changes that `foo()` makes to the contents of `pfoo` also affect the contents of `pa`.

Now comes the difficult task—passing references across machine boundaries. How should you represent references on the wire? Obviously it makes no sense to marshal an address because the address has no meaning to the other machine. The only reasonable alternative is to follow the reference to its value (also known as *dereferencing* the value) in order to transmit it to the other machine, as shown in Figure 7.5. The receiving machine must reciprocate when altering the parameter value so that the calling machine will see the value change.

As the number of parameters increases on a given interface, it becomes difficult to read and manage the interface. One approach is to encapsulate multiple parameters within a single data structure that can be passed to the procedure.

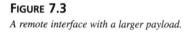

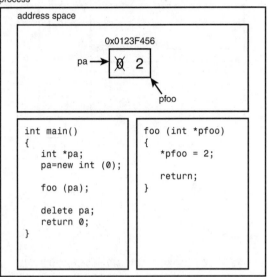

FIGURE 7.4

References in same address space.

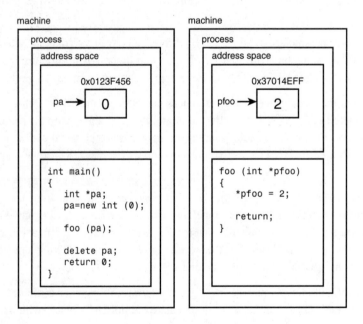

FIGURE 7.5

References across machines.

Passing Data Structures and Graphs

An alternative to passing large numbers of parameters is to wrap the data items into a structure, as shown in Listing 7.2. In this way, the procedure is more readable and can usually be changed with very little effort.

LISTING 7.2 Passing Data Structures

```
MoveImage1(int x, int y, int z);



typedef struct {
    int x;
    int y;
    int z;
} Point3D;

MoveImage2(Point3D p);
```

Another situation that must be dealt with is the passing of multiple items within a structure, as in the case of a graph.

When passing graphs such as trees, linked-lists, and so on, it is important for the remoting architecture to understand how to traverse the graph while marshalling its contents. Consider the following structure and remote procedure call:

```
typedef struct {
    int nValue;
    Node* pNext;
} Node;

foo(Node *p);
```

The question then becomes, should the remoting architecture marshal just the Node that p points to, or should it marshal p and the chain of Nodes that follow?

Unfortunately, there is no programmatic way to determine the correct behavior without some intervention from the developer. Each situation can require different behavior, and the marshalling code has no way to correctly guess what you want. Therefore, DCOM uses IDL to define how pointers (that is, graphs) should be marshalled.

As discussed in Chapter 6, IDL uses the attributes [ptr], [ref], and [unique] to describe how parameters should be treated. Although the specifics of DCOM are not important for this

7

SOAP AND
COMMUNICATIONS

discussion, the marshalling behavior of DCOM using these attributes *is* very important. The following describes IDL's attribute behavior:

- The [ptr] attribute is used to describe a *full pointer*. This pointer can be NULL, and the identity of the data is maintained across the call. This form of marshalling is somewhat slower, because of the extra memory work necessary.

- The [ref] attribute identifies a reference pointer that will always point to the same storage both before and after a procedure call. Therefore, reference pointers can never be NULL, and they do not maintain identity.

- The [unique] attribute specifies a unique pointer that can be NULL, but its identity is not maintained.

The entire purpose of these three attributes is to give the developer complete control over memory behavior during the marshalling process. Although SOAP doesn't have IDL to describe intent, it does require similar constructs to establish predictable behavior.

When dealing with memory pointers or networks, it's common practice to expect errors to occur during processing. These errors are called *exceptions* and require the developer to handle erroneous events that take place in an RPC.

Exception Handling

When making remote procedure calls, there's always the possibility that some error can occur that is outside the realm of the application. This might be a network error, a low resource issue, or some other infrastructure anomaly.

In order to have network transparency, applications don't always provide mechanisms for accepting these errors. Rather, many programming languages enable developers to take advantage of robust exception handling facilities built in to the language.

> **NOTE**
>
> In the case of DCOM development in C++, you are required to build interface methods that return a 32-bit value (called an HRESULT) in order for your application to receive COM runtime or network errors.
>
> When using DCOM interfaces from runtime environments such as Visual Basic, the VB runtime monitors the HRESULT return values and throws VB exceptions when appropriate.

RPC addressed everything that was needed for building robust applications using procedural-based programming syntax. However, as object-oriented development gained acceptance, the need arose for a network layer that could play in the object-oriented sandbox. Fortunately, RPC was fairly extensible and led to the development of Object RPC, or ORPC.

Object Remote Procedure Call (ORPC)

With the advent of object-oriented programming languages, RPC assumed the look and feel of an object-oriented network protocol called ORPC. With this came the notion of object semantics spliced into the existing RPC protocol. The basic ORPC request packet as implemented by DCOM looks something like Figure 7.6.

version
packet type
packet flags
data representation
object identifier (UUID)
interface identifier (UUID)
activity identifier (UUID)
sequence number
operation number
ORPCTHIS
payload…

FIGURE 7.6
ORPC request packet layout.

As you can see from Figure 7.6, the ORPC request packet consists of several fields, most significantly an object identifier, interface identifier, and operation number. These fields represent a particular object, interface, and method on the remote system, respectively.

The ORPCTHIS field, as shown in Figure 7.7, is used to communicate protocol extensions such as the causality identifier, which maintains a logical thread of execution across network calls.

Finally, the payload of the ORPC request packet contains the [in] and [in, out] method parameters required by the remote object.

The ORPC *response* packet is very similar to Figure 7.6, with the exception of the ORPCTHIS field. Instead of an ORPCTHIS field, the response has an ORPCTHAT field. Figure 7.8 shows the ORPCTHAT field, which is also used to communicate protocol extensions.

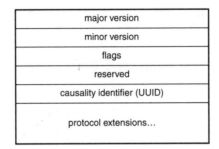

FIGURE 7.7
The contents of the ORPCTHIS *field.*

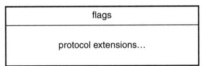

FIGURE 7.8
The ORPCTHAT *field.*

More importantly, the response packet is used to transfer the [out] and [in, out] parameters back to the client within the payload.

A common practice in object-oriented systems is passing object references or interfaces as method parameters. In a distributed environment, this is not such an easy task.

Object References

In the case of DCOM, any server that provides objects for a remote client to use is called an *object exporter*. In order for a client to obtain an interface to a remote object, it must be given the necessary information that describes the remote object.

Figure 7.9 shows the Object Reference used by DCOM to represent a unique object endpoint.

The most interesting fields in the Object Reference are the interface ID, object exporter ID, object ID, interface pointer ID, and host addresses.

Obviously, a host address identifies the actual machine where the remote object resides, and the port number on that machine is represented by the object ID. The interface ID identifies the type of interface to be used by the client, whereas the interface pointer ID denotes the actual interface that will be used on a unique object. The object exporter ID is used to distinguish between different contexts within the system. The context might be a particular thread, transaction, or other component property.

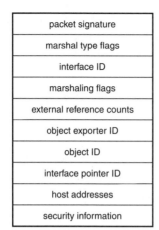

packet signature
marshal type flags
interface ID
marshaling flags
external reference counts
object exporter ID
object ID
interface pointer ID
host addresses
security information

7

SOAP AND COMMUNICATIONS

FIGURE 7.9
DCOM Object Reference.

When clients request a particular object, the server resolves the object reference so that the client can be serviced.

As clients use remote objects, the server is responsible for controlling the lifetime (and thus the object state) of the objects it exports. Managing this state and ensuring that orphaned objects are properly destroyed is a key feature of any rich component system.

State Management and Garbage Collection

Managing state and performing garbage collection go hand in hand when dealing with remote systems. It's fairly obvious why a server needs to maintain state across multiple client requests, but actually implementing such a mechanism can be complex and resource intensive.

Each client requires an open connection with the server in order to retain the state of any object it is using. This requires the two systems to constantly monitor the connection through network *pinging*, which ultimately generates an increasing amount of network traffic for each client that connects.

The server runtime is responsible for acting as a stand-in, thus holding references to objects for the client. COM/DCOM uses a reference counting paradigm for controlling object lifetime. When all clients have decremented the reference count to zero, the server is able to release the object and all associated state.

In some situations, it's possible for clients to terminate without properly adjusting the outstanding reference counts. If this happens, the server is responsible for releasing the orphaned object so system resources can be reclaimed.

By this time, you are probably asking yourself why a book on SOAP has spent so much time covering RPC and ORPC protocols. The fact is, SOAP can be used as another form of ORPC. Many of the mechanisms built in to the existing ORPC systems must also be included in rich SOAP implementations.

The remainder of this chapter will inspect how these mechanisms are discussed in the SOAP specification, and how they might be implemented.

SOAP and ORPC

The basic functions of any remoting architecture are to convert a call stack into a wire representation, to transmit the data across a network connection, and to reconstruct a call stack at the other end before executing the requested method. Figure 7.10 shows an example of a foo() method call with this behavior.

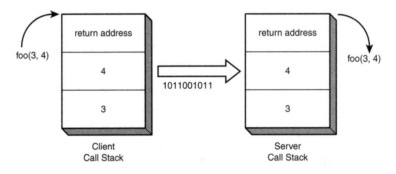

FIGURE 7.10

Remoting method call stacks.

In modern remoting architectures, translating between call stacks and wire representation is the job of the proxy (or an equivalent). The proxy uses type definition information so it can interpret the method parameters and map them to well-understood binary wire representations. Proxies calculate exactly how much space needs to be allocated in the outgoing network payload and place the parameters onto the wire.

> **NOTE**
>
> Although proxies have many uses, one of the most important is to de-couple the client application from the network layer. This enables the client to be unaware of the fact that the method call is being remoted to another thread, process, or machine.

How parameter type information is gathered depends on the component architecture you choose. For instance, contemporary DCOM proxies that are built with the /oicf MIDL compiler option contain format strings that define the parameter types. An interpreter evaluates the interface definition strings as the proxy builds the outgoing payload. This data is then packaged and transmitted to a remote machine where the stub reverses the process before the DCOM runtime makes the method call on behalf of the client.

Implementations built upon SOAP can work in a similar fashion, as can be seen in Figure 7.11.

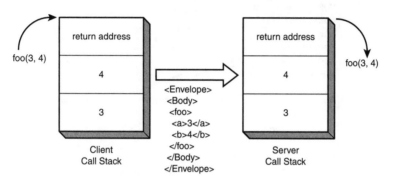

FIGURE 7.11
Remoting SOAP method calls

Instead of building binary network payloads, the Serializer (the SOAP equivalent to a proxy) follows the constructs described in Chapters 5, "SOAP and Data: The XML Payload," and 6, "SOAP and Data: Data Types," to build an XML payload from the method name, parameter types, and parameter values.

Given a well-formed SOAP payload, the next logical step is to transfer it from the client to the server so that a remote method can be executed.

The SOAP Object Reference

The previous section covering ORPC described the basic information needed to reference a particular remote object. SOAP for RPC requires the same types of information but in a slightly different form:

- Transport protocol
- Port number
- IP address
- Object identifier
- Interface and method identifier

Figure 7.12 shows the Object Reference as it exists in a typical SOAP request (namespace information omitted for brevity).

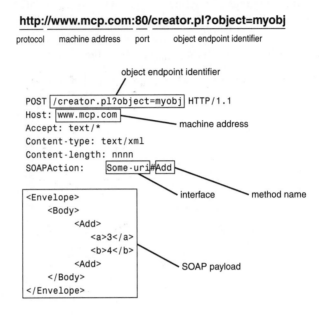

FIGURE 7.12
SOAP Object Reference and Request.

The data found on the URL and within the HTTP header are extremely important for specifying a remote object, as shown in Figure 7.12.

Initially the remoting layer must select the appropriate transport protocol for communication. In order for the connection to work properly, the remote machine must also understand this transport. In the case of SOAP, the transport can be one of many transport protocols, but for sake of this discussion it is HTTP.

Standardized transport protocols have default port numbers assigned to them for ease of use. For instance, HTTP is typically provided on port 80 and serviced by a Web server. Remember that a server exposes a transport protocol by binding an application (that understands the transport) to a socket. The application listens to the socket for incoming connections and responds to service requests as necessary. When specifying a SOAP endpoint for HTTP, you will typically not need to supply a port number because the transport's default port will be exactly what you want.

The next thing you need to know is where the remote machine is located on the network. In the most basic sense, this is determined by an IP address. An IP address has an inherent uniqueness that guarantees only one machine on a given network will respond to this address.

> **NOTE**
>
> Although hostnames can be used to specify a particular machine on a network, host-names are ultimately resolved into IP addresses prior to making a request.

As was previously mentioned, in order to connect to the appropriate endpoint, you need a port number that uniquely identifies the service that will execute the method on behalf of the client. In this case, the default port 80 has been explicitly specified on the URL.

The next pertinent bit of information needed by the server is the object endpoint identifier. This usually comes in the form of a *file path* and *query string* that uniquely identifies the object on that server (that is, `/creator.pl?object=myobj`). This path can be used by a Web server to execute a server-side script that actually creates or obtains the object.

When executing a method on an object in standard object-oriented programming languages, you must reference the method based on a particular interface. The same can be true for SOAP, although the approach is slightly different—the interface and method name are specified in the SOAPAction HTTP header field.

Together, these components make up a SOAP object reference that can be used for client requests, as shown in Listing 7.3. HTTP is one of the existing mechanisms for making such requests with SOAP, which leads into the next topic, wire representation.

LISTING 7.3   A Complete HTTP Request *Packet*

```
POST /creator.pl?object=myobj HTTP/1.1
Host: www.mcp.com
Accept: text/*
Content-type: text/xml
Content-length: nnnn
SOAPAction: Some-uri#Add

<SOAP-ENV:Envelope
        xmlns:SOAP-ENV="http://schemas.xmlsoap.org/soap/envelope/"
        SOAP-ENV:encodingStyle="http://schemas.xmlsoap.org/soap/encoding/">
    <SOAP-ENV:Body>
        <m:Add xmlns:m="Some-uri">
            <a>3</a>
            <b>4</b>
        </m:Add>
    </SOAP-ENV:Body>
</SOAP-ENV:Envelope>
```

Wire Representation

Any ORPC protocol must define the wire representation that will be used for communicating between systems. As you've already seen in Chapter 2, "SOAP and XML: The Foundation of SOAP", and Chapter 4, "SOAP and Data: Protocol Transports", HTTP and XML can provide the protocol transport and payload data representation for SOAP on RPC, respectively.

Building interfaces for SOAP has many parallels to building interfaces for other ORPC protocols, with a few distinct exceptions as described in the following sections.

SOAP Interface Design

Because SOAP on RPC can be built on a stateless request/response protocol, you need to consider how interfaces should be designed. This is not to say that a SOAP runtime could not provide state management, it just means that you, as a SOAP developer, need to design accordingly as will be discussed later in this chapter.

Consider the example of iterating through a list of items contained on a server. Because each client connection is closed after iteration, the server does not know what value any particular client last received, so it can never accurately return the next value in the list. One way to circumvent this problem involves state management, which will be discussed later in this section.

Another difference between SOAP on RPC and existing ORPC protocols is the issue of passing object references or interfaces.

Passing References and Interfaces

Unlike DCOM, there is no easy way for interfaces to be passed at will. Under normal circumstances, clients will have no means for servers to initiate a conversation. Therefore, there is no way that a client-side object can be exported for server-side use. Of course, this would not necessarily be the case if a SOAP implementation were based upon a messaging system.

The other requirement for this to work involves state management. In the stateless request/response model, objects live and die with each request, so there is no concept of holding an interface to an object. For this to be successful, clients require that objects maintain state, which also dictates the need for lifetime management and garbage collection.

State Management and Garbage Collection

Because SOAP can rely heavily on HTTP as a base transport, there are several properties of HTTP that SOAP can utilize, such as redirection services, secure connections, and cookies.

Cookies offer the unique capability of the server to maintain state on the client, without requiring the client to do anything special. Each subsequent call that the client makes provides enough information for the server to reconstitute its last known state. This can be done be storing all the necessary information in the cookie, or by storing an identifier in the cookie that can be linked to a database entry. When done properly, cookies provide a scalable environment that enables any server machine that exports the particular object to behave as if it were the original.

You can also accomplish similar behavior by using the SOAP header, as shown in Listing 7.4.

LISTING 7.4   Request with a SOAP Header

```
<SOAP-ENV:Envelope
      xmlns:SOAP-ENV="http://schemas.xmlsoap.org/soap/envelope/"
      SOAP-ENV:encodingStyle="http://schemas.xmlsoap.org/soap/encoding/">
   <SOAP-ENV:Header>
      <oi:ObjectIdentity xmlns:oi="object-identity-uri"
             SOAP-ENV:mustUnderstand="1">
          591043623
      </oi:ObjectIdentity>
   </SOAP-ENV:Header>
   <SOAP-ENV:Body>
      <m:SomeMethod xmlns:m="Some-uri">
          <Param>1</Param>
      </m:SomeMethod>
   </SOAP-ENV:Body>
</SOAP-ENV:Envelope>
```

In this case, the client SOAP implementation needs to understand the semantics behind the ObjectIdentity element. The server must also understand these semantics, and honor the request using this additional header information.

Assuming that the server stores one or more database entries for each client, how then can the server relinquish this and any other resources that are no longer needed?

The answer to garbage collection of this sort lies in the system requirements. Sometimes state information can be released based on application semantics, such as when a client calls an application-defined method such as Release(). Another way to control the lifetime of state is to implement a timeout period, during which the server guarantees to retain the object's state for a short period of time, but after which the server can delete this state. Let's take a closer look at how state can be managed.

Implementing State Management

Managing state across calls can be accomplished in a couple of different ways. The first option is to use cookies, a well-known tool used in the Web development paradigm. The second option that can be used is the inherent SOAP headers that carry extended information within SOAP calls.

Both mechanisms will get the job done. You are faced with the question of whether it's easier to implement a cookie-based solution from your server environment, or if it's more important for your implementation to support a generic SOAP approach.

Cookies

Cookies provide a means of persisting state on the client machine using standard HTTP mechanisms. One benefit of using cookies is that they are easily persisted across instances of the client application. In other words, you can run the client application, close it, and restart a completely new instance of the application and still maintain state.

The biggest problem with using cookies to persist state is that they are directly tied to HTTP. If you were to use the SOAP protocol with another transport layer, you would probably not find a cookie equivalent in that paradigm.

Rather than use cookies, SOAP headers offer a solution that does require the client-side SOAP plumbing to do a little more work, but provides a mechanism that is portable to any transport layer that might carry SOAP calls.

The SOAP Header

An alternative to using cookies is to store state information in the SOAP headers. To do this, the server sends a response with state information in the SOAP header. The client is responsible for understanding the information and persisting it appropriately, as shown in Listing 7.5.

LISTING 7.5   Placing State in the SOAP Header

```
<SOAP-ENV:Envelope
        xmlns:SOAP-ENV="http://schemas.xmlsoap.org/soap/envelope/"
        SOAP-ENV:encodingStyle="http://schemas.xmlsoap.org/soap/encoding/">
    <SOAP-ENV:Header>
        <st:LongTermState xmlns:st="state-uri"
                SOAP-ENV:mustUnderstand="1">
            1
        </st:LongTermState>
        <st:ShortTermState xmlns:st="state-uri"
                SOAP-ENV:mustUnderstand="1">
            2
        </st:ShortTermState>
    </SOAP-ENV:Header>
    <SOAP-ENV:Body>
        <m:SomeMethod xmlns:m="Some-uri">
            <SomeParam>abcd</SomeParam>
        </m:SomeMethod>
    </SOAP-ENV:Body>
</SOAP-ENV:Envelope>
```

By declaring that the client must understand (that is, `mustUnderstand="1"`) each header element, the server can assume that the client will take the appropriate actions when dealing with these elements. This means that the client application is responsible for ensuring that any work associated with the header elements is performed.

For instance, in Listing 7.5 the server has requested that the value 1 be persisted in a long-term repository such as a database. The client must reciprocate by making the appropriate database calls to store this information. The server has also requested that the value 2 be stored in a short-term repository such as memory. Once again, the client must perform the requested task.

Just as a Web browser is responsible for understanding and properly handling cookies from a server, the client-side SOAP plumbing should be expected to handle mandatory header elements.

Now that you've seen the concept, let's see this approach in action.

An Example of State Management

Earlier in the chapter, some discussion was given concerning interface design issues. Specifically, I said that a remotable interface that forces clients to iterate over elements in a list is not usually an optimal design. However, for the sake of this example, please disregard the original warning.

Listing 7.6 shows some Visual Basic code that is used by a client application to iterate through values supplied by a remote server. The called `GetNextItem()` function is provided by a proxy-like implementation, as shown in Listing 7.7.

LISTING 7.6   `CLIENT.FRM`—Client Application

```
Private Sub GetNext_Click()
On Error GoTo Error_Click

Me.Value = GetNextItem()
Exit Sub

Error_Click:
MsgBox Err.Description

End Sub
```

LISTING 7.7   `PROXY.BAS`—Client Proxy Code

```
Dim ClientState As Long

Function GetNextItem() As Integer
```

continues

LISTING 7.7   Continued

```
Dim reqdom As New msxml.DOMDocument
Dim reqstring As String
Dim inetctl As New XMLHTTPRequest


'Build the request string
reqstring = "<SOAP-ENV:Envelope " + _
    "xmlns:SOAP-ENV='http://schemas.xmlsoap.org/soap/envelope/' " + _
    "SOAP-ENV:encodingStyle='http://schemas.xmlsoap.org/soap/encoding/'>" + _
    "<SOAP-ENV:Header>" + _
    "<myns:CurrIndex xmlns:myns='My-uri' SOAP-ENV:mustUnderstand='1'>" + _
    Str(ClientState) + "</myns:CurrIndex></SOAP-ENV:Header>" + _
    "<SOAP-ENV:Body><m:GetNext xmlns:m='Some-uri' />" + _
    "</SOAP-ENV:Body></SOAP-ENV:Envelope>"

'Load the request string into the DOM
reqdom.loadXML (reqstring)

'Build a temporary file for displaying the request message
'in a browser window
Dim reqfile As String
reqfile = "C:\_Client_req.xml"

'Save the request file
reqdom.save reqfile

'Navigate the first browser window to this file
Form1.WebBrowser1.Navigate2 reqfile

'Wait for the browser to finish navigation
Do While Form1.WebBrowser1.readyState < READYSTATE_COMPLETE
    DoEvents
Loop

'Delete the file (it's been cached in the browser)
Kill reqfile

'Build an HTTP object for making the remote method call
Dim inet As New msxml.XMLHTTPRequest

'Open the POST connection to the URL
Dim post As String
Dim url As String
post = "POST"
url = "http://localhost/iterator.asp"
```

```
inet.open post, url

'Send the request DOM
inet.send reqdom.xml

'Wait for the response string
Do While inet.readyState < READYSTATE_COMPLETE
    DoEvents
Loop

'Load the response into the DOM
Dim respdom As New msxml.DOMDocument
respdom.loadXML inet.responseText

'Save response to a temporary file for displaying the
'response in a browser window
Dim respfile As String
respfile = "C:\_Client_resp.xml"

'Save the response file
respdom.save respfile

'Navigate the second browser window to this file
Form1.WebBrowser2.Navigate2 respfile
Do While Form1.WebBrowser2.readyState < READYSTATE_COMPLETE
    DoEvents
Loop

'Delete the file (it's been cached in the browser)
Kill respfile

'Maintain state for the next call
ClientState = respdom.documentElement. _
        getElementsByTagName("CurrIndex")(0).nodeTypedValue

'Return the next number
GetNextItem = respdom.documentElement. _
        getElementsByTagName("Value")(0).nodeTypedValue

End Function
```

There is nothing special about the way the proxy was implemented, and a large majority of the code exists only to display the outgoing XML request and incoming XML response. More importantly, you should recognize the use of the ClientState variable. This is an in-memory global variable that has been used to persist the client's state across each call.

The client code uses the current state value to build an XML request document that is sent to the server. The XML is also saved to a temporary file, which is used to populate a browser control for visual purposes only. The `inet` object (of type XMLHTTPRequest) is used to POST the request data to the server for processing. The client then waits for the server's response, places the response in a DOM, and also uses a temporary file for displaying the response in another browser window. The state is extracted from the server's response and persisted within the client for the next method call.

Now that you've seen what the client software is required to do, consider the server application. Listing 7.8 shows the server-side ASP code used to simulate a server application, which contains a list of integer values.

LISTING 7.8   `ITERATOR.ASP`—Server Application

```
<%@ LANGUAGE=VBScript %>

<%
Dim r
Dim val
dim xmlDoc

'Create a free threaded request DOM
set xmlDoc = Server.CreateObject("Microsoft.FreeThreadedXMLDOM")
if (xmlDoc is Nothing) then
    'Release the DOM
    set xmlDoc = nothing

    'Return an error
    Response.Write Err.description
End if

'Load the request DOM
xmlDoc.load Request
if (Err.Number <> 0) then
    'Release the DOM
    set xmlDoc = Nothing

    'Return an error
    Response.Write Err.description
End if

'Create a free threaded response DOM
dim xmlResp
set xmlResp = Server.CreateObject("Microsoft.FreeThreadedXMLDOM")
if (Err.Number <> 0) then
```

```
    'Release the DOM
    set xmlResp = Nothing

    'Return an error
    Response.Write Err.description
End if

dim resp
dim docelement
dim currindex
dim retval

'Get the root node (i.e. document element)
set docelement = xmlDoc.documentElement

'Locate the current state information
set elementlist = docelement.getElementsByTagName("myns:CurrIndex")

'Extract the state value
currindex = elementlist(0).nodeTypedValue

'Simulate a list (i.e. array)
if (currindex = 0) then
        retval = 3
        currindex = 1
elseif (currindex = 1) then
        retval = 7
        currindex = 2
elseif (currindex = 2) then
        retval = 9
        currindex = 3
else
        retval = 11
        currindex = 0
end if


if (Err.Number <> 0) then
    'Release the DOM
    set xmlResp = Nothing

    'Return an error
    Response.Write Err.description
End if
```

continues

LISTING 7.8 Continued

```
'Build the response string
resp = "<SOAP-ENV:Envelope " + _
    "xmlns:SOAP-ENV='http://schemas.xmlsoap.org/soap/envelope/' " + _
    "SOAP-ENV:encodingStyle='http://schemas.xmlsoap.org/soap/encoding/'>" + _
    "<SOAP-ENV:Header>" + _
    "<myns:CurrIndex xmlns:myns='My-uri' SOAP-ENV:mustUnderstand='1'>" + _
    cstr(currindex) + "</myns:CurrIndex></SOAP-ENV:Header>" + _
    "<SOAP-ENV:Body><m:GetNextResponse xmlns:m='Some-uri'><Value>" + _
    cstr(retval) + _
    "</Value></m:GetNextResponse></SOAP-ENV:Body></SOAP-ENV:Envelope>"

'Load the response string into the response DOM
xmlResp.loadXML(resp)
if (Err.Number <> 0) then
    'Release the DOM
    set xmlResp = Nothing

    'Return an error
    Response.Write Err.description
End if

'Send the response to the client
Response.write xmlResp.xml

%>
```

The server ASP code is quite simple. It starts by creating a FreeThreadedXMLDOM object, which provides multi-threaded access to DOM data (although this example only uses a single thread). Next, the ASP code extracts the state information from the SOAP header and simulates iteration by using a simple if-then-else condition. Finally, the response is constructed and sent to the client application.

Now let's look at how the client and server interact in a SOAP conversation.

Because the client application is aware of the mandatory CurrIndex header from the start, it initially populates this element with the existing *ClientState* value (0), as follows:

```
<SOAP-ENV:Envelope
        xmlns:SOAP-ENV="http://schemas.xmlsoap.org/soap/envelope/"
        SOAP-ENV:encodingStyle="http://schemas.xmlsoap.org/soap/encoding/">
    <SOAP-ENV:Header>
        <myns:CurrIndex xmlns:myns="My-uri"
            SOAP-ENV:mustUnderstand="1">0</myns:CurrIndex>
    </SOAP-ENV:Header>
    <SOAP-ENV:Body>
```

```
            <m:GetNext xmlns:m="Some-uri" />
        </SOAP-ENV:Body>
</SOAP-ENV:Envelope>
```

First, notice the mustUnderstand="1" attribute used to signify that the server must understand the CurrIndex element. Also notice that the GetNext() method has no parameters, only a return value.

Upon each request, the server searches the request payload header for the CurrIndex element, which it uses to index into the list of integers. When found, the return value is encoded in the appropriate response payload and returned to the client, as follows:

```
<SOAP-ENV:Envelope>
    <SOAP-ENV:Header>
        <myns:CurrIndex xmlns:myns="My-uri"
            SOAP-ENV:mustUnderstand="1">1</myns:CurrIndex>
    </SOAP-ENV:Header>
    <SOAP-ENV:Body>
        <m:GetNextResponse xmlns:m="Some-uri">
            <Value>3</Value>
        </m:GetNextResponse>
    </SOAP-ENV:Body>
</SOAP-ENV:Envelope>
```

When the client receives the server response, it is responsible for persisting the CurrIndex value in the *ClientState* global variable such that the next request contains the updated value (1), as follows:

```
<SOAP-ENV:Envelope
        xmlns:SOAP-ENV="http://schemas.xmlsoap.org/soap/envelope/"
        SOAP-ENV:encodingStyle="http://schemas.xmlsoap.org/soap/encoding/">
    <SOAP-ENV:Header>
        <myns:CurrIndex xmlns:myns="My-uri"
            SOAP-ENV:mustUnderstand="1">1</myns:CurrIndex>
    </SOAP-ENV:Header>
    <SOAP-ENV:Body>
        <m:GetNext xmlns:m="Some-uri" />
    </SOAP-ENV:Body>
</SOAP-ENV:Envelope>
```

This mechanism provides a way to transmit information without the client having explicit knowledge of the payload content.So far you've seen how state can be managed across SOAP calls so that the server can expect the client to do a little bit of work to facilitate the server's state needs.

The final topic that needs to be discussed in order to invoke remote methods is that of object activation.

Understanding Object Activation

There are a variety of ways that you can implement an activation scheme for SOAP. Deciding how to implement such a system depends a lot on the environment in which you develop server components. Fortunately, SOAP for RPC doesn't really care *how* you activate objects. Instead, SOAP's only requirement is that both client and server follow the rules set forth in the SOAP specification. Outside of that, the rest is up to you.

So far, the examples of server implementations in this book have been object specific; in other words, a single object is served by a single Active Server Page (ASP). Another simplification is the integration of the XML parsing within the object doing the actual work. Although this is fine for simple examples and application-specific approaches, it doesn't provide a generic architecture that can be used by any generic object.

One key service that an activation system should have is a way for objects to *register* with the server to be made available to clients. For example, in COM, this might be done through a set of registry settings listing the available classes (that is, CLSIDs) of client-accessible objects.

Regardless of how you choose to activate objects, keep the following in mind—your SOAP implementation will likely be used by client applications that have been developed in different programming languages, various component runtimes, and system platforms. Don't build constructs into your system that preclude a client from working with your implementation.

Summary

Invoking remote methods is the ultimate goal of SOAP for RPC. By looking at existing RPC and ORPC protocols, you can discern a great deal from the historical approaches and begin to understand the work that needs to be done in order to build a robust SOAP infrastructure.

This chapter provided a detailed discussion about RPC and the concepts behind its design. Many of the complex issues that are handled by RPC were introduced, as a way to understand what services a new RPC protocol such as SOAP must perform. Aspects of interface design were discussed as a general rule for any distributed programming that you do.

ORPC protocols were also discussed in order to see how existing systems, such as DCOM, operate. Referencing objects using ORPC mechanisms is a fairly simple process, but when translated to SOAP and HTTP, this is not necessarily an easy task to perform.

State management is a key concept to understand when dealing with the stateless paradigm of HTTP. Both cookies and SOAP headers are viable ways to manage state, each with some pros and cons.

The last topic of discussion, object activation. requires you to inspect the server architecture and environment that you'll be working with, before building the appropriate SOAP plumbing.

The most important idea that you should leave this chapter with is that history repeats itself. At the end of the day, SOAP for RPC is just another ORPC protocol that requires the same tactics for remoting method calls as do DCOM and CORBA.

7

SOAP AND COMMUNICATIONS

SOAP: BizTalk and the SOAP Toolkit

IN THIS CHAPTER

This chapter describes some of the technologies that Microsoft is building, and how they relate to the SOAP protocol. These include

- BizTalk.org—An organization that provides a repository for XML Schemas, which can be shared between common business groups
- BizTalk Server—A Microsoft product aimed at moving XML documents between systems
- BizTalk Framework—A protocol that defines a standard way for information to be easily communicated
- SOAP Toolkit for Visual Studio 6—Initially called Web Services, it is a set of tools that allow you to build Web-enabled systems using SOAP

BizTalk.org

The business world longs for computer systems of all kinds to co-exist and naturally share information through a seamless binding. Unfortunately, nobody can seem to agree on data formats, and even when they do, new and better protocols are developed making older protocols incompatible and eventually obsolete.

Common interfaces are needed for systems to share information in a clear and concise way. However, defining interfaces can be a difficult task because you try to accommodate every possible need you can fathom, so you don't end up changing the interface later. You may find yourself including *reserved* fields to be used by some future data elements that you haven't even thought of yet. Or worse, you abandon the data in one field so you can use that same field for something completely different, thus voiding any documentation that may exist.

Microsoft's goal in building BizTalk is to employ only "best-of-breed" technologies (using Microsoft's terminology). This means that Microsoft will strive to use standardized mechanisms for implementing the BizTalk Framework.

Some obvious "best-of-breed" technologies include XML, XML Namespaces, XML Schemas, and other related topics. These are the foundations for building a system that will integrate well with other platforms. You already understand XML's extensibility, and you also know that any document built with XML can be converted into any other XML or ASCII format necessary using XSL or XSLT. Assuming that everyone can conform to these limits, all that is left to do is define and publish the interfaces being used through schemas or DTDs. BizTalk.org and OASIS have emerged to act as interface repositories for the business community. Both organizations have a common goal—to provide a formal mechanism for exchanging XML interfaces. Both groups aim to provide common vocabularies that can be shared among businesses thus improving the overall compatibility of data. For instance, all Accounting systems understand *debits* and *credits*, all Graphics systems understand *lines* and *circles*, and so on. Allowing these business groups to develop their own interfaces should lead to successful interaction between systems.

Not only does the BizTalk.org Web site (www.biztalk.org) act as a repository for schemas, it is also a source of information concerning XML as it applies to the BizTalk initiative.

Just having a published schema doesn't solve all of your problems. What you need is a mechanism for moving data between systems with minimal congestion and zero data loss. This is where the BizTalk Server comes into play.

The BizTalk Server

Microsoft has an e-commerce product called *BizTalk Server*. Its goal is to use the other BizTalk initiatives to interchange business documents between disparate systems.

BizTalk Server aims at supporting Electronic Data Interchange (EDI) flat files, ADO record-sets, and other data formats. Several of the proposed features of this new product include document routing, delivery, and translation, over the standard Internet transport protocols such as HTTP and SMTP. All of this is done using reliable and secure mechanisms to provide guaranteed and protected delivery.

The BizTalk Server Architecture

As you would expect, Windows 2000 Server is the base operating system for BizTalk Server 2000, and the database facilities are provided by SQL Server.

BizTalk uses the concept of a *server group* to organize servers that have a common *Shared Queue* database, as well as a *Document Tracking and Activity* (DTA) database.

The Shared Queue database is used for providing a scalable and fault-tolerant way (assuming Microsoft's clustering technology is used) to interchange work information, while the DTA database can track the interchange activity.

Another key piece to the BizTalk architecture is that multiple server groups share document specifications and maps through the Web Distributed Authoring and Versioning (WebDAV) service.

Given any XML, text, or EDI document, the document specification describes how the original data format can be converted or transformed into an internal XML format for BizTalk Server processing.

Microsoft is also providing several tools to help build document specifications and maps. The next section briefly discusses these tools.

The BizTalk Server Tools

BizTalk Editor lets you apply the business document structure to document specifications. A typical Windows GUI application, the Editor enables you to create document specifications manually, by using one of the predefined specifications, or by importing DTDs, XDR schemas, or XML document instances.

The BizTalk Mapper lets you define how one format of an inbound document can be mapped to an outbound document format. Recall that these formats are internal representations used by the BizTalk Server, and not necessarily the format of the original data.

Finally, the BizTalk Management Desk is an MMC snap-in (similar to the IIS snap-in), and enables you to administer server groups, message queues, and so on.

The BizTalk Framework

Microsoft's BizTalk Framework is a work in progress that uses XML as an encoding protocol for exchanging data. An approach was taken to define XML elements that would delineate various portions of an XML message.

The goal is to define an acceptable interface that can easily move data between disparate systems using a messaging paradigm. The framework itself does not define the particular manner to which data is moved; it simply defines a way for the data to be packaged for wire representation. This de-coupling of messages allows the application to specify the destination or endpoint, and the transport mechanism to be responsible for moving the data.

Consider how Internet applications work today. An application requests a particular hostname from the DNS server. In turn, DNS resolves the hostname to a unique IP address at runtime, to which the application can connect and carry out its work. De-coupling systems in this way provides great flexibility because applications are not bound to the communications layer.

The BizTalk Framework is described in two parts. The first part specifies a particular XML tagging scheme that differentiates a BizTalk document from any other type of XML document.

The second part of the framework is a design guide for building XML documents and schemas. This part takes a more subjective approach to applying standard methods for the construction of readable and understandable documents.

The BizTalk Framework: XML Tag Specifications

According to the currently proposed BizTalk Framework, the specification calls for all BizTalk documents to conform to XML-Data Reduced (XDR) as proposed by Microsoft. This is necessary until the XML Schemas working draft becomes a formal standard.

The tagging scheme required by the BizTalk Framework is as follows. A mandatory *root tag* called <biztalk_1> is to contain all other elements in the document. Notice in the following example that this element selects a default namespace, which references version 1.0 of the BizTalk specification:

```
<?xml version="1.0" ?>
<biztalk_1 xmlns="urn:biztalk-org:biztalk:biztalk_1">
```

```
    <!-- ...etc... -->
</biztalk_1>
```

This unique identifier communicates to the receiver that this is a true BizTalk document conforming to the 1.0 Framework document.

A mandatory <body> element must appear at the next level of the hierarchy:

```
<?xml version="1.0" ?>
<biztalk_1 xmlns="urn:biztalk-org:biztalk:biztalk_1">
    <body>
        <!-- ...etc... -->
    </body>
</biztalk_1>
```

The specification allows for additional elements to be included at the same level as <body>, as shown in the following:

```
<?xml version="1.0" ?>
<biztalk_1 xmlns="urn:biztalk-org:biztalk:biztalk_1">
    <SomeTag>
        <!-- ...etc... -->
    </SomeTag>
    <body>
        <!-- ...etc... -->
    </body>
    <SomeOtherTag>
        <!-- ...etc... -->
    </SomeOtherTag>
</biztalk_1>
```

Following the <body> element, you specify the *message type* using a descriptive element name. You must only reference a namespace for this element, no other attributes are allowed:

```
<?xml version="1.0" ?>
<biztalk_1 xmlns="urn:biztalk-org:biztalk:biztalk_1">
    <body>
        <PO xmlns="urn:biztalk-org:biztalk:my_po_1">
            <!-- This is my purchase order document -->
        </PO>
    </body>
</biztalk_1>
```

At this point, you have a valid BizTalk document that can be understood by any BizTalk compatible application.

As with SOAP, there are times when you need to attach additional information to the message prior to sending it. The BizTalk Framework also supports the concept of a header as follows:

```
<?xml version="1.0" ?>
<biztalk_1 xmlns="urn:biztalk-org:biztalk:biztalk_1">
    <header>
        <!-- ...etc... -->
    </header>
</biztalk_1>
```

Assuming that you have a predefined means for delivering data to its intended endpoint, nothing further must be done. However it is reasonable that you would like to reference an endpoint and let some service deliver the message for you. To do this, you must provide delivery tags that describe the location, process, and instance of the receiver. You also must include delivery information that can be used to return back to the sender. Delivery information is shown in the following fragment:

```
<header>
    <delivery>
        <message>...</message>
        <to>...</to>
        <from>...</from>
    </delivery>
</header>
```

Although the `<delivery>` element is completely optional, if you choose to use it, you are required to provide all its required child elements as well. These are the `<message>`, `<to>`, and `<from>` elements.

The `<message>` element requires a `<messageID>`, `<sent>`, and an optional `<subject>` element as shown in the following:

```
<message>
    <messageID>3454376364534</messageID>
    <sent>2000-02-21T19:00:01+02:00</sent>
    <subject>This is my message</subject>
</message>
```

The `<messageID>` element is an implementation-specific value that can be used for logging, message tracking, and so on. Its value can be generated from a Globally Unique Identifier (GUID) or possibly a sequential message number.

The `<sent>` element contains the sending time stamp of the message using ISO 8601 format. One should not count on this information being accurate enough to use for anything beyond information purposes.

Finally, the optional `<subject>` element is used for providing a brief description of the message.

Additionally, the `<to>` and `<from>` elements are used to specify address information for proper delivery without regard for the transport being used. The following is a sample `<to>` element, but the `<from>` element has a similar form:

```
<to>
    <address>http://www.mcp.com/bt.asp</address>
    <state>...</state>
</to>
```

The `<address>` element is used for denoting the Uniform Resource Indicator (URI) of the logical address. The `<state>` element contains additional message information for use within a BizTalk Server. These additional elements are shown in the following fragment:

```
<state>
    <referenceID>345</referenceID>
    <handle>4</handle>
    <process>myprocess</process>
</state>
```

Together, these elements refine the state of interchange by identifying a specific business process.

Along with the delivery information, BizTalk also defines optional document manifest information, which also travels in the header:

```
<header>
    <delivery>...</delivery>
    <manifest>
        <document>...</document>
        <attachment>...</attachment>
    </manifest>
</header>
```

The `<manifest>` element contains one or more `<document>` elements, followed by optional `<attachment>` elements.

The `<document>` element contains the document name and description, as follows:

```
<document>
    <name>my_po_1</name>
    <description>A purchase order</description>
</document>
```

The `<attachment>` element contains an index number for ordering the attachments, a filename, a description, and an attachment type, as follows:

```
<attachment>
    <index>1</index>
    <filename>threeiron.bmp</filename>
```

```
    <description>Golf club picture</description>
    <type>bmp</bmp>
</attachment>
<attachment>
    <index>2</index>
    <filename>scorecard.rtf</filename>
    <description>My scorecard</description>
    <type>rtf</bmp>
</attachment>
```

Overall, the BizTalk specification addresses message structure and delivery constructs. The next section provides some guidelines that have been provided at www.biztalk.org.

The BizTalk Framework: Document Design Guide

Microsoft's next step to creating a usable framework is to provide guidelines for developers to follow that suggest ways to properly construct XML documents and schemas. Understand that most of these are only recommendations and do not need to be followed to properly conform to the BizTalk Framework. However, there are three requirements to this framework that must be adhered to:

- Use the BizTalk tagging specifications.
- Schemas must use XML-Data Reduced (XDR) until the XML Schema Definition Language becomes a W3C recommendation.
- Schemas must be documented for automatic cataloging.

Together, these three items will help you ensure that others can understand your documents.

You've already seen how the BizTalk tagging specification works, now consider how XML-Data and schema documentation apply.

Schemas and XML-Data

XML-Data is a schema vocabulary that Microsoft submitted as a note to the W3C. Later, this evolved into the XML Schema working draft that is currently being developed.

> **NOTE**
>
> Since XML-Data resembles XML Schemas, you should refer to Chapter 2, "SOAP and XML: The Foundation of SOAP," for more information about schemas.

XML-Data allows you to declare elements and attributes to be used in your XML documents. XML-Data schemas provide data types that can be used to type-check element and attribute values, and by using the Microsoft XML parser you can validate your XML documents against these schemas.

Schema Documentation

The BizTalk Framework requires that information be provided with a schema so that it can be properly documented and classified. This allows vocabularies in a given business group to be shared and understood by all interested parties.

As schemas are developed, other business groups may find use for particular structures that others have created. If the need arises, this should prove very useful when sharing data between different business groups.

Style

Although not a requirement, BizTalk suggests that authors follow a few simple guidelines when developing schemas and XML tags.

When naming elements and attributes you should try to provide as much information as possible (or is reasonable) to the reader. Object names should follow the convention of *UpperCamelCase* whereas the properties of objects should use *lowerCamelCase* notation.

> **NOTE**
>
> Camel case refers to the uppercase *humps* that you see in a name. UpperCamelCase starts with an uppercase letter, whereas lowerCamelCase starts with a lowercase letter.

Consider the following:

```
<SnowBall>
    <radius>4</radius>
    <packingDensity>917</packingDensity>
    <horizontalVelocity>65</horizontalVelocity>
    <temperature>23</temperature>
</SnowBall>
```

Based on this XML, you cannot be exactly sure how to interpret these values. Instead, a more descriptive approach could be taken:

```
<SnowBall>
    <radiusInches>4</radiusInches>
    <packingDensityKgPerMCubed>917</packingDensityKgPerMCubed>
    <horizontalVelocityMPH>65</horizontalVelocityMPH>
    <temperatureDegF>23</temperatureDegF>
</SnowBall>
```

By naming elements in this way, it is more obvious as to how the snowball has been constructed. A more elaborate way to do this is as follows:

```
<SnowBall>
    <radius>
        <value>4</value>
        <unit>inches</unit>
    </radius>
    <packingDensity>
        <value>917</value>
        <unit>Kg per M Cubed</unit>
    </packingDensity>
    <horizontalVelocity>
        <value>65</value>
        <unit>MPH</unit>
    </horizontalVelocity>
    <temperature>
        <value>23</value>
        <unit>DegF</unit>
    </temperature>
</SnowBall>
```

Ultimately it is a choice that you have to make when designing your XML structure and schemas. An honorable approach is to evaluate other XML documents that are used in your industry or business group for improved conformance and understanding.

Comparing the BizTalk Framework to SOAP

With the release of SOAP v1.1, there is little difference between SOAP and the BizTalk Framework v1.0a specification. Now that SOAP v1.1 enables one-way transmission of SOAP packets, SOAP has become a messaging protocol like the BizTalk Framework. In fact, BizTalk's message structure is essentially a superset of SOAP 1.1.

This basically means that the BizTalk Server will likely use SOAP to encode XML documents that are transferred between systems. Since SOAP can now travel across protocols other than HTTP, this fits into the BizTalk architecture of providing multiple types of connections for BizTalk Servers to communicate.

From the application perspective, XML documents can be generated based on the associated business logic, and using SOAP, transferred to the BizTalk Server for delivery to some other location.

The SOAP Toolkit for Visual Studio 6

During the course of writing this book, we were very fortunate to make contact with the people at Microsoft that were involved with the SOAP Toolkit effort. Microsoft was generous enough to provide portions of their SOAP Toolkit software to us, so that we can evaluate the product and document some of our findings. This proved to be a valuable asset in understanding Microsoft's commitment to this effort. The remainder of this chapter focuses on the more interesting aspects of the SOAP Toolkit, as it existed at the time of our analysis.

> ### CAUTION
>
> The information contained herein is based on a prerelease version of the SOAP Toolkit. Readers are advised that this information is subject to change.

Microsoft's approach to SOAP Toolkit is to build development tools that make it easier to develop SOAP-compatible services on the Web. Microsoft has made several announcements concerning integration of SOAP with their Visual Studio products. The following sections describe Microsoft's latest tool, some of which may be available before the release of Visual Studio 7.0.

Service Description Language (SDL)

Just as Interface Definition Language (IDL) is used to describe COM (and DCE RPC) interfaces, SDL can be used to describe services that are accessible via the Web. SDL solves a practical issue: How can someone use your Web service if they have no knowledge of the properties and methods you support? An interesting side effect is that you can control what gets exposed; hence, a given service may only expose one of several methods.

SDL is little more than an XML Schema that describes a Web service—usually a COM object if it's running on a Microsoft system (however, SDL can describe any type of Web service) and the interfaces that the object exposes. The SOAP Toolkit comes with a wizard that can be used to interrogate any COM object (with a type library) or an existing SDL file, and build an associated SDL file and ASP listener script. The ASP listener script ties your service into the generic SOAP listener and provides you with a starting framework. Listing 8.1 shows the SDL that was generated for a single interface, Microsoft's XML HTTPRequest interface, on the Microsoft XML parser.

LISTING 8.1   XMLHTTPRequest SDL

```xml
<?xml version='1.0' ?>
<serviceDescription name='MSXML'
    xmlns='urn:schemas-xmlsoap-org:servicedesc/2000-1-17'
    xmlns:dt='http://www.w3.org/1999/XMLSchema'
    xmlns:XMLHttpRequest='XMLHttpRequest'>
    <import namespace='XMLHttpRequest' location='#XMLHttpRequest'/>

    <soap xmlns='urn:schemas-xmlsoap-org:soap-sdl-2000-01-25'>
        <interface name='XMLHttpRequest'>
            <requestResponse name='open'>
                <request ref='XMLHttpRequest:open'/>
                <response ref='XMLHttpRequest:openResponse'/>
            </requestResponse>
            <requestResponse name='setRequestHeader'>
                <request ref='XMLHttpRequest:setRequestHeader'/>
                <response
                    ref='XMLHttpRequest:setRequestHeaderResponse'/>
            </requestResponse>
            <requestResponse name='getResponseHeader'>
                <request ref='XMLHttpRequest:getResponseHeader'/>
                <response
                    ref='XMLHttpRequest:getResponseHeaderResponse'/>
            </requestResponse>
            <requestResponse name='getAllResponseHeaders'>
                <request ref='XMLHttpRequest:getAllResponseHeaders'/>
                <response
                    ref='XMLHttpRequest:getAllResponseHeadersResponse'/>
            </requestResponse>
            <requestResponse name='send'>
                <request ref='XMLHttpRequest:send'/>
                <response ref='XMLHttpRequest:sendResponse'/>
            </requestResponse>
            <requestResponse name='abort'>
                <request ref='XMLHttpRequest:abort'/>
                <response ref='XMLHttpRequest:abortResponse'/>
            </requestResponse>
        </interface>
        <service>
            <!-- apply to all interactions -->
            <addresses>
                <location url='http://localhost'/>
            </addresses>
            <implements name='XMLHttpRequest'/>
```

```
            </service>
</soap>


<XMLHttpRequest:schema id='XMLHttpRequest'
                       targetNamespace='XMLHttpRequest'
                       xmlns='http://www.w3.org/1999/XMLSchema'>
    <element name='open'>
        <type>
            <element name='bstrMethod' type='dt:string'/>
            <element name='bstrUrl' type='dt:string'/>
            <element name='varAsync' type='dt:variant'/>
            <element name='bstrUser' type='dt:variant'/>
            <element name='bstrPassword' type='dt:variant'/>
        </type>
    </element>
    <element name='openResponse'>
        <type>
            <element name='varAsync' type='dt:variant'/>
            <element name='bstrUser' type='dt:variant'/>
            <element name='bstrPassword' type='dt:variant'/>
        </type>
    </element>
    <element name='setRequestHeader'>
        <type>
            <element name='bstrHeader' type='dt:string'/>
            <element name='bstrValue' type='dt:string'/>
        </type>
    </element>
    <element name='setRequestHeaderResponse'>
        <type>
        </type>
    </element>
    <element name='getResponseHeader'>
        <type>
            <element name='bstrHeader' type='dt:string'/>
        </type>
    </element>
    <element name='getResponseHeaderResponse'>
        <type>
            <element name='return' type='dt:string'/>
        </type>
    </element>
    <element name='getAllResponseHeaders'>
    </element>
```

8

SOAP: BizTalk
AND THE SOAP
Toolkit

continues

LISTING 8.1 Continued

```
            <element name='getAllResponseHeadersResponse'>
                <type>
                    <element name='return' type='dt:string'/>
                </type>
            </element>
            <element name='send'>
                <type>
                    <element name='varBody' type='dt:variant'/>
                </type>
            </element>
            <element name='sendResponse'>
                <type>
                    <element name='varBody' type='dt:variant'/>
                </type>
            </element>
            <element name='abort'>
            </element>
            <element name='abortResponse'>
                <type>
                </type>
            </element>
        </XMLHttpRequest:schema>


</serviceDescription>
```

LISTING 8.2 Basic Structure of SDL

```
<?xml version='1.0' ?>
<serviceDescription name='type-library-name'
    xmlns='urn:schemas-xmlsoap-org:servicedesc/2000-1-17'
    xmlns:dt='http://www.w3.org/1999/XMLSchema'
    xmlns:interface-name='interface-name'>
    <soap xmlns='urn:schemas-xmlsoap-org:soap-sdl-2000-01-25'>
        <interface name='Interface-Name'>
            <requestResponse name='method'>
                <request ref='interface-name:method'/>
                <response ref='interface-name:methodResponse'/>
            </requestResponse>
        </interface>
        <service>
            <addresses>
                <location url='http://some-url'/>
            </addresses>
            <implements name='interface-name'/>
```

```
        </service>
    </soap>
    <interface-name:schema id='interface-name'
                           targetNamespace='interface-name'
                           xmlns='http://www.w3.org/1999/XMLSchema'>
        <element name='method'>
            <type>
                <element name='param1' type='dt:string'/>
                <element name='param2' type='dt:string'/>
            </type>
        </element>
    </interface-name:schema>
</serviceDescription>
```

Listing 8.2 shows the basic structure of an SDL description. There are several interesting properties that make this XML extremely valuable to both the client and the server. Before we get into the specifics, consider Listing 8.3, which is the SDL for a simple math object that exposes the ICalculate interface. ICalculate has a single Add method that accepts two input values and returns a single output value.

LISTING 8.3   The Math Object SDL

```
<?xml version='1.0' ?>
<serviceDescription name='MATHOBJECTLib'
    xmlns='urn:schemas-xmlsoap-org:servicedesc/2000-1-17'
    xmlns:dt='http://www.w3.org/1999/XMLSchema'
    xmlns:Calculate='Calculate'>
    <import namespace='Calculate' location='#Calculate'/>
    <soap xmlns='urn:schemas-xmlsoap-org:soap-sdl-2000-01-25'>
        <interface name='Calculate'>
            <requestResponse name='Add'>
                <request ref='Calculate:Add'/>
                <response ref='Calculate:AddResponse'/>
            </requestResponse>
        </interface>
        <service>
            <!-- apply to all interactions -->
            <addresses>
                <location url='http://localhost/listener.asp'/>
            </addresses>
            <implements name='Calculate'/>
        </service>
    </soap>
```

continues

LISTING 8.3   Continued

```
    <Calculate:schema id='Calculate' targetNamespace='Calculate'
        xmlns='http://www.w3.org/1999/XMLSchema'>
        <element name='Add'>
            <type>
                <element name='a' type='dt:integer'/>
                <element name='b' type='dt:integer'/>
                <element name='c' type='dt:integer'/>
            </type>
        </element>
        <element name='AddResponse'>
            <type>
                <element name='c' type='dt:integer'/>
            </type>
        </element>
    </Calculate:schema>
</serviceDescription>
```

First, request/response pairs are used to describe interfaces exposed by the object. For example, as you've already seen in many other examples, the client uses the `<Add>` element to request that the `Add` method be called. However, the server must respond with results using the `<AddResponse>` element. There are no rules that state you must use the word *Response* in the response element, this is simply a convention that is very clear.

In order for the client to find the Web service, it uses the `<location>` element to obtain the associated URL.

Given this information, the client can invoke methods as described in the `<Calculate>` element. It must use the parameters as described in the `<element name='Add'>` element. The server, on the other hand, uses the `<element name='AddResponse'>` element to determine what needs to be sent back to the client.

The interface information alone is not very helpful, this is where the Remote Object Proxy Engine comes into play.

Remote Object Proxy Engine (ROPE)

ROPE was built to make life easier for developers who are used to programming in Visual Basic. It abstracts all SOAP's implementation details and allows developers to use the techniques they're comfortable with: instantiating an object, calling a method, and using the results. ROPE is a powerful COM component, which provides several distinct objects that can be used by both the client and server:

- The Proxy object—Provides a client-side proxy that exposes COM interfaces based on SDL input

- The ServiceDescriptors object—A collection of method and endpoint objects

- The SOAPPackager object—Provides a robust interface for building SOAP packets

- The SDMethodInfo object—Contains method information about a SOAP message and is contained within the ServiceDescriptors object

- The SDEndPointInfo object—Describes a SOAP endpoint URI

- The SDParameterInfo object—Describes the parameters for an SDMethodInfo object

- The Wire Transfer object—Provides the capability of performing HTTP GET and POST methods

- The Base64 object—Encodes binary data into an HTTP-compatible form

Together, these objects are used to provide seamless integration between the client application and the Web service.

Proxy

Proxy is designed to expose COM interfaces based on SDL that is either located at a particular URI or passed as a character string:

```
Dim Proxy As New ROPE.Proxy

Retcode = Proxy.LoadServicesDescription 1,
                "http://www.mcp.com/soap/object.xml"
Retcode = Proxy.LoadServicesDescription 2,
                "<?xml version='1.0' ?>..."
```

Once the LoadServicesDescription method is called, the Proxy object can then assume the look and feel of the remote Web Service as described by the SDL. The Proxy object does not maintain state across method calls and subsequent calls to LoadServicesDescription result in the old SDL being purged from the object to make room for the new SDL. If you wish to view the SDL that the Proxy retrieved, you can use the ServicesDescription property as follows:

```
Dim mySDL As String
MySDL = Proxy.ServicesDescription
```

Another nice feature about Proxy is that it allows you to retrieve a copy of the actual SOAP payload (excluding the HTTP headers) by using the DataSent property. This hidden property returns a BSTR containing the SOAP payload XML, which allows you to easily debug your systems.

The Proxy Engine also exposes the DataReceived hidden property, which allows you to see the SOAP response that the server returned.

The ServiceDescriptors, SDMethodInfo, and SDEndPointInfo Objects

The ServiceDescriptors object is a collection of `SDMethodInfo` or SDEndPointInfo objects. Its `CollectionType` property tells you which type of object it contains. As with any automation collection, you can determine the total number of items in the collection, as well as iterate over the collection, using the `Count` and `Item` methods, respectively.

The SDMethodInfo object provides properties such as the method name, its input and output structure, a return type, and so on.

The SDEndPointInfo object has only one property, `URI`, which returns the Uniform Resource Indicator for the given endpoint.

SOAP Packager

The SOAP Packager provides a detailed interface that allows you to work directly with the SOAP payload. You can easily iterate over method parameters, SOAP Header attributes, and SDL methods.

If the LoadServicesDescription call on the Proxy fails (that is, returns `FALSE`), the `GetFaultString`, `GetFaultCode`, `GetFaultActor`, and `GetFaultDetail` methods on the SOAP Packager can be used to obtain SOAP fault information.

The SOAP Packager also maintains both the request and response SOAP packets. Many of the methods require that you specify the *payload type* (0 for request, 1 for response) so the SOAP Packager will operate on the correct SOAP packet.

Given a fully constructed SOAP payload, the next step is to transmit the request to the remote Web service.

SDParameterInfo

This object describes very specific information about a parameter in the SDMethodInfo object. This includes the parameter's name, type, and direction. Here, direction specifies whether the parameter is incoming, outgoing, or both.

Wire Transfer

The Wire Transfer object exposes much of the behavior of Microsoft's XML parser with regard to HTTP requests and responses. It also provides mechanisms for inserting and retrieving header fields in the HTTP packet using `SetHeader` and `GetHeader`, respectively, among other HTTP header-related methods.

Wire Transfer also allows you to insert standard SOAP and SDL header fields into the SOAP payload, and it provides a variety of properties that you can use to debug the HTTP packets.

Finally, and most importantly, Wire Transfer provides the `GetPageByURI` and `PostDataToURI` methods that allow you to retrieve and send XML, respectively, with `PostDataToURI` not only posting data but also retrieving a response.

Base64

The Base64 object provides the simple function of encoding and decoding strings and byte arrays using Base 64. This is very important for sending binary data within your SOAP payloads. Binary data is converted into a textual format that conforms to the XML specification. However, the Base64 version will be much larger than its binary counterpart.

Listeners

As was mentioned earlier, the SDL Wizard also generates an ASP listener for you to include with your SDL file. When it is generated and properly updated with your changes, you can place this file and the generic SOAP listener ASP file in a Web-accessible directory under the IIS Web Server. Your new service is then in place. Listing 8.4 shows the SDL Wizard–generated ASP code for the Math Object.

LISTING 8.4   The Math Object ASP Listener

```
<%@ Language=VBScript %>
<% Option Explicit

Response.Expires = 0

'.....................................
' SOAP ASP Interface file Calculate.asp
' Generated 5/29/00 9:48:27 PM
'.....................................

Const SOAP_SDLURI = "http://localhost/soap/Calculate.xml"
'URI of service description file
%>
<!--#include file="listener.asp"-->

<%

Public Function Add (ByVal a, ByVal b)
        Dim objAdd
        Set objAdd = Server.CreateObject("MATHOBJECTLib.Calculate")

        Add = objAdd.Add(a, b, c)
```

8

SOAP: BizTalk
AND THE SOAP
TOOLKIT

continues

LISTING 8.4   Continued

```
      'Insert additional code here

      Set objAdd = NOTHING

    'Parameter c is output only
End Function


%>
```

Microsoft is also providing an ISAPI Extension listener, which will monitor requests for .SOD files. The .SOD files are nothing more than XML documents, which relate COM ProgIDs to their associated SDL files. Although the ISAPI listener is faster, it does not provide the same level of flexibility as the ASP version.

As you already know, the SOAP Toolkit Wizard allows you to easily generate the necessary code and XML files for your service. However, it also allows you to immediately publish your services to the Web (assuming that you can write to the Web Server's file system).

SOAP Toolkit Benefits and Limitations

One of the benefits (and limitations) of the SOAP Toolkit is that it does not use WinInet. If you are not familiar with WinInet, it is the common component that provides the HTTP, HTTPS, FTP, and Gopher protocols to client applications. Unfortunately, WinInet has some scalability issues with its threading capabilities. Fortunately, because the SOAP Toolkit does not use WinInet, it will not have this problem. However, WinInet did provide secure connections via SSL (that is, HTTPS), which the SOAP Toolkit does not yet provide.

The current implementation of the SOAP Toolkit only supports scalar data types. These are types such as strings, integers, and so on. If you need to pass recordsets, arrays, and other complex data types, your application is responsible for building the XML that represents your data. Then your application must package the XML with CDATA. (ROPE provides a convenient CDATAize method.) The far end must process the CDATA payload.

Summary

The BizTalk effort seems to be one of the ways Microsoft is committing to the XML revolution. As schemas become the interface definition language of the future, it is obvious that a mechanism needs to be in place to easily publish and obtain this information, and Microsoft is clearly trying to fill that void.

As far as SOAP is concerned, it would be unreasonable for Microsoft to advertise two competing efforts at defining a wire protocol that uses XML. Based on Microsoft's involvement in the SOAP movement, it's possible that SOAP may ultimately replace the existing BizTalk Framework tagging scheme.

Microsoft's SOAP Toolkit allows you to generate SDL, which describes interfaces found in COM object type libraries. SDL simply contains interface information with an associated XML Schema. Also included in the toolkit is ROPE, a COM object that provides SOAP services to clients and servers. Most importantly, it provides the binding between the client and the wire representation of the method call, using SDL to construct the SOAP payload.

Microsoft has always been known for their easy-to-use software development tools. Given their efforts with BizTalk and the SOAP Toolkit, developers should find these new products invaluable as the Internet development paradigm evolves.

The Future of SOAP

IN THIS CHAPTER

Make no mistake—the future of SOAP is more in your hands and those of the specification author's than in the hands of the authors of this book. However, there are some areas the SOAP specification does not address, and some technologies clearly await implementation to bring SOAP to the general public.

This chapter brings together a wide range of thoughts concerning the SOAP concepts. Some believe that SOAP has many shortcomings because it explicitly avoids addressing component runtime services. Others believe that overloading the SOAP specification with too many services will complicate the protocol and inhibit developers from building extensions to the SOAP framework. Regardless of which side you choose, these services will no doubt grab the attention of specification developers and product vendors alike. Either way, with luck (and a quick committee consensus), SOAP developers win.

SOAP is, by design, not an object-based transport. Rather, it was originally designed to be purely an RPC protocol, which is to say that you call a remote method and receive a response. If the method is related in any way to some object you've created, that is purely coincidental as far as SOAP is concerned. It wouldn't be a tremendous stretch of the imagination to incorporate object-based services into SOAP, perhaps as a new, higher-level specification that uses SOAP as a foundational technology.

Further, SOAP is a concept that is identified in a specification. It is *not* an implementation of a given technology. Although a specification is nice to have, at some point bits and bytes must find their way from one location to another. This means that underlying plumbing code and tools will be required, many of which will be provided by the operating system vendors (such as Microsoft with their Web Services toolkit). Some other possible tools and technologies are presented here, although this list is by no means complete.

Protocol Acceptance

As with any technology, it is only as good as the acceptance it has gained in the market. Nothing about SOAP should prevent developers from adopting it as a valid and useful protocol, but you should always expect some negative reaction from groups that either don't believe the protocol has merit or think their way is simply better. This is the nature of the business and something that the industry should be accustomed to.

Fortunately SOAP, as its name implies, is simple. And simplicity is the catalyst for acceptance. Most business system developers are not interested in wading through complex architectures that require years to develop. The business world changes too rapidly for this process to be successful. Rather, these developers need tools that facilitate rapid development and ease of use. This is why Visual Basic, Java, and, more importantly, the Web have become so popular—they provide an easy way to develop systems quickly and efficiently.

It's possible that SOAP will need some fine-tuning over the next year or so. However, many of the top distributed object developers have been involved with this effort, and it would be ridiculous to claim that they've totally missed the mark with SOAP. You can see that the SOAP creators have already made great strides towards improvement by simply comparing version 0.9 of the SOAP specification to version 1.0, and by then comparing the 1.0 version to the (current draft) 1.1 specification. Not only did they improve the overall XML structure, but they also avoided creating yet another interface definition language (CDL) and chose to use XML Schemas.

The beauty of SOAP is that its architects have clearly chosen to build the specification for the development community at large, rather than as a Microsoft-centric technology. Of course this doesn't mean that Microsoft won't capitalize on SOAP's capabilities, but it does mean that absolutely any platform, any language, and any developer can leverage SOAP to build success- ful distributed applications on the Internet—with or without the help of Microsoft. This also gives other vendors an opportunity to build applications and tools for SOAP for any language, operating system, or platform.

Regardless of the business motivation, developers should see SOAP as an opportunity to stan- dardize on a protocol that will serve them well. As more developers begin to use SOAP, more and more opportunities will arise to build cohesive systems that can cross platform, vendor, and Internet boundaries.

In order for SOAP to gain a strong acceptance in the developer communities, several important events need to take place. They are as follows:

- Open standardization
- Additional research and development
- Extensions and derivations
- Sufficient development tools and documentation
- Product development

Although this is not an all-inclusive list, when you consider the other Internet technologies that have been adopted in the past, these events always took place.

Take XML for instance—no single vendor owns XML or can control its direction, which guar- antees that the technology benefits the full spectrum of developers. The W3C ensures that XML addresses the most important needs of the development community as a whole, not just some vendor's marketing department.

Research and development of XML is an ongoing effort and has resulted in many new exten- sions to (and derivations of) the language. These include XSL, XML Schemas, and more importantly for this discussion, SOAP.

9

THE FUTURE OF
SOAP

When given a new technology such as XML, developers are tasked with using it to the best of their ability. This requires good documentation and ultimately useful tools, which make it less difficult for developers to incorporate the technology into their current projects. To see this in action, look at the number of XML books, training courses, parser implementations, and so on that are available today.

Finally, when developers can properly apply a given technology, they can begin to incorporate it into the products they build. This is where the "rubber meets the road." If a technology is truly of great value, it will be obvious to developers that this is so when they see how the technology reacts to and interacts with the real world.

Let's now apply these ideas to SOAP to see how it compares to the way XML has been adopted.

Building SOAP's Future Acceptance with an Open Standardization

In some ways it is unfortunate that SOAP is being touted as a new "Microsoft technology." Many developers will simply avoid the protocol just because Microsoft has been involved with its development. However, a closer inspection of the SOAP specification will reveal that nothing in the specification provides any advantage to Microsoft that isn't also provided to the entire development community. This is the whole idea behind the IETF task force projects—to investigate proposed standards that will improve the overall interoperability of Internet-related technologies. It's because of these standards that your system can communicate (via TCP/IP) with other systems on the Internet.

SOAP plays a very vendor-neutral role in today's market. SOAP works between UNIX, Windows 9x/NT, Linux, MacOS, and so on. SOAP is compatible with Intel, Sun, IBM, HP, and every other hardware vendor on the market. It doesn't care if you write C++, Java, Visual Basic, Perl, or even Assembler. Finally, SOAP is unbiased when it comes to component run-times—DCOM, CORBA, and Java, are all equivalent when using SOAP.

Several CORBA vendors are already building SOAP implementations that will allow their products to inter-operate with diverse SOAP systems. Microsoft has also been developing products to facilitate SOAP on the Windows platforms, and most likely will integrate SOAP into their BizTalk Framework very soon. Another company that should be mentioned is DevelopMentor. Not only has DevelopMentor spearheaded the development of SOAP, but they also created the first partial Java and Perl implementations that many new SOAP developers have used to study the SOAP protocol and have used for early-adoption experiments.

Architecting SOAP's Future Through Additional Research and Development

Although the SOAP specification version 1.0 has solidified a great deal as compared to its earlier version, and version 1.1 adds even more capability, there are still those that hope to sway its direction. It takes the blood, sweat, and tears of many talented architects and developers to bring an idea such as SOAP to fruition and meet the needs of the larger populous.

The only way to ensure that SOAP continues down the correct path is for developers from different problem domains to participate and contribute to the specification process. This is a time-consuming effort that usually forces the specification to grow in size and complexity. The purpose should not be to design a utopian protocol that meets everyone's needs, but the goal should be to meet the needs of the majority while providing means to build new, specialized versions of the protocol to meet the needs of the minority.

Extensions and Derivations

As mentioned in previous chapters, SOAP's basic principles can be used to build new protocols for transports other than HTTP. Probably the most interesting transport that has been discussed is SMTP messaging systems, and clearly this was in the minds of the SOAP architects as they crafted the 1.1 version (see especially the SOAP actor concept).

Because HTTP is strictly request/response, it doesn't fit the messaging or queuing paradigm. Many systems operate on messaging architectures and require this type of support from its infrastructure. It is unlikely that the SOAP specification will be modified to account for the SMTP transport in particular (an addendum would make more sense), but it was not surprising to see the new (proposed) version 1.1 of the specification build in the foundational capabilities for messaging protocols in general.

Messaging with SOAP, in particular, has been the topic of many interesting discussions on the SOAP mailing list. Asynchronous communications can solve a variety of problems that the request/response model cannot. Also, the current Internet messaging infrastructure (for example, SMTP servers) already exists as a means for bi-directional communication, so very little work must be done to tap into this resource. Considering SMTP in particular, SOAP could easily tap into this already-proven, feature rich and robust technology, which is also a technology that developers are familiar with (as with HTTP).

Consider Listing 9.1, which shows a SOAP message that deposits money into a bank account.

9

THE FUTURE OF SOAP

LISTING 9.1   Deposit Message with SOAP Encoding

```
To: object@mcp.com
From: client-app@endurasoft.com
Subject: Some-uri#Deposit
Content-Type: text/xml

<SOAP-ENV:Envelope
        xmlns:SOAP-ENV="http://schemas.xmlsoap.org/soap/envelope/"
        SOAP-ENV:encodingStyle="http://schemas.xmlsoap.org/soap/encoding/">
    <SOAP-ENV:Body>
        <m:Deposit xmlns:m="Some-uri">
            <AccountNo>12345</AccountNo>
            <Amount>500.00</Amount>
        </m:Deposit>
    </SOAP-ENV:Body>
</SOAP-ENV:Envelope>
```

Notice that the HTTP form of SOAP maps very well to a messaging format. Every HTTP header field has an associated SMTP field to facilitate the required parameters of an RPC call. The host IP address, port number, object endpoint, and interface-method pair can all be provided in the request.

For example, given the following HTTP URL, `http://www.mcp.com/object.pl`, the URL path `object.pl` represents the object endpoint. When using messaging constructs, the object endpoint `object@mcp.com` can be placed in the `To` field as shown in Listing 9.1.

However, there is an implied behavior given to SMTP that the request/response model does not provide. The client application must provide a return address that uniquely identifies from whom the request originated. Because the sender's address is provided in the `From` field, the recipient has a means for responding directly to the message creator.

Although HTTP allows the server to determine the IP address and client application from the HTTP headers, it has no guaranteed way (especially with proxies in the middle) to resolve a return address that uniquely identifies the client application. Even if the server could uniquely identify the client, there is most likely no way for the server to open a communication link to the client because the client generally will not have an HTTP server available.

With the asynchronous communication model, clients now have a choice between waiting for the server's response and continuing with other work until the server is finished. Clients can also register for notification when certain events take place on the server, and they can operate in a disconnected mode when no communication is available by queuing all request messages.

Yet all these features come with a price of complexity. Recall the example from Listing 9.1 in which a client wants to deposit money into an account. Listing 9.2 shows a similar request for *withdrawing* money from the account. Assume that the account has no initial balance and that the client wants to make both a deposit and a withdrawal. Because a messaging system doesn't guarantee any particular order of delivery, it's possible that the withdrawal might be processed *before* the deposit. If this occurs, the customer will be charged for overdrawing on the account. Although this might be a profitable side effect for the bank owner, it probably is not going to be acceptable to bank customers.

Listing 9.2   Withdrawal Message with SOAP Encoding

```
To: object@mcp.com
From: client-app@endurasoft.com
Subject: Some-uri#Withdraw
Content-Type: text/xml

<SOAP-ENV:Envelope
        xmlns:SOAP="http://schemas.xmlsoap.org/soap/envelope/"
        SOAP-ENV:encodingStyle="http://schemas.xmlsoap.org/soap/encoding/">
    <SOAP-ENV:Body>
        <m:Withdraw xmlns:m="Some-uri">
            <AccountNo>12345</AccountNo>
            <Amount>300.00</Amount>
        </m:Withdraw>
    </SOAP-ENV:Body>
</SOAP-ENV:Envelope>
```

There are basically two ways that this problem can be solved. The first way is to force the client to wait for each financial transaction to be processed. This guarantees that the server will process the requests in the same order the client submitted them (assuming for the moment they are delivered in the correct order). However, this is slow and defeats the purpose of having a messaging system in the first place.

The second way to resolve the problem is to include a transaction ID and sequence number to each request as shown in Listings 9.3 and 9.4.

Listing 9.3   Sequenced Deposit

```
To: object@mcp.com
From: client-app@endurasoft.com
Subject: Some-uri#Deposit
Content-Type: text/xml

<SOAP-ENV:Envelope
        xmlns:SOAP="http://schemas.xmlsoap.org/soap/envelope/"
        SOAP-ENV:encodingStyle="http://schemas.xmlsoap.org/soap/encoding/">
    <SOAP-ENV:Header>
```

continues

9

LISTING 9.3 Continued

```
        <t:Transaction xmlns:t="transaction-uri"
                SOAP-ENV:mustUnderstand="true">
            1
        </t:Transaction>
        <seq:SequenceNumber xmlns:seq="sequence-uri"
                SOAP-ENV:mustUnderstand="true">
            1
        </seq:SequenceNumber>
    </SOAP-ENV:Header>
    <SOAP-ENV:Body>
        <m:Deposit xmlns:m="Some-uri">
            <AccountNo>12345</AccountNo>
            <Amount>500.00</Amount>
        </m:Deposit>
    </SOAP-ENV:Body>
</SOAP-ENV:Envelope>
```

LISTING 9.4 Sequenced Withdrawal

```
To: object@mcp.com
From: client-app@endurasoft.com
Subject: Some-uri#Withdraw
Content-Type: text/xml

<SOAP-ENV:Envelope
        xmlns:SOAP="http://schemas.xmlsoap.org/soap/envelope/"
        SOAP-ENV:encodingStyle="http://schemas.xmlsoap.org/soap/encoding/">
    <SOAP-ENV:Header>
        <t:Transaction xmlns:t="transaction-uri"
                SOAP-ENV:mustUnderstand="true">
            1
        </t:Transaction>
        <seq:Sequence xmlns:seq="sequence-uri"
                SOAP-ENV:mustUnderstand="true">
            2
        </seq:Sequence>
    </SOAP-ENV:Header>
    <SOAP-ENV:Body>
        <m:Withdraw xmlns:m="Some-uri">
            <AccountNo>12345</AccountNo>
            <Amount>300.00</Amount>
        </m:Withdraw>
    </SOAP-ENV:Body>
</SOAP-ENV:Envelope>
```

By using the `Transaction` and `Sequence` fields in the SOAP header, the server is able to reconstruct the true order of the calls regardless of the order that they're received. The onus is now on the server to guarantee correct processing of the requests so that the client application can operate asynchronously.

Sufficient Development Tools and Documentation

Every programming language has its own mechanisms to describe objects and interfaces. An object's interface schema should look the same, or practically so, regardless of the language from which it was generated.

One way to make objects available through SOAP is by somehow translating the object interface definitions into SOAP-compatible XML schemas.

Building XML Schemas from Programming Languages

Listing 9.5 and 9.6 show a C++ abstract base class and a Visual Basic class module, respectively, that defines the `IAnimal` interface. It's important to note that both languages define the interface in a similar manner, but the only way to guarantee compatibility across all languages is to represent the interface in a common language, hence an XML Schema. The associated XML Schema for the `IAnimal` interface is shown in Listing 9.7.

LISTING 9.5 C++ Abstract Base Class

```cpp
class IAnimal
{
public:
    virtual void Eat(void) = 0;
    virtual void Sleep(int nHours) = 0;
    virtual void Talk(std::string strWords) = 0;
};
```

LISTING 9.6 IAnimal.cls—Visual Basic Class Module

```vb
Public Sub Eat()
End Sub

Public Sub Sleep(nHours as Integer)
End Sub

Public Sub Talk(strWords as String)
End Sub
```

LISTING 9.7   IAnimal XML Schema

```
<schema targetNamespace="IAnimal"
        xmlns="http://www.w3.org/1999/XMLSchema">
    <type name="Eat" />
    <type name="Sleep">
        <element name="nHours" type="integer">
    </type>
    <type name="Talk">
        <element name="strWords" type="string">
    </type>

    <element name="Eat" type="Eat" />
    <element name="Sleep" type="Sleep" />
    <element name="Talk" type="Talk" />
</schema>
```

One way to generate the XML Schema is by using a tool that can translate programming language definitions of interfaces into schema representations. This topic is revisited in the upcoming "Automated Schema Generation" section.

In the COM world, this can also be done through the use of type libraries. Type libraries provide the metadata necessary to describe the interface including the method names, arguments, and argument types. In fact, this is the approach taken in the next chapter, "Implementing SOAP: The COM Language Binding," where you see a SOAP implementation that works in conjunction with COM.

Rather than working from the language to build the interface definition, it's more reasonable to build the interface definition first and generate the language-specific constructs from this schema.

Building XML Schemas from Interface Definitions

DCE and COM developers are very familiar with building C/C++ language bindings from IDL. You start by defining the IDL to describe your interfaces and objects; you then execute an IDL compiler to generate the appropriate header files and proxy/stub code that are linked into the application.

A similar tool would be just as useful for generating language bindings from XML Schemas. In this case, developers would start by defining interfaces in a schema, compiling the schema into a language-specific binding, and then linking the binding into their application code. This is the approach taken, at least at this early stage, by Microsoft's Web Services.

Although it's uncertain whether XML Schemas will actually replace IDL, there's a lot of merit to having a generic mechanism for describing distributed objects.

SOAP-Enabled Operating System Services

Operating system vendors could take the ultimate step and incorporate SOAP into their operating system infrastructures. Given Microsoft's enthusiastic support for SOAP, for example, it wouldn't be surprising to find SOAP woven into a Windows operating system object/component in the future that makes your job, that of communicating with SOAP, much easier. You might also note that IBM joined Microsoft in authoring the 1.1 version of the specification, and IBM, too, is enthusiastically supporting SOAP as a technology.

Product Development

A very important step in the lifecycle of any technology is to actually use it in real-life applications. Without this experience, it is very difficult to find the benefits and deficiencies of the technology.

At the time of this writing, the majority of the SOAP specific implementations can be found at the main SOAP specification author's Internet site, `www.develop.com/soap`. There is a plethora of SOAP information available there, to include the SOAP discussion group itself. In addition to SOAP general information, you can access live SOAP objects to test your own implementation(s) and to build your SOAP development experience.

Current Issues SOAP Does Not Address

SOAP has been criticized for not addressing several distributed services that are typically found in robust distributed systems. However, this has never been the goal of SOAP. Rather than seeing the "big bang" theory in action, SOAP's architects took the approach of layering the protocols so that a common infrastructure can be constructed to support new protocols that address more specific needs and requirements.

Security

SOAP does not directly address security; instead it provides mechanisms that can be used to implement various types of security.

Security is a broad topic and can relate to authentication, access control, data encryption, and so on. Each of these requires a different solution but can be incorporated at the same time.

Secure Socket Layer

Because SOAP is based on standard HTTP constructs, it operates just as well over an SSL connection as it does a standard unsecured connection, albeit somewhat more slowly. Assuming that your client interface to HTTP supports SSL, your application gains this functionality for free.

NOTE

Microsoft's *WinInet* library that ships with Internet Explorer allows you to enable SSL connections for your client application. Other libraries, such as *libwww*, can also provide SSL functionality, but care must be taken when using such libraries given the existing U.S. import/export regulations.

SSL ensures that your data cannot be easily viewed as it moves across the wire, but it provides no mechanism to ensure that the user is correctly authenticated.

Authentication

The SOAP header acts as a generic container that can carry application security information and other call-related data with each method call. With regard to authentication, the goal is to ensure that clients are who they say they are.

In the DCOM challenge/response model, the client makes a method call in the form of an RPC request. For the server to authenticate the client, it sends a *WAY request* to the client with a *challenge* message. *WAY*, if you're unfamiliar with the term, stands for "Who are you?" The client must then construct a response code and send the *WAY response* back to the server, hence the name challenge/response. If the server approves of the security response, it can then continue with the client's original request; otherwise, it must fail the method call and return an error.

In SOAP, because the server has no mechanism for calling-back to the client with a WAY request, the challenge/response model as it exists in DCOM will not suffice. Rather, the HTTP model of authentication makes more sense in this case. The client application makes an anonymous request for which the server can fail if it requires authentication information. Upon authentication failure, the client first adds this server to its "requires authentication" cache and resubmits the request with the appropriate security information in the HTTP header.

This type of authentication already exists in current Web infrastructures. Whether inspecting IP addresses, employing cookies, or using other forms of authentication, SOAP can operate equally well on top of these foundations.

If you require application-level security, one solution is to again use the SOAP header. Listing 9.8 shows a client request to log on to the application. Notice that this should be done over an SSL connection so that the password is not transmitted over the wire in clear text. Listing 9.9 shows the server response with an authentication code in the SOAP header. The client can then use the authentication code in subsequent requests with or without the use of SSL, as shown in Listing 9.10. This authentication code could be expired after a period of time, requiring the client to reauthenticate.

LISTING 9.8   Client Logon

```
<SOAP-ENV:Envelope
        xmlns:SOAP="http://schemas.xmlsoap.org/soap/envelope/"
        SOAP-ENV:encodingStyle="http://schemas.xmlsoap.org/soap/encoding/">
    <SOAP-ENV:Body>
        <m:Logon xmlns:m="Some-uri">
            <UserID>joeuser</UserID>
            <Password>somepw</Password>
        </m:Logon>
    </SOAP-ENV:Body>
</SOAP-ENV:Envelope>
```

LISTING 9.9   Server Response

```
<SOAP-ENV:Envelope
        xmlns:SOAP="http://schemas.xmlsoap.org/soap/envelope/"
        SOAP-ENV:encodingStyle="http://schemas.xmlsoap.org/soap/encoding/"
        xmlns:xsi="http://www.w3.org/1999/XMLSchema/instance">
    <SOAP-ENV:Header>
        <a:Authentication xmlns:a="authenticate-uri"
                SOAP-ENV:mustUnderstand="true"
                xsi:type="binary">
            a3ad899ff63f70e
        </a:Authentication>
    </SOAP-ENV:Header>
    <SOAP-ENV:Body>
        <m:LogonResponse xmlns:m="Some-uri">
            <return>1</return>
        </m:LogonResponse>
    </SOAP-ENV:Body>
</SOAP-ENV:Envelope>
```

LISTING 9.10   Subsequent Client Requests

```
<SOAP-ENV:Envelope
        xmlns:SOAP="http://schemas.xmlsoap.org/soap/envelope/"
        SOAP-ENV:encodingStyle="http://schemas.xmlsoap.org/soap/encoding/"
        xmlns:xsi="http://www.w3.org/1999/XMLSchema/instance">
    <SOAP-ENV:Header>
        <a:Authentication xmlns:a="authenticate-uri"
                SOAP-ENV:mustUnderstand="true"
                xsi:type="binary">
```

9

THE FUTURE OF SOAP

continues

LISTING 9.10   Continued

```
                a3ad899ff63f70e
            </a:Authentication>
        </SOAP-ENV:Header>
        <SOAP-ENV:Body>
            <m:DoWork xmlns:m="Some-uri">
                <arg1>30</arg1>
            </m:DoWork>
        </SOAP-ENV:Body>
    </SOAP-ENV:Envelope>
```

Obviously, this is just a simplified example that shows you how the headers can be used to include security information. More elaborate measures could be taken to ensure that the user information is never directly transmitted over the wire.

In this case the client transmits their user identification and password as arguments to a (remote) Logon method (shown prototyped in Visual Basic):

```
Public Function Logon(UserID as String, Password as String) as Boolean
```

The arguments are encoded as you see in Listing 9.8. The server's response includes the return value ('1' in this case, indicating the user was validated), which you see in Listing 9.9. In this case, the server adds an independent SOAP header element `Authentication` that represents a security cookie or authentication key to be used for all subsequent SOAP requests. Not surprisingly, you see the cookie returned to the server in Listing 9.10 using the same SOAP header element.

Access Control

When the server knows *who* is requesting its services, it can then control *how much* access should be granted to the user. Fortunately, this is fairly simple to add to your SOAP implementation. Because the interface and method name are provided in the HTTP header, assuming that the HTTP header also includes authentication information, you can very inexpensively control this access without having to parse the SOAP payload.

Consider the pseudo-code in Listing 9.11 as one way that you could control access to a particular method.

LISTING 9.11   Access Control

```
UserCred = GetUserCredentials(HTTP.cookie)
If AllowedToExecute(UserCred, HTTP.SOAPAction)
    DispatchRequest(HTTP.SOAPAction, HTTP.Body)
Else
    Return(AccessDenied)
```

Overall, security is a difficult issue that will require a great deal of work from vendors who plan to integrate existing security models with SOAP.

Object Activation and Garbage Collection

Object activation is the process of taking an object identifier (and possibly an interface) and creating the requested object for client use. Not only do you need to be concerned with creating the object, but you also need to know when it can be deleted. In the HTTP paradigm, which is the SOAP paradigm most commonly in use today (at least in public forums), the HTTP server performs the activation by loading the requested resource as specified in the URL path. Security measures might come into play, but in the general case, the server simply pulls the resource into memory and sends it to the client. Other than caching the resource for further requests, no state is maintained, and the only garbage collection that must be done is when the resource is purged from the cache to make room for new resources.

In the case of SOAP, this is a perfectly reasonable approach. But then again, SOAP could also support rich object systems that manage object lifetime and maintain state information across multiple method calls. (Of course, this is beyond the scope of the SOAP specification and of this book.)

How you choose to implement your SOAP system is up to you. However, when it comes to system scalability, the more state that you try to maintain, the less scalable your system becomes.

Another design question you should ask yourself is "How do I want objects to be accessible?" One way is to build a generic object activation server that uses an object database to map object identifiers to actual server objects. Consider the following URL:

```
http://www.mcp.com/bin/activate.pl?objectid=calc
```

In this case, the activation script `activate.pl` can use the `objectid` field to perform a database lookup where the script can ultimately load the real object. In the COM world, for example, this could be done using a class ID (CLSID) and the system Registry.

Objects and Object Discovery

Another area that your SOAP implementation will likely need to address is that of discovering remote objects and providing object-based plumbing. CORBA and RMI, to use two contemporary examples, both support dynamic object discovery through various means (they clearly support object-based data transmission). With CORBA, you identify the object of interest and the local ORB locates the server for the remote object. In a similar manner, RMI stores object-server mappings in the RMI Registry.

SOAP is itself an RPC mechanism, at least as originally envisioned, and is therefore (by original design and intent) ignorant of the location of remote servers, and even of the data it is transporting. SOAP is not object-based but is designed to transport data from here to there. How you arrive at *what* data to transport is completely up to you. This supports protocol layering, which is a big part of the overall SOAP design, especially for version 1.1.

Turning SOAP into an object-based transport mechanism doesn't require modifications to the specification. Rather, you add the additional information you require in the SOAP header. Most object-based implementations will need to add an endpoint identifier and some information to identify precisely which client is making the given request. The implementation you will see in Chapter 10 uses a COM CLSID/IID combined with the host's URL as the endpoint information and the client's process/thread identifiers together formed the client ID. (In the strictest sense, SOAP doesn't require this information because it is designed to be a request/response RPC layer, so it is assumed that the client will block while waiting for the server's response packet.) The location of the host was stored in a specialized SOAP database, to be used by the client serialization code when making the SOAP request.

The point is that SOAP by itself is truly an RPC mechanism that neither hinders nor overtly helps you implement object-based data transfer, and the concept of object discovery is completely foreign to the protocol. Any such mechanism you require will need to be provided to you (perhaps by some SOAP vendor), or you will need to code it for yourself.

Direct Interface to SOAP Translation

Although SOAP does not mandate the use of an XML schema, at least as they pertain to the given method, incorporating one into the protocol-processing loop makes sense. Given a schema, certain pieces of the SOAP infrastructure can be forearmed with knowledge regarding the method and request. For example, the server could easily validate the incoming request packet. Or, the method could be somehow pre-processed to create a schema that the client-side serialization code would use to quickly generate the XML packet information. Let's look at two related technologies that one could easily envision.

Automated Schema Generation

There are at least two points in the SOAP data transport process in which it makes sense to inject code to automatically create a schema to describe the method and its parameters. The first point would be when the object itself was created, perhaps when the IDL file was compiled. The second is when the object is used, either on the client or the server end of the process.

Direct IDL to Schema Compilation

At the time you create the IDL file that describes your remote method, you have enough information to create a schema that also describes your method. For example, consider the (COM)
IDL definition you see in Listing 9.12.

LISTING 9.12   Example (COM) IDL Interface and Method Definition

```
typedef struct tag_MyStruct
{
    int i;
    int j;
    int* pk;
} MyStruct;

 [
    object,
    uuid(5948031F-E097-11D3-0000-000000000000),

    helpstring("IAnotherAnimal Interface"),
    pointer_default(unique)
]
interface IAnotherAnimal : IUnknown
{
    [helpstring("method Fight")] HRESULT Fight([in] MyStruct* pStruct,
                                               [out] long lnResult);
    [helpstring("method Flight")] HRESULT Flight([in,out] long* plnShipNum);
};
```

In this case, there are two methods defined, Fight() and Flight(). Listing 9.12 would be compiled to create a schema such as you see in Listing 9.13.

LISTING 9.13   Resulting IDL Interface and Method Schema Definition

```
<?xml version="1.0"?>

<Schema name="IAnotherAnimal"
    xmlns="http://www.w3.org/1999/xmlschema"
    xmlns:xsd="http://www.w3.org/1999/xmlschema"
    xmlns:SOAP-ENV="http://schemas.xmlsoap.org/soap/envelope/"
    targetNamespace="www-myurl-com:ISomeInterface">

<!-- typedef struct tagMyStruct -->
<type name="tagMyStruct">
```

continues

9

THE FUTURE OF
SOAP

LISTING 9.13   Continued

```
    <element name="i" xsd:type="integer"/>
    <element name="j" xsd:type="integer"/>
    <element name="pk" xsd:type="integer"/>
</type>


<!-- Fight([in] MyStruct* pStruct, [in] long lnData) -->
<type name="Fight">
    <element name="pStruct" xsd:type="tagMyStruct"
        ➥hreftype="MyStruct_1"/>
    <element name="lnData" xsd:type="integer"/>
</type>


<!-- Flight([in,out] long* plnShipNum) -->
<type name="lnShipNum" xsd:type="integer"/>
<type name="Flight">
    <element name="plnShipNum" xsd:type="lnShipNum"
        ➥hreftype="lnShipNum_1"/>
</type>

<!-- SOAP Body -->
<type name="SOAP-ENV:Body">
    <element type="Fight" minOccurs="0" maxOccurs="1"/>
    <element ref="MyStruct_1" minOccurs="0" maxOccurs="1"/>
    <element type="Flight" minOccurs="0" maxOccurs="1"/>
    <element ref="lnShipNum_1" minOccurs="0" maxOccurs="1"/>
    <extends type="SOAP-ENV:Body"/>
</type>

</Schema>
```

Of course, this is simply a by-hand translation of the IDL file using the current schema specification. You can expect things to change as the schema specification solidifies and schemas are more widely supported in validating XML processors. In any case, the IDL-to-schema compiler would provide the schema a name, which in this case is the interface name:

```
<Schema name="IAnotherAnimal"
```

It would then add other relevant schemas, to include the schema definition schema and the SOAP schema:

```
xmlns:xsd="http://www.w3.org/1999/xmlschema"
xmlns:SOAP-ENV="http://schemas.xmlsoap.org/soap/envelope/"
```

It would also likely provide a default target namespace:

```
targetNamespace="www-myurl-com:ISomeInterface">
```

Element types would then be identified, and in this case the compiler would encounter the structure definition first. In this case, the compiler might note that the structure is in [in] argument, so the value indicated by the pk structure member could in fact be sent by value instead of by reference (an optimization). The result of this is the value of the integer is transported rather than the pointer reference:

```
<element name="pk" xsd:type="integer"/>
```

After parsing the IDL interface attributes, the compiler would next encounter the methods that compose the interface. Fight()'s first argument is a multi-reference accessor simply because a pointer to a structure is being serialized. So the compiler would emit this element definition:

```
<element name="pStruct" xsd:type="tagMyStruct" hreftype="MyStruct_1"/>
```

Flight() also has a multi-reference accessor as an argument because a pointer to a long value is being serialized. You see the schema representation here:

```
<element name="plnShipNum" xsd:type="lnShipNum" hreftype="lnShipNum_1"/>
```

Of course, with the methods and structures defined, you'll need to subclass the SOAP Body element to incorporate the methods and their arguments:

```
<!-- SOAP Body -->
<type name="SOAP-ENV:Body">
    <element type="Fight" minOccurs="0" maxOccurs="1"/>
    <element ref="MyStruct_1" minOccurs="0" maxOccurs="1"/>
    <element type="Flight" minOccurs="0" maxOccurs="1"/>
    <element ref="lnShipNum_1" minOccurs="0" maxOccurs="1"/>
    <extends type="SOAP-ENV:Body"/>
</type>
```

This allows you to tailor the SOAP body to your particular interface, thus constraining the interpretation of the XML representation of a particular interface's method call.

Language to Schema Interpretation

Another alternative to IDL compilation is to read type information at runtime. Three examples of this include Java's Object.getClass(), C++'s RTTI, and COM's type library (which will be used in the sample SOAP implementation in Chapter 10). The first two require some cooperation from the object itself, but the third, as you'll see in Chapter 10, can be used ubiquitously.

At the time serialization is required, you could overtly pass your object to a SOAP serialization object (instead of transparently as you will in Chapter 10). The DevelopMentor Java SOAP serializer works in this fashion, for example. The serialization object would then request the pertinent type information from your object and create a schema on-the-fly. The schema could then be used for both client and server-side SOAP packet creation and validation. If version information is available, the schema could be cached for later use, thus improving efficiency in subsequent method invocations.

Automated Serializer Generation

Certainly another step to take would be to create the SOAP serializer as the object requires serialization. For example, the method arguments and their types could be queried (using Object.getClass(), RTTI, or type libraries), and a table created so that a generic table-driven serializer could encode and transport the information.

One benefit of this is the serialization information is encoded at runtime rather than when the object is compiled (or interpreted). Not all architectures support blind delegation and will require support from both object and client in this fashion to be moderately coupled rather than tightly coupled.

Summary

Don't let the simplicity of the SOAP specification fool you into believing the protocol is inherently limited or incapable of handling more complex tasks. If you incorporate SOAP as a low-level protocol and layer more complex protocols atop SOAP, such as for object-based method invocation and messaging, SOAP provides the foundation you'll require to efficiently transport your data from location to location.

Also, as SOAP gains popularity, you'll see an explosion of tools and information regarding the protocol itself and innovative ways the protocol can be used. Several major systems vendors are working on SOAP implementations at this time, even though the latest specification submittal hasn't been ratified by the W3C (as of this writing).

SOAP is not a Microsoft technology, so don't let those who claim that it is sway your interest if you don't work in a Microsoft environment. To the contrary, the SOAP specification authors worked hard to be sure that the protocol was fair to all vendors and easily implementable even by casual weekend hobbyists.

And finally, if you like what you see but want to instigate change, join the SOAP discussion group at http://discuss.develop.com and voice your opinion. Suggest innovative change. Review the archives to see if your suggestion wasn't previously voiced and discarded for one reason or another. See if other suggestions that might complement yours aren't already in process. Although you might not be one of the founding SOAP architects, SOAP is *your* protocol.

The final chapter of the book is where you'll see a concrete SOAP implementation, that of applying SOAP to the Component Object Model in Windows. There is much more in that chapter than Windows code, however, so even if you work in UNIX, read on!

Implementing SOAP: The COM Language Binding

IN THIS CHAPTER

It all comes down to this—at some point you need to take the specification and turn it into real code that actually sends data over the wire. There are several approaches you can take when it comes to using SOAP:

- You can simply create the SOAP packets directly from objects you are creating today.
- You can create intermediate objects that accept method parameter data and that submit remote SOAP calls on your behalf.
- You can create a full-fledged language binding.

The implications of each approach are such that the amount of code you must write to support each increases as you progress through the list. However, a tremendous benefit of writing this additional code is that you decouple your workhorse objects from SOAP implementations.

In the first approach, your object has full knowledge of the SOAP information to be transmitted between the client and the server. If the SOAP specification changes, so must *all* your objects. In many situations this is not only unappealing but also is quite impractical.

You could write intermediary SOAP objects that implement a standard interface and enable your primary object to access the remote server method through these middleware objects. Although this does separate your primary object(s) from the SOAP aspects of the invocation, you still must maintain the SOAP-to-object interface and hope that it never requires change. In that case, once again, *all* your objects will likely change to derive any benefit from the use of the newer SOAP interface.

The last approach is by far the most complicated of the three approaches. You ultimately want to fool your primary objects into believing they are executing local methods (versus remote methods) and that their entire life cycle exists within the sphere of their language or default architecture. Put another way, your primary objects never know (or knew) a given method call went off-system, much less that the remote method was invoked using SOAP.

In this chapter you will explore one such language binding, that of the Windows Component Object Model. If you are very interested in SOAP but have little interest in COM, fear not. There is information in this chapter you can use as well as reusable (pure) C++ code you can drop into your own SOAP implementations. Before you look at the implementation contained within this chapter, let's first mention some of the existing SOAP language bindings.

NOTE

In other words, you will see in this chapter *how to completely replace DCOM* on a Windows system in favor of a remote processing architecture that implements SOAP. If you're looking for gnarly, deep, systems-level code, you'll find it in this chapter.

Existing Language Bindings

Several language bindings exist and are readily available for you to use and experiment with. The first two are currently available, whereas the third should be available by the time this book is published. Note that the implementations you see in this section won't be discussed further here because descriptions of their use and architecture are available from various sources, including online at their download site(s).

DevelopMentor's Perl SOAP Language Binding

You can download the UNIX SOAP Perl implementation from DevelopMentor's Web site at `http://soapl.develop.com/SOAP-0.23.tar.gz` or the Windows (32-bit) version from `http://soapl.develop.com/SOAP-0.23.zip`. These URLs are subject to change as version updates to the Perl implementation arrive, so be sure to see `http://www.develop.com/soap` for any late-breaking information.

DevelopMentor's Java SOAP Language Binding

The Java language binding is suitable for either UNIX or 32-bit Windows use and can be found at `http://www.develop.com/soap/soap.jar`.

Microsoft's Visual Basic SOAP Language Binding

Microsoft has entered the SOAP tools market with the introduction of SOAP SDK, which you saw in Chapter 8, "SOAP: BizTalk and the SOAP Toolkit." For more information about SOAP SDK, refer to the Microsoft Web site `http://msdn.microsoft.com`.

The COM Language Binding

The Windows Component Object Model is probably the most successful commercial object technology ever created. Every Windows-based system, starting with Windows 3.1, has at least some support for COM, and nearly everything Microsoft creates relies upon COM for its very existence.

It isn't surprising to find both Microsoft and DevelopMentor are working on their own COM language bindings. In fact, you might have their implementations by the time you read this chapter. In all likelihood, what you won't figure out is the *source code* they used or, more importantly, *how* they made such magic work. The magic behind the scenes is precisely what this chapter is all about.

The overall goal of this implementation of the COM language binding is to shield any given COM object from the knowledge that it is being used remotely or is using remote objects. This is all too often an ideal goal, as practical matters often intercede and cause you to make adjustments or concessions because of the myriad of issues remote methods introduce.

Latency and security are but two issues that often stand in your way. However, it is a good goal to shoot for when designing remote architectures, if for no other reason than to decouple the primary objects from the remoting layers (as mentioned previously).

A secondary goal is to provide a modular approach to serialization, both to provide as much pure C++ code as possible and to allow for future COM innovations that might otherwise not be so easily injected into this architecture. An example of the first case is the C++-based SOAP objects and object model to be discussed in the upcoming "Reusable SOAP C++ Objects" section. An example of the second case is that the type information necessary to interpret the method call stack is encoded in a byte stream that serves as an interface to the serialization state machine. Today, COM uses the type library to store object type information. However, this information could easily come from some other source in the future, such as an XML Schema. Given any such source, all that needs to be done is to create the type byte stream and to feed it to the serialization code. This is almost certainly less efficient from a processing perspective, but the benefits of decoupling components seem to prove that it is ultimately the better design approach.

Let's first examine the COM language binding architecture, and then look at some of the details involved with interception, delegation, and type determination. If the terms are unfamiliar to you, don't worry…they will become clearer shortly.

The COM Language Binding Architecture

If you refer back to Chapter 1, "Essential SOAP: A Comparison of SOAP to Existing Distributed Object Technologies," you'll recall that there is a distributed version of COM in addition to the localized version. The distributed version of COM is quite complicated and, as a result, does not scale well. This (rather severe) limitation is offset by what DCOM does well, which is to maintain object identity, system security, activity causality, and to decouple objects from the remoting plumbing as much as possible.

SOAP, on the other hand, is designed to be inter-operable with *any* other remote system, not just systems using COM or DCOM. SOAP is highly scalable and has no implicit support for system security or object identity, all of which conflict with the primary objectives of DCOM. How is this ultimately reconciled?

The solution to this apparent disparity is to forego the goals of DCOM and use only objects that match the goals of the SOAP architecture. If you look at the other language bindings mentioned earlier, you'll find they also take this approach. The COM language binding described here, creates a connection with the remote computer, executes the remote method, and returns the results to the caller. There is no provision for subsequent calls, such as a transactional cookie or some other similar mechanism. You call the remote computer, ask it to do something for you, and then terminate the connection. (This, by its nature, eliminates causality issues!) This architecture also doesn't provide a full security implementation, although security is nontrivially considered and addressed by the (remote) server.

The essential components of the client-side processing architecture are shown in Figure 10.1. The Application layer is the true object client—the application program or other object invokes the remote object. The Application layer might or might not be aware the object it is using has been accessed remotely, although an interactive application might present the user with a delay as the remote object is accessed.

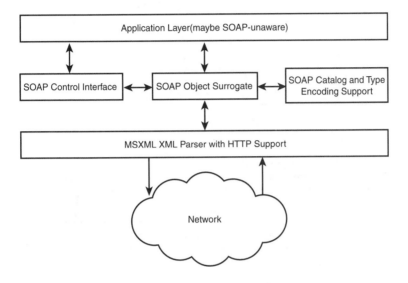

FIGURE 10.1
The COM language binding's client-side architecture.

The processing architecture exposes an interface to interact with the SOAP aspects of the remote method call. Currently the interface provides the namespace and the endpoint URL that are being used, as well as a method to create a new object with SOAP support (delegation). The architecture relies heavily upon the SOAP Catalog and type library encoding objects. The SOAP Catalog is used to record which object/interfaces are to be remoted (as a client or as a server) and to store the germane endpoint URL and namespace associated with the object/interface. Without the associated type information, the SOAP encoding is not possible. This is the role of the type library encoder. Both the SOAP Catalog and type library encoder objects are shared by the client- and server-side architectures.

The serializer object manages the brunt of the SOAP work. The serializer object acts as the state machine for SOAP processing—it encodes the type library, creates the SOAP request packet (filled with data from the method's call stack), ships the packet to the remote server, interprets the method results, and returns those results to the application layer.

The server-side architecture mirrors the client-side architecture in that it has to deserialize the SOAP payload in order to reconstruct the original method call.

10

As you can see in Figure 10.2, an ISAPI extension is used to tie SOAP into the Web server. ISAPI extensions provide a robust environment for integration with the IIS Web server, however, ASP could have also been used in this architecture.

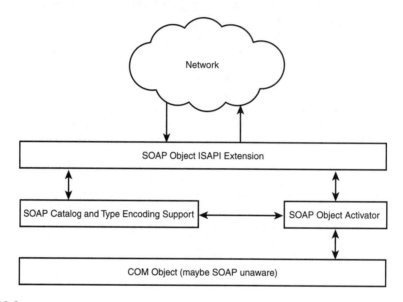

FIGURE 10.2
The COM language binding's server-side architecture.

Upon receiving a SOAP request, the ISAPI extension forwards the call to the activation code for processing. The activation code deserializes the SOAP payload, gathering pertinent method information as needed.

The server architecture, like the client architecture, relies heavily on the SOAP Catalog and type library decoding objects to interpret the incoming request. Assuming the request is destined for a publicly exposed interface, the activation code creates the client-requested object and obtains the appropriate interface.

Given the method signature, the activation code parses the SOAP payload while creating a call stack from the list of method parameters. It then executes the object's method and retrieves the method results from the stack.

At this point, a SOAP response can be constructed, which contains *all* the necessary outgoing method parameters and the return code. This is sent back to the client for final processing.

With a basic understanding of the goals of the architecture—chief among them to be an unobtrusive remoting layer for existing COM objects—it's important to understand how the architecture can be made unobtrusive. That's the topic of the next section.

The Essentials of Interception and Delegation

If you are familiar with the Microsoft Transaction Server (MTS), you are familiar with the concept of *interception*. When building transactional objects, you first create them as you would any other object. However, after they have been created and debugged, you "register" them with MTS. When an object is registered, MTS grabs the object as an instance is being created before that instance is returned to you. MTS *intercepts* the object's creation.

Of course, MTS does this to provide the transactional environment you require. To your object (for the most part), this environment appears to be an integral part of the COM runtime environment. Obvious extensions include the transactional methods you must invoke to commit or abort the transaction and the special marshalling requirement you must meet when passing out object references. Your objects must also be written as stateless because they could be participating in many transactions at any one time.

And what does this have to do with SOAP? Actually, there are two areas in which MTS sets interesting precedences when implementing COM-based interception architectures. First, an object designed for transaction processing is an ideal candidate for SOAP processing. But more importantly, the MTS interception model is ideal for creating instances of remote objects.

> **NOTE**
>
> You could easily argue that intercepting the object as a whole is far less useful than intercepting a given COM interface the object exposes. This is the essential difference between interception (which provides you control of the whole object) and delegation (which provides you the control of a given interface), and both mechanisms are supported with this architecture.

When you register your object with MTS, MTS does several things, two of which are particularly interesting. In order for MTS to create your object, MTS must step between your application and COM. To do this, MTS modifies the Registry for your object. Specifically, the path to your object is removed from the Registry altogether and stored in the MTS Catalog. (MTS still needs to know where your object resides on disk.) When you try to create an instance of your object, COM reads the Registry and instead creates a special MTS object, which in turn creates an instance of your object. MTS has effectively wedged itself between your application and the object you want to use.

When MTS is in place between your application and the object, MTS can control the environment in which the object executes. For example, MTS provides an alternative *context*, which you can access to retrieve the transactional and security aspects of the object's lifetime. MTS also provides other services your object can call upon to help with its transactional processing.

10

IMPLEMENTING
SOAP

As a result of its previous actions, MTS *intercepts* your object and controls the object at a higher level than otherwise possible. Naturally, there is a lot involved with this, and the transactional objects must obey certain rules as well. For example, the object can't simply provide its own interface pointer for other objects to use. Instead, it must rely upon MTS to properly marshal the interface pointer *and* context (a tightly coupled situation). Consequently, interception is rarely a perfect solution, but it has its place.

Delegation, in COM terms, is similar to interception in that third-party code injects itself between the client and the server object. The primary differences are twofold. MTS intercepts the entire object rather than just an interface the object exports. Delegation offers a finer level of control in that you only delegate a single interface and not the entire object. Delegation also is traditionally a cooperative effort. The client code usually invokes a third-party method to create an instance of the delegated object, or it provides an existing interface pointer to the delegator and enables the delegator to deal with the object as required. This means that the client is aware of the delegation, and it can take measures to exploit or ignore the delegation.

You'll revisit both interception and delegation later in the chapter when the COM SOAP processing architecture is introduced, in the "SOAP from the Client—the SOAP Object Surrogate" section. There is another aspect of SOAP encoding that must be addressed first, that is, method argument type determination.

Determining Method Parameter Type

Because SOAP is directed towards remote method invocation, it makes sense that the runtime environment must have access to method argument type information. How SOAP encodes argument relies heavily upon the argument's data type.

The Perl and Java language bindings use their respective languages' built-in type information retrieval methods when they encode the method arguments. This is a good and effective use of the languages.

C++ has a limited capability to determine runtime data type discovery through Run Time Type Information (RTTI). RTTI enables you to use the `typeid(type_id)` operator, which returns an instance of the `type_info` class filled with information regarding the given parameter (*type-id*). Although this is fine for vanilla C++ implementations, COM implementations can take the additional step of using the COM *type library*.

The COM MIDL compiler creates the COM type library when it takes the IDL file that denotes the interfaces the object supports and creates the other files you require when creating C++-based COM objects. Type libraries are optional unless your object supports scripting, for which you must provide a type library. A type library enables the script engine to access the argument type information at runtime. Most developers create type libraries as a matter of course, even if the object isn't destined for scripting. Microsoft recommends you do so. (They actually recommend all objects be script compatible, but that's another argument.)

Type libraries are tokenized type information streams you access using two primary COM interfaces, ITypeInfo and ITypeLib. You'll see how these interfaces are used in gory detail later in the section "Encoding Type Libraries." Given the rich type detail stored within the COM type library, it probably won't be too surprising that COM language bindings make extensive use of the type library data.

Reusable SOAP C++ Objects

Just because this book discusses a COM language binding doesn't mean generic C++ SOAP support couldn't be written to provide some reusable class assistance to other developers not interested in supporting SOAP over COM. When using SOAP on the client, you need some mechanism to create the outgoing XML, ship it, and interpret the results. On the server, you need tools to interpret the incoming SOAP method information, process it, and create the response packet.

It makes sense that the transmission mechanism is platform-dependent. You'll send an HTTP packet one way using Windows and Internet Information Services, whereas Linux and Apache require a different code base. This part of the SOAP language binding is, therefore, not an ideal candidate for generic C++ unless you simply want to lay out the basic object model using virtual base classes.

Furthermore, because there are many quality XML parsers available, it doesn't make sense to reinvent a SOAP-specific XML parser to interpret the response packet. Simply choose your favorite and dive into the response packet yourself. A recommendation is to use the SAX parser and set up an element stack to properly cover namespace scope issues as well as multi-reference accessor relationships.

The part of the overall process for which it does make sense to provide generic C++ support is certainly the creation of the initial SOAP XML encoding. The layout of the SOAP packet makes for an obvious object model—envelope, body, header, and so on. This is precisely what you will find in the SOAPObjectLib project, included with the book's sample code.

> **NOTE**
>
> The SOAPObjectLib project is a Visual C++ project, rather than a generic make project. However, it is a simple matter to take the C++ files from the Visual C++ project and provide your own SOAPObjectLib.make file to compile them into a library of your own, if you don't intend to use Visual C++.

10

IMPLEMENTING
SOAP

The basic SOAP object model is shown in Figure 10.3.

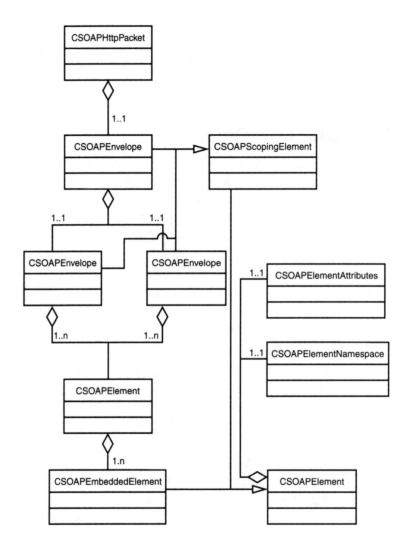

FIGURE 10.3

SOAPObjectLib SOAP object model.

As you can see from Figure 10.3, there are objects for the envelope, the header, and the body. There are also objects for independent and embedded elements, namespaces, attributes, and other support classes to include the main container class, CSOAPHttpPacket. The C++ SOAP object model is restated in Table 10.1.

TABLE 10.1 The C++ SOAP Object Model

Object	Purpose
CSOAPHTTPPacket	Container object for HTTP request and SOAP XML information
CSOAPElement	Base class for all SOAP (XML) elements
CSOAPElementAttributes	Class to manage SOAP (XML) attributes
CSOAPElementNamespace	Class to manage SOAP (XML) namespaces
CSOAPScopingElement	Base class for SOAP envelope, header, and body (drives from CSOAPElement)
CSOAPScopingElement	Base class for SOAP envelope, header, and body (drives from CSOAPElement)
CSOAPEnvelope	Implements SOAP envelope functionality, acts as container for header and body
CSOAPHeader	Implements SOAP header functionality
CSOAPBody	Implements SOAP body functionality
CSOAPIndependentElement	Implements SOAP independent element functionality
CSOAPEmbeddedElement	Implements SOAP embedded element functionality

Let's examine each class in some detail, starting with the base class for all SOAP XML nodes, CSOAPElement.

The SOAP Base Class: CSOAPElement

The layout of the CSOAPElement class is shown in Listing 10.1.

LISTING 10.1 CSOAPElement Definition

```
// SOAPElement.h
//
// Kenn Scribner
// Understanding SOAP, March 2000
//
// Basic SOAP XML element object definition.
// Implements the basic SOAP (XML) node and acts
// as the base class for all derived SOAP elements
// (envelope, header, body, independent, and
// embedded).
//
#if !defined __SOAPELEMENT_H
#define __SOAPELEMENT_H
```

10

IMPLEMENTING
SOAP

continues

LISTING 10.1   Continued

```cpp
#include <string>
#include <iostream>
#include <strstream>
#include "SOAPElementAttributes.h"
#include "SOAPElementNamespace.h"

// SOAP error codes
#define SOAP_S_OK           0x00000000
#define SOAP_S_FALSE        0x00000001
#define SOAP_E_POINTER      0x80004003
#define SOAP_E_OUTOFMEMORY  0x8007000E
#define SOAP_E_INVALIDARG   0x80070057
#define SOAP_E_UNEXPECTED   0x8000ffff


class CSOAPElement
{
public:
    CSOAPElement(CSOAPElement* pParent = NULL);
    virtual ~CSOAPElement();

// Methods
public:
    void SetTagText(const std::string& strTagText);
    void SetTagNamespace(long iNamespaceCookie);
    bool EnableStdAttribute(long iStdAttributeCookie, bool bEnable);
unsigned long InsertAttribute(long iNamespaceCookie,
➥std::string& strAttrName, std::string& strAttrValue);
    void SetElementData(const std::string& strData,
➥bool bIsCDATA = false);
    bool EnableStdNamespace (long iStdNamespaceCookie, bool bEnable);
unsigned long InsertNamespace(const std::string& strLongName,
➥const std::string& strShortName, long* piNamespaceCookie);
    unsigned long GetNamespace(long iNamespaceCookie,
➥std::string& strNamespace);
    virtual unsigned long WriteToStream(std::ostrstream& ostr);
    virtual unsigned long StreamContents(std::ostrstream& ostr);
    virtual unsigned long StreamOpenTag(std::ostrstream& ostr,
➥bool bWriteStdNS = false);
    virtual unsigned long StreamCloseTag(std::ostrstream& ostr);

    CSOAPElement* GetParent() { return m_pParent; }

// Attributes
protected:
    CSOAPElement* m_pParent;
```

```
    CSOAPElementAttributes m_CAttributes;
    CSOAPElementNamespace m_CNamespaces;

    long m_iTagNamespaceCookie;

    std::string m_strTagText;
    std::string m_strData;

};


#endif // __SOAPELEMENT_H
```

The functionality you see in CSOAPElement will find its way to *all* the other SOAP element types. It makes sense that you can do such things as set the SOAP tag name and namespace, add (scoped) namespaces (as attributes) to the element, and be provided some mechanism for retrieving the SOAP packet information. In this case, the Standard Template Library (STL) and the modern C++ ostrstream stream class are used in lieu of some other COM-based interfaces that provide similar functionality.

The output methods (WriteToStream() and so on) are virtual, which enables you to tailor derived implementations. The SOAP envelope has very different streaming requirements than an embedded element does, for example. This design detail enables the majority of SOAP objects to simply stream their contents while providing a way for more intricate objects to adjust how their content is streamed.

CSOAPElement aggregates two supporting classes, CSOAPElementNamespace and CSOAPElementAttributes. Namespaces are also related to the CSOAPElement::m_iTagNamespaceCookie class attribute.

The Mechanics of CSOAPElementNamespace

Cookies represent Namespaces in this SOAP object model implementation. The term *cookie* here is used in the same spirit as the Win32 API rather than as the term is associated with Internet programming. A cookie in Win32 terms is simply a 32-bit value of some significance. The use of a cookie here precludes you from having to carry strings around in your code to be inserted into tags and attributes. You simply tell a given SOAP element to insert a namespace, and, from then on, you use the cookie it passes back to identify the particular namespace. Each element also has a namespace it will associate with its tag, which is the purpose of CSOAPElement::m_iTagNamespaceCookie.

You can insert as many namespaces as you like, although the binding implementation you'll see shortly in "SOAP from the Server—The Object Activator" only uses the namespace associated with the method. The MSXML parser does not support namespace parsing, so other namespaces are ignored.

10

You can see the basic functions CSOAPElementNamespace provides by examining Listing 10.2.

LISTING 10.2 CSOAPElementNamespace Definition

```cpp
// SOAPElementNamespace.h
//
// Kenn Scribner
// Understanding SOAP, March 2000
//
// SOAP XML element namespace object definition.
//
#if !defined __SOAPELEMENTNAMESPACE_H
#define __SOAPELEMENTNAMESPACE_H

#include <vector>
#include <string>
#include <map>
#include <iostream>
#include <strstream>

// Standard namespace cookies
#define NULLNSCOOKIE   -1
#define ENVNSCOOKIE     0
#define ENCNSCOOKIE     1
#define XSINSCOOKIE     2
#define COMNSCOOKIE     3

// Fwd declaration
class CSOAPElement;

class CSOAPElementNamespace
{
public:
    CSOAPElementNamespace(CSOAPElement* pParent = NULL,
➥long iBaseNSCookie = NULLNSCOOKIE);
    virtual ~CSOAPElementNamespace();

// Methods
public:
    bool EnableStdNamespace(long iNamespaceCookie, bool bEnable);
unsigned long InsertNamespace(const std::string& strLongName,
➥const std::string& strShortName, long* piNamespaceCookie);
    unsigned long GetNamespace(long iNamespaceCookie,
➥std::string& strNamespace);
    unsigned long WriteToStream(std::ostrstream& ostr,
➥bool bWriteStdNS = false);
```

```
    void SetBaseNSCookie(long iNamespaceCookie = NULLNSCOOKIE)
    {
        m_iBaseNSCookie = iNamespaceCookie;
    }
    void SetParent(CSOAPElement* pNewParent) { m_pParent =
                                        ↪pNewParent; }
    CSOAPElement* GetParent() { return m_pParent; }

// Attributes
protected:
    CSOAPElement* m_pParent;

    std::vector<std::string> m_vecNamespaces;

    long m_iBaseNSCookie;
    long m_iNextCookie;

    bool m_bStdNamespaces[4];
    std::map<long,std::string> m_mapNSFull;
    std::map<long,std::string> m_mapNSShort;

};

#endif // __SOAPELEMENTNAMESPACE_H
```

The format of the XML namespace follows this pattern:

```
xmlns:short_namespace="full_namespace"
```

The *short_namespace* is commonly used throughout the XML document, but it is really a placeholder for the `full_namespace` and is interpreted as such when parsed. CSOAPElementNamespace stores both namespace formats in STL maps, hence the use of the cookie. The cookie actually represents the map hash key the object will use to extract the associated namespace string.

CSOAPElementNamespace::m_vecNamespaces is an STL vector that contains the full XML namespace definition(s) for this element, if any. The vector's (preformatted) contents are streamed to the HTTP packet when the element is streamed.

With the exception of the standard cookies, CSOAPElementNamespace maintains a counter it uses to create new cookies, starting with CSOAPElementNamespace:: m_iBaseNSCookie. Different elements are assigned differing base cookies to enable namespace scope resolution. This arrangement enables you to easily insert namespace delineated items in subordinate elements and have the SOAP object model resolve (and correctly expand) the namespaces for you.

10

IMPLEMENTING
SOAP

Listing 10.3 shows you the namespace object constructor and how it inserts the default SOAP namespace cookies.

LISTING 10.3   CSOAPElementNamespace Class Constructor

```
CSOAPElementNamespace::CSOAPElementNamespace(CSOAPElement* pParent
➥/*=NULL*/, long iBaseNSCookie /*=NULLNSCOOKIE*/) :
  m_pParent(pParent),
  m_iBaseNSCookie(iBaseNSCookie),
  m_iNextCookie(0)
{
    // Insert the standard namespaces into the maps
    m_mapNSFull[ENVNSCOOKIE] =
      "http://schemas.xmlsoap.org/soap/envelope/";
    m_mapNSShort[ENVNSCOOKIE] = "SOAP-ENV";
    m_bStdNamespaces[ENVNSCOOKIE] = false;
    ++m_iNextCookie;
    m_mapNSFull[ENCNSCOOKIE] =
      "http://schemas.xmlsoap.org/soap/encoding/";
    m_mapNSShort[ENCNSCOOKIE] = "SOAP-ENC";
    m_bStdNamespaces[ENCNSCOOKIE] = false;
    ++m_iNextCookie;
    m_mapNSFull[XSINSCOOKIE] =
      "http://www.w3.org/1999/XMLSchema/instance";
    m_mapNSShort[XSINSCOOKIE] = "xsi";
    m_bStdNamespaces[XSINSCOOKIE] = false;
    ++m_iNextCookie;
    m_mapNSFull[COMNSCOOKIE] =
      "urn:www-microsoft-com:com";
    m_mapNSShort[COMNSCOOKIE] = "COM";
    m_bStdNamespaces[COMNSCOOKIE] = false;
    ++m_iNextCookie;
}
```

As you can see, inserting new namespaces is a simple matter of inserting the namespace strings into STL maps using the cookie as the key:

```
m_mapNSShort[ENVNSCOOKIE] = "SOAP-ENV";
```

When the default SOAP namespaces are inserted, they are marked as unused by the current SOAP element. (The corresponding m_bStdNamespaces array element is set to false.) You can enable or disable the default SOAP namespaces by using the CSOAPElementNamespace::EnableStdNamespace() method, which simply toggles the respective default namespace array element (true or false). This encapsulates the SOAP default namespaces and relieves you from the burden of properly encoding them when you create your SOAP packets—let the namespace object do that for you.

Arbitrary namespaces are a bit more complicated, as you can see from Listing 10.4.

LISTING 10.4   CSOAPElementNamespace Arbitrary Namespace Insertion

```
unsigned long CSOAPElementNamespace::InsertNamespace(const
➥std::string& strLongName, const std::string& strShortName,
➥long* piNamespaceCookie)
{
    // A quick check
    if ( piNamespaceCookie == NULL ) return SOAP_E_POINTER;

    // Insert the namespace
    m_mapNSFull[m_iNextCookie] = strLongName;
    m_mapNSShort[m_iNextCookie] = strShortName;

    // Assign the cookie
    *piNamespaceCookie = (m_iNextCookie | m_iBaseNSCookie);
    ++m_iNextCookie;

    return SOAP_S_OK;
}
```

In InsertNamespace(), the strings are inserted into the map using incremental cookie values. However, the value passed to the consumer is logically OR'ed with the base cookie to produce a unique cookie value (assuming you assign unique base cookie values when you instantiate the object model):

```
*piNamespaceCookie = (m_iNextCookie | m_iBaseNSCookie);
```

Retrieving the requested namespace involves a similar, though reverse, process. Things do get a bit more complicated because of namespace scope resolution, as you can discern from Listing 10.5.

LISTING 10.5   CSOAPElementNamespace Namespace Retrieval

```
unsigned long CSOAPElementNamespace::GetNamespace(long
➥iNamespaceCookie, std::string& strNamespace)
{
    // Look up namespace given the cookie
    unsigned long res = SOAP_S_OK;

    if ( iNamespaceCookie != NULLNSCOOKIE ) {
        // The cookie isn't asking for a null namespace, so
        // now check for the default SOAP namespace case
```

continues

10

IMPLEMENTING SOAP

LISTING 10.5 Continued

```
            if ((iNamespaceCookie >= ENVNSCOOKIE) && (iNamespaceCookie <=
➥COMNSCOOKIE)) {
                // SOAP-ENV, SOAP-ENC, XSI, or COM
                strNamespace = m_mapNSShort[iNamespaceCookie];
            } // if
            else if (((unsigned long)iNamespaceCookie &
                    (unsigned long)m_iBaseNSCookie) == m_iBaseNSCookie) {
                // The cookie wasn't a standard namespace, so see if it
                // lies within the scope of this object. If the test above
                // passed, it does, so mask the scoping value and look
                // up the namespace.
                iNamespaceCookie &= 0x0000FFFF; // strip off scoping value
                strNamespace = m_mapNSShort[iNamespaceCookie];
            } // else if
            else {
                // The cookie wasn't a standard cookie, nor was it in
                // the scope of this element, so check to see if it
                // is registered with the parent node.
                if ( m_pParent != NULL ) {
                    CSOAPElement* pNextParent = m_pParent->GetParent();
                    if ( pNextParent != NULL ) {
                        res = pNextParent->GetNamespace(iNamespaceCookie,
                                                        strNamespace);
                    } // if
                    else {
                        // The cookie must be invalid!
                        res = SOAP_E_INVALIDARG; // invalid argument
                    } // else
                } // if
                else {
                    // The cookie must be invalid!
                    res = SOAP_E_INVALIDARG; // invalid argument
                } // else
            } // else
        } // if

    return res;
}
```

To resolve a namespace, the first thing done is to see if the cookie represents one of the intrinsic namespaces, SOAP-ENV, SOAP-ENC, xsi, or COM. If so, the corresponding cookie is returned. If not, the cookie is scoped by logically AND'ing the base cookie with the given cookie value. If the result is not zero, the given cookie represents namespace strings residing in this element's namespace container. If this fails, the next parent element is checked. Checks bubble up from the most subordinate element to the document element (the SOAP envelope). If ultimately the cookie can't be resolved, GetNamespace() returns an invalid argument error.

As mentioned, the namespaces are streamed into the HTTP packet. Their external representations are stored as STL strings in an STL vector. This code actually spits them into the (provided) output stream:

```
std::string strNamespace;
if ( m_bStdNamespaces[ENVNSCOOKIE] ) {
    // Stream the SOAP-ENV namespace
    strNamespace = " xmlns:";
    strNamespace += m_mapNSShort[ENVNSCOOKIE];
    strNamespace += "=\"";
    strNamespace += m_mapNSFull[ENVNSCOOKIE];
    strNamespace += "\"";
    ostr << strNamespace.c_str();
} // if

if ( m_bStdNamespaces[ENCNSCOOKIE] ) {
    (Code similar to ENVNSCOOKIE)
} // if

if ( m_bStdNamespaces[XSINSCOOKIE] ) {
    (Code similar to ENVNSCOOKIE)
} // if

if ( m_bStdNamespaces[COMNSCOOKIE] ) {
    (Code similar to ENVNSCOOKIE)
} // if

// Stream any other namespaces
for ( long i = COMNSCOOKIE+1; i < m_mapNSShort.size() ; i++ ) {
    strNamespace = " xmlns:";
    strNamespace += m_mapNSShort[i];
    strNamespace += "=\"";
    strNamespace += m_mapNSFull[i];
    strNamespace += "\"";

    // Write the namespace
    ostr << strNamespace.c_str();
} // for
```

The stream is filled with namespace strings from the STL maps, with the appropriate attribute formatting applied.

The next functional aspect of a SOAP element is that it can contain attributes, which themselves can be scoped by a namespace. Let's examine attributes now.

10

IMPLEMENTING
SOAP

The Mechanics of `CSOAPElementAttributes`

Any XML node can contain attributes, which are in the form:

```
namespace:attribute_name="attribute_value"
```

The `CSOAPElementAttributes` object maintains a collection of element attributes, each with associated namespaces, names, and values. The class definition is shown in Listing 10.6.

LISTING 10.6   `CSOAPElementAttributes` Definition

```cpp
// SOAPElementAttributes.h
//
// Kenn Scribner
// Understanding SOAP, March 2000
//
// SOAP XML element attribute object definition
//
#if !defined __SOAPELEMENTATTRIBUTES_H
#define __SOAPELEMENTATTRIBUTES_H

#include <vector>
#include <string>
#include <iostream>
#include <strstream>

// Fwd declaration
class CSOAPElement;

class CSOAPElementAttributes
{
public:
    CSOAPElementAttributes(CSOAPElement* pParent = NULL);
    virtual ~CSOAPElementAttributes();

// Methods
public:
    bool EnableStdAttribute(long iStdAttributeCookie, bool bEnable);
    unsigned long InsertAttribute(long iNamespaceCookie,
➥std::string& strAttrName, std::string& strAttrValue);
    unsigned long WriteToStream(std::ostrstream& ostr);

    void SetParent(CSOAPElement* pNewParent) { m_pParent =
                                               ➥pNewParent; }
    CSOAPElement* GetParent() { return m_pParent; }
```

```
// Attributes
protected:
    CSOAPElement* m_pParent;

    bool m_bStdAttributes[4];
    std::vector<std::string> m_vecAttributes;

};

#endif // __SOAPELEMENTATTRIBUTES_H
```

The attributes themselves are stored as strings in an STL vector,
CSOAPElementAttributes::m_vecAttributes. The attribute strings are created when the
attribute is inserted, using InsertAttribute():, the implementation for which is shown in
Listing 10.7.

LISTING 10.7   CSOAPElementAttributes::InsertAttribute() Implementation

```
unsigned long
➥CSOAPElementAttributes::InsertAttribute(long iNamespaceCookie,
➥std::string& strAttrName, std::string& strAttrValue)
{
    // First find the namespace
    std::string strNamespace;
    unsigned long res = SOAP_S_OK;
    if ( m_pParent != NULL ) {
        res = m_pParent->GetNamespace(iNamespaceCookie,strNamespace);
        if ( res ) return res;
    } // if

    // Create the attribute, starting with the namespace
    std::string strAttr(" "); // leading space

    // Add the namespace, if any
    if ( strNamespace.length() ) {
        strAttr += strNamespace;

        // Add the colon
        strAttr += ":";
    } // if

    // Add the name
    strAttr += strAttrName;
```

continues

10

IMPLEMENTING
SOAP

LISTING 10.7 Continued

```
    // Add the '='
    strAttr += "=\"";

    // Add the value
    strAttr += strAttrValue;

    // Add the final quote
    strAttr += "\"";

    // Stuff in the storage vector
    m_vecAttributes.push_back(strAttr);

    return res;
}
```

The attribute string creation begins with the derivation of the appropriate namespace:

```
res = m_pParent->GetNamespace(iNamespaceCookie,strNamespace);
```

With the namespace in hand, the remainder of the attribute is built by combining the various input parameters. For example, here the namespace is combined with a colon and the attribute name:

```
if ( strNamespace.length() ) {
    strAttr += strNamespace;

    // Add the colon
    strAttr += ":";
} // if

// Add the name
strAttr += strAttrName;
```

The rest of the attribute is processed similarly. After the attribute string is completely built, it is inserted into the attribute storage vector:

```
// Stuff in the storage vector
m_vecAttributes.push_back(strAttr);
```

Later, when the attributes are streamed out, the vector is again accessed (from `CSOAPElementAttributes::WriteToStream()`):

```
// From WriteToStream(std::ostrstream& ostr)
if ( m_bStdAttributes[ENCATTRCOOKIE] ) {
    // Stream the encodingStyle attribute
    res = StreamStdAttribute(ostr,ENCATTRCOOKIE);
```

```
    if ( res ) throw res;
} // if

if ( m_bStdAttributes[MUNDATTRCOOKIE] ) {
    (Code similar to ENCATTRCOOKIE)
} // if

if ( m_bStdAttributes[ACTNXTATTRCOOKIE] ) {
    (Code similar to ENCATTRCOOKIE)
} // if

if ( m_bStdAttributes[ROOTATTRCOOKIE] ) {
    (Code similar to ENCATTRCOOKIE)
} // if

// Write any instance-specific attributes
for ( long i = 0; i < m_vecAttributes.size() ; i++ ) {
    // Retrieve the element
    std::string strAttr = m_vecAttributes[i];

    // Write the attribute
    ostr << strAttr.c_str();
} // for
```

In this manner, arbitrary element attributes are streamed in a first-in, first-out basis behind the standard SOAP element attributes. (These are enabled using CSOAPElementAttributes::EnableStdAttribute(), similarly to how the default SOAP namespaces are enabled.)

Now that you've seen the base classes the SOAP objects use, it's time to turn to the primary derived classes.

Primary Derived SOAP Classes

The primary derived SOAP classes consist of the scoping element (a base class for the SOAP envelope, header, and body), the independent element, and the embedded element. The independent and embedded elements were discussed in Chapter 5, "SOAP and Data: The XML Payload." The *scoping element* serves as a base class for the envelope, the header, and the body, which have special meaning to the protocol.

The embedded element class is little more than a thin veneer class that derives from the base SOAP element class and isn't especially interesting. The independent element class is a bit more interesting, in that it contains embedded elements, as you see from Listing 10.8.

10

IMPLEMENTING
SOAP

LISTING 10.8   CSOAPIndElement Definition

```cpp
// SOAPIndElement.h
//
// Kenn Scribner
// Understanding SOAP, March 2000
//
// SOAP independent element object definition
//
#if !defined __SOAPINDELEMENT_H
#define __SOAPINDELEMENT_H

#include <vector>
#include <string>
#include <iostream>
#include <strstream>
#include "SOAPElement.h"

class CSOAPEmbeddedElement;
class CSOAPIndElement : public CSOAPElement
{
public:
    CSOAPIndElement(CSOAPElement* pParent);
    virtual ~CSOAPIndElement();

// Methods
public:
    virtual unsigned long InsertElement(const std::string& strTagText,
➡long iNamespaceCookie, CSOAPEmbeddedElement** ppElement);
    virtual unsigned long StreamContents(std::ostrstream& ostr);
    virtual unsigned long StreamOpenTag(std::ostrstream& ostr);
    virtual unsigned long StreamCloseTag(std::ostrstream& ostr);

// Attributes
protected:
    std::vector<CSOAPEmbeddedElement*> m_vecElements;
};

#endif // __SOAPINDELEMENT_H
```

The embedded elements this independent element contains are kept in the STL vector CSOAPIndElement::m_vecElements. Embedded elements are created by the independent element object using the InsertElement() method you see in Listing 10.9.

LISTING 10.9   CSOAPIndElement::InsertElement() Implementation

```
unsigned long CSOAPIndElement::InsertElement(const std::string&
➥strTagText, long iNamespaceCookie, CSOAPEmbeddedElement**
➥ppElement)
{
    // A quick check
    if ( ppElement == NULL ) return SOAP_E_POINTER;

    // Create a new independent element
    CSOAPEmbeddedElement* pEE = new CSOAPEmbeddedElement(this);
    if ( pEE == NULL ) return SOAP_E_OUTOFMEMORY;

    // Establish its name and namespace
    pEE->SetTagText(strTagText);
    pEE->SetTagNamespace(iNamespaceCookie);

    // Assign out value
    *ppElement = pEE;

    // Stuff in the storage vector
    m_vecElements.push_back(pEE);

    return S_OK;
}
```

The independent element's streaming methods are also provided as virtual methods (WriteToStream() and so on), as the independent element must diverge from the base class' implementation and stream its contained embedded elements as well as its own tags.

The scoping element is very similar to the independent element. The primary difference is CSOAPScopingElement::InsertElement() creates independent elements rather than the embedded elements CSOAPIndElement creates. Otherwise, the classes have very similar implementations. The reasoning for having two separate base classes—one for scoping elements and one for independent elements—is that SOAP interprets the meaning of independent and embedded elements differently, thus enabling the individual base classes to manage them differently, if desired.

The scoping element, as previously mentioned, serves as the base class for the secondary derived SOAP classes, the envelope, the header, and the body, which are examined next.

Secondary Derived SOAP Classes

Because all of the processing is handled by CSOAPScopingElement, the CSOAPHeader and CSOAPBody classes are very thin wrappers that merely delegate the work to the base class. These derived classes do need to identify their base cookie. The SOAP header's definition is shown in Listing 10.10, whereas the body's is shown in Listing 10.11.

LISTING 10.10   CSOAPHeader Class Definition

```cpp
// SOAPHeader.h
//
// Kenn Scribner
// Understanding SOAP, March 2000
//
// SOAP Header object definition
//
#if !defined __SOAPHEADER_H
#define __SOAPHEADER_H

#include "SOAPScopingElement.h"

#define HEADERBASECOOKIE  0x00020000

class CSOAPEnvelope;
class CSOAPHeader : public CSOAPScopingElement
{
public:
    CSOAPHeader(CSOAPEnvelope* pEnvelope);
    virtual ~CSOAPHeader();

// Methods
public:
    CSOAPEnvelope* GetEnvelope() { return m_pEnvelope; }

// Attributes
protected:
    CSOAPEnvelope* m_pEnvelope;

};

#endif // __SOAPHEADER_H
```

LISTING 10.11   CSOAPBody Class Definition

```cpp
// SOAPBody.h
//
// Kenn Scribner
// Understanding SOAP, March 2000
//
// SOAP Body object definition
//
```

```
#if !defined __SOAPBODY_H
#define __SOAPBODY_H

#include "SOAPScopingElement.h"

#define BODYBASECOOKIE  0x00040000

class CSOAPEnvelope;
class CSOAPHeader;
class CSOAPBody : public CSOAPScopingElement
{
public:
    CSOAPBody(CSOAPEnvelope* pEnvelope, CSOAPHeader* pHeader = NULL);
    virtual ~CSOAPBody();

// Methods
public:
    CSOAPEnvelope* GetEnvelope() { return m_pEnvelope; }
    CSOAPHeader* SetHeader(CSOAPHeader* pHeader) {
        CSOAPHeader* pHeaderTemp = m_pHeader;
        m_pHeader = pHeader;
        return pHeaderTemp;
    }
    CSOAPHeader* GetHeader() { return m_pHeader; }

// Attributes
protected:
    CSOAPEnvelope* m_pEnvelope;
    CSOAPHeader* m_pHeader;

};

#endif // __SOAPBODY_H
```

The major difference between the header and body objects is that the body can access (directly) both the header and envelope objects, whereas the header can access only the envelope object. Of course, this is consistent with the specification's guidelines for header access. The SOAP header is in itself a complete entity and must not reference information stored in external elements. The body, of course, can access information in the header, and as a result it has a direct link to the header object (via a pointer).

The SOAP body also has a special method to assign the SOAP header, `CSOAPBody::SetHeader()`. SOAP requires a body element, but the header element is optional and might not be created at the same time as the body element. If the header element is created after the body is created, you can still link the body to the header using this method.

10

IMPLEMENTING
SOAP

The SOAP envelope is more complex because the specification rules that govern its behavior are more complex. The envelope object's definition is shown in Listing 10.12.

LISTING 10.12 CSOAPEnvelope Class Definition

```cpp
// SOAPEnvelope.h
//
// Kenn Scribner
// Understanding SOAP, March 2000
//
// SOAP Envelope object definition
//
#if !defined __SOAPENVELOPE_H
#define __SOAPENVELOPE_H

#include <iostream>
#include <strstream>
#include "SOAPScopingElement.h"

#define ENVELOPEBASECOOKIE  0x00010000

class CSOAPHeader;
class CSOAPBody;
class CSOAPHttpPacket;
class CSOAPEnvelope : public CSOAPScopingElement
{
public:
    CSOAPEnvelope(CSOAPHttpPacket* pParent);
    virtual ~CSOAPEnvelope();

// Methods
public:
    virtual unsigned long InsertElement(const std::string& strTagText,
    ➥long iNamespaceCookie, CSOAPElement** ppElement);
    virtual unsigned long WriteToStream(std::ostrstream& ostr);
    virtual unsigned long StreamOpenTag(std::ostrstream& ostr);
    virtual unsigned long StreamCloseTag(std::ostrstream& ostr);
    CSOAPHttpPacket* GetHttpPacket() { return m_pParent; }
    CSOAPHeader* GetHeader() { return m_pHeader; }
    CSOAPBody* GetBody() { return m_pBody; }

// Attributes
protected:
    CSOAPHttpPacket* m_pParent;
    CSOAPHeader* m_pHeader;
```

```
CSOAPBody* m_pBody;

};
```

```
#endif // __SOAPENVELOPE_H
```

The envelope maintains links to its constituent header and body as well as to the containing HTTP packet object (to be discussed in the next section). The `InsertElement()` method might seem incongruous at first because the body object is created in the envelope class's constructor, like this:

```
// From CSOAPEnvelope's constructor
m_pBody = new CSOAPBody(this,NULL);
```

and the header is created in GetHeader(), like this:

```
// If there is no SOAP header, create one
// now...
if ( m_pHeader == NULL ) {
    m_pHeader = new CSOAPHeader(this);
    m_pBody->SetHeader(m_pHeader);
} // if

return m_pHeader;
```

The `InsertElement()` method is actually in Listing 10.12 to *prevent* insertion of new elements. (Elements at this level aren't necessarily precluded by the SOAP specification, but for nominal SOAP encoding they are undefined.) The implementation of `InsertElement()` is shown in Listing 10.13.

LISTING 10.13   `CSOAPEnvelope::InsertElement()` Implementation

```
unsigned long CSOAPEnvelope::InsertElement(const std::string&
➥strTagText, long iNamespaceCookie, CSOAPElement** ppElement)
{
    // You can't add independent elements to the envelope, so this
    // method simply returns a NULL element and SOAP_S_FALSE;
    if ( *ppElement == NULL ) return SOAP_E_POINTER;

    *ppElement = NULL;
    return SOAP_S_FALSE;
}
```

The envelope also has different streaming requirements when requested to provide the XML document. The envelope's `WriteToStream()` implementation is shown in Listing 10.14.

10

LISTING 10.14 CSOAPEnvelope::WriteToStream() Implementation

```
unsigned long CSOAPEnvelope::WriteToStream(std::ostrstream& ostr)
{
    // Nothing to write if the external stream is NULL
    if ( ostr == NULL ) return SOAP_E_POINTER;

    unsigned long res = SOAP_S_OK;
    try {
        // Write the opening envelope tag text to the
        // local stream
        res = StreamOpenTag(ostr);
        if ( res ) throw res;

        // Stream the header into the local stream, if
        // one has been created.
        if ( m_pHeader != NULL ) {
            res = m_pHeader->WriteToStream(ostr);
            if ( res ) throw res;
        } // if

        // Stream the body into the local stream
        res = m_pBody->WriteToStream(ostr);
        if ( res ) throw res;

        // Write the closing envelope tag text to the
        // local stream
        res = StreamCloseTag(ostr);
        if ( res ) throw res;
    } // try
    catch(unsigned long resErr) {
        // Some internal error...
        res = resErr; // normalize to this error...
        char szErr[256] = {0};
        sprintf(szErr,"Internal error while streaming
                ➥envelope data, %#08x.",resErr);
        std::cerr << szErr << std::endl;
    } // catch
    catch(...) {
        // Some error...
        res = SOAP_E_UNEXPECTED;
        std::cerr << "Unexpected application error while
        ➥streaming envelope data" << std::endl;
    } // catch

    return res;
}
```

The envelope is responsible for writing the header and body. Note that if the header pointer is NULL (there is no header), no header data will be streamed. The envelope element is also the singular element that (by default) streams the standard SOAP namespaces.

All SOAP objects are responsible for maintaining SOAP information within their scope. However, the HTTP packet object, `CSOAPHttpPacket`, maintains the SOAP packet as a whole. `CSOAPHttpPacket` is discussed next.

C++ HTTP Packet Support

In addition to the XML payload, the HTTP packet must have at least five headers—POST, HOST, Content-Type, Content-Length, and the SOAP action header. The `CSOAPHttpPacket` object maintains these headers as well as contains the SOAP envelope object. Its class definition is shown in Listing 10.15.

LISTING 10.15 `CSOAPHttpPacket` Class Definition

```
// SOAPHttpPacket.h
//
// Kenn Scribner
// Understanding SOAP, March 2000
//
// SOAP HTTP object definition
//
#if !defined __SOAPHTTPPACKET_H
#define __SOAPHTTPPACKET_H

#include <string>
#include <iostream>
#include <strstream>
#include "SOAPEnvelope.h"

typedef struct tagSOAPCallInfo {
    std::string strHost;
    std::string strPostHdr;
    std::string strActionData;
    std::string strMethod;
} SOAPCALLINFO, *LPSOAPCALLINFO;

class CSOAPHttpPacket
{
public:
    CSOAPHttpPacket(LPSOAPCALLINFO pci);
    virtual ~CSOAPHttpPacket();
```

continues

10

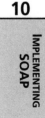

IMPLEMENTING
SOAP

LISTING 10.15 Continued

```cpp
// Methods
public:
    unsigned long WriteToStream(std::ostrstream& ostr,
    ➥bool bEnvelopeOnly = false);
    CSOAPEnvelope* GetEnvelope() { return m_pEnvelope; }
    void GetMethodName(std::string& str)
    {
        str = m_strMethodName;
    }
    void GetEndpointURL(std::string& str)
    {
        str = m_strEndpointURL;
    }
    void GetPostText(std::string& str)
    {
        str = m_strPostText;
    }
    void GetPostHdr(std::string& str)
    {
        str = m_strPostHdr;
    }
    void GetHostText(std::string& str)
    {
        str = m_strHostText;
    }
    void GetHostHdr(std::string& str)
    {
        str = m_strHostHdr;
    }
    void GetContentTypeText(std::string& str)
    {
        str = m_strContentTypeText;
    }
    void GetContentTypeHdr(std::string& str)
    {
        str = m_strContentTypeHdr;
    }
    void GetContentLenText(std::string& str)
    {
        str = m_strContentLenText;
    }
    void GetContentLenHdr (std::string& str)
    {
        str = m_strContentLenHdr;
```

```
    }
    void GetSoapActionText(std::string& str)
    {
        str = m_strSOAPActionText;
    }
    void GetSoapActionHdr(std::string& str)
    {
        str = m_strSOAPActionHdr;
    }

// Attributes
protected:
    CSOAPEnvelope* m_pEnvelope;

    // Incoming HTTP informational strings
    std::string m_strEndpointURL;
    std::string m_strPostData;
    std::string m_strActionData;
    std::string m_strMethodName;

    // HTTP header strings
    int m_iPacketSize;
    std::string m_strPostHdr; // string in header form
    std::string m_strPostText; // header data only
    std::string m_strHostHdr;
    std::string m_strHostText;
    std::string m_strContentTypeHdr;
    std::string m_strContentTypeText;
    std::string m_strContentLenHdr;
    std::string m_strContentLenText;
    std::string m_strSOAPActionHdr;
    std::string m_strSOAPActionText;

};

#endif // __SOAPHTTPPACKET_H
```

For the most part the class accepts input information, such as the method name and endpoint URL, and creates the necessary headers. You can retrieve the header information either as the content of the header or as the header itself. For example, if you use the GetContentLenText() method, you would receive a string with an integer value representing the length of the packet in bytes (say "412"). Calling the GetContentLenHdr() method, on the other hand, returns the entire header ("Content-Length: 412"). Of course, you retrieve the SOAP envelope object using the GetEnvelope() method.

10

IMPLEMENTING
SOAP

You've seen a lot of objects and definitions, so it's probably a good time to show you how the objects are used to create a SOAP request packet. That's the goal of the next section.

Using the SOAP Object Model

If you've had the opportunity to review the SOAP specification (an annotated copy of which is in Appendix A, "The SOAP 1.1 Specifications"), you've undoubtedly seen the sample method that requests the latest stock price for some imaginary stock. You'll find the example in Section 1.3 of the SOAP specification as well as in the appendix. The code shown in Listing 10.16 uses the SOAP object model to re-create the SOAP packet described in Section 1.3 with the addition of a transaction ID (also an example from the specification) and a couple of other slight alterations (such as the addition of the xsi namespace). The transaction ID was added to provide header data so that the header would also be streamed.

LISTING 10.16   SOAPObjectsTest SOAP Object Model Test Driver Implementation

```cpp
// SOAPObjectsTest.cpp
//
// Kenn Scribner
//
// Understanding SOAP
// March 2000
//
// Test driver for the SOAPObjectsLib SOAP object
// model library.
//
#include <string>
#include <iostream>
#include <strstream>
#include <atlbase.h>
#include "..\SOAPObjectLib\SOAPEnvelope.h"
#include "..\SOAPObjectLib\SOAPHeader.h"
#include "..\SOAPObjectLib\SOAPBody.h"
#include "..\SOAPObjectLib\SOAPIndElement.h"
#include "..\SOAPObjectLib\SOAPEmbeddedElement.h"
#include "..\SOAPObjectLib\SOAPHttpPacket.h"
using namespace std;

int main(int argc, char* argv[])
{
    cout << "Testing HTTP/SOAP Packet Objects" << endl;
    cout << "+----------------------------+" << endl;

    SOAPCALLINFO ciInfo;
    ciInfo.strHost = "www.stockquoteserver.com";
```

```
ciInfo.strPostHdr = "StockQuote";
ciInfo.strActionData = "Some-Namespace-URI#GetLastTradePrice";
ciInfo.strMethod = "GetLastTradePrice";
CSOAPHttpPacket* pPacket = new CSOAPHttpPacket(&ciInfo);

// Add some stuff to the envelope
CSOAPEnvelope* pEnvelope = pPacket->GetEnvelope();

long iCookie = NULLNSCOOKIE;
unsigned long hr = pEnvelope->InsertNamespace(string("Some-
➥Namespace-URI "),string("m"),&iCookie);
if ( FAILED(hr) ) {
    cout << "Failed to insert namespace." << endl;
    return -1;
} // if

CSOAPHeader* pHeader = pEnvelope->GetHeader();
CSOAPIndElement* pTXElement = NULL;
hr = pHeader->InsertElement(string("TransactionID"),
                            ➥iCookie,&pTXElement);
if ( FAILED(hr) ) {
    cout << "Failed to insert new header element." << endl;
    return -1;
} // if

// Set the root attribute
pTXElement->EnableStdAttribute(ROOTATTRCOOKIE,true);

// Set the mustUnderstand attribute
pTXElement->EnableStdAttribute(MUNDATTRCOOKIE,true);

pTXElement->SetElementData(_T("1265777831"));

CSOAPBody* pBody = pEnvelope->GetBody();
CSOAPIndElement* pMethodElement = NULL;
hr = pBody->InsertElement(string("GetLastTradePrice"),
             ➥iCookie,&pMethodElement);
if ( FAILED(hr) ) {
    cout << "Failed to insert body method element." << endl;
    return -1;
} // if

CSOAPEmbeddedElement* pEmbedded = NULL;
hr = pMethodElement->InsertElement(string("symbol"),
                     ➥NULLNSCOOKIE,&pEmbedded);
```

continues

10

IMPLEMENTING
SOAP

LISTING 10.16 Continued

```
if ( FAILED(hr) ) {
    cout << "Failed to insert new embedded element." << endl;
    return -1;
} // if

pEmbedded->SetElementData(_T("DIS"));

// Stream packet
ostrstream ostr;
hr = pPacket->WriteToStream(ostr);
if ( FAILED(hr) ) {
    cout << "Failed to stream packet." << endl;
    return -1;
} // if

CRegKey rkRoot;
long lRes = rkRoot.Open(HKEY_LOCAL_MACHINE,
                        ➥_T("Software\\MCP\\SOAP"));
if ( lRes != ERROR_SUCCESS ) return HRESULT_FROM_WIN32(lRes);

CRegKey rkFile;
lRes = rkFile.Open(rkRoot,_T("HttpRequestFile"));
if ( lRes != ERROR_SUCCESS ) return HRESULT_FROM_WIN32(lRes);

TCHAR szFile[_MAX_PATH+1] = {0};
DWORD dwBytesRead = _MAX_PATH;
lRes = rkFile.QueryValue(szFile,NULL,&dwBytesRead);
if ( lRes == ERROR_SUCCESS ) {
    HANDLE hFile = CreateFile(szFile,
                             GENERIC_WRITE,
                             0,
                             NULL,
                             CREATE_ALWAYS,
                             FILE_ATTRIBUTE_NORMAL,
                             NULL);

    WriteFile(hFile,ostr.str(),ostr.pcount(),&dwBytesRead,NULL);

    CloseHandle(hFile);
} // if

delete pPacket;

cout << "Complete." << endl;

return 0;
}
```

The program begins by completing a SOAPCALLINFO structure, which is passed to a new SOAP HTTP Packet object:

```
SOAPCALLINFO ciInfo;
ciInfo.strHost = "www.stockquoteserver.com";
ciInfo.strPostHdr = "StockQuote";
ciInfo.strActionData = "Some-Namespace-URI#GetLastTradePrice";
ciInfo.strMethod = "GetLastTradePrice";
CSOAPHttpPacket* pPacket = new CSOAPHttpPacket(&ciInfo);
```

With the packet itself created, the SOAP envelope is retrieved to begin completing the XML document creation:

```
// Add some stuff to the envelope
CSOAPEnvelope* pEnvelope = pPacket->GetEnvelope();
```

The method namespace is inserted into the envelope, and a cookie is returned for later use:

```
long iCookie = NULLNSCOOKIE;
unsigned long hr = pEnvelope->InsertNamespace(string("Some-
➥Namespace-URI "),string("m"),&iCookie);
if ( FAILED(hr) ) {
    cout << "Failed to insert namespace." << endl;
    return -1;
} // if
```

Then the test application retrieves the header object and inserts an independent element that will contain an imaginary transaction ID:

```
CSOAPHeader* pHeader = pEnvelope->GetHeader();
CSOAPIndElement* pTXElement = NULL;
hr = pHeader->InsertElement(string("TransactionID"),
                            ➥iCookie,&pTXElement);
if ( FAILED(hr) ) {
    cout << "Failed to insert new header element." << endl;
    return -1;
} // if
```

The transaction ID element is then given the SOAP-ENV:root and SOAP-ENV:mustUnderstand attributes and some data:

```
    // Set the root attribute
    pTXElement->EnableStdAttribute(ROOTATTRCOOKIE,true);

    // Set the mustUnderstand attribute
    pTXElement->EnableStdAttribute(MUNDATTRCOOKIE,true);


pTXElement->SetElementData(_T("1265777831"));
```

10

IMPLEMENTING
SOAP

With the header complete, the test application turns to the body. The body element is retrieved from the envelope, and the method's independent element is created in this manner:

```
CSOAPBody* pBody = pEnvelope->GetBody();
CSOAPIndElement* pMethodElement = NULL;
hr = pBody->InsertElement(string("GetLastTradePrice"),
            ➥iCookie,&pMethodElement);
if ( FAILED(hr) ) {
    cout << "Failed to insert body method element." << endl;
    return -1;
} // if
```

Note that the method element is given the namespace associated with the cookie (Some-Namespace-URL as m).

The method's single argument is inserted as an embedded element, like so:

```
CSOAPEmbeddedElement* pEmbedded = NULL;
hr = pMethodElement->InsertElement(string("symbol"),
                    ➥NULLNSCOOKIE,&pEmbedded);
if ( FAILED(hr) ) {
    cout << "Failed to insert new embedded element." << endl;
    return -1;
} // if

pEmbedded->SetElementData(_T("DIS"));
```

Namespaces are not required in embedded elements because the containing independent element's namespace encompasses all subordinate embedded elements. However, the object model does not preclude you from inserting a namespace if you choose. If you do not want a namespace applied to any element, simply use the standard namespace cookie NULLNSCOOKIE.

At this point all the SOAP information has been recorded in the SOAP object model. All that is left is to stream the contents of the C++ objects into an XML format. This is done using CSOAPHttpPacket::WriteToStream():

```
// Stream packet
ostrstream ostr;
hr = pPacket->WriteToStream(ostr);
if ( FAILED(hr) ) {
    cout << "Failed to stream packet." << endl;
    return -1;
} // if
```

The next few lines of code write the HTTP information to a file you can review. In fact, the contents of this file, which represent the resulting SOAP HTTP packet, are shown in Listing 10.17. Instead of coding a filename into the application, the test program reads a special Registry key to determine where to save the file data. You'll see this Registry key again when you examine the SOAP Object Surrogate in the upcoming "Using the SOAP Object Surrogate" section. The code is vanilla Win32 programming with some Registry help from ATL, so the details are left for you to review in Listing 10.17.

LISTING 10.17   SOAPObjectsTest, the Resulting SOAP HTTP Packet

```
POST /StockQuote HTTP/1.1
HOST: http://www.stockquoteserver.com
Content-Type: text/xml
Content-Length: 414
SOAPAction: "Some-Namespace-URI#GetLastTradePrice"

<SOAP-ENV:Envelope
  xmlns:SOAP-ENV="http://schemas.xmlsoap.org/soap/envelope/"
  xmlns:m="Some-Namespace-URI"
  SOAP-ENV:encodingStyle="http://schemas.xmlsoap.org/soap/encoding/">
    <SOAP-ENV:Header>
        <m:TransactionID SOAP-ENV:mustUnderstand="1"
          SOAP-ENV:root="1">
            1265777831
        </m:TransactionID>
    </SOAP-ENV:Header>
    <SOAP-ENV:Body>
        <m:GetLastTradePrice>
            <symbol>DIS</symbol>
        </m:GetLastTradePrice>
    </SOAP-ENV:Body>
</SOAP-ENV: Envelope>
```

The SOAP object model is a pure C++ implementation of objects that help you assemble SOAP requests and responses. The COM language binding takes a more COM-based approach, starting with the next section.

Reusable SOAP COM Objects

To properly encode a given COM object's method call stack, you must have two things. First, you must have some meta-information regarding the method call, such as the namespace to associate with the method and the URL to where the call should be remoted. The second critical piece of information is the type information associated with the method arguments. Without that information, the call stack is little more than random bit patterns.

The meta-information associated with a given COM interface is stored in the SOAP Catalog, much as transactional data is stored in the MTS Catalog, or COM+ information is stored in the Class Store. The Catalog is managed by the SOAP Catalog Manager, which is an in-process COM object.

10

The type information is recorded in the COM object's type library. Although you could easily rummage through the type library while consuming bytes in the call stack, the type library encoder (also an in-process COM object) handles this for you and presents you with a stream of tokenized type information, much like the "OICF" strings MIDL uses in contemporary proxy DLLs. If you're not familiar with OICF strings, a detailed explanation is well beyond the scope of this book. However, to state their purpose concisely, the type information gleaned from the IDL file is tokenized as a byte stream, which ultimately is fed to a general-purpose proxy state machine. The state machine reads the byte stream and marshals the method arguments accordingly. In a similar manner, the Encoder does the same thing as MIDL when it creates a tokenized byte stream the serializer uses to encode the call stack data.

Let's take a closer look at the SOAP Catalog and meta-information, as they are used both on the server and the client computers.

The SOAP Catalog

The SOAP Catalog could be nearly anything, from data stored in the Registry to an old-fashioned Windows .INI file. It could be a database, or a simple flat file. But because SOAP makes heavy use of XML, and because the MSXML parser is so readily available, the SOAP Catalog is actually an XML document.

The purpose of the Catalog is twofold. First, you need to persist information regarding the remote method invocations *somewhere*. After all, the idea behind language binding is to enable objects to operate nearly seamlessly with the remoting architecture. If that is the case, then you don't want to have the object itself worry about URLs and namespace. Your remoting architecture should manage those details. And second, you need to easily and effectively determine at runtime which interfaces are marked as remoted and which are not. A corollary to this is the indication as to whether the interface is to be remoted (as a server) or to be used remotely (as a client).

Hence the SOAP Catalog. The general layout of the Catalog is shown in Listing 10.18.

LISTING **10.18**   The SOAP Catalog General Layout

```
<?xml version="1.0"?>
<SOAPCat>
    <Object CLSID="{CLSID}">
        <Interface IID="{IID1}" isOutgoing="true">
            <EndpointURL>{URL}</EndpointURL>
            <Namespace>{namespace}</Namespace>
        </Interface>
        <Interface IID="{IID2}" isOutgoing="false"/>
        <TLB>{file location}</TLB>
    </Object>
</SOAPCat>
```

The XML document tag is `<SOAPCat />`, and each registered COM coclass is stored in its own `<Object />` tag. There is only one object registered in Listing 10.18. However, this one coclass (identified by its CLSID, which is a 128-bit unique number stemming from the RPC UUID) has two interfaces registered. The first interface, IID1, is used as a remote interface. (The isOutgoing attribute is true.) You also know this because this interface has associated `<EndpointURL />` and `<Namespace />` tags. The second interface, IID2, is to be served to other remote clients. (Its isOutgoing attribute is false.)

Ultimately the MSXML parser is used to maintain the Catalog, which is the purpose of the SOAP Catalog Manager, SOAPCatMan. SOAPCatMan is actually an ATL COM object that exports several useful Catalog-related methods. The IDL for the object is shown in Listing 10.19.

LISTING 10.19   The SOAPCatMan Interface Definition

```
// SOAPCatMan.idl : IDL source for SOAPCatMan.dll
//
// Kenn Scribner
//
// Understanding SOAP
// March 2000
//

// This file will be processed by the MIDL tool to
// produce the type library (SOAPCatMan.tlb) and marshalling code.

import "oaidl.idl";
import "ocidl.idl";
    [
        object,
        uuid(CD12406D-E92A-11D3-87C0-20610CC1FFFF),
        dual,
        helpstring("ISOAPCatalog Interface"),
        pointer_default(unique)
    ]
    interface ISOAPCatalog : IDispatch
    {
        [id(1), helpstring("Adds new object/interface by type library
➥version"), local] HRESULT Add([in] BSTR bstrCLSID, [in] BSTR
➥bstrIID, [in] long iTLBMajVer, [in] long iTLBMinVer, [in]
➥VARIANT bIsRemote );
        [id(2), helpstring("Adds new object/interface by type library
➥file"), local] HRESULT Add2([in] BSTR bstrCLSID, [in] BSTR
➥bstrIID, [in] BSTR bstrTLBFile, [in] VARIANT bIsRemote );
        [id(3), helpstring("Removes interface (and object if last
➥interface)"), local] HRESULT Remove([in] BSTR bstrCLSID, [in]
➥BSTR bstrIID, [in] VARIANT bIsRemote);
```

continues

10

IMPLEMENTING
SOAP

LISTING 10.19   Continued

```
        [id(4), helpstring("Retrieves namespace string (per
➥interface)"), local]  HRESULT GetNamespace([in] BSTR bstrCLSID,
➥ [in] BSTR bstrIID, [in] VARIANT bIsRemote, [out, retval] BSTR*
➥pbstrMethodNamespace);
        [id(5), helpstring("Sets namespace string (per interface)"),
➥local] HRESULT PutNamespace([in] BSTR bstrCLSID, [in] BSTR
➥bstrIID, [in] VARIANT bIsRemote, [in] BSTR
➥bstrMethodNamespace);
        [id(6), helpstring("Retrieves endpoint URL"), local] HRESULT
➥GetEndpointURL([in] BSTR bstrCLSID, [in] BSTR bstrIID, [in]
➥VARIANT bIsRemote, [out, retval] BSTR* pbstrEndpointURL);
        [id(7), helpstring("Sets endpoint URL"), local] HRESULT
➥PutEndpointURL([in] BSTR bstrCLSID, [in] BSTR bstrIID, [in]
➥VARIANT bIsRemote, [in] BSTR bstrEndpointURL);
        [id(8), helpstring("Retrieves type library file path"), local]
➥HRESULT GetTLBFile([in] BSTR bstrCLSID, [out, retval] BSTR*
➥pbstrTLBFile);
        [id(9), helpstring("Returns true if the object (coclass)
➥is registered"), local]
➥HRESULT IsRegisteredObject([in] BSTR bstrCLSID);
        [id(10), helpstring("Returns true if the interface is
➥registered"), local]
➥HRESULT IsRegisteredInterface([in] BSTR bstrCLSID,
➥[in] BSTR bstrIID, [in] VARIANT bIsRemote);
    };

[
    uuid(CD124061-E92A-11D3-87C0-20610CC1FFFF),
    version(1.0),
    helpstring("SOAPCatMan 1.0 Type Library")
]
library SOAPCATMANLib
{
    importlib("stdole32.tlb");
    importlib("stdole2.tlb");

    [
        uuid(CD12406E-E92A-11D3-87C0-20610CC1FFFF),
        helpstring("SOAPCat Class")
    ]
    coclass SOAPCatManager
    {
        [default] interface ISOAPCatalog;
    };
};
```

Of the ten SOAPCatMan methods, two are used for adding new entries (Add() and Add2()),and one removes an entry (Remove()). Four deal with inserting and querying for method meta-information (setting and putting namespaces and endpoint URLs). One returns the associated type library file path (GetTLBFile()), and the remaining two simply test a given CLSID or IID to see if it is currently in the Catalog.

The primary difference among the insertion methods is the arguments regarding the type library. If you know the version numbers associated with the particular type library, you would use the Add() method. This method manages the grungy Registry access code to pull the type library file path from the interface's stored information. With the type library path in hand, Add() invokes Add2(), which is used when you have the path versus the version information. The type library's path is stored in the Catalog as a convenience, as type libraries are versioned. In this manner, you can store the user's desired type library version information and speed things up a bit by pre-loading the file path (versus accessing the Registry each time you require the type library).

All the methods involve relatively mundane DOM access code used to read or write the Catalog file. A good example is the Add2() method you see in Listing 10.20.

LISTING 10.20   ISOAPCatalog::Add2() Implementation

```
STDMETHODIMP CSOAPCat::Add2(BSTR bstrCLSID, BSTR bstrIID,
➥BSTR bstrTLBFile, VARIANT bIsRemote)
{
    // Manage multithreaded access
    m_cs.Lock();

    // Try to add a new object to the catalog
    HRESULT hr = S_OK;
    try {
        // First, open the catalog
        CComPtr<IXMLDOMDocument> spCatalog;
        hr = OpenCatFile(&spCatalog);
        if ( FAILED(hr) ) throw hr;

        // Then, see if any elements exist with the given
        // CLSID
        CComQIPtr<IXMLDOMNode> spObjNode;
        hr = FindCLSID(bstrCLSID,spCatalog,&spObjNode);
        if ( FAILED(hr) ) throw hr;

        if ( hr == S_FALSE ) {
            // Node doesn't exist, so create it as an
```

10

continues

LISTING 10.20   Continued

```cpp
// element
CComPtr<IXMLDOMElement> spObjElement;
hr = CreateObjectNode(bstrCLSID,spCatalog,
                        &spObjElement);
if ( FAILED(hr) )  throw hr;

// Now convert it to a node
spObjNode = spObjElement;

// Next add the IID node
CComPtr<IXMLDOMNode> spItfNode;
CComBSTR bstrItfTag;
bstrItfTag.LoadString(IDS_ITFTAG);
hr = CreateChildNode(bstrItfTag,NULL,spCatalog,
                        spObjNode,&spItfNode);
if ( FAILED(hr) ) throw hr;

// Set the IID as the attribute
CComQIPtr<IXMLDOMElement> spItfElement;
spItfElement = spItfNode;
CComBSTR bstrAttr;
bstrAttr.LoadString(IDS_IIDTAG);
hr = spItfElement->setAttribute(bstrAttr,
                        CComVariant(bstrIID));
if ( FAILED(hr) ) throw hr;

// Add the attribute to tell if the interface is
// incoming or outgoing
bstrAttr.LoadString(IDS_ISOUTGOTAG);
CComVariant var(bIsRemote);
var.ChangeType(VT_BOOL);
if ( var.bVal ) {
    hr = spItfElement->setAttribute(bstrAttr,
                        CComVariant("true"));
} // if
else {
    hr = spItfElement->setAttribute(bstrAttr,
                        CComVariant("false"));
} // else
if ( FAILED(hr) ) throw hr;

// Finally add the TLB node
IID iid = GUID_NULL;
hr = IIDFromString(bstrIID,&iid);
if ( FAILED(hr) ) throw hr;
```

```
        CComPtr<IXMLDOMNode> spTLBNode;
        CComBSTR bstrTLBTag;
        bstrTLBTag.LoadString(IDS_TLBTAG);
        hr = CreateChildNode(bstrTLBTag,bstrTLBFile,
                        spCatalog,spObjNode,&spTLBNode);
        if ( FAILED(hr) ) throw hr;


        hr = spCatalog->save(CComVariant(m_strCatFile));
        if ( FAILED(hr) ) throw hr;
    } // if
    else {
        // Search for the given IID value...you can
        // assume the TLB data is already there or there
        // wouldn't be an object node...
        CComPtr<IXMLDOMNode> spItfNode;
        hr = FindIID(bstrIID,spObjNode,bIsRemote,
                                    &spItfNode);
        if ( FAILED(hr) ) throw hr;


        if ( hr == S_FALSE ) {
            // Add the new IID
            CComBSTR bstrItfTag;
            bstrItfTag.LoadString(IDS_ITFTAG);
            hr = CreateChildNode(bstrItfTag,NULL,
                        spCatalog,spObjNode,&spItfNode);
            if ( FAILED(hr) ) throw hr;


            // Set the IID as the attribute
            CComQIPtr<IXMLDOMElement> spItfElement;
            spItfElement = spItfNode;
            CComBSTR bstrAttr;
            bstrAttr.LoadString(IDS_IIDTAG);
            hr = spItfElement->setAttribute(bstrAttr,
                            CComVariant(bstrIID));
            if ( FAILED(hr) ) throw hr;


            // Add the attribute to tell if the
            // interface is incoming or outgoing
            bstrAttr.LoadString(IDS_ISOUTGOTAG);
            CComVariant var(bIsRemote);
            var.ChangeType(VT_BOOL);
            if ( var.bVal ) {
                hr = spItfElement->setAttribute(bstrAttr,
                                CComVariant("true"));
            } // if
```

continues

10

IMPLEMENTING SOAP

LISTING 10.20   Continued

```
                    else {
                        hr = spItfElement->setAttribute(bstrAttr,
                                            CComVariant("false"));
                    } // else
                    if ( FAILED(hr) ) throw hr;

                    hr = spCatalog->
                        ➥save(CComVariant(m_strCatFile));
                    if ( FAILED(hr) ) throw hr;
                } // if
            } // else
        } // try
        catch(HRESULT hrErr) {
            // Some COM error
            hr = hrErr;
            ATLTRACE("SOAPCat: error adding object to catalog
                                ➥file, %#08x\n",hr);
            ATLASSERT(SUCCEEDED(hr));
        } // catch
        catch(...){
            // Some error
            hr = E_UNEXPECTED;
            ATLTRACE("SOAPCat: unspecified error adding object
                        ➥to catalog file, %#08x\n",hr);
            ATLASSERT(SUCCEEDED(hr));
        } // catch

        // Manage multithreaded access
        m_cs.Unlock();

        return hr;
}
```

Most of the SOAPCatMan methods are similar to Add2(). The method begins by locking an object-wide critical section to prevent multithreaded concurrent access:

```
// Manage multithreaded access
m_cs.Lock();
```

The meat of the method begins by opening the Catalog file, which is accomplished by a helper function OpenCatFile():

```
// First, open the catalog
CComPtr<IXMLDOMDocument> spCatalog;
hr = OpenCatFile(&spCatalog);
if ( FAILED(hr) ) throw hr;
```

Next, the given CLSID is located (or not), using another helper function, FindCLSID():

```
// Then, see if any elements exist with the given CLSID
CComQIPtr<IXMLDOMNode> spObjNode;
hr = FindCLSID(bstrCLSID,spCatalog,&spObjNode);
if ( FAILED(hr) ) throw hr;
```

If the CLSID node is not located—FindCLSID() returns S_FALSE—, a new node is created using the CreateObjectNode() helper function:

```
// Node doesn't exist, so create it as an element
CComPtr<IXMLDOMElement> spObjElement;
hr = CreateObjectNode(bstrCLSID,spCatalog,&spObjElement);
if ( FAILED(hr) ) throw hr;
```

To be inserted, the new node (which is a DOM element) must be added as a DOM node, so a new XML DOM interface is queried and added. Remember that spObjNode is an IXMLDOMNode interface (smart) pointer, and that the assignment you see actually is an overloaded assignment operator that performs a QueryInterface(). CreateChildNode() is yet another helper function that creates subordinate nodes given a parent node:

```
// Now convert it (the element) to a node
spObjNode = spObjElement;


// Next add the IID node
CComPtr<IXMLDOMNode> spItfNode;
CComBSTR bstrItfTag;
bstrItfTag.LoadString(IDS_ITFTAG);
hr = CreateChildNode(bstrItfTag,NULL,spCatalog,
                        spObjNode,&spItfNode);
if ( FAILED(hr) )  throw hr;
```

Because a new interface node was created, you must also set the IID and isOutgoing attributes:

```
// Set the IID as the attribute
CComQIPtr<IXMLDOMElement> spItfElement;
spItfElement = spItfNode;
CComBSTR bstrAttr;
bstrAttr.LoadString(IDS_IIDTAG);
hr = spItfElement->setAttribute(bstrAttr,
                                CComVariant(bstrIID));
if ( FAILED(hr) ) throw hr;

// Add the attribute to tell if the interface is
// incoming or outgoing
bstrAttr.LoadString(IDS_ISOUTGOTAG);
CComVariant var(bIsRemote);
var.ChangeType(VT_BOOL);
```

10

```
if ( var.bVal ) {
hr = spItfElement->setAttribute(bstrAttr,
                                CComVariant("true"));
} // if
else {
hr = spItfElement->setAttribute(bstrAttr,
                                CComVariant("false"));
} // else
if ( FAILED(hr) )  throw hr;
```

Because the object node did not exist, you must finally add the type library's path node:

```
// Finally add the TLB node
IID iid = GUID_NULL;
hr = IIDFromString(bstrIID,&iid);
if ( FAILED(hr) ) throw hr;

CComPtr<IXMLDOMNode> spTLBNode;
CComBSTR bstrTLBTag;
bstrTLBTag.LoadString(IDS_TLBTAG);
hr = CreateChildNode(bstrTLBTag,bstrTLBFile,
                     spCatalog,spObjNode,&spTLBNode);
if ( FAILED(hr) ) throw hr;
```

With all this new Catalog information just inserted, don't forget to save it:

```
hr = spCatalog->save(CComVariant(m_strCatFile));
if ( FAILED(hr) ) throw hr;
```

All the preceding code is executed if the CLSID (object) node didn't exist. It is also possible that FindCLSID() *did* find the object node. (The given CLSID has already been inserted.) In that case, you must also test to see if the interface has been added by searching for the interface node. Note that an interface marked as isOutgoing="true" is different from an interface marked "false". If you search for one and the other already exists in the Catalog, the search will return with no node found.

As with locating object nodes, you use a helper function to search for interface nodes—FindIID():

```
// Search for the given IID value...you can
// assume the TLB data is already there or there
// wouldn't be an object node...
CComPtr<IXMLDOMNode> spItfNode;
hr = FindIID(bstrIID,spObjNode,bIsRemote,&spItfNode);
if ( FAILED(hr) ) throw hr;
```

And as with object nodes, the interface node might or might not already exist in the Catalog. If it does exist, no action is taken. Add2() merely returns with a successful completion result code. If the node does not exist, Add2() executes logic very similar to what you saw when adding a new object node.

As previously mentioned, Add2() is representative of the other SOAPCatMan methods. The myriad of helper functions serves to make the code a bit more readable and to encapsulate relatively short, cohesive blocks of XML DOM–oriented functionality that is reused in many places. For example, if you want to know if a given CLSID is registered, which is the purpose of ISoapCatalog::IsRegisteredObject(), all you need to do is call FindCLSID():

```
// (This code from IsRegisteredObject())
// First, open the catalog
CComPtr<IXMLDOMDocument> spCatalog;
hr = OpenCatFile(&spCatalog);
if ( FAILED(hr) ) throw hr;

// Then, see if any elements exist with the given CLSID
CComQIPtr<IXMLDOMNode> spObjNode;
hr = FindCLSID(bstrCLSID,spCatalog,&spObjNode); // S_OK or
                                                // S_FALSE
if ( FAILED(hr) ) throw hr;
```

The last piece of information you should know is whether the Catalog file's location is persisted in the Registry under this Registry key:

```
HKLM/
    Software/
        MCP/
            SOAP/
                CatalogFile
```

The file's path is stored as the default string of the CatalogFile key. The Catalog Manager locates the file's path value when it executes FinalConstruct(), as you see in Listing 10.21.

LISTING 10.21   ISOAPCatalog::FinalConstruct() Implementation

```
HRESULT FinalConstruct()
{
    // Manage multithreaded access
    m_cs.Unlock();

    HRESULT hr = S_OK;
    try {
        // Locate catalog file
        CRegKey rkRoot;
        long lRes = rkRoot.Open(HKEY_LOCAL_MACHINE,
```

continues

LISTING 10.21 Continued

```
                                _T("Software\\MCP\\SOAP"));
        if ( lRes != ERROR_SUCCESS ) throw
                        ➥HRESULT_FROM_WIN32(lRes);

        CRegKey rkFile;
        lRes = rkFile.Open(rkRoot,_T("CatalogFile"));
        if ( lRes != ERROR_SUCCESS ) throw
                        ➥HRESULT_FROM_WIN32(lRes);

        TCHAR szFile[_MAX_PATH+1] = {0};
        DWORD dwBytesRead = _MAX_PATH;
        lRes = rkFile.QueryValue(szFile,NULL,&dwBytesRead);
        if ( lRes != ERROR_SUCCESS ) throw
                        ➥HRESULT_FROM_WIN32(lRes);

        // Persist the location
        _tcscpy(m_strCatFile,szFile);
    } // try
    catch(HRESULT hrErr) {
        // Some COM error
        hr = hrErr;
        ATLTRACE("SOAPCat: error loading catalog file,
                ➥%#08x\n",hr);
    } // catch
    catch(...){
        // Some error
        hr = E_UNEXPECTED;
        ATLTRACE("SOAPCat: unspecified error loading
                ➥catalog file, %#08x\n",hr);
    } // catch

    // Manage multithreaded access
    m_cs.Unlock();

    return hr;
}
```

The first thing to do is lock the object's critical section to prevent multithreaded access in the rare occurrence of simultaneous object creation:

```
// Manage multithreaded access
m_cs.Lock();
```

Then the base Registry key is opened for reading:

```
// Locate catalog file
CRegKey rkRoot;
long lRes = rkRoot.Open(HKEY_LOCAL_MACHINE,
                        _T("Software\\MCP\\SOAP"));
if ( lRes != ERROR_SUCCESS ) throw HRESULT_FROM_WIN32(lRes);
```

Assuming this was successful, the Catalog key is opened:

```
CRegKey rkFile;
lRes = rkFile.Open(rkRoot,_T("CatalogFile"));
if ( lRes != ERROR_SUCCESS ) throw HRESULT_FROM_WIN32(lRes);
```

Finally, the key's default string is read and stored as the Catalog's file path:

```
TCHAR szFile[_MAX_PATH+1] = {0};
DWORD dwBytesRead = _MAX_PATH;
lRes = rkFile.QueryValue(szFile,NULL,&dwBytesRead);
if ( lRes != ERROR_SUCCESS ) throw HRESULT_FROM_WIN32(lRes);

// Persist the location
_tcscpy(m_strCatFile,szFile);
```

The SOAP Catalog is accessed by much of the architecture and is a key piece of the language binding. Another key piece uses the Catalog to locate the type library and extract the type information. This is the TLBEncoder object, which is discussed next.

The Type Library Encoder

The encoder object's singular purpose is to access the type library and extract type information pertinent to the given interface/method pair. The tokenized type information stored in the type library is read to create a more concise byte stream that contains certain key pieces of type information. This byte stream also serves as a type interface (of sorts) to the SOAP serialization logic, such that, in the future, other forms of type data might be similarly encoded (such as an interface schema).

Code that reads type libraries is not pretty. A type library contains a lot of information, and most of it is recorded in various structures that contain pointers to other structures. Because the code is so grungy, the overall design of the encoder object differs from the design of the Catalog object. The Catalog object uses inline method code. (Granted, the XMLDOM work is also relatively grungy and could probably benefit from the same architecture.) The encoder object, on the other hand, delegates the work (in the C++ sense) to an aggregated encoder C++ object, CEncoder. Perhaps this is made clearer by Figure 10.4.

10

IMPLEMENTING
SOAP

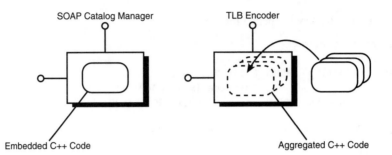

SOAP Catalog Manager

TLB Encoder

Embedded C++ Code

Aggregated C++ Code

FIGURE 10.4

The Catalog Manager's architecture versus the encoder's architecture.

What Figure 10.4 shows you is that the encoder's COM functionality is split from its encoding functionality. Let's look at the encoder's basic COM functionality first.

The Encoder's COM Functionality

The encoder has three basic capabilities, depending upon the information you have and what you require. Its interface definition file is shown in Listing 10.22.

LISTING 10.22   `ISOAPCatalog::FinalConstruct()` Implementation

```
// TLBEncoder.idl : IDL source for TLBEncoder.dll
//
// Kenn Scribner
//
// Understanding SOAP
// March, 2000
//

// This file will be processed by the MIDL tool to
// produce the type library (TLBEncoder.tlb) and marshalling
// code.

// Tokens
cpp_quote("#define TLB_NUL    0x00000000")
cpp_quote("#define TLB_SIG1   0x6E6E654B")
cpp_quote("#define TLB_SIG2   0x6B72614D")
cpp_quote("#define TLB_VMAJ   0x00000001")
cpp_quote("#define TLB_VMIN   0x00000000")
cpp_quote("#define TLB_ITF    0x00000001")
cpp_quote("#define TLB_MTD    0x00000002")
cpp_quote("#define TLB_IN     0x00000004")
cpp_quote("#define TLB_OUT    0x00000008")
cpp_quote("#define TLB_IOUT   0x00000010")
```

```
cpp_quote("#define TLB_I2     0x00000012")
cpp_quote("#define TLB_I4     0x00000014")
cpp_quote("#define TLB_UI2    0x00000018")
cpp_quote("#define TLB_UI4    0x00000020")
cpp_quote("#define TLB_INT    0x00000022")
cpp_quote("#define TLB_UINT   0x00000024")
cpp_quote("#define TLB_FLT    0x00000028")
cpp_quote("#define TLB_DBL    0x00000030")
cpp_quote("#define TLB_BSTR   0x00000032")
cpp_quote("#define TLB_BOOL   0x00000034")
cpp_quote("#define TLB_HRESULT 0x00000038")
cpp_quote("#define TLB_VOID   0x00000040")
cpp_quote("#define TLB_PTR    0x00000042")
cpp_quote("#define TLB_EOF    0x000000FF")

import "oaidl.idl";
import "ocidl.idl";
    [
        object,
        uuid(3E0DFF2D-E2E1-11D3-87C0-90610CC1FFFF),

        helpstring("IEncodeTLB Interface"),
        pointer_default(unique)
    ]
    interface IEncodeTLB : IUnknown
    {
        [helpstring("Encodes a method based upon it's vtable
➥offset"), local] HRESULT EncodeMethod([in] ITypeLib*
➥lpItlb, [in] BSTR bstrCLSID, [in] BSTR bstrIID, [in]
➥long iMethod, [out] long* piStackSize, [out]
➥IStream* pRemStream);
        [helpstring("Encodes a method based upon it's
➥name"), local] HRESULT EncodeMethod2([in] ITypeLib*
➥lpItlb, [in] BSTR bstrCLSID, [in] BSTR bstrIID, [in]
➥BSTR bstrMethodName, [out] long* piMethodNum, [out]
➥long* piStackSize,  [out] IStream* pRemStream);
        [helpstring("Determines if an interface is encodable
➥(S_FALSE if not)"), local] HRESULT
➥IsEncodableInterface([in] ITypeLib* lpItlb, [in]
➥BSTR bstrCLSID, [in] BSTR bstrIID);
    };

[
    uuid(3E0DFF21-E2E1-11D3-87C0-90610CC1FFFF),
    version(1.0),
```

continues

10

LISTING 10.22   Continued

```
        helpstring("TLBEncoder 1.0 Type Library")
]
library TLBENCODERLib
{
    importlib("stdole32.tlb");
    importlib("stdole2.tlb");

    [
        uuid(3E0DFF2E-E2E1-11D3-87C0-90610CC1FFFF),
        helpstring("TLBEncoder Class")
    ]
    coclass TLBEncoder
    {
        [default] interface IEncodeTLB;
    };
};
```

IEncodeTLB exposes three methods, EncodeMethod(), EncodeMethod2(), and
IsEncodableInterface(). The two method encoding functions are very similar in that they
are the encoder functions that produce the type byte stream. The difference between them is
EncodeMethod() takes the method's vtable offset, whereas EncodeMethod2() takes the method
name (as a string) and determines the vtable offset, then looks up the method type information.
IsEncodableInterface() examines the given interface to see if it is a candidate for SOAP
encoding.

> **NOTE**
>
> COM is many things, butcertainly one important aspect regarding COM is its object
> model, which mirrors the C++ object model. The C++ object model is based upon *vir-
> tual function pointer tables*, or *vtables* for short. A requirement the COM specifica-
> tion levies upon all COM-producing languages is that the language must be compiled
> into, or accessed by, a vtable binary format. If you are unfamiliar with vtables and
> how COM uses them, a good reference is Don Box's excellent book *Essential COM*
> from Addison-Wesley (ISBN 0-201-63446-5). You will also see a great deal more about
> vtables, starting with the upcoming "SOAP from the Client—The SOAP Object
> Surrogate" section.

In reality, each of the three COM methods delegates the hard work to the CEncoder C++
object. EncodeMethod() is as representative as any, as shown in Listing 10.23.

LISTING 10.23   `IEncodeTLB::EncodeMethod()` Implementation

```
STDMETHODIMP CEncoder::EncodeMethod(ITypeLib *lpItlb, BSTR
➥bstrCLSID, BSTR bstrIID, long iMethod, long*
➥piStackSize, IStream *pRemStream)
{
    // Multithread lock
    m_cs.Lock();

    HRESULT hr = S_OK;
    try {
        // Check the pointers...
        if ((lpItlb == NULL) || (piStackSize == NULL))
            ➥throw E_POINTER;

        // Assume errors
        *piStackSize = 0;

        // Create a stream object on a memory block.
        LPSTREAM lpStream = NULL;
        HGLOBAL hGlobal = GlobalAlloc(GMEM_MOVEABLE |
                                      GMEM_SHARE,0);
        if ( hGlobal != NULL ) {
            hr = CreateStreamOnHGlobal(hGlobal,TRUE,
                                       &lpStream);
            if ( FAILED(hr) ) {
                ATLTRACE("CreateStreamOnHGlobal failed.\n");
                GlobalFree(hGlobal);
                throw hr;
            } // if
        } // if
        else {
            ATLTRACE("Failed to allocate memory for
                      ➥stream.\n");
            throw hr;
        } // if

        // Extract the CLSID/IID
        CLSID clsid;
        hr = CLSIDFromString(bstrCLSID,&clsid);
        if ( FAILED(hr) ) {
            ATLTRACE("CLSID extraction failed.\n");
            lpStream->Release();
            GlobalFree(hGlobal);
            throw hr;
        } // if
```

10

IMPLEMENTING SOAP

continues

LISTING 10.23   Continued

```
IID iid;
hr = IIDFromString(bstrIID,&iid);
if ( FAILED(hr)  ) {
    ATLTRACE("IID extraction failed.\n");
    lpStream->Release();
    GlobalFree(hGlobal);
    throw hr;
} // if

// Encode the method
long iStackSize = -1;
hr = m_CEncoder.EncodeMethod(lpItlb,clsid,iid,
                    iMethod,&iStackSize,lpStream);
if ( FAILED(hr) ) {
    ATLTRACE("Method encoding failed.\n");
    lpStream->Release();
    GlobalFree(hGlobal);
    throw hr;
} // if

// Move seek pointer to beginning of stream
LARGE_INTEGER liBeg = {0};
hr = lpStream->Seek(liBeg,STREAM_SEEK_SET,NULL);
if ( FAILED(hr) ) {
    ATLTRACE("IStream::Seek to beginning
                ➥failed.\n");
    lpStream->Release();
    GlobalFree(hGlobal);
    throw hr;
} // if

// Return the stream contents
if ((pRemStream != NULL) && (hr == S_OK)) {
    // Copy the stream contents to the destination
    // stream...
    ULARGE_INTEGER liCpy = {0xFFFFFFFF,0};
    hr = lpStream->CopyTo(pRemStream,liCpy,
                    NULL,NULL);
    if ( FAILED(hr) ) {
        ATLTRACE("IStream::CopyTo failed.\n");
        lpStream->Release();
        GlobalFree(hGlobal);
        throw hr;
    } // if
```

```
        } // if

        // Free the stream and memory
        lpStream->Release();
        GlobalFree(hGlobal);

        // Return the stack size for this method
        if ( piStackSize != NULL ) {
            *piStackSize = iStackSize;
        } // if
    } // try
    catch(HRESULT hrErr) {
        // Some COM error...
        hr = hrErr;
    } // catch
    catch(...) {
        // Some error
        hr = E_UNEXPECTED;
    } // catch

    m_cs.Unlock();

    returnhr;
}
```

As with the SOAP Catalog Manager, the first thing to do is manage potential multithreaded access by locking up a critical section:

```
// Multithread lock
m_cs.Lock();
```

After checking for NULL return pointers and clearing the return address's data for the stack size, EncodeMethod() creates an instance of an IStream object. The object will be used to contain the (arbitrary length) byte stream. The nice thing about using IStream is that it grows as you add information, unlike a conventional memory buffer wherein *you* manage the growth aspects. The stream is created in heap memory:

```
// Create a stream object on a memory block.
LPSTREAM lpStream = NULL;
HGLOBAL hGlobal = GlobalAlloc(GMEM_MOVEABLE|GMEM_SHARE,0);
if ( hGlobal != NULL ) {
    hr = CreateStreamOnHGlobal(hGlobal,TRUE, &lpStream);
    if ( FAILED(hr) ) {
        ATLTRACE("CreateStreamOnHGlobal failed.\n");
        GlobalFree(hGlobal);
        throw hr;
```

10

IMPLEMENTING SOAP

```
    } // if
} // if
else {
    ATLTRACE("Failed to allocate memory for stream.\n");
    throw hr;
} // if
```

Then you must pull the CLSID and IID from the strings used to pass them into the method:

```
// Extract the CLSID/IID
CLSID clsid;
hr = CLSIDFromString(bstrCLSID,&clsid);
if ( FAILED(hr) ) {
    ATLTRACE("CLSID extraction failed.\n");
    lpStream->Release();
    GlobalFree(hGlobal);
    throw hr;
} // if

IID iid;
hr = IIDFromString(bstrIID,&iid);
if ( FAILED(hr) ) {
    ATLTRACE("IID extraction failed.\n");
    lpStream->Release();
    GlobalFree(hGlobal);
    throw hr;
} // if
```

At this time you have a stream and a CLSID and IID, which is enough information to pass to the (delegated) encoder C++ object:

```
// Encode the method
long iStackSize = -1;
hr = m_CEncoder.EncodeMethod(lpItlb,clsid,iid,
                              iMethod,&iStackSize,lpStream);
if ( FAILED(hr) ) {
    ATLTRACE("Method encoding failed.\n");
    lpStream->Release();
    GlobalFree(hGlobal);
    throw hr;
} // if
```

Assuming the encoding was successful, you then move the stream's seek pointer to the beginning to enable eventual persistence:

```
// Move seek pointer to beginning of stream
LARGE_INTEGER liBeg = {0};
hr = lpStream->Seek(liBeg,STREAM_SEEK_SET,NULL);
```

```
if ( FAILED(hr) ) {
    ATLTRACE("IStream::Seek to beginning failed.\n");
    lpStream->Release();
    GlobalFree(hGlobal);
    throw hr;
} // if
```

And, finally, you return the stream to the caller. Presumably, the caller will determine the persistence requirements.

```
// Return the stream contents
if ((pRemStream != NULL) && (hr == S_OK)) {
    // Copy the stream contents to the destination
    // stream...
    ULARGE_INTEGER liCpy = {0xFFFFFFFF,0};
    hr = lpStream->CopyTo(pRemStream,liCpy,NULL,NULL);
    if ( FAILED(hr) ) {
        ATLTRACE("IStream::CopyTo failed.\n");
        lpStream->Release();
        GlobalFree(hGlobal);
        throw hr;
    } // if
} // if
```

Of course, CEncoder manages the lion's share of the tricky work, which is the topic of the next section.

Encoding Type Libraries

The code necessary to read the type information is encapsulated in CEncoder (found in the TLBEncoderObj.h/cpp files). CEncoder has several methods, most of them protected, that either break the type information apart or spit the relevant token(s) to the type information stream that will later be used by the serialization code.

Client-side encoding typically requires the EncodeMethod(), whereas the remote server will probably find EncodeMethod2() more useful. The difference is that, when encoding the client object's method invocation, you know the vtable offset and can calculate the method number:

```
method number = vtable offset / sizeof(void*);
```

Given the method number, you can move directly to that method's type information and begin encoding.

The remote server has a different problem. The method comes in as an XML document, which means the method's name is available instead of the actual vtable offset. In this case, the encoder loops through the set of interface method names, comparing each to the method name that came over the wire. After the name is found, the method number is simply the loop counter's value, and encoding proceeds as it does for the client.

10

IMPLEMENTING SOAP

A detailed description of type libraries and how they are accessed is well beyond the space constraints of an already lengthy chapter. The EncodeMethod() method is shown in Listing 10.24, however, and each subsequent helper method will also be shown in listing form.

LISTING 10.24   CTLBEncoder::EncodeMethod() Implementation

```
HRESULT CTLBEncoder::EncodeMethod(ITypeLib *lpTypeLib,
➥const CLSID& clsid, const IID& iid, DWORD dwMethod,
➥long* piStackSize, IStream* lpStream)
{
    // Check the pointers
    if ((lpTypeLib == NULL) ||
        (piStackSize == NULL) ||
        (lpStream == NULL)) {
        // NULL pointers
        return E_POINTER;
    } // if

    HRESULT hr = S_OK;
    try {
        // Save values.
        m_spITypeLib = lpTypeLib; // will AddRef()
        m_clsid = clsid;
        m_iid = iid;
        m_dwMethod = dwMethod;
        m_iStackSize = 4; // account for implicit "this"
                          // pointer on stack
        m_pIStream = lpStream;

        // Lock the stream
        m_pIStream->AddRef();

        // Encode the method
        hr = ShredTLB();
        if ( FAILED(hr) ) throw hr;

        // Return the stack size
        *piStackSize = m_iStackSize;

        // Rewind the stream
        STATSTG statstg;
        hr = m_pIStream->Stat(&statstg,STATFLAG_NONAME);
         if ( FAILED(hr) ) throw hr;

         // Adjust stream pointer
         LARGE_INTEGER li = {0};
```

```
        hr = m_pIStream->Seek(li,STREAM_SEEK_SET,NULL);
        if ( FAILED(hr) ) throw hr;

        // Clear the stream if the interface didn't encode
        // properly.
        if ( hr != S_OK ) {
            // Clear the stream...ignore the HRESULT...
            ULARGE_INTEGER uli = {0};
            m_pIStream->SetSize(uli);
        } // else
    } // try
    catch(HRESULT hrErr) {
        // Some COM error...
        hr = hrErr;
    } // catch
    catch(...) {
        // Some error...
        hr = E_UNEXPECTED;
    } // catch

    // Release the type library
    m_spITypeLib = NULL;

    // Unlock the stream
    if ( m_pIStream != NULL ) m_pIStream->Release();

    return hr;
}
```

After some basic pointer checking and class attribute assignments, EncodeMethod() calls the first level helper function ShredTLB():

```
// Encode the method
hr = ShredTLB();
if ( FAILED(hr) ) throw hr;
```

Assuming ShredTLB() was successful, the stack size is returned, and the stream seek pointer is set to the beginning of the stream. The stack size is the total size of the method's call stack, which will be at least 4 bytes (storage for the implicit this pointer). The serializer will use this information to clean the call stack as required by COM rules. The stream represents the tokenized type information, which will be in this form:

```
TLB_SIG1 (signature bytes)
TLB_SIG2
TLB_VMAJ
TLB_VMIN
```

```
offset to method args (4 bytes)
TLB_ITF
Interface name string
TLB_NUL
TLB_MTD
Method Ordinal (1 byte)
Number of arguments (1 byte)
Method return value type (1 byte)
Method name string
TLB_NUL

(method arguments, 0-n)
TLB_IN (if necesary)
TLB_OUT (if necessary)
TLB_IOUT (if necessary)
Argument type (1 byte)
Argument name string
TLB_NUL

(EOF, after last argument)
TLB_EOF
```

The tokens themselves are recorded in the TLBEncoder.idl file, which is handy because any object that uses the encoder will already include this file to obtain the header information for IEncodeTLB.

ShredTLB()is shown in Listing 10.25. Its main purpose is to locate the storage for the SOAP'ed interface in preparation for pulling the individual method's information.

LISTING 10.25   CTLBEncoder::ShredTLB() Implementation

```
HRESULT CTLBEncoder::ShredTLB()
{
    CComPtr<ITypeInfo> pIti;
    TYPEATTR* pattr = NULL;
    HRESULT hr = S_OK;
    try {
        // Emit signature bytes
        hr = EmitSignature();
        if ( FAILED(hr) ) throw hr;

        // Save seek pointer, as the offset to the
        // method args must be inserted
        LARGE_INTEGER liNull = {0};
        ULARGE_INTEGER uliPtr = {0};
        ULARGE_INTEGER uliArgs = {0};
        hr = m_pIStream->Seek(liNull,STREAM_SEEK_CUR,
```

```
                    &uliPtr);
if ( FAILED(hr) ) throw hr;

// Now emit placholder bytes that will eventually
// represent the offset into the stream for the
// method args.  Later this will be used as a
// pointer offset into the stream to more easily
// extract the argument information when
// serializing.
hr = EmitArgPointer(0);
if ( FAILED(hr) ) throw hr;

BOOL bItfShredded = FALSE;
UINT uiInfos = m_spITypeLib->GetTypeInfoCount();
for (UINT i = 0 ; i < uiInfos ; i++) {
    hr = m_spITypeLib->GetTypeInfo(i,&pIti);
    if ( FAILED(hr) ) throw hr;

    hr = pIti->GetTypeAttr(&pattr);
    if ( FAILED(hr) ) throw hr;

    switch ( pattr->typekind ) {
        case TKIND_DISPATCH:
        case TKIND_INTERFACE:
            // The interface of interest?
            if ( pattr->guid == m_iid ) {
                if ( bRequiresAdjustment ) {
                    // Next pull the base interface. If the
                    // base interface it IDispatch, the type
                    // library will have already accounted for
                    // the IUnknown methods in the vtable. If
                    // the base interface is IUnknown, the type
                    // library has no such adjustment and you'll
                    // need to deduct three methods from the
                    // overall method count in order to select
                    // the type information for the proper
                    // method.
                    HREFTYPE href = NULL;
                    hr = pIti->GetRefTypeOfImplType(i-1,&href);
                    if ( FAILED(hr) ) throw hr;

                    CComPtr<ITypeInfo> pItiImpl;
                    hr = pIti->GetRefTypeInfo(href,&pItiImpl);
                    if ( FAILED(hr) )  throw hr;
```

continues

10

LISTING 10.25   Continued

```
CComBSTR bstrName;
hr = pItiImpl->GetDocumentation(MEMBERID_NIL,
                    &bstrName,NULL,NULL,NULL);
if ( FAILED(hr) ) throw hr;

// Now check the base...
if ( !_wcsicmp(bstrName,L"IUnknown") ) {
    // IUnknown-based...deduct three methods
    // from the total number of available
    // methods and then search for the proper
    // method type information.
    m_dwMethod -= 3;
} // if
if ( FAILED(hr) )  throw hr;
} // if

// Pull the interface information
hr = ShredInterface(pIti,&uliArgs);
if ( FAILED(hr) ) throw hr;

// See if the interface encoded
// properly
if ( hr == S_OK ) {
    // It did...
    bItfShredded = TRUE;

    // Store the offset to the
    // method arguments
    LARGE_INTEGER liPtr =
                {uliPtr.LowPart,0};
    hr = m_pIStream->Seek(liPtr,
            STREAM_SEEK_SET,NULL);
    if ( FAILED(hr) ) throw hr;

    hr = EmitArgPointer(
         ➥uliArgs.LowPart);
    if ( FAILED(hr) ) throw hr;
    } // if
} // if
break;

default:
// Ignore these...
```

```
                break;
          } // switch

          // Release the attribute
          pIti->ReleaseTypeAttr(pattr);
          pattr = NULL;

          // Release the ITypeInfo
          pIti.Release();

          // Done?
          if ( bItfShredded ) {
              // Got it...
              break;
          } // if
      } // for

      // If the interface wasn't encoded properly (was it
      // in the type library?),  return S_FALSE.
      if ( !bItfShredded ) {
          hr = S_FALSE;
      } // if
  } // try
  catch(HRESULT hrErr) {
      // Some COM error...
      hr = hrErr;
  } // catch
  catch(...) {
      // Some error...
      hr = E_UNEXPECTED;
  } // catch

  // Check to see if we need to release things...
  if ( pattr != NULL ) {
      // Release the attribute...
      pIti->ReleaseTypeAttr(pattr) ;
      pattr = NULL;
  } // if

  // Release the ITypeInfo...
  pIti.Release();

  return hr;
}
```

`ShredTLB()` begins by placing the signature bytes and version information in the output byte stream:

```
// Emit signature bytes
hr = EmitSignature();
if ( FAILED(hr) ) throw hr;
```

The meat of `EmitSignature()` looks like this:

```
// Write a DWORD
DWORD term = (DWORD)TLB_SIG1;
hr = m_pIStream->Write(&term,4,NULL);  // 4 bytes
if ( FAILED(hr) ) throw hr;

term = (DWORD)TLB_SIG2;
hr = m_pIStream->Write(&term,4,NULL); // 4 bytes
if ( FAILED(hr) ) throw hr;

hr = EmitToken(TLB_VMAJ);
if ( FAILED(hr) ) throw hr;
hr = EmitToken(TLB_VMIN);
if ( FAILED(hr) ) throw hr;
```

The code to emit a token, from `EmitToken()`, is simply

```
// Write a byte
BYTE term = (BYTE)iToken;
hr = m_pIStream->Write(&term,1,NULL);
if ( FAILED(hr) ) throw hr;
```

In fact, all the "emit" methods simply execute an `IStream::write()` with the appropriate buffer and buffer size information.

The next data stored in the stream will be a four-byte offset to the method argument information. This is done for efficiency. At times you want the interface and method name information, and at other times you do not. For those times you do not, such as at runtime when you are working directly with the method arguments and the call stack, you can skip the intervening ancillary information and get right to the method arguments. This should save some processing time.

When creating the data stream, however, the precise offset to the method arguments is not known. That's because the interface and method names are variable length strings (which will be zero-terminated in the byte stream). Therefore, you must temporarily save the stream's seek pointer for later modification. This is accomplished by this code (from Listing 10.25):

```
// Save seek pointer, as the offset to the
// method args must be inserted
LARGE_INTEGER liNull = {0};
ULARGE_INTEGER uliPtr = {0};
```

```
ULARGE_INTEGER uliArgs = {0};
hr = m_pIStream->Seek(liNull,STREAM_SEEK_CUR,&uliPtr);
if ( FAILED(hr) ) throw hr;
```

Then, you should emit four dummy bytes that are to be overwritten when you do know the method argument's precise location in the byte stream:

```
// Now emit placholder bytes that will eventually
// represent the offset into the stream for the
// method args.  Later this will be used as a
// pointer offset into the stream to more easily
// extract the argument information when
// serializing.
hr = EmitArgPointer(0);
if ( FAILED(hr) ) throw hr;
```

Next comes the actual type library work. The first action you must take is to examine the type library for the interface in question. The search key you have is the method's unique identifier, known as an *Interface Identifier* or *IID*. The type library maintains the IIDs for all the interfaces that its related COM object exports, and these are stored in a type attribute structure, TYPEATTR. The basic search algorithm is to simply loop through all the TYPEATTR structures contained in the type library and examine each for the given IID value. If it's found, you burrow deeper into the type library. If the IID isn't found in the type library, you return an error. This pseudocode further describes the process:

```
for each TYPEATTR
    retrieve current TYPEATTR
    if TYPEATTR represents an interface
        check the interface IID against the desired IID
        if found, encode the interface, then break loop
    end if
next TYPEATTR
```

There is one interesting fact about how type libraries are created that you should know. The type library isn't designed to give you true vtable information. Put another way, the type library is created by MIDL in different ways depending upon the base interface for each interface stored in the table. If your interface is a dual interface (one based upon IDispatch), then the method's offset, as reported by the type library, is the same as that you would find in the original vtable. On the other hand, if your interface was custom (based upon IUnknown directly), then you need to add the three IUnknown methods to your method's vtable offset to account for IUnknown. The type library will begin your method offsets from 0 (zero), rather than from 3, which will cause you to invoke methods at the incorrect vtable entry when you later delegate the COM method call. The code you find in ShredTLB() accounts for this base interface dependency and makes the adjustment as required.

10

IMPLEMENTING
SOAP

Assuming the interface is found, it is encoded using `ShredInterface()`, which you see in Listing 10.26.

LISTING 10.26 CTLBEncoder::ShredInterface() Implementation

```
HRESULT CTLBEncoder::ShredInterface(ITypeInfo* pIti,
➥ULARGE_INTEGER* puliArgs)
{
    TYPEATTR* pattr = NULL;
    HRESULT hr = S_OK;
    try {
        // Indicate a new interface stream
        hr = EmitToken(TLB_ITF);
        if ( FAILED(hr) ) throw hr;

        // Pull the interface's attributes
        hr = pIti->GetTypeAttr(&pattr);
        if ( FAILED(hr) ) throw hr;

        // Pull interface name
        CComBSTR bstrName;
        hr = pIti->GetDocumentation(MEMBERID_NIL,&bstrName,
                                    NULL,NULL,NULL);
        if ( FAILED(hr) ) throw hr;

        // Emit interface name
        hr = EmitBSTR(bstrName);
        if ( FAILED(hr) ) throw hr;

        // Emit end-of-string
        hr = EmitToken(TLB_NUL);
        if ( FAILED(hr) ) throw hr;

        // Shred the interface methods
        hr = ShredMethod(pIti,pattr,puliArgs);
    } // try
    catch(HRESULT hrErr) {
        // Some COM error...
        hr = hrErr;
    } // catch
    catch(...) {
        // Some error...
        hr = E_UNEXPECTED;
    } // catch
```

```
    // Release the type attributes
    if ( pattr != NULL ) {
        pIti->ReleaseTypeAttr(pattr);
    } // if

    return hr;
}
```

Because the interface is recorded in the type library, you first emit a token indicating the beginning of the interface type stream:

```
// Indicate a new interface stream
hr = EmitToken(TLB_ITF);
if ( FAILED(hr) ) throw hr;
```

Then you access the interface's TYPEATTR structure to obtain the interface's name using ITypeInfo::GetDocumentation():

```
// Pull the interface's attributes
hr = pIti->GetTypeAttr(&pattr);
if ( FAILED(hr) ) throw hr;

// Pull interface name
CComBSTR bstrName;
hr = pIti->GetDocumentation(MEMBERID_NIL,&bstrName,NULL,NULL,NULL);
if ( FAILED(hr) ) throw hr;
```

Assuming the name is retrieved, you emit that to the byte stream along with a NULL terminator token:

```
// Emit interface name
hr = EmitBSTR(bstrName);
if ( FAILED(hr) ) throw hr;

// Emit end-of-string
hr = EmitToken(TLB_NUL);
if ( FAILED(hr) ) throw hr;
```

Finally, you extract the method's type information by using ShredMethod():

```
// Shred the interface methods
hr = ShredMethod(pIti,pattr,puliArgs);
```

ShredMethod() is shown in Listing 10.27. The method level is the lowest you will need to go into the type library, as it contains references to all the method arguments as well as to the return type of the method itself.

LISTING 10.27 CTLBEncoder::ShredMethod() Implementation

```
#define _MAX_NAMES    64 // max parameters to a function

...
HRESULT CTLBEncoder::ShredMethod(ITypeInfo* pIti, TYPEATTR*
►pattr, ULARGE_INTEGER* puliArgs)
{
    HRESULT hr = S_OK;
    try {
        for (UINT i = 0; i < pattr->cFuncs; i++) {
            if ( i == m_dwMethod ) {
                // Found it!
                hr = EmitMethod(pIti,pattr,puliArgs);
                if ( FAILED(hr) ) throw hr;
                break;
            } // if
        } // for
    } // try
    catch(HRESULT hrErr) {
        // Some COM error...
        hr = hrErr;
    } // catch
    catch(...) {
        // Some error...
        hr = E_UNEXPECTED;
    } // catch

    return hr;
}
```

As with the interface, you loop through all the available methods and jump out of the loop when you find the correct one. Unlike the interface encoding, however, the method loop simply checks that the method exists (or at least that there is a method in the type library with that method number). The following pseudocode describes this process:

```
for each method in the given TYPEATTR
    if the requested method number is the same as an existing one
        emit the method information, then break loop
    end if
next method in TYPEATTR
```

The EmitMethod() helper function actually extracts the type data and emits it to the stream. You can see this in Listing 10.28.

LISTING 10.28   CTLBEncoder::EmitMethod() Implementation

```
HRESULT CTLBEncoder::EmitMethod(ITypeInfo* pIti, TYPEATTR*
➥pattr, ULARGE_INTEGER* puliArgs)
{
    FUNCDESC* pFuncDesc = NULL;
    BSTR rgbstrNames[_MAX_NAMES] = {0};
    HRESULT hr = S_OK;
    try {
        // Get method's descriptive information
        hr = pIti->GetFuncDesc(m_dwMethod,&pFuncDesc);
        if ( FAILED(hr) ) throw hr;

        // Get argument names...do this first so we can record
        // how many arguments we're dealing with
        UINT cNames = 0;
        hr = pIti->GetNames(pFuncDesc->memid,rgbstrNames,
                            _MAX_NAMES,&cNames);
        if ( FAILED(hr) ) throw hr;

        // fix for 'rhs' problem (well-known type library
        // bug...)
        if ((int)cNames < pFuncDesc->cParams + 1) {
            rgbstrNames[cNames] =
                            ::SysAllocString(OLESTR("rhs"));
            ++cNames;
        } // if

        // Emit method token
        hr = EmitToken(TLB_MTD);
        if ( FAILED(hr) ) throw hr;

        // Emit method number
        hr = EmitToken((UINT)m_dwMethod);
        if ( FAILED(hr) ) throw hr;

        // Emit number of arguments
        hr = EmitToken(pFuncDesc->cParams);
        if ( FAILED(hr) ) throw hr;

        // Get return value type
        hr = EmitType(&pFuncDesc->elemdescFunc.tdesc,FALSE);
        if ( FAILED(hr) ) throw hr;

        // Pull method name and emit
        CComBSTR bstrName;
```

continues

LISTING 10.28   Continued

```
hr = pIti->GetDocumentation(pFuncDesc->memid,
                        &bstrName,NULL,NULL,NULL);
if ( FAILED(hr) ) throw hr;
hr = EmitBSTR(bstrName);
if ( FAILED(hr) ) throw hr;
hr = EmitToken(TLB_NUL);
if ( FAILED(hr) ) throw hr;

// Save seek pointer, as the offset to the
// method args must be inserted
LARGE_INTEGER liNull = {0};
hr = m_pIStream->Seek(liNull,STREAM_SEEK_CUR,
                        puliArgs);
if ( FAILED(hr) ) throw hr;

// Pull arguments: attr type name
for (int i = 0; i < pFuncDesc->cParams; i++) {
    // Look for [in] attr
    BOOL bIn = FALSE;
    if (pFuncDesc->lprgelemdescParam[i].idldesc.
                ➥wIDLFlags & IDLFLAG_FIN) {
        bIn = TRUE;
    } // if

    // Look for [out] attr
    BOOL bOut = FALSE;
    if (pFuncDesc->lprgelemdescParam[i].idldesc.
                ➥wIDLFlags & IDLFLAG_FOUT) {
        bOut = TRUE;
    } // if

    // Now see which attributes were present
    if ( bIn && bOut ) {
        // [in,out]
        hr = EmitToken(TLB_IOUT);
        if ( FAILED(hr) ) throw hr;
    } // if
    else if ( bIn ) {
        // [in] only
        hr = EmitToken(TLB_IN);
        if ( FAILED(hr) ) throw hr;
    } // else if
    else if ( bOut ) {
```

```
                        // [out] only
                        hr = EmitToken(TLB_OUT);
                        if ( FAILED(hr) ) throw hr;
                } // else if

                // Emit type
                hr = EmitType(&pFuncDesc->
                        ➥lprgelemdescParam[i].tdesc);
                if ( FAILED(hr) ) throw hr;

                // Emit arg name
                hr = EmitBSTR(rgbstrNames[i+1]);
                if ( FAILED(hr) )  throw hr;
                hr = EmitToken(TLB_NUL);
                if ( FAILED(hr) ) throw hr;
        } // for

        // Emit EOF
        hr = EmitToken(TLB_EOF);
        if ( FAILED(hr) ) throw hr;
} // try
catch(HRESULT hrErr) {
    // Some COM error...
    hr = hrErr;
} // catch
catch(...) {
    // Some error...
    hr = E_UNEXPECTED;
} // catch

// Release the function description
if ( pFuncDesc != NULL ) {
   pIti->ReleaseFuncDesc(pFuncDesc);
} // if

// Release any BSTRs
for (UINT i = 0; i < _MAX_NAMES; i++) {
    // Free the string...note SysFreeString(NULL) is OK...
    ::SysFreeString(rgbstrNames[i]);
} // if

return hr;
}
```

10

IMPLEMENTING
SOAP

A given method's type information is stored in a FUNCDESC structure, so the first thing to do is retrieve the FUNCDESC data for the particular method in question:

```
FUNCDESC* pFuncDesc = NULL;
...
// Get method's descriptive information
hr = pIti->GetFuncDesc(m_dwMethod,&pFuncDesc);
if ( FAILED(hr) ) throw hr;
```

Given the method's function description structure, you can retrieve the number and names of all the arguments:

```
BSTR rgbstrNames[_MAX_NAMES] = {0};
...
// Get argument names...do this first so we can record
// how many arguments we're dealing with
UINT cNames = 0;
hr = pIti->GetNames(pFuncDesc->memid,rgbstrNames,_MAX_NAMES,&cNames);
if ( FAILED(hr) ) throw hr;
```

Then, after adjusting the last argument name (if required), the method token and the method number are emitted:

```
// Emit method token
hr = EmitToken(TLB_MTD);
if ( FAILED(hr) ) throw hr;

// Emit method number
hr = EmitToken((UINT)m_dwMethod);
if ( FAILED(hr) ) throw hr;
```

These tokens are followed by the number of arguments, the method return type, and the method name:

```
// Emit number of arguments
hr = EmitToken(pFuncDesc->cParams);
if ( FAILED(hr) ) throw hr;

// Get return value type
hr = EmitType(&pFuncDesc->elemdescFunc.tdesc,FALSE);
if ( FAILED(hr) ) throw hr;

// Pull method name and emit
CComBSTR bstrName;
hr = pIti->GetDocumentation(pFuncDesc->memid,&bstrName,NULL,NULL,NULL);
if ( FAILED(hr) ) throw hr;
hr = EmitBSTR(bstrName);
```

```
if ( FAILED(hr) ) throw hr;
hr = EmitToken(TLB_NUL);
if ( FAILED(hr) ) throw hr;
```

The method's name is extracted in the same manner as the interface name, by using ITypeInfo->GetDocumentation(). A NULL terminator follows the name.

As you might remember, there is a four-byte offset to the method arguments at the beginning of the stream. At this point, you have the correct offset. Save the stream seek pointer at this point so you can later insert its value in the earlier portion of the stream:

```
// Save seek pointer, as the offset to the
// method args must be inserted
LARGE_INTEGER liNull = {0};
hr = m_pIStream->Seek(liNull,STREAM_SEEK_CUR,puliArgs);
if ( FAILED(hr) ) throw hr;
```

Finally, it's time to process the method arguments themselves. The number of arguments is given in the FUNCDESC structure, so it's a simple matter to set up a loop and run through the arguments from first to last:

```
// Pull arguments: attr type name
for (int i = 0; i < pFuncDesc->cParams; i++) {
    (process an argument)
}
```

The individual argument's marshalling information is stored in an IDLDESC structure, which you access through the method's FUNCDESC structure. Here, you need to determine the marshalling requirements of the argument, whether [in], [out], or [in,out]. This information affects how you serialize the argument information. This code looks for the marshalling information for the given argument:

```
BOOL bIn = FALSE;
BOOL bOut = FALSE;
...
// Look for [in] attr
BOOL bIn = FALSE;
if (pFuncDesc->lprgelemdescParam[i].idldesc.
                        ➥wIDLFlags & IDLFLAG_FIN) {
bIn = TRUE;
} // if

// Look for [out] attr
BOOL bOut = FALSE;
if (pFuncDesc->lprgelemdescParam[i].idldesc.
                        ➥wIDLFlags & IDLFLAG_FOUT) {
```

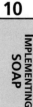

```
        bOut = TRUE;
} // if

// Now see which attributes were present
if ( bIn && bOut ) {
    // [in,out]
    hr = EmitToken(TLB_IOUT);
    if ( FAILED(hr) ) throw hr;
} // if
else if ( bIn ) {
    // [in] only
    hr = EmitToken(TLB_IN);
    if ( FAILED(hr) ) throw hr;
} // else if
else if ( bOut ) {
    // [out] only
    hr = EmitToken(TLB_OUT);
    if ( FAILED(hr) ) throw hr;
} // else if
```

Next look for the argument return value type in the associated PARAMDESC structure (also from the method's FUNCDESC structure):

```
// Emit type
hr = EmitType(&pFuncDesc->
                    ➥lprgelemdescParam[i].tdesc);
if ( FAILED(hr) ) throw hr;
```

Finally, emit the argument's name, which was recorded in a name array by ITypeInfo::GetNames():

```
// Emit arg name
hr = EmitBSTR(rgbstrNames[i+1]);
if ( FAILED(hr) ) throw hr;
hr = EmitToken(TLB_NUL);
if ( FAILED(hr) ) throw hr;
```

You might have noticed an innocent-looking method call mixed into the method type determination called EmitType(). This is actually a crucial helper function; in it, you calculate the size of the method's call stack. It is here that you also determine what data types you are willing to encode. In this case, only simple data types are handled. Arrays and structures, although fascinating, are just too complicated to implement and still publish in this book. However, you are free to modify the code in EmitType(), shown in Listing 10.29, to handle arrays and structures. It is also important to note that EmitType() is recursive. This encoder does handle the simple data types as well as pointers to those types , which it would have to do to encode [out] and [in,out] arguments.

LISTING 10.29   CTLBEncoder::EmitType() Implementation

```
HRESULT CTLBEncoder::EmitType(TYPEDESC* ptdesc, BOOL
➥bIncrementStack /*=TRUE*/, BOOL bAsPointer
➥/*=FALSE*/)
{
    HRESULT hr = S_OK;
    switch ( ptdesc->vt ) {
        case VT_I2:
            hr = EmitToken(TLB_I2);
            break;

        case VT_I4:
            hr = EmitToken(TLB_I4);
            break;

        case VT_UI2:
            hr = EmitToken(TLB_UI2);
            break;

        case VT_UI4:
            hr = EmitToken(TLB_UI4);
            break;

        case VT_INT:
            hr = EmitToken(TLB_INT);
            break;

        case VT_UINT:
            hr = EmitToken(TLB_UINT);
            break;

        case VT_R4:
            hr = EmitToken(TLB_FLT);
            break;

        case VT_R8:
            // Add the extra 4 bytes for the double data,
            // except if a pointer was called for...
            if ( bIncrementStack || !bAsPointer )
                m_iStackSize += 4;
            hr = EmitToken(TLB_DBL);
            break;
```

continues

10

IMPLEMENTING
SOAP

LISTING 10.29 Continued

```
        case VT_BSTR:
            hr = EmitToken(TLB_BSTR);
            break;

        case VT_BOOL:
            hr = EmitToken(TLB_BOOL);
            break;

        case VT_HRESULT:
            hr = EmitToken(TLB_HRESULT);
            break;

        case VT_VOID:
            hr = EmitToken(TLB_VOID);
            break;

        case VT_PTR:
            // Emit the pointer token
            hr = EmitToken(TLB_PTR);
            if ( FAILED(hr) ) throw hr;

            // Is a pointer to some type, so crack the type
            // stack already accounted for!
            hr = EmitType(ptdesc->lptdesc,FALSE,TRUE);
            if ( FAILED(hr) ) throw hr;
            break;

        default:
            return E_INVALIDARG;
    } // switch

    // Adjust the stack size
    if ( bIncrementStack ) m_iStackSize += 4;

    return hr;
}
```

Generally, to emit a type token, the argument's TYPEDESC structure is accessed and the type emitted is based upon the contents. The type is recorded as a VARIANT type. A big switch() statement manages emitting the type, based upon its VARIANT descriptor:

```
switch ( ptdesc->vt ) {
    case VT_I2:
        hr = EmitToken(TLB_I2);
```

```
        break;

    case VT_I4:
        hr = EmitToken(TLB_I4);
        break;

... (and so on for all supported types)

} // switch
```

However, this is complicated somewhat by references to argument data, so if the VARIANT descriptor is VT_PTR, the type descriptor for the referenced value is accessed and EmitType() is recursed:

```
case VT_PTR:
    // Emit the pointer token
    hr = EmitToken(TLB_PTR);
    if ( FAILED(hr) ) throw hr;

    // Is a pointer to some type, so crack the type
    // stack already accounted for!
    hr = EmitType(ptdesc->lptdesc,FALSE,TRUE);
    if ( FAILED(hr) ) throw hr;
    break;
```

In this way, all argument types are retrieved and stored in the type byte stream.

Returning to Listing 10.28, after all the argument information has been recorded in the type byte stream, a final token is emitted that signifies the end of the data:

```
// Emit EOF
hr = EmitToken(TLB_EOF);
if ( FAILED(hr) ) throw hr;
```

At this point you have extracted all the relevant type information needed to encode a method's call stack. The serialization/deserialization code will act as state machines and act upon the type information byte stream and call stack as appropriate.

From an administrative perspective, there must be an easier way to add and remove interfaces and objects from the SOAP Catalog. And, because not every conceivable interface can be encoded using this encoder, there should be an application available to test a set of interfaces to see which is encodable. If a selected interface can be encoded, the application should be able to add it to, or remove it from, the SOAP Catalog. This is the purpose of the SOAP Configuration utility, which is the topic of the next section.

10

IMPLEMENTING
SOAP

The SOAP Configuration Utility

If you are familiar with DCOM, you are probably also familiar with DCOMCnfg.exe, the DCOM configuration utility application. DCOMCnfg.exe enables you to do many things to configure a given object or system for remote object activation and use. For example, you can add or change security settings for a given object, or you can determine how the object is to be remotely activated and by whom.

For the purposes of this book, the SOAP implementation, although large and complex, is not nearly as complex as DCOM. But there still had to be a way to view the SOAP Catalog, make changes, and determine which interfaces in which objects were candidates for encoding and serialization given the data types the SOAP implementation could handle. This is the purpose of the SOAP Configuration utility, SOAPCnfg.

SOAPCnfg lets you select potential objects/interfaces from the list of objects and interfaces registered on your system. If you elect to use the interface remotely, you provide the endpoint URL and namespace qualifier. You also decide how to use the interface, as an intercepted interface or by delegation. To the system configuration, the difference amounts to choosing to modify the system Registry or not (more on this later in the chapter).

If you elect to authorize the interface to be served to remote clients, you have a drop-down list that lets you choose the default access. Actually, the control is completely ignored by the architecture at this time—it is a placeholder to remind everyone of the security considerations that should be considered but that are not part of this implementation currently. If you select an interface to be served, it is added to the SOAP Catalog; that's all that happens. The security and activation information is completely ignored at this time.

Returning to the client, you might choose to use a given interface by interception or by delegation. Both cases cause the interface to be added to the SOAP Catalog. The interception takes a further step and modifies the system Registry entry for the object (in HKCR/CLSID/{clsid}) to force COM to load the SOAP Object Surrogate, instead of the actual COM object. The COM object never loads on the local system. More details regarding object activation can be found in the upcoming section "SOAP from the Client—The SOAP Object Surrogate."

The user interface for SOAPCnfg is shown in Figure 10.5.

Some capabilities of the user interface are unavailable until you select a valid SOAP interface. (A valid interface is one encodable by this implementation.) For example, buttons to add, remove, or update the SOAP Catalog are hidden until an encodable interface is selected from the tree control. Even then, some of the buttons might be disabled depending upon other factors, such as the state and contents of the SOAP Catalog.

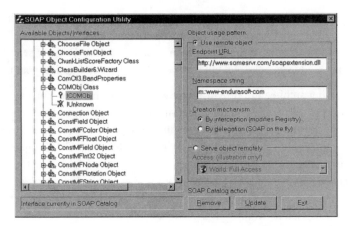

FIGURE 10.5
SOAPCnfg *user interface.*

The code for the utility isn't particularly interesting from a SOAP perspective and will be largely omitted here. There are a few items to note, however.

First, the interfaces you see listed in the tree control come from the interfaces registered in HKCR/Interface. If you have a custom interface COM object that has no proxy/stub DLL, you won't find it listed in the tree control. (It won't be registered in HKCR/Interface.) To register your custom interface in this location, you must do one of two things. Either you must create and register the proxy/stub DLL, or you must convert the custom interface into a dual interface (derived from IDispatch rather than IUnknown) and reregister the COM object after compilation.

Second, the user interface has no facility to send SOAP information from arbitrary interface IDs, though this could be added. Therefore, you must ship and register the proxy/stub DLL or dual interface object on the client for the utility to be able to configure the system. This isn't too stringent a requirement, as you'd need to do this for a DCOM-based object also.

Finally, SOAPCnfg uses both the SOAPCatMan and TLBEncoder objects, just as the serialization/deserialization code does. If you're interested in seeing how these objects can be used in situations other than serialization, be sure to examine the utility source code (especially CObjTreeCtrl in ObjTreeCtrl.cpp).

SOAP from the Client—The SOAP Object Surrogate

All that you have read to this point is in preparation for object method serialization and deserialization. In this section, you see the serialization process and code in action.

While reading this section, keep in mind the overall goal of this architecture, which is to be as unobtrusive as possible when making SOAP calls using existing COM objects. The COM object developers should not have to modify their code to use SOAP. Truly seamless distributed processing is not always possible, but it is nonetheless a good design goal to try to obtain.

This SOAP processing architecture provides you with two mechanisms you can use to instantiate your COM objects with SOAP support. The first is interception, and the second is delegation. With interception, you fool COM into creating a surrogate instead of the true COM object. With delegation, you use a special SOAP interface to create COM objects that are SOAP enabled under the covers. Interception controls the entire COM object, whereas delegation lets you manage the object on an interface-by-interface basis. Let's look at how interception is managed, and then move to delegation. As you'll see when you tackle interception, delegation is nearly tackled as well.

The Mechanics of Interception

To effectively manage interception of arbitrary COM objects, you need to do at least two things. First, you must convince COM to invoke a surrogate object in lieu of the true COM object. The surrogate object manages the true object, or, in this case, bypasses it altogether. Second, you must have the surrogate object.

The first action is accomplished by the SOAP Configuration utility when you select a COM object/interface and add it to the SOAP Catalog with the interception radio button selected. After you press the Add button, the utility modifies the Registry.

As you know, the location of a given COM object is stored in a specific Registry location. Precisely which location depends upon the object, and is determined by its executable image. If the object is an in-process server (a DLL), the DLL's file location is stored as the default key in this Registry key:

```
HKCR/
    CLSID/
        {clsid}/
            InprocServer32
```

On the other hand, if the object is an executable file (an EXE), the EXE's file location is stored in the LocalServer32 key under the object's CLSID.

If you change the file stored in either of these Registry keys, you affect the invocation of the given COM object. COM will blindly activate any file stored in these keys, whether or not the file represents the true COM object. If you place the file location of a different COM object in these keys, the different COM object will be created in lieu of the original COM object.

That is the purpose of a COM surrogate, and this is a common practice when using the Microsoft Transaction Server. However, your surrogate must understand that any COM interface could be requested, and that it is impossible to build a surrogate that could handle every conceivable COM interface a priori. The surrogate will need to handle interface queries dynamically at runtime, or have foreknowledge of the interfaces in use. MTS follows the second practice. When you code an object for use in MTS, you link in a special MTS library and provide a type library. This gives MTS an edge at runtime.

The SOAP surrogate has no such luxury. The goal of this SOAP processing architecture was to accept existing COM objects as they are. Therefore, no special library could be compiled into the SOAP-enabled objects before entering their information into the Registry. The SOAP surrogate must handle interface queries and respond appropriately.

This is precisely what the SOAP surrogate does. To understand the SOAP surrogate, you must also understand a bit more about the COM architecture.

When you try to create a COM object, COM reads the location of the COM server's file from the Registry, as you've seen. After the file is loaded into memory (and executed, if an EXE), COM requests the object's *class object*, also referred to as its *class factory*.

The class factory is responsible for creating COM co-classes, or in other words, the class factory creates instances of the object. You provide COM with the specific class factory interface you wish to use, such as `IClassFactory` or `IClassFactory2`, as well as the CLSID of the object to create. Then, you use the class factory that COM returns to you to create as many instance objects as you desire (assuming the object supports the class factory interface you requested). It's this two-step creation process the SOAP surrogate must manage.

Things are further complicated by apartments and threading issues. COM objects are classified in several ways, such as in-process servers (DLLs) or local servers (EXEs). But they are also classified by threading models. Some COM objects are completely thread-safe and can exist in multithreaded environments without a problem. Other COM objects are very thread-hostile and must have synchronized access; some are even tied to a specific Windows thread.

COM manages threading issues by placing COM objects into *apartments*. Which apartment a COM object enters depends upon the `ThreadingModel` value found under its file location key (`InprocServer32` or `LocalServer32`). If a given thread that invokes a COM object has a compatible apartment, the COM object and the thread coexist in the apartment with minimal COM intervention. If the thread and the COM object have incompatible apartment types, COM will create a new apartment for the COM object and typically marshal information as it passes between the calling thread and the COM object.

There are five basic threading models and three apartment types. The threading models include *single*, *apartment*, *free*, *both*, and *neutral* (COM+ only) The apartment types include the *single threaded apartment* (STA), the *multithreaded apartment* (MTA), and the *thread-neutral apartment* (TNA, COM+ only). The details of apartment selection and thread model selection are beyond the scope of this discussion. What is important is that the surrogate must deal with threading and apartment issues.

It does this by overwriting the original COM object's threading model value with its own, which must be the *both-threaded* model. By marking the surrogate object's threading model as *both*, you're saying that the object will happily reside in the apartment of the calling thread. This eliminates the need for a proxy/stub DLL to marshal information if the apartment types differ significantly.

This is important because the SOAP surrogate is an in-process server, not a local server. (MTS uses a local server as the surrogate and therefore can choose the *free* threaded model.). COM will load the DLL into the client's address space and apartment when the original COM object is requested, no matter what the original COM object's intent is. Consequently, the SOAP surrogate can snuggle as close as possible to the client, thus improving performance. (COM local servers incur performance degradation when crossing process boundaries.)

To distill all of this into a single thought, remember that the SOAP Configuration utility modifies the Registry to overwrite an original COM object's file and the threading information to reflect that of the SOAP surrogate. (The original values are saved so that they can be more easily recovered.) The utility does this to both intercept the original object's invocations and to force the highest-performance COM threading configuration possible.

Now that the Registry has been appropriately modified, let's turn to the SOAP Object Surrogate to see how it deals with arbitrary COM objects and SOAP. The best place to begin is with the Surrogate's class factory.

The SOAP Object Surrogate Class Factory

The SOAP Object Surrogate class factory has two main parts. First, as with all COM in-process servers, the Surrogate exports the well-known method `DllGetClassObject()`, which returns to the COM infrastructure a pointer to a class object. Second, there is the class object itself.

In traditional C++–based COM programming, the class object is simply a static object. When COM calls `DllGetClassObject()`, you merely return a pointer to the static object. There is no requirement that this be so, however. The Surrogate takes advantage of this by creating class objects on-the-fly, depending upon the requested object's CLSID.

The code for `DllGetClassObject()` is shown in Listing 10.30 and can be found in the `SOAPObjSurMain.cpp` file.

LISTING 10.30   The SOAP Object Surrogate's `DllGetClassObject()` Implementation

```
// The surrogate doesn't "know" beforehand what objects it
// can create, so it will create them dynamically (up to
// g_iMaxClassObjects of them...if you want more, then
// increase this value).
const int g_iMaxClassObjects = 8;
LPCLASSSTORE g_pClassStore[g_iMaxClassObjects] = {0};


...


STDAPI DllGetClassObject(REFCLSID rclsid,
                         REFIID riid,
                         void **ppv)
{
    // Check the pointer
    if ( ppv == NULL ) {
        return E_POINTER;
    } // if

    HRESULT hr = S_OK;
    try {
        // Clear return pointer
        *ppv = NULL;

        // Check for the surrogate's CLSID, as they may be
        // trying to CoCreate SoapObjectSurrogate::ISoapControl...
        if ( rclsid != __uuidof(SoapObjectSurrogate) ) {
            // CoCreate the catalog
            CComPtr<ISOAPCatalog> spISOAPCatalog;
            hr = spISOAPCatalog.CoCreateInstance(
                            ➥__uuidof(SOAPCatManager));
            if ( FAILED(hr) ) throw hr;

            OLECHAR wszCLSID[64] = {0};
            StringFromGUID2(rclsid,wszCLSID,64);
            CComBSTR bstrCLSID(wszCLSID);
            hr = spISOAPCatalog->IsRegisteredObject(bstrCLSID);
            if ( FAILED(hr) ) throw hr;
        } // if

        if ( hr == S_OK ) {
            // CLSID is in the catalog, so create a new class
            // factory and return it to the caller
            CSOAPObjSurFactory* pCF = NULL;
```

continues

10

IMPLEMENTING
SOAP

LISTING 10.30   Continued

```
                for ( int i = 0; i < g_iMaxClassObjects; i++ ) {
                    // See if this one is NULL
                    if ( g_pClassStore[i] == NULL ) {
                        // Available slot, so create a class store
                        // node and a class factory object
                        pCF = new CSOAPObjSurFactory(rclsid);
                        g_pClassStore[i] = new CLASSSTORE;
                        g_pClassStore[i]->clsid = rclsid;
                        g_pClassStore[i]->iid = GUID_NULL;
                        g_pClassStore[i]->pCF = pCF;
                        break;
                    } // if
                } // for

                // If no slots, return CLASS_E_CLASSNOTAVAILABLE
                if ( pCF != NULL ) {
                    // Create a new object through the class factory
                    // we just created
                    hr = pCF->QueryInterface(riid, ppv);
                } // if
                else {
                    // No slots
                    hr = CLASS_E_CLASSNOTAVAILABLE;
                } // else
            } // if
            else {
                // CLSID not registered...
                hr = CLASS_E_CLASSNOTAVAILABLE;
            } // else
        } // try
        catch(HRESULT hrErr) {
            // Some COM error...
            hr = CLASS_E_CLASSNOTAVAILABLE; // normalize to this error...
            TCHAR strErrMsg[256] = {0};
            wsprintf(strErrMsg,"COM error obtaining class
                            ➥factory%#08x\n",hrErr);
            OutputDebugString(strErrMsg);
        } // catch
        catch(...) {
            // Some error...
            hr = CLASS_E_CLASSNOTAVAILABLE;
            OutputDebugString(_T("Unexpected application error obtaining
                            ➥ class factory\n"));
        } // catch

        return hr;
}
```

The Surrogate keeps a small cache of known class objects:

```
const int g_iMaxClassObjects = 8;
LPCLASSSTORE g_pClassStore[g_iMaxClassObjects] = {0};
```

A more robust implementation would remove the hard-coded value for the cache size, but this number should suffice for most instances. In any case, when COM asks for a class object via DllGetClassObject(), it provides the CLSID of the object in question, the IID of the class object, and a pointer to some preallocated storage to receive the pointer to the class object. DllGetClassObject() first checks for the validity of the return pointer storage:

```
// Check the pointer
if ( ppv == NULL ) {
    return E_POINTER;
} // if
```

If for some odd reason COM passes in a NULL value, DllGetClassObject() will return an error result (E_POINTER). If the address is non-NULL, DllGetClassObject() clears the return variable:

```
// Clear return pointer
*ppv = NULL;
```

If there is no error, a valid class object's address will overwrite this variable. If there is an error, COM can't execute code at some arbitrary address that might have been stored randomly in the pointer variable.

The next task is to check for the CLSID of the object in question. If it's not the SOAP Object Surrogate, then you open the SOAP Catalog and check to see whether the object is registered:

```
// Check for the surrogate's CLSID, as they may be
// trying to CoCreate SoapObjectSurrogate::ISoapControl...
if ( rclsid != __uuidof(SoapObjectSurrogate) ) {
    // CoCreate the catalog
    CComPtr<ISOAPCatalog> spISOAPCatalog;
    hr = spISOAPCatalog.CoCreateInstance(
                            ➥__uuidof(SOAPCatManager));
    if ( FAILED(hr) ) throw hr;

    OLECHAR wszCLSID[64] = {0};
    StringFromGUID2(rclsid,wszCLSID,64);
    CComBSTR bstrCLSID(wszCLSID);
    hr = spISOAPCatalog->IsRegisteredObject(bstrCLSID);
    if ( FAILED(hr) ) throw hr;
} // if
```

10

If the object is registered, or if the object to be created is the Surrogate itself (for delegation purposes), then a new CSOAPObjSurFactory object is created and added to the Surrogate class object cache:

```
// CLSID is in the catalog, so create a new class
// factory and return it to the caller
CSOAPObjSurFactory* pCF = NULL;
for ( int i = 0; i < g_iMaxClassObjects; i++ ) {
    // See if this one is NULL
    if ( g_pClassStore[i] == NULL ) {
        // Available slot, so create a class store
        // node and a class factory object
        pCF = new CSOAPObjSurFactory(rclsid);
        g_pClassStore[i] = new CLASSSTORE;
        g_pClassStore[i]->clsid = rclsid;
        g_pClassStore[i]->iid = GUID_NULL;
        g_pClassStore[i]->pCF = pCF;
        break;
    } // if
} // for
```

At this point, you have a class object, so you call its QueryInterface() method to see if it supports the class object interface in question:

```
// If no slots, return CLASS_E_CLASSNOTAVAILABLE
if ( pCF != NULL ) {
    // Create a new object through the class factory
    // we just created
    hr = pCF->QueryInterface(riid, ppv);
} // if
else {
    // No slots
    hr = CLASS_E_CLASSNOTAVAILABLE;
} // else
```

At the point of the QueryInterface(), the SOAP object class factory takes over. Its class definition is shown in Listing 10.31.

LISTING 10.31   CSOAPObjSurFactory Class Definition

```
// CSOAPObjSurFactory is used to produce the class
// object for the SoapObjectSurrogate coclass
class CSOAPObjSurFactory : public IClassFactory
{
public:
    CSOAPObjSurFactory(REFCLSID rclsid);
```

```
// IUnknown methods
   STDMETHODIMP QueryInterface(REFIID riid, void **ppv);
   STDMETHODIMP_(ULONG) AddRef(void);
   STDMETHODIMP_(ULONG) Release(void);

// IClassFactory methods
   STDMETHODIMP CreateInstance(IUnknown *pUnkOuter, REFIID riid, void **ppv);
   STDMETHODIMP LockServer(BOOL bLock);

protected:
   const CLSID m_clsid;
};
```

If you're familiar with C++–based COM programming, you'll recognize the class definition in Listing 10.31 as a fairly standard `IClassFactory` definition. Note that the object's CLSID is stored in `m_clsid` for later reference. This enables the class object to be tailored by CLSID.

The two most interesting class object methods are `QueryInterface()` and `CreateInstance()`. `QueryInterface()` is shown in Listing 10.32, and `CreateInstance()` is shown in Listing 10.33.

LISTING 10.32 `CSOAPObjSurFactory::QueryInterface()` Implementation

```
STDMETHODIMP CSOAPObjSurFactory::QueryInterface(REFIID riid,
                                                void **ppv)
{
    // Check the pointer
    if ( ppv == 0 ) {
        return E_POINTER;
    } // if

    // Assume failure...
    *ppv = NULL;

    // Which (class object) interface?
    if (riid == IID_IClassFactory)
        *ppv = static_cast<IClassFactory*>(this);
    else if (riid == IID_IUnknown)
        *ppv = static_cast<IClassFactory*>(this);
    else
        // Interface is not supported
        return E_NOINTERFACE;

    // Interface is supported
    reinterpret_cast<IUnknown*>(this)->AddRef();
    return S_OK;
}
```

10

IMPLEMENTING
SOAP

LISTING 10.33   CSOAPObjSurFactory::CreateInstance() Implementation

```
STDMETHODIMP CSOAPObjSurFactory::CreateInstance (IUnknown *pUnkOuter,
                                                 REFIID riid,
                                                 void **ppv)
{
    // Check the pointer
    if ( ppv == 0 ) {
        return E_POINTER;
    } // if

    // Assume failure...
    *ppv = NULL;

    // Disallow aggregation
    if ( pUnkOuter != NULL ) {
        return CLASS_E_NOAGGREGATION;
    } // if

    // So far so good, so create a new instance of the
    // CSOAPObjectSurrogate C++ class.
    CSOAPObjectSurrogate *pObj = new CSOAPObjectSurrogate(m_clsid);

    // If  new fails, return E_OUTOFMEMORY.
    if ( pObj == NULL ) {
        return E_OUTOFMEMORY;
    } // if

    // Stabilize the object's reference count.
    pObj->AddRef();

    // Retrieve an interface pointer for the caller.
    HRESULT hr = pObj->QueryInterface(riid,ppv);

    // If QueryInterface failed, then this Release will destroy
    // the object, ensuring no resources are leaked.
    pObj->Release();

    return hr; // hr from QI()
}
```

The meat of the QueryInterface() is to check for the IClassFactory (or IUnknown) interface:

```
// Which (class object) interface?
if (riid == IID_IClassFactory)
    *ppv = static_cast<IClassFactory*>(this);
else if (riid == IID_IUnknown)
    *ppv = static_cast<IClassFactory*>(this);
```

```
else
    // Interface is not supported
    return E_NOINTERFACE;
```

If the client requests any other class object interface (such as IClassFactory2, for example), the query will fail, and the object will not be created.

When the client does attempt to create an instance of the object, it calls CreateInstance(). CreateInstance() first disallows aggregation:

```
// Disallow aggregation
if ( pUnkOuter != NULL ) {
    return CLASS_E_NOAGGREGATION;
} // if
```

Aggregation is a COM-based form of object reuse; describing it in depth would require a more involved discussion than space here permits. Simply put, the SOAP Object Surrogate does not support aggregation.

Assuming the client didn't want aggregation, an instance of the Surrogate is created:

```
// So far so good, so create a new instance of the
// CSOAPObjectSurrogate C++ class.
CSOAPObjectSurrogate *pObj = new CSOAPObjectSurrogate(m_clsid);
```

If the object is created (there is no memory problem, for example), then the object is queried for a given interface:

```
// Stabilize the object's reference count.
pObj->AddRef();

// Retrieve an interface pointer for the caller.
HRESULT hr = pObj->QueryInterface(riid,ppv);

// If QueryInterface failed, then this Release will destroy
// the object, ensuring no resources are leaked.
pObj->Release();
```

It's common practice to use the object itself to fill the client's interface pointer with a pointer to the requested interface using the object's QueryInterface() method. If the object does support the interface, the trailing Release() call offsets the AddRef() found in QueryInterface(). The overall reference count remains at one. If the QueryInterface() fails, the trailing Release() will cause the object to destroy itself and reclaim any resources.

If the call to the Surrogate's QueryInterface() is successful, the job of the Surrogate's class object is done, and the client will deal with the Surrogate itself from then on.

The mechanics of the Surrogate's QueryInterface() will be examined in the upcoming "Using the SOAP Object Surrogate" section. First, take a brief look at delegation.

The Mechanics of Delegation

Everything need to support delegation is in place, with the exception of a special interface that creates delegated objects. This interface is ISoapControl. In addition to the standard IUnknown methods, it supports three methods of its own (from SOAPObjectSurrogate.h):

```
// ISoapControl methods
STDMETHODIMP GetEndpointURL(/*[out]*/ BSTR* pbstrEndptURL);
STDMETHODIMP GetNamespace(/*[out]*/ BSTR* pbstrNamespace);
STDMETHODIMP CreateInstance(/*[in]*/ REFCLSID rclsid,
                            /*[in]*/ REFIID riid,
                            /*[out, iid_is(riid)]*/ IUnknown**
                                                    ➥ppvObject);
```

GetEndpointURL() and GetNamespace() are merely convenience functions that return the SOAP Catalog information for the delegated object. It's the CreateInstance() method that is far more interesting. Its implementation is shown in Listing 10.34.

LISTING 10.34   CSOAPObjectSurrogate::CreateInstance() Implementation

```
STDMETHODIMP CSOAPObjectSurrogate::CreateInstance(REFCLSID rclsid,
                                ➥REFIID riid, IUnknown** ppvObject)
{
    // Check the pointer
    if ( ppvObject == NULL ) {
        return E_POINTER;
    } // if

    HRESULT hr = S_OK;
    try {
        // Store the CLSID
        m_clsid = rclsid;

        // Simply do a QI()...
        hr = QueryInterface(riid,
                            reinterpret_cast<void**>(ppvObject));
        if ( FAILED(hr) ) throw hr;
    } // try
    catch(HRESULT hrErr) {
        // Some COM error...
        hr = hrErr; // normalize to this error...
        TCHAR strErrMsg[256] = {0};
        wsprintf(strErrMsg,"COM error in ISoapControl::CreateInstance
                    ➥ %#08x\n",hrErr);
        OutputDebugString(strErrMsg);
    } // catch
```

```
catch(...) {
    // Some error...
    hr = E_UNEXPECTED;
    OutputDebugString(_T("Unexpected application error in
                    ➥ ISoapControl::CreateInstance\n"));
} // catch

return hr;
}
```

Given the work done to support interception, delegation is easy. Simply store the CLSID of the object in question and execute a QueryInterface():

```
// Store the CLSID
m_clsid = rclsid;

// Simply do a QI()...
hr = QueryInterface(riid, reinterpret_cast<void**>(ppvObject));
```

The resulting interface pointer will be an instance of the SOAP Object Surrogate that manages SOAP calls for the referenced COM object. A client application would delegate a SOAP call like so:

```
CComPtr<ISoapControl> spSoapControl;
hr = spSoapControl.CoCreateInstance(__uuidof(SoapObjectSurrogate));
if ( FAILED(hr) ) throw hr;

CComPtr<ISomeInterface> spSomeInterface;
hr = spSoapControl->CreateInstance(&spSomeInterface);
if ( FAILED(hr) ) throw hr;
if (spSomeInterface.p == NULL ) throw E_POINTER;

// Instance of spSomeInterface is now remoted...
```

That's all there is to delegation. Most of the magic happens in the Surrogate's QueryInterface(), as you'll see in the next section.

Creating SOAP-Enabled Objects

When it comes to creating instances of SOAP-enabled objects, the SOAP Object Surrogate's magic is in its QueryInterface() implementation, which you see in Listing 10.35. The basis of the SOAP encoding is wrapped in a *serializer object*, which is created and stored in a serializer cache (by interface). The serializer object is discussed in detail in the upcoming "Encoding Type Libraries" section.

10

IMPLEMENTING
SOAP

LISTING 10.35 CSOAPObjectSurrogate::QueryInterface() Implementation

```
typedef struct tagSerializerStore {
    IID iid;
    CSOAPSerializer* pSerializer;
} SERIALIZERSTORE, FAR* LPSERIALIZERSTORE;

...

STDMETHODIMP CSOAPObjectSurrogate::QueryInterface(REFIID riid,
                                                  void **ppv)
{
    // Check the pointer
    if ( ppv == NULL ) {
        return E_POINTER;
    } // if

    // Which interface?
    HRESULT hr = S_OK;
    if (riid == __uuidof(ISoapControl)) {
        *ppv = static_cast<ISoapControl*>(this);
        (reinterpret_cast<IUnknown*>(*ppv))->AddRef();
    } // if
    else if (riid == __uuidof(IUnknown)) {
        *ppv = static_cast<ISoapControl*>(this);
        (reinterpret_cast<IUnknown*>(*ppv))->AddRef();
    } // else if
    else {
        // Check for existance of CLSID/IID combination
        // in the SOAP catalog and retrieve the type
        // library filename.
        try {
            // Assume failure
            *ppv = NULL;

            // CoCreate the catalog
            CComPtr<ISOAPCatalog> spISOAPCatalog;
            hr = spISOAPCatalog.CoCreateInstance(
                    __uuidof(SOAPCatManager));
            if ( FAILED(hr) ) throw hr;

            OLECHAR wszCLSID[64] = {0};
            StringFromGUID2(m_clsid,wszCLSID,64);
            CComBSTR bstrCLSID(wszCLSID);
            OLECHAR wszIID[64] = {0};
            StringFromGUID2(riid,wszIID,64);
            CComBSTR bstrIID(wszIID);
```

```
        // See if the interface is available
        hr = spISOAPCatalog->IsRegisteredInterface(bstrCLSID,
                                   bstrIID,CComVariant(false));
        if ( FAILED(hr) ) throw hr;
        if ( hr == S_OK ) {
            // It is, so load the type library
            CComBSTR bstrTLBFile;
            hr = spISOAPCatalog->GetTLBFile(bstrCLSID,
                                        &bstrTLBFile);
            if ( FAILED(hr) ) throw hr;

            if ( hr == S_OK ) {
                // CLSID/IID is in the catalog...if you've seen
                // these before, you should have already loaded
                // the type library and obtained the ITypeLib
                // interface pointer (you went through the
                // searching to validate the CLSID/IID
                // combination).  If you've not loaded the type
                //  library, do so now...
                if ( m_pITypeLib.p == NULL ) {
                    // Load the type library...
                    hr = LoadTypeLibEx(bstrTLBFile,
                                REGKIND_REGISTER,&m_pITypeLib);
                    if ( FAILED(hr) ) throw hr;
                } // if

                // Here you create a new serializer object and
                // stuff it into the array of serializers if
                // the interface hasn't already been exported.
                LPSERIALIZERSTORE pSerializer = NULL;
                for ( int i = 0; i < g_iMaxSerializers; i++ ) {
                if ( m_pSerializers[i] != NULL ) {
                    // Non-NULL element, so check for this
                        // IID
                        if ( m_pSerializers[i]->iid == riid ) {
                            // Found it...
                            pSerializer = m_pSerializers[i];
                            break;
                        } // if
                    } // if
                } // for

                // If you didn't find the serializer, create one
                // in the first NULL slot
                if ( pSerializer == NULL ) {
```

continues

LISTING 10.35   Continued

```
for ( i = 0; i < g_iMaxSerializers; i++ ) {
    if ( m_pSerializers[i] == NULL ) {
        // First NULL element, so create a
        // new serializer
        pSerializer = new SERIALIZERSTORE;
        if ( pSerializer == NULL )
            throw E_OUTOFMEMORY;

        pSerializer->iid = riid;
        pSerializer->pSerializer = new
                ➥CSOAPSerializer(this,
                m_clsid,riid,m_pITypeLib);
        if ( pSerializer->pSerializer == NULL )
            throw E_OUTOFMEMORY;

        m_pSerializers[i] = pSerializer;
        break;
    } // if
} // for
} // if

// Pass back the serializer pointer...this will have
// the appropriate vtable...  In this case you have
// to handle the this pointer yourself, hence the
// additional parameter.  The client will interact
// with this method as you'd expect.
*ppv = pSerializer->pSerializer;
Serializer_AddRef(pSerializer->pSerializer);

// Pull the endpoint and namespace information
// for later use
CComBSTR bstrEndPointURL;
hr = spISOAPCatalog->GetEndpointURL(bstrCLSID,
        bstrIID,CComVariant(true),&bstrEndPointURL);
if ( hr == S_OK ) {
    USES_CONVERSION;
    LPTSTR pszEndpointURL = W2T(bstrEndPointURL);
    _tcsncpy(m_strEndpointURL,pszEndpointURL,
                _MAX_PATH);
} // if
CComBSTR bstrNamespace;
hr = spISOAPCatalog->GetNamespace(bstrCLSID,
        bstrIID,CComVariant(true),&bstrNamespace);
if ( hr == S_OK ) {
    USES_CONVERSION;
    LPTSTR pszNamespace = W2T(bstrNamespace);
```

```
                _tcsncpy(m_strNamespace,pszNamespace,_MAX_PATH);
            } // if

            // Call the serializer's initialization method
            hr = pSerializer->pSerializer->Init();
            if ( FAILED(hr) )  throw hr;

            // Lock the module...Release() will eventually
            // unlock it
            LockModule ();
        } // if
        else {
            // CLSID/IID not registered...
            throw = E_NOINTERFACE;
        } // else
    } // if
    else {
        // CLSID/IID not registered...
        throw E_NOINTERFACE;
    } // else
} // try
catch(HRESULT hrErr) {
    // Some COM error...
    hr = hrErr; // normalize to this error...
    TCHAR strErrMsg[256] = {0};
    wsprintf(strErrMsg,"COM error in object QueryInterface
                    ➥%#08x\n",hrErr);
    OutputDebugString(strErrMsg);
} // catch
catch(...) {
    // Some error...
    hr = E_UNEXPECTED;
    OutputDebugString(_T("Unexpected application error in
                        ➥object QueryInterface\n"));
} // catch
} // else

return hr;
}
```

After clearing the returned pointer's storage, the Surrogate checks to see if the requested interface is in any way special (ISoapControl, IUnknown, or something else):

```
if (riid == __uuidof(ISoapControl)) {
    *ppv = static_cast<ISoapControl*>(this);
    (reinterpret_cast<IUnknown*>(*ppv))->AddRef();
} // if
```

```
else if (riid == __uuidof(IUnknown)) {
    *ppv = static_cast<ISoapControl*>(this);
    (reinterpret_cast<IUnknown*>(*ppv))->AddRef();
} // else if
else {
    // Something else...
} // else
```

If the interface is either ISoapControl or IUnknown, then standard COM programming takes effect and the appropriate vtable is returned (more on vtables in the "Encoding Type Libraries" section). However, if the interface is something else, the SOAP Catalog is queried for the interface, and, if the interface is registered in the SOAP Catalog, a serializer is created:

```
// CoCreate the catalog
CComPtr<ISOAPCatalog> spISOAPCatalog;
hr = spISOAPCatalog.CoCreateInstance(__uuidof(SOAPCatManager));
if ( FAILED(hr) ) throw hr;

OLECHAR wszCLSID[64] = {0};
StringFromGUID2(m_clsid,wszCLSID,64);
CComBSTR bstrCLSID(wszCLSID);
OLECHAR wszIID[64] = {0};
StringFromGUID2(riid,wszIID,64);
CComBSTR bstrIID(wszIID);

// See if the interface is available
hr = spISOAPCatalog->IsRegisteredInterface(bstrCLSID,
                        bstrIID,CComVariant(false));
if ( FAILED(hr) ) throw hr;
if ( hr == S_OK ) {
    // Create a serializer
} // if
```

Assuming the interface is registered in the SOAP Catalog (you receive an E_NOINTERFACE error if not), its type library is loaded for encoding:

```
if ( m_pITypeLib.p == NULL ) {
    // Load the type library...
    hr = LoadTypeLibEx(bstrTLBFile,REGKIND_REGISTER,&m_pITypeLib);
    if ( FAILED(hr) ) throw hr;
} // if
```

Then, the serializer cache is checked to see if a serializer already exists for this interface:

```
LPSERIALIZERSTORE pSerializer = NULL;
for ( int i = 0; i < g_iMaxSerializers; i++ ) {
    if ( m_pSerializers[i] != NULL ) {
        // Non-NULL element, so check for this IID
```

```
            if ( m_pSerializers[i]->iid == riid ) {
                // Found it...
                pSerializer = m_pSerializers[i];
                break;
            } // if
        } // if
    } // for
```

If a serializer already exists, its pointer will be returned. If not, one is created:

```
// If you didn't find the serializer, create one
// in the first NULL slot
if ( pSerializer == NULL ) {
    for ( i = 0; i < g_iMaxSerializers; i++ ) {
        if ( m_pSerializers[i] == NULL ) {
            // First NULL element, so create a new serializer
            pSerializer = new SERIALIZERSTORE;
            if ( pSerializer == NULL ) throw E_OUTOFMEMORY;

            pSerializer->iid = riid;
            pSerializer->pSerializer = new CSOAPSerializer(this,
                                    m_clsid,riid,m_pITypeLib);
            if ( pSerializer->pSerializer == NULL )
                throw E_OUTOFMEMORY;

            m_pSerializers[i] = pSerializer;
            break;
        } // if
    } // for
} // if
```

With a serializer pointer in hand (whether you created it or found it in the serializer cache), you must assign the client's [out] pointer value and AddRef() the serializer:

```
*ppv = pSerializer->pSerializer;
Serializer_AddRef(pSerializer->pSerializer);
```

After pulling the interface's endpoint URL and namespace, the serializer's initialization method is called:

```
hr = pSerializer->pSerializer->Init();
if ( FAILED(hr) ) throw hr;
```

Finally, the DLL is secured in memory by a call to the LockModule() helper function (found in SOAPObjSurMain.cpp).

At this point, if there were no errors, you have a serializer object ready to encode the interface's methods. Before discussing the serializer object itself, there are some details you should be aware of when using the SOAP Object Surrogate; these are discussed next.

10

IMPLEMENTING
SOAP

Using the SOAP Object Surrogate

There are a few Registry settings you should be aware of that govern some aspects of the Surrogate's operations. All of them are found under this Registry hierarchy:

```
HKLM/
    Software/
        MCP/
            SOAP/
                CatalogFile (key)
                HttpRequestFile (key)
                HttpResponseFile (key)
                Settings/
                    ResponseTimeout (DWORD value)
```

The location of the SOAP Catalog is stored as the default string in the CatalogFile key. If you want to see the contents of the SOAP packets as they leave and return, create the HttpRequestFile and HttpResponseFile keys and assign their default strings a path to a text file. If the keys exist, the processing architecture will read the file location and write the packet contents for either the request or the response data (or both). This enables you to debug the SOAP streams. The final key is the Settings key, which has a single entry, ResponseTimeout. ResponseTimeout, a DWORD value, contains the length of time (in milliseconds)that the processing architecture will wait for the remote server's response. A value of 0xFFFFFFFF is essentially an infinite wait period (also good for debugging).

Interpreting the COM Method Call Stack

As you recall, the Surrogate's implementation of QueryInterface() created a serializer object and stuffed it into a serializer cache. It is the serializer that actually mimics the operation of the true COM object. It does so by providing a dummy vtable filled with methods that do nothing but call a serialization method, remserialize(), and then wipe out the call stack. Let's look at the details.

First, remember that COM objects at the binary level provide C++–compatible vtables, a diagram of which you see in Figure 10.6.

The pointer to the COM object actually points to a vptr (virtual [table] pointer), which is a pointer to a table containing still other pointers to the object's methods. If you are familiar with assembly language, you might refer to this table as a *jump table*. If you know which method you want to execute, you simply calculate the offset into the jump table, load the address you find there, and begin execution at the new location. This offset calculation is simply the method number multiplied by the size of a pointer, which for Intel 32-bit platforms is 32 bits (4 bytes, or sizeof(long)).

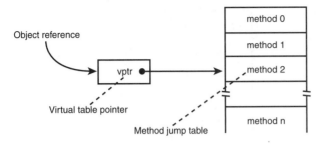

FIGURE 10.6

The COM virtual pointer table.

By definition, the C++ vptr is the first piece of class data. Whenever you create C++ classes with virtual functions, you automatically generate a vptr that points to a table of your class's virtual functions. Other class state information will follow (in memory). The vtable is easily found using this arrangement.

In COM, every COM object has one or more vtables, with each vtable representing an interface supported by the COM object. (In fact, that's what the C++ implementation of QueryInterface() does—it gives you the vtable for the requested interface, just as dynamic_cast<>() does for C++ objects.) Therefore, the Surrogate must somehow re-create the true object's vtable.

The Surrogate is also responsible for clearing the call stack. That is, COM methods are invoked using __stdcall, which means the arguments are pushed onto a stack from right to left (making variable numbers of arguments difficult).The stack is cleaned up by the recipient of the call, not the caller. This means the Surrogate had better know precisely how many bytes were pushed onto the call stack, so that the proper amount can be removed.

A call stack is simply a chunk of memory, like a scratch pad, that is used to store temporary information. It gets its name from *"calling* a function." The arguments to be passed to the function are placed in the scratch memory (as a stack) to be used by the called function. A typical call stack could be graphically depicted as you see in Figure 10.7.

The caller pushes a return address onto the stack, followed by an implicit this pointer (for C++ or COM call stacks), which is then followed by any method arguments. In the case of __stdcall methods, the call recipient pulls the arguments from the stack, removes the implicit this pointer, and returns to the address that remains on the stack.

All this tedious work, and more, is accomplished by the SOAP serializer object, CSOAPSerializer (found in SOAPSerializer.h/.cpp). For example, note the location of the vptr variable in CSOAPSerializer's definition, shown in Listing 10.36.

10

IMPLEMENTING
SOAP

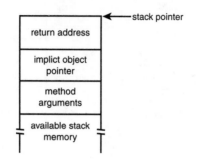

FIGURE 10.7
Nominal call stack layout.

LISTING 10.36 CSOAPSerializer Object Definition

```
// SOAPSerializer.h
//
// Kenn Scribner
// Understanding SOAP, March 2000
//
// SOAP serialization object definition
//
#ifndef _SOAPSERIALIZER_H
#define _SOAPSERIALIZER_H

#include <atlbase.h>
#include "..\TLBEncoder\TLBEncoder.h"
#include "StackCruncher.h"
#include "SOAPHttpTransaction.h"

class CSOAPObjectSurrogate;
class CSOAPSerializer
{
public:
    CSOAPSerializer(CSOAPObjectSurrogate* pParent,
                    const CLSID& clsid,
                    const IID& iid,
                    ITypeLib* pITypeLib) :
        m_pParent(pParent),
        m_clsid(clsid),
        m_iid(iid),
        m_spTypeLib(pITypeLib),
        m_cRefs(0),
        m_vptr(s_vptr)
```

```
    {
    }

    ~CSOAPSerializer()
    {
    }

// Operations
    HRESULT Init();
    HRESULT GetCallInfo(LPSOAPCALLINFO pInfo, LPSTREAM lpStream);
    HRESULT ParseArgs(int** ppArgs, CStackCruncher* pCruncher,
                      ➥LPSTREAM lpStream);
    HRESULT SoapEncode(CStackCruncher* pCruncher,
                       ➥CSOAPHttpTransaction* pTransaction);
    HRESULT SendReceive(CSOAPHttpTransaction* pTransaction);
    HRESULT SoapDecode(CStackCruncher* pCruncher,
                       ➥CSOAPHttpTransaction* pTransaction,
                       ➥HRESULT& hrFromSerialization);

// Attributes
    const void* const m_vptr; // <─vtable, this + 0 bytes
    CSOAPObjectSurrogate* m_pParent;
    const CLSID m_clsid;
    CComBSTR m_bstrCLSID;
    const IID m_iid;
    CComBSTR m_bstrIID;
    long m_cRefs;
    CComPtr<ITypeLib> m_spTypeLib;
    CComPtr<IEncodeTLB> m_spEncoder;
    CComAutoCriticalSection m_cs;
    TCHAR m_strEndpointURL[_MAX_PATH];
    TCHAR m_strNamespace[_MAX_PATH];

    static const void* const s_vptr; // virtual functions

};

#endif // _SOAPSERIALIZER_H
```

Note this italicized line from Listing 10.36:

```
const void* const m_vptr; // <─vtable, this + 0 bytes
```

This is the vptr, which is the first class attribute (followed by many more). The vptr is
assigned a value in the class constructor

```
m_vptr(s_vptr)
```

10

IMPLEMENTING
SOAP

wherein s_vptr is given by this line of code:

```
static const void* const s_vptr; // virtual functions
```

This is the virtual function table, which is static to the class. And, as is mandatory in C++, the static variable must be initialized. This is done in SOAPSerializer.inc using this line of code:

```
const void* const CSOAPSerializer::s_vptr = vtbl;
```

The vtbl variable is an array of SERIALIZER_ENTRY_POINT values:

```
#define SERIALIZER_ENTRY_POINT(n) \
static void __declspec(naked) ser_##n(void)   \
{ __asm push (n*4) __asm jmp serialize }


...

static const void* const vtbl[] = {
    Serializer_QueryInterface,
    Serializer_AddRef,
    Serializer_Release,
    ser_3,
    ser_4,
    ser_5,
...
    ser_29,
    ser_30,
    ser_31 };
```

There are currently 32 entries in the serializer's vtable, but this is easily extended. For demonstration purposes, 32 interface methods or fewer should suffice. A more robust implementation would increase this number to 256, or even 1024.

The SOAP Serializer and IUnknown

Serializer_QueryInterface(), Serializer_AddRef(), and Serializer_Release() are functions implemented in SOAPSerializer.cpp, rather than as macro expansions. By COM rules, these must be the first three methods in every interface's vtable (and in the order listed as well). Serializer_AddRef() and Serializer_Release() are relatively straightforward implementations. (You'll find them in SOAPSerializer.cpp.) As a handy feature, Serializer_Release() calls its parent surrogate's OnSerializerFinalRelease() method after decrementing the last reference count. The surrogate can then remove the serializer from its serializer cache.

Serializer_QueryInterface() is a bit more interesting, as you can see from Listing 10.37.

LISTING 10.37 CSOAPSerializer::Serializer_QueryInterface() Implementation

```
STDMETHODIMP Serializer_QueryInterface(CSOAPSerializer* pThis,
                                       REFIID riid, void** ppv)
{
    // Check the pointer
    if ( ppv == NULL ) {
        return E_POINTER;
    } // if

    // Which interface?
    HRESULT hr = S_OK;
    if (riid == __uuidof(ISoapControl)) {
        // Interface managed strictly by the parent...marshalling
        // the interface pointer should not be required as the
        // surrogate is marked as Both threaded (no proxy).
        *ppv = static_cast<ISoapControl*>(pThis->m_pParent);
        (reinterpret_cast<IUnknown*>(*ppv))->AddRef();
    } // if
    else if (riid == __uuidof(IUnknown)) {
        // Must give out parent's IUnknown pointer (rule of COM
        // that you must pass out same IUnknown pointer for each
        // QI), but AddRef() this object to keep this object
        // alive...
        *ppv = static_cast<ISoapControl*>(pThis->m_pParent);
        Serializer_AddRef(pThis);
    } // if
    else if (riid == pThis->m_iid ) {
        // This interface
        *ppv = pThis;
        Serializer_AddRef(pThis);
    } // else if
    else {
        *ppv = NULL;
        return E_NOINTERFACE;
    } // else

    return S_OK;
}
```

The serializer's interface query implementation supports three interfaces: ISoapControl, IUnknown, and the serializer's known interface IID. Other interface requests result in an E_NOINTERFACE error.

10

This poses interesting problems with interface identity. The Surrogate exports `ISoapControl` and `IUnknown`, not the serializer instance object. Therefore, the serializer must return to the caller the interface pointers associated with its parent Surrogate, unless the serialized interface is specifically requested.

To clarify things a bit, this code returns the `ISoapControl` interface pointer:

```
if (riid == __uuidof(ISoapControl)) {
    // Interface managed strictly by the parent...marshalling
    // the interface pointer should not be required as the
    // surrogate is marked as Both threaded (no proxy).
    *ppv = static_cast<ISoapControl*>(pThis->m_pParent);
    (reinterpret_cast<IUnknown*>(*ppv))->AddRef();
 } // if
```

`ISoapControl` is managed entirely by the Surrogate, not by the serializer object. Therefore, when the serializer is asked for an `ISoapControl` pointer, it returns a pointer to its parent surrogate and `AddRef()`s through the interface pointer. Note that, because the Surrogate is marked as both-threaded, no further interface pointer marshalling should be required when passing out the parent surrogate's interface pointer. (No proxy/stub DLL is required.)

The serializer does, however, handle `IUnknown`, but the `IUnknown` pointer must be identical to the parent surrogate. (This a COM interface identity rule.) Therefore, the serializer returns the parent surrogate's `IUnknown` pointer but `AddRef()`s itself instead of the parent. (The parent won't be destroyed until the serializer calls the `OnSerializerFinalRelease()` method.) This code returns the `IUnknown` pointer for the serializer:

```
else if (riid == __uuidof(IUnknown)) {
    // Must give out parent's IUnknown pointer (rule of COM
    // that you must pass out same IUnknown pointer for each
    // QI), but AddRef() this object to keep this object
    // alive...
    *ppv = static_cast<ISoapControl*>(pThis->m_pParent);
    Serializer_AddRef(pThis);
} // if
```

Also remember the Surrogate's implementation of `QueryInterface()`—it will search its serializer cache for any existing instance of a serializer. So, the rules of COM are maintained, and you can negotiate interfaces at will, no matter which object you happen to be working with (Surrogate or serializer).

If the serializer is queried for the interface it is currently serializing, this code takes effect:

```
else if (riid == pThis->m_iid ) {
    // This interface
    *ppv = pThis;
```

```
    Serializer_AddRef(pThis);
} // else if
```

In this case, the serializer simply returns a pointer to itself and increments its reference count.

The Serializer's Entry Point

As you might recall, the `SERIALIZER_ENTRY_POINT(n)` macro expands to this:

```
push (n*4)
jmp serialize
```

This pushes the method number onto the call stack and then jumps (executes) `serialize()`. The code for `serialize()` can be found in Listing 10.38.

LISTING 10.38 `CSOAPSerializer::serialize()` Implementation

```
static __declspec(naked) void serialize(void)
{
    __asm {
        push ebp // set up simple stack frame
        mov  ebp, esp

        sub  esp, 8  // Obtain 8 bytes of stack frame to
                     // set up local and register vars:
                     // ebp-8  = local variable:
                     //    ➥hrFromSerialization
                     // ebp-4  = local variable: stackSize
                     // ebp+0  = ebp
                     // ebp+4  = local variable: vtbl offset
                     //    ➥(in bytes)
                     // ebp+8  = return address
                     // ebp+12 = this (CSOAPSerializer&)
                     // ebp+16 = begin method args


        call remserialize // function shares the stack frame for efficiency

        push esi
        mov  esi, [ebp-4]   // esi = stackSize (clear stack)
        add  esi, 8
        add  esi, ebp // esi points to bottom arg on stack

        mov  eax, [ebp+8] // copy retaddr down
        mov  [esi], eax
        sub  esi, 4
        mov  eax, [ebp-8] // copy hrFromSerialization down
        mov  [esi], eax
```

10

IMPLEMENTING SOAP

continues

LISTING 10.38 Continued

```
        mov  eax, esi // reset stack and return to caller
        pop  esi
        mov  ebp, [ebp]
        mov  esp, eax
        pop  eax // pull hrFromSerialization into accumulator
        ret
    } // __asm
}
```

Assembly language often scares people, but there really isn't that much to serialize(). The first thing to do is to reserve some stack memory for local variable storage:

```
push ebp // set up simple stack frame
mov  ebp, esp

sub  esp, 8  // Obtain 8 bytes of stack frame to
             // set up local and register vars
```

This first opcode saves the (extended) base pointer so it can be restored when returning to the caller. Then, it moves the stack pointer to the base pointer so that local variables can be referenced from the stack's memory. It finally reserves eight bytes of local variable memory. The first four bytes will be used to return the result of the serialization process. The second four bytes will eventually contain the stack size, so that the serialize() method can clean up the stack (as is required with COM method calling conventions).

Then the serialization process is executed:

```
call remserialize // function shares the stack frame for efficiency
```

You'll examine the remserialize() method shortly.

Finally, the stack is cleaned by removing the memory associated with the local variables, the COM method's arguments (if any), the implicit this pointer, and any other information that might have been recorded onto the stack:

```
push esi
mov  esi, [ebp-4] // esi = stackSize (clear stack)
add  esi, 8
add  esi, ebp // esi points to bottom arg on stack

mov  eax, [ebp+8] // copy retaddr down
mov  [esi], eax
sub  esi, 4
mov  eax, [ebp-8] // copy hrFromSerialization down
mov  [esi], eax
```

```asm
mov  eax, esi // reset stack and return to caller
pop  esi
mov  ebp, [ebp]
mov  esp, eax
pop  eax // pull hrFromSerialization into accumulator
ret
```

The `remserialize()` method is where the (SOAP) action is, as you can see from Listing 10.39. A good and sneaky trick—first implemented by Keith Brown's Universal Delegator—is that the `remserialize()` method overlays the COM method's call stack. This is the purpose of the `__cdecl` calling convention, which states the caller cleans the stack. The stack is actually untouched by `remserialize()`, which is critical to the operation of the serialization routines. The stack will later be returned to its original state when the remote method call has completely finished. This means the method arguments for `remserialize()` are shared by the arguments to the COM method. Furthermore, because you reserved eight bytes of stack memory for local variable storage, these eight bytes also show up as `remserialize()` arguments. (They are indicated by the `volatile` keyword in the argument list.)

LISTING 10.39   `CSOAPSerializer::remserialize()` Implementation

```cpp
DWORD __cdecl remserialize(volatile HRESULT hrFromSerialization,
                           volatile DWORD dwStackSize,
                           DWORD /*ebp*/,
                           DWORD dwVtblOffset,
                           void* /*retaddr*/,
                           CSOAPSerializer& me,
                           void* pvArgs)
{
    // Lock critical section...
    me.m_cs.Lock();

    const DWORD dwMethod = dwVtblOffset / sizeof(void*);

    HGLOBAL hTypeStream = NULL;
    LPSTREAM lpTypeStream = NULL;
    CStackCruncher* pCruncher = NULL;
    CSOAPHttpTransaction* pTransaction = NULL;
    DWORD dwReturn = 0;
    try {
        // Create a stream for processing the type information
        hTypeStream = GlobalAlloc(GMEM_MOVEABLE|GMEM_SHARE,0);
        if ( hTypeStream != NULL ) {
            HRESULT hr = CreateStreamOnHGlobal(hTypeStream,TRUE,
                                               &lpTypeStream);
```

continues

10

IMPLEMENTING
SOAP

LISTING **10.39** Continued

```
        if ( FAILED(hr) ) throw -1;
    } // if
    else {
        throw -1;
    } // if

    // Encode the type library information for this method
    hrFromSerialization = me.m_spEncoder->EncodeMethod(
                        ➥me.m_spTypeLib,me.m_bstrCLSID,
                        me.m_bstrIID,dwMethod,
                        (long*)&dwStackSize,lpTypeStream);
    if ( FAILED(hrFromSerialization) ) throw -1;

    // Extract the pertinent SOAP call information and set
    // the seek pointer on the type stream for parsing the
    // call stack.
    SOAPCALLINFO ciInfo;
    hrFromSerialization = me.GetCallInfo(&ciInfo,lpTypeStream);
    if ( FAILED(hrFromSerialization) ) throw -1;

    // Parse the stack and extract information from method args
    pCruncher = new CStackCruncher;
    hrFromSerialization = me.ParseArgs((int**)&pvArgs,pCruncher,
                                        lpTypeStream);
    if ( FAILED(hrFromSerialization) ) throw -1;

    // With the stack information in hand, create the SOAP packet
    pTransaction = new CSOAPHttpTransaction(&ciInfo);
    hrFromSerialization = me.SoapEncode(pCruncher,pTransaction);
    if ( FAILED(hrFromSerialization) ) throw -1;

    // Send the SOAP information to the remote server
    hrFromSerialization = me.SendReceive(pTransaction);
    if ( FAILED(hrFromSerialization) ) throw -1;

    // Pull the return value and store any [out] data
    HRESULT hrApp = hrFromSerialization = E_FAIL;
    HRESULT hrDecode = me.SoapDecode(pCruncher,pTransaction,
                                        hrApp);
    if ( FAILED(hrDecode) ) throw -1;

    hrFromSerialization = hrApp;
    if ( FAILED(hrFromSerialization) ) throw -1;
} // try
catch(...) {
```

```
    // Some error
    dwReturn = -1;
    OutputDebugString(_T("Unexpected application error in
     ➡serialization object while serializing\n"));
} // catch

// Release the stream objects
if ( lpTypeStream != NULL ) {
    lpTypeStream->Release();
    lpTypeStream = NULL;
} // if

// Free the stream memory
if ( hTypeStream != NULL ) {
    GlobalFree(hTypeStream);
    hTypeStream = NULL;
} // if

// Free the remaining objects
if ( pCruncher != NULL ) {
    delete pCruncher;
    pCruncher = NULL;
} // if
if ( pTransaction != NULL ) {
    delete pTransaction;
    pTransaction = NULL;
} // if

// Unlock critical section...
me.m_cs.Unlock();

return dwReturn;
}
```

Finally, after nearly 100 pages of background, you are ready to serialize a COM call stack!
The serialization process begins with the method number calculation:

```
const DWORD dwMethod = dwVtblOffset / sizeof(void*);
```

This will be used to encode the type information for the call stack. The next step is to create
the stream for the encoded type information:

```
// Create a stream for processing the type information
hTypeStream = GlobalAlloc(GMEM_MOVEABLE|GMEM_SHARE,0);
if ( hTypeStream != NULL ) {
    HRESULT hr = CreateStreamOnHGlobal(hTypeStream,TRUE,
                                       &lpTypeStream);
```

```
    if ( FAILED(hr) ) throw -1;
} // if
else {
    throw -1;
} // if
```

The stream pointer and method number are then passed to the TLBEncoder object so that the type information can be accessed as the call stack is accessed. Note that the overall call stack size is returned by the encoder to facilitate stack cleanup:

```
// Encode the type library information for this method
hrFromSerialization = me.m_spEncoder->EncodeMethod(me.m_spTypeLib,
                               me.m_bstrCLSID,
                               me.m_bstrIID,dwMethod,
                               (long*)&dwStackSize,lpTypeStream);
if ( FAILED(hrFromSerialization) ) throw -1;
```

It's also interesting to note that the implicit this pointer isn't implicit when used in remserialize(), hence the reference me. (The variable name was used, tongue-in-cheek, from Visual Basic.)

With the encoded type information in hand, the SOAP method call information is determined by a call to CSOAPSerializer::GetCallInfo():

```
// Extract the pertinent SOAP call information and set
// the seek pointer on the type stream for parsing the
// call stack.
SOAPCALLINFO ciInfo;
hrFromSerialization = me.GetCallInfo(&ciInfo,lpTypeStream);
if ( FAILED(hrFromSerialization) ) throw -1;
```

GetCallInfo() is a helper function that extracts information from the type byte stream, such as the interface and method names. It also locates the namespace and the endpoint URL values. All this information is recorded in a SOAPCALLINFO structure that will eventually be passed to the SOAP encoding logic. You'll find GetCallInfo() implemented in SOAPSerializer.cpp.

The magic moment has arrived. It's time to dig the method arguments from the call stack and encode them in a SOAP format. This code initiates the call stack parsing:

```
// Parse the stack and extract information from method args
pCruncher = new CStackCruncher;
hrFromSerialization = me.ParseArgs((int**)&pvArgs,pCruncher,
                                   lpTypeStream);
if ( FAILED(hrFromSerialization) ) throw -1;
```

A new object, the stack cruncher, is created and passed to CSOAPSerializer::ParseArgs(). The stack cruncher will actually consume the stack information and maintain a queue of stack data. But, first, let's examine ParseArgs(),shown in Listing 10.40.

LISTING 10.40   CSOAPSerializer::ParseArgs() Implementation

```
HRESULT CSOAPSerializer::ParseArgs(int** ppArgs,
                                   CStackCruncher* pCruncher,
                                   LPSTREAM lpStream)
{
    // pvArgs points to the first argument, so index
    // from there depending upon what the encoding string
    // tells you.  The stack size always starts at 4, and
    // add the appropriate number of bytes depending upon
    // what is pushed onto the stack.
    //
    // | this | <-- implicit stack size (first 4 bytes of stack)
    // | arg0 |
    // | arg1 |
    // | .... |
    // | argn | <-- last argument (rightmost in method prototype
    // +------+     because of __stdcall call declaration)

    if ( pCruncher == NULL ) return E_OUTOFMEMORY;

    // Interpret the call stack
    HRESULT hr = pCruncher->Crunch(ppArgs,lpStream);
    if ( FAILED(hr) ) {
        return hr;
    } // if

    return hr;
}
```

ParseArgs() delegates call stack information removal to the CStackCruncher object:

```
HRESULT hr = pCruncher->Crunch(ppArgs,lpStream);
```

The call stack is examined, and the data retrieved in the CStackCruncher::Crunch() method, which you see in Listing 10.41.

LISTING 10.41   CStackCruncher::Crunch() Implementation

```
HRESULT CStackCruncher::Crunch(int** ppArgs, LPSTREAM lpStream)
{
    HRESULT hr = S_OK;
    int** pEBP = ppArgs;

    // Pull the stream information and allocate the type buffer
    LARGE_INTEGER li = {0};
    lpStream->Seek(li,STREAM_SEEK_SET,NULL);
```

10

IMPLEMENTING
SOAP

continues

LISTING 10.41   Continued

```
STATSTG statstg;
lpStream->Stat(&statstg,STATFLAG_NONAME);

m_iTypeStringLen = statstg.cbSize.LowPart;
m_pTypeString = new BYTE[m_iTypeStringLen];
lpStream->Read((void*)(m_pTypeString),statstg.cbSize.LowPart,NULL);

m_pSeekPtr = m_pTypeString;
int iS1 = *((int*)m_pSeekPtr);
int iS2 = *((int*)(m_pSeekPtr+4));
if ((iS1 != TLB_SIG1) || (iS2 != TLB_SIG2)) {
    // Incorrect signature
    return E_INVALIDARG;
} // if

// Skip signature
m_pSeekPtr += 2*sizeof(int);

// Check version (1.0)
BYTE iV1 = *m_pSeekPtr;
BYTE iV2 = *(m_pSeekPtr+1);
if ((iV1 != 1) || (iV2 != 0)) {
    // Incorrect version
    return E_INVALIDARG;
} // if

// Skip version
m_pSeekPtr += 2; // skip 2 bytes

// Add offset to obtain pointer to argument information...
// This skips all of the interface/method junk to get right
// to the meat of the argument processing.
hr = Seek((int)(*m_pSeekPtr));
if ( FAILED(hr) ) return E_INVALIDARG;

// Parse the stack...
while ( *m_pSeekPtr != TLB_EOF ) {
    // While you have tokens to parse, you have
    // argument data, so create a new STACKDATA
    // and complete.
    LPSTACKDATA pStackData = new STACKDATA;

    // Initialize it
    pStackData->iType = TLB_NUL;
    pStackData->nNumRefs = 0;
```

```
pStackData->mdType = MD_NUL;
pStackData->strName[0] = '\0';
pStackData->pValPtr = NULL;
pStackData->dblVal = 0.0; // clears all 8 bytes...

// Now parse the marshal information
switch (*m_pSeekPtr ) {
    case TLB_IN:
        pStackData->mdType = MD_IN;
        break;
    case TLB_OUT:
        pStackData->mdType = MD_OUT;
        break;
    case TLB_IOUT:
        pStackData->mdType = MD_INOUT;
        break;
} // switch

// Move the seek pointer to the type byte
++m_pSeekPtr;

// ExtractStackData() pulls the information from
// the stack and stuffs it into the provided
// STACKDATA record.
ExtractStackData(pEBP,pStackData);

// Move the seek pointer to the name
++m_pSeekPtr;

// Copy the name
_tcscpy(pStackData->strName,
        reinterpret_cast<char*>(m_pSeekPtr));

// Skip the name
m_pSeekPtr += (_tcslen(pStackData->strName) + 1);
                              ➥// skip trailing TLB_NUL

// At this point the seek pointer will either be
// pointing to another marshal parameter or TLB_EOF
//
// Bump the count
++m_iNumArgs;

// Bump the pointer (increments by four bytes...)
++pEBP;
if ((pStackData->iType == TLB_DBL) &&
```

10

IMPLEMENTING
SOAP

continues

LISTING 10.41   Continued

```
                (!pStackData->nNumRefs)) ++pEBP;
                              ➡// account for additional 4 bytes

        // Enqueue the stack data record
        if ( !EnqueueArg(pStackData) ) {
            // Couldn't queue up the record???
            hr = E_INVALIDARG;
            break;
        } // if
    } // while

    return hr;
}
```

The stack crunching begins by rewinding the type information stream and retrieving the stream information into a local buffer:

```
// Pull the stream information and allocate the type buffer
LARGE_INTEGER li = {0};
lpStream->Seek(li,STREAM_SEEK_SET,NULL);
STATSTG statstg;
lpStream->Stat(&statstg,STATFLAG_NONAME);

m_iTypeStringLen = statstg.cbSize.LowPart;
m_pTypeString = new BYTE[m_iTypeStringLen];
lpStream->Read((void*)(m_pTypeString),statstg.cbSize.LowPart,NULL);

m_pSeekPtr = m_pTypeString;
```

Then, the type information byte stream is examined byte by byte, starting with the signature and version bytes:

```
int iS1 = *((int*)m_pSeekPtr);
int iS2 = *((int*)(m_pSeekPtr+4));
if ((iS1 != TLB_SIG1) || (iS2 != TLB_SIG2)) {
    // Incorrect signature
    return E_INVALIDARG;
} // if

// Skip signature
m_pSeekPtr += 2*sizeof(int);

// Check version (1.0)
BYTE iV1 = *m_pSeekPtr;
BYTE iV2 = *(m_pSeekPtr+1);
if ((iV1 != 1) || (iV2 != 0)) {
```

```
    // Incorrect version
    return E_INVALIDARG;
} // if

// Skip version
m_pSeekPtr += 2; // skip 2 bytes
```

Assuming the signature and version bytes are as expected, the type byte buffer pointer is moved past the ancillary method information (interface and method name, for example) to place the pointer at the first byte of argument type data:

```
// Add offset to obtain pointer to argument information...
// This skips all of the interface/method junk to get right
// to the meat of the argument processing.
hr = Seek((int)(*m_pSeekPtr));
if ( FAILED(hr) ) return E_INVALIDARG;
```

Next, a loop begins to extract the stack data and creates stack data records for each argument:

```
// Parse the stack...
while ( *m_pSeekPtr != TLB_EOF ) {
    // Process each argument individually
} // while
```

The argument processing begins with the creation of a stack data record:

```
// While you have tokens to parse, you have
// argument data, so create a new STACKDATA
// and complete.
LPSTACKDATA pStackData = new STACKDATA;

// Initialize it
pStackData->iType = TLB_NUL;
pStackData->nNumRefs = 0;
pStackData->mdType = MD_NUL;
pStackData->strName[0] = '\0';
pStackData->pValPtr = NULL;
pStackData->dblVal = 0.0; // clears all 8 bytes...
```

Then the argument marshalling information is determined:

```
// Now parse the marshal information
switch (*m_pSeekPtr ) {
    case TLB_IN:
        pStackData->mdType = MD_IN;
        break;
    case TLB_OUT:
        pStackData->mdType = MD_OUT;
        break;
    case TLB_IOUT:
```

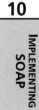

10

IMPLEMENTING
SOAP

```
        pStackData->mdType = MD_INOUT;
        break;
} // switch
```

Then, the call stack is accessed, and the data contained there is retrieved:

```
// Move the seek pointer to the type byte
++m_pSeekPtr;

// ExtractStackData() pulls the information from
// the stack and stuffs it into the provided
// STACKDATA record.
ExtractStackData(pEBP,pStackData);
```

Keep the ExtractStackData() method in mind for a moment. Assuming the data was extracted, the argument name is pulled from the type information:

```
// Move the seek pointer to the name
++m_pSeekPtr;

// Copy the name
_tcscpy(pStackData->strName,
        reinterpret_cast<char*>(m_pSeekPtr));

// Skip the name
m_pSeekPtr += (_tcslen(pStackData->strName) + 1);
                            ➥// skip trailing TLB_NUL
```

At this point, this argument has been parsed. There might be more, or this might be the last. (It depends upon the method.) In any case the number of arguments parsed must be incremented, and the data pointer to the next argument, bumped:

```
// Bump the count
        ++m_iNumArgs;

        // Bump the pointer (increments by four bytes...)
        ++pEBP;
        if ((pStackData->iType == TLB_DBL) &&
            (!pStackData->nNumRefs)) ++pEBP;
                        ➥// account for additional 4 bytes
```

The stack argument pointer (pEBP) is incremented again if the stack data contained double information, which requires eight bytes of stack storage.

The argument information, now stored in the stack data record, is placed on a data queue for later SOAP encoding:

```
// Enqueue the stack data record
if ( !EnqueueArg(pStackData) ) {
```

```
    // Couldn't queue up the record???
    hr = E_INVALIDARG;
    break;
} // if
```

The meat of the stack data extraction was performed in ExtractStackData(). This method has a switch() statement that directs stack processing depending upon the data type of the argument. For all (supported) data types except double and pointers, ExtractStackData() executes a macro:

EXTRACTDATA

The macro expands to this:

```
if ( !pStackData->nNumRefs ) {
    __asm push ebp
    __asm mov ebp,pEBP
    __asm mov eax,dword ptr [ebp]
    __asm pop ebp
    __asm mov dword ptr [ebp-0Ch],eax
}
else {
    __asm push ebp
    __asm mov ebp,pEBP
    __asm mov ecx,dword ptr [ebp]
    __asm pop ebp
    __asm mov edx,dword ptr [ecx]
    __asm mov dword ptr [ebp-0Ch],edx
}
```

Yes, more assembly language! But, once again, it isn't too difficult to understand when you see what it is doing. The stack data is extracted differently if it is by value or by reference. If by value, the stack contains the data itself. If by reference, the stack contains a pointer that indicates where in memory the actual data resides.

If the argument is passed by value, this code is executed:

```
push ebp
mov ebp,pEBP
mov eax,dword ptr [ebp]
pop ebp
mov dword ptr [ebp-0Ch],eax
```

The current base pointer is saved (push ebp), and the pointer to the stack argument is stuffed into the base pointer to facilitate the data extraction (mov ebp,pEBP). The data residing at pEBP is loaded into the accumulator (mov eax,dword ptr [ebp]). eax now holds the stack data! Finally, the original base pointer is restored (pop ebp), and the data in the accumulator is stored in a local variable defined in ExtractStackData() (mov dword ptr [ebp-0Ch],eax).

10

Referenced data must first be dereferenced, so there is an additional step that loads the data pointer (mov ecx,dword ptr [ebp]) and then accesses the data located in some arbitrary memory address (mov edx,dword ptr [ecx]).

Now let's look at ExtractStackData(), shown in Listing 10.42.

LISTING 10.42   CStackCruncher::ExtractStackData() Implementation

```
void CStackCruncher::ExtractStackData(int** ppArg,
                                        LPSTACKDATA pStackData)
{
    // Allocate some scratch memory to be used when dereferencing
    // stack data. 8 bytes is required as that's the largest data
    // size (sizeof(double)). The memory is referenced (via the base
    // pointer) at an offset of 0Ch, hence this assembly language:
    //
    // mov dword ptr [ebp-0Ch],eax
    //
    // which says to move the data in the eax register into the
    // memory pointed to by the base pointer less 12 bytes (0Ch).
    // If you change this code and insert new local variables,
    // do so after the scratch memory or you'll need to recalculate
    // the appropriate offset (the 0Ch value will change).
    BYTE scratch[8] = {0}; // scratch memory
    int** pEBP = ppArg;

    // Pull the stack data
    switch ( *m_pSeekPtr ) {
        case TLB_I2:
            {
                pStackData->iType = TLB_I2;
                EXTRACTDATA;
                pStackData->iVal = *((short*)scratch);
            }
            break;

        case TLB_UI2:
            {
                pStackData->iType = TLB_UI2;
                EXTRACTDATA;
                pStackData->uiVal = *((unsigned short*)scratch);
            }
            break;

        case TLB_I4:
            {
                pStackData->iType = TLB_I4;
```

```
        EXTRACTDATA;
        pStackData->lVal = *((long*)scratch);
    }
    break;

case TLB_UI4:
    {
        pStackData->iType = TLB_UI4;
        EXTRACTDATA;
        pStackData->ulVal = *((unsigned long*)scratch);
    }
    break;

case TLB_INT:
    {
        pStackData->iType = TLB_INT;
        EXTRACTDATA;
        pStackData->intVal = *((int*)scratch);
    }
    break;

case TLB_UINT:
    {
        pStackData->iType = TLB_UINT;
        EXTRACTDATA;
        pStackData->uintVal = *((unsigned int*)scratch);
    }
    break;

case TLB_FLT:
    {
        pStackData->iType = TLB_FLT;
        EXTRACTDATA;
        pStackData->fltVal = *((float*)scratch);
    }
    break;

case TLB_DBL:
    {
        pStackData->iType = TLB_DBL;
        if ( !pStackData->nNumRefs ) {
            // Double data is a bit different in that it
            // consumes 8 bytes on the stack, whereas all
            // of the other data types handled consume 4
            // (including pointers). So, The first thing to
            // do is determine how much stack was consumed.
            // If this was a reference to a double, that means
```

10

IMPLEMENTING
SOAP

continues

LISTING 10.42   Continued

```
        // a pointer was on the stack, so return 4 bytes
        // consumed (which was done when the pointer was
        // handled). If, on the other hand, the actual
        // double value was pushed onto the stack, then
        // pop off 8 bytes later when the stack is
        // cleaned.
        //
        // Is direct value
        __asm {
            push ebp
            mov ebp,pEBP
            mov eax,dword ptr [ebp] // first 4 bytes
            pop ebp
            mov dword ptr [ebp-0Ch],eax // &scratch[0]
            push ebp
            mov ebp,pEBP
            mov ecx,dword ptr [ebp+04h] // last 4 bytes
            pop ebp
            mov dword ptr [ebp-08h],ecx // &scratch[4]
        } // __asm
    } // if
    else {
        // Is referenced value
        __asm {
            push ebp
            mov ebp,pEBP
            mov eax,dword ptr [ebp] // address of double
            mov ecx,dword ptr [eax] // first 4 bytes
            pop ebp
            mov dword ptr [ebp-0Ch],ecx // &scratch[0]
            push ebp
            mov ebp,pEBP
            mov edx,dword ptr [eax+4] // second 4 bytes
            pop ebp
            mov dword ptr [ebp-08h],edx // &scratch [4]
        } // __asm
    } // else

    // If the double value was referenced, it is entirely
    // possible the value read will be something
    // completely useless, like 5.3476831e-348 (as an
    // example), because the memory was not initialized.
    // This should really be interpreted as zero,
    // but the conversion back to a true double will
    // suffice.
```

```
                pStackData->dblVal = *((double*)scratch);
        }
        break;

case TLB_BSTR:
        {
                pStackData->iType = TLB_BSTR;
                EXTRACTDATA;
                pStackData->bstrVal = *((BSTR*)scratch);
        }
        break;

case TLB_BOOL:
        {
                pStackData->iType = TLB_BOOL;
                EXTRACTDATA;
                pStackData->boolVal = *((bool*)scratch);
        }
        break;

case TLB_HRESULT:
        {
                pStackData->iType = TLB_HRESULT;
                EXTRACTDATA;
                pStackData->ulVal = *((unsigned long*)scratch);
        }
        break;

case TLB_PTR:
        {
                // Chase the pointer.  The final recurse
                // will adjust the stack size as well as
                // complete the stack data structure.
                ++pStackData->nNumRefs;
                ++m_pSeekPtr;
                __asm {
                        push ebp
                        mov  ebp,pEBP
                        mov  eax,dword ptr [ebp]
                        pop  ebp
                        mov  dword ptr [ebp-0Ch],eax
                } // asm

                // The pointer is in eax, so store it as the last
                // known pointer. You'll need this to fill the
                // [in,out] or [out] argument with data when the
```

continues

10

IMPLEMENTING
SOAP

LISTING 10.42 Continued

```
                    // SOAP call returns... The interesting casting
                    // tells the compiler to take the contents of
                    // the scratch memory as 4 bytes instead of
                    // one:
                    //
                    // *(int*)scratch
                    // |   |       |
                    // |   |       +-----data is at this address
                    // |   +-----------pretend the data is int (4 bytes)
                    // +--------------return the contents of the address
                    //
                    // You then must convert that to a BYTE* to
                    // stuff it into the stack data structure:
                    //
                    // (BYTE*)(...)
                    //      |
                    //      +-----------pretend data is a ptr to BYTE info
                    //
                    // What gets stored in pValPtr is the last pointer
                    // reference to the data, which is where the [in,out]
                    // and [out] data will eventually be stored.
                    pStackData->pValPtr = (BYTE*)(*(int*)scratch);
                    ExtractStackData((int**)scratch,pStackData);
                }
                break;

        case TLB_VOID:
        default:
            {
                pStackData->iType = TLB_VOID;
                EXTRACTDATA;
                pStackData->ulVal = *((unsigned long*)scratch);
            }
            break;
    } // switch
}
```

As you can see from Listing 10.42, `ExtractStackData()` is somewhat lengthy, but it is also relatively straightforward if you understand the assembly language contained in the `EXTRACTDATA` macro (as discussed previously).

First, carve out an additional eight bytes of local storage to be used as scratch memory:

```
BYTE scratch[8] = {0}; // scratch memory
```

Then assign the argument pointer to be an `int**`, which allows you to access the stack data four bytes at a time:

```
int** pEBP = ppArg;
```

Based upon the type information, pull the stack data in a big `switch()` statement:

```
switch ( *m_pSeekPtr ) {
    case TLB_I2:
        // short
    case TLB_UI2:
        // unsigned short

    ...

    case TLB_VOID:
        // void (or HRESULT return type)
} // switch
```

With a couple of notable exceptions, the data comes from the stack as follows. (This example is for `long` data.)

```
case TLB_I4:
    {
        pStackData->iType = TLB_I4;
        EXTRACTDATA;
        pStackData->lVal = *((long*)scratch);
    }
break;
```

In the this case, the type is recorded in the stack data record:

```
pStackData->iType = TLB_I4;
```

Then, pull the relevant four bytes from the stack and place them into the scratch memory. (Remember that the macro expands to the assembly language you saw previously.)

```
EXTRACTDATA;
```

Finally, copy the scratch memory to the stack data record.

```
pStackData->lVal = *((long*)scratch);
```

The casting (`*((long*)scratch)`) is required to make sure the correct data is placed in the stack data record. The cast essentially says `scratch` is a `long*` variable, so dereference that pointer to obtain the `long` data. Most of the other data types are the same.

The two notable exceptions are `double` values and pointers. `double` values are actually eight bytes of data, instead of four, so the generic stack-access macro `EXTRACTDATA` won't work in this case. Instead, it is modified slightly to pull the first and then the second four-byte chunks of the `double` value. You can see this in Listing 10.42.

10

IMPLEMENTING
SOAP

Pointers require additional processing because the stack data represents a reference to some data, rather than to the data itself. In this case, ExtractStackData() recurses itself using the pointer value as the base pointer:

```
case TLB_PTR:
    {
        // Chase the pointer.  The final recurse
        // will adjust the stack size as well as
        // complete the stack data structure.
        ++pStackData->nNumRefs;
        ++m_pSeekPtr;
        __asm {
            push ebp
            mov  ebp,pEBP
            mov  eax,dword ptr [ebp]
            pop  ebp
            mov  dword ptr [ebp-0Ch],eax
        } // asm

        // The pointer is in eax, so store it as the last
        // known pointer. You'll need this to fill the
        // [in,out] or [out] argument with data when the
        // SOAP call returns... The interesting casting
        // tells the compiler to take the contents of
        // the scratch memory as 4 bytes instead of
        // one:
        //
        // *(int*)scratch
        // |  |      |
        // |  |      +-----data is at this address
        // |  +-----------pretend the data is int (4 bytes)
        // +--------------return the contents of the address
        //
        // You then must convert that to a BYTE* to
        // stuff it into the stack data structure:
        //
        // (BYTE*)(...)
        //    |
        //    +-----------pretend data is a ptr to BYTE info
        //
        // What gets stored in pValPtr is the last pointer
        // reference to the data, which is where the [in,out]
        // and [out] data will eventually be stored.
        pStackData->pValPtr = (BYTE*)(*(int*)scratch);
        ExtractStackData((int**)scratch,pStackData);
    }
break;
```

Here, the fact that the data is referenced is recorded in the stack data record:

```
++pStackData->nNumRefs;
```

Then the pointer is retrieved and placed into `scratch`:

```
__asm {
    push ebp
    mov   ebp,pEBP
    mov   eax,dword ptr [ebp]
    pop   ebp
    mov   dword ptr [ebp-0Ch],eax
} // asm
```

The pointer is saved, so that at a later time any `[out]` or `[in,out]` data can be placed into the variable:

```
pStackData->pValPtr = (BYTE*)(*(int*)scratch);
```

Finally `ExtractStackData()` recurses itself based upon the pointer it found on the stack:

```
ExtractStackData((int**)scratch,pStackData);
```

Referring again to Listing 10.39 (`remserialize()`), the stack (argument) parsing is now complete, and any argument data is queued to be encoded in the SOAP protocol. (Remember: The data queue is held by the stack crunching object.) Assuming there was no error while pulling the stack data, `remserialize()` creates an HTTP transaction object and calls the serializer's `SoapEncode()` method:

```
// With the stack information in hand, create the SOAP packet
pTransaction = new CSOAPHttpTransaction(&ciInfo);
hrFromSerialization = me.SoapEncode(pCruncher,pTransaction);
if ( FAILED(hrFromSerialization) ) throw -1;
```

`SoapEncode()` combines the queued stack information and the SOAP object model code you saw previously to form a SOAP request packet. You can see this in Listing 10.43.

LISTING 10.43 CSOAPSerializer::SoapEncode() Implementation

```
HRESULT CSOAPSerializer::SoapEncode(CStackCruncher* pCruncher,
                                    CSOAPHttpTransaction* pTransaction)
{
    HRESULT hr = S_OK;
    try {
        // Retrieve the envelope
        CSOAPHttpPacket* pPacket = pTransaction->GetPacket();
        if ( !pPacket ) throw E_OUTOFMEMORY;
```

10

IMPLEMENTING
SOAP

continues

LISTING 10.43 Continued

```
// Retrieve the envelope
CSOAPEnvelope* pEnvelope = pPacket->GetEnvelope();
if ( !pEnvelope ) throw E_OUTOFMEMORY;

// Insert the namespace...note the defined namespace
// is not used in its entirety...the short namespace is
// used in conjunction with the IID.
TCHAR strNamespace[_MAX_PATH];
_tcscpy(strNamespace,m_strNamespace); // work with a copy...
LPTSTR pszShortNamespace = _tcstok(strNamespace,_T(":"));
USES_CONVERSION;
std::string strMainNamespace(W2T(m_bstrIID));

std::string strMethod;
pPacket->GetMethodName(strMethod);
strMainNamespace += _T(":");
strMainNamespace += strMethod;
long iCookie = NULLNSCOOKIE;
HRESULT hr = pEnvelope->InsertNamespace(strMainNamespace,
                    std::string(pszShortNamespace),&iCookie);
if ( FAILED(hr) ) throw hr;

// Enable the COM namespace
pEnvelope->EnableStdNamespace(COMNSCOOKIE,true);

// Insert a header element that represents the object
// ID...in this case the CLSID.
CSOAPHeader* pHeader = pEnvelope->GetHeader();
CSOAPIndElement* pObjID = NULL;
hr = pHeader->InsertElement(std::string("CLSID"),
                                COMNSCOOKIE,&pObjID);
if ( FAILED(hr) )  throw hr;

// Set the root attribute
pObjID->EnableStdAttribute(ROOTATTRCOOKIE,true);

// Set the mustUnderstand attribute
pObjID->EnableStdAttribute(MUNDATTRCOOKIE,true);

LPTSTR pstrCLSID = W2T(m_bstrCLSID);
pObjID->SetElementData(std::string(pstrCLSID));

// TODO: enter a call (or causality) ID?
```

```
// Next insert the method's independent element into the
// body
CSOAPBody* pBody = pEnvelope->GetBody();
CSOAPIndElement* pMethodElement = NULL;
pPacket->GetMethodName(strMainNamespace); // memory reuse...
hr = pBody->InsertElement(strMainNamespace,iCookie,
                          &pMethodElement);
if ( FAILED(hr) ) throw hr;


// The call stack has been interpreted and the data and data
// types are stuffed in the cruncher's queue, so dequeue the
// stack data and create SOAP independent elements from what
// is stored there.
LPSTACKDATA pStackData = pCruncher->DequeueArg();
while ( pStackData != NULL ) {
    // Don't encode [out]-only arguments...
    if ( pStackData->mdType != MD_OUT ) {
        // For each argument an embedded method element will
        // need to be created. However, it depends upon what
        // type of data is stored. If the data is single-ref,
        // then the data goes directly into the element. If
        // the data is multi-ref or string, then a reference
        // element is inserted and the data becomes a new
        // independent element under the body.
        CSOAPEmbeddedElement* pArgument = NULL;
        hr = pMethodElement->InsertElement(
                        ➥std::string(pStackData->strName),
                        NULLNSCOOKIE,&pArgument);
        if ( FAILED(hr) ) throw hr;


        // Check for multi-ref status
        if ((pStackData->nNumRefs) ||
            (pStackData->iType == TLB_BSTR)) {
            // Either a referenced value or a string, so the
            // element gets an href attribute.
            static int iCount = 1;
            TCHAR strHrefId[8] = {0};
            wsprintf(strHrefId,"#ID%03d",iCount++);
            hr = pArgument->InsertAttribute(NULLNSCOOKIE,
                        std::string("href"),
                        std::string(strHrefId));
            if ( FAILED(hr) ) throw hr;


            // The data needs to be placed in a new
            // independent element.
```

continues

LISTING 10.43   Continued

```
                 CSOAPIndElement* pArgData = NULL;
                 hr = pBody->InsertElement(pStackData->strName,
                                           iCookie,&pArgData);
                 if ( FAILED(hr) ) throw hr;

                 hr = pArgData->InsertAttribute(NULLNSCOOKIE,
                         std::string("id"),
                         std::string(&strHrefId[1])); // skip '#'
                 if ( FAILED(hr) ) throw hr;

                 // The data and data type depend...
                 if ( pStackData->iType == TLB_BSTR ) {
                    // Is string type
                    hr = pArgData->InsertAttribute(XSINSCOOKIE,
                                    std::string("type"),
                                    std::string("string"));
                    if ( FAILED(hr) ) throw hr;

                    pArgData->SetElementData(
          ➡std::string(W2T((BSTR)pStackData->bstrVal)),true);
                 } // if
                 else if ((pStackData->iType == TLB_FLT) ||
                         (pStackData->iType == TLB_DBL)) {
                    // Is floating point type
                    hr = pArgData->InsertAttribute(XSINSCOOKIE,
                                    std::string("type"),
                                     std::string("number"));
                    if ( FAILED(hr) ) throw hr;

                    double dVal = pStackData->dblVal;
                    if ( pStackData->iType == TLB_FLT ) {
                        // Adjust...value is float, not double
                        dVal = (double)pStackData->fltVal;
                    } // if

                    TCHAR dblValBuf[256] = {0};
                    _gcvt(dVal,10,dblValBuf);
                    pArgData->SetElementData(std::string(dblValBuf));
                 } // else if
                 else {
                    // Is integer type
                    hr = pArgData->InsertAttribute(XSINSCOOKIE,
                                    std::string("type"),
                                    std::string("int"));
                    if ( FAILED(hr) ) throw hr;
```

```
              TCHAR intValBuf[64] = {0};
              long iVal = (long)pStackData->lVal;
              if ((pStackData->iType == TLB_I2) ||
                  (pStackData->iType == TLB_UI2)) {
                  // Adjust...value is short, not 32 bits
                  iVal = (long)pStackData->iVal;
                           ➥// handles unsigned case...
              } // if

              itoa(iVal,intValBuf,10);
              pArgData->SetElementData(
                                ➥std::string(intValBuf));
         } // else
  } // if
  else {
      // Single-ref value, so stuff into independent
      // element
      if ((pStackData->iType == TLB_FLT) ||
          (pStackData->iType == TLB_DBL)) {
          // Is floating point type
          double dVal = pStackData->dblVal;
          if ( pStackData->iType == TLB_FLT ) {
              // Adjust...value is float, not double
              dVal = (double)pStackData->fltVal;
          } // if

          TCHAR dblValBuf[256] = {0};
          _gcvt(dVal,10,dblValBuf);
          pArgument->SetElementData(
                        ➥std::string(dblValBuf));
      } // else if
      else {
          // Is integer type
          TCHAR intValBuf[64] = {0};
          long iVal = (long)pStackData->lVal;
          if ((pStackData->iType == TLB_I2) ||
              (pStackData->iType == TLB_UI2)) {
              // Adjust...value is short, not 32 bits
              iVal = (long)pStackData->iVal;
                       ➥// handles unsigned case...
          } // if

          itoa(iVal,intValBuf,10);
  pArgument->SetElementData(std::string(intValBuf));
      } // else
```

continues

10

LISTING 10.43 Continued

```
                } // else
            } // if

            // If the data is out or in/out, save the stack data
            // to later stuff the return value
            if ((pStackData->mdType == MD_OUT) ||
                (pStackData->mdType == MD_INOUT)) {
                // Save the stack data
                pCruncher->EnqueueOutArg(pStackData);
            } // if
            else {
                // Done with this stack data, so delete the record
                delete pStackData;
            } // else

            // Get the next stack record...
            pStackData = pCruncher->DequeueArg();
        } // while
    } // try
    catch(HRESULT hrErr) {
        // Some COM error...
        hr = hrErr; // normalize to this error...
        TCHAR strErrMsg[256] = {0};
        wsprintf(strErrMsg,"COM error in serialization object while
                        ➥encoding SOAP packet %#08x\n",hrErr);
        OutputDebugString(strErrMsg);
    } // catch
    catch(...) {
        // Some error...
        hr = E_UNEXPECTED;
        OutputDebugString(_T("Unexpected application error in
                ➥serialization object while encoding SOAP packet\n"));
    } // catch

    return hr;
}
```

The `CSOAPHttpTransaction` object aggregates the SOAP object model library, so the first thing to do is retrieve the SOAP HTTP packet object:

```
// Retrieve the envelope
CSOAPHttpPacket* pPacket = pTransaction->GetPacket();
if ( !pPacket ) throw E_OUTOFMEMORY;
```

Of course, given the HTTP packet, you next retrieve the SOAP envelope object:

```
// Retrieve the envelope
CSOAPEnvelope* pEnvelope = pPacket->GetEnvelope();
if ( !pEnvelope ) throw E_OUTOFMEMORY;
```

Then you add the method's namespace:

```
// Insert the namespace...note the defined namespace
// is not used in its entirety...the short namespace is
// used in conjunction with the IID.
TCHAR strNamespace[_MAX_PATH];
_tcscpy(strNamespace,m_strNamespace); // work with a copy...
LPTSTR pszShortNamespace = _tcstok(strNamespace,_T(":"));
USES_CONVERSION;
std::string strMainNamespace(W2T(m_bstrIID));

std::string strMethod;
pPacket->GetMethodName(strMethod);
strMainNamespace += _T(":");
strMainNamespace += strMethod;
long iCookie = NULLNSCOOKIE;
HRESULT hr = pEnvelope->InsertNamespace(strMainNamespace,
                   std::string(pszShortNamespace),&iCookie);
if ( FAILED(hr) ) throw hr;
```

> **NOTE**
>
> The remote processing architecture for this language binding assumes the namespace prefix is "m". The only enforcement of this on the client end is in the SOAPCnfg SOAP Configuration Utility, which you will typically use to add entries to the SOAP Catalog. If you add entries to the SOAP Catalog using your own client application but intend to use the remote processing architecture presented here, remember to use the m prefix also.

> **NOTE**
>
> The namespace entered into the SOAP Catalog is ignored in lieu of the interface's IID value (in string form). This enables the remote processing architecture to more easily extract the relevant IID value and invoke the object on the client's behalf.

10

IMPLEMENTING
SOAP

Next, the COM namespace is inserted into the envelope:

```
// Enable the COM namespace
      pEnvelope->EnableStdNamespace(COMNSCOOKIE,true);
```

This enables passing the object's CLSID/IID to the remote processing architecture. Because the COM namespace isn't part of the SOAP specification, you must explicitly activate it. In order for the remote processing architecture to also know what CLSID to use, the object's CLSID is inserted into the SOAP header:

```
// Insert a header element that represents the object
// ID...in this case the CLSID.
CSOAPHeader* pHeader = pEnvelope->GetHeader();
CSOAPIndElement* pObjID = NULL;
hr = pHeader->InsertElement(std::string("CLSID"),
                            COMNSCOOKIE,&pObjID);
if ( FAILED(hr) ) throw hr;

hr = pObjID->InsertAttribute(SOAPNSCOOKIE,
                std::string("rootWithId"),std::string("1"));
if ( FAILED(hr) ) throw hr;

// Set the root attribute
pObjID->EnableStdAttribute(ROOTATTRCOOKIE,true);

// Set the mustUnderstand attribute
pObjID->EnableStdAttribute(MUNDATTRCOOKIE,true);
```

With the SOAP header in place, it's time to turn to the SOAP body. Retrieve the body object from the SOAP envelope object and create and insert the method's independent element, as follows:

```
// Next insert the method's independent element into the
// body
CSOAPBody* pBody = pEnvelope->GetBody();
CSOAPIndElement* pMethodElement = NULL;
pPacket->GetMethodName(strMainNamespace); // memory reuse...
hr = pBody->InsertElement(strMainNamespace,iCookie,
                          &pMethodElement);
if ( FAILED(hr) ) throw hr;
```

Finally, a while loop processes the queued argument stack data records:

```
// The call stack has been interpreted and the data and data
// types are stuffed in the cruncher's queue, so dequeue the
// stack data and create SOAP independent elements from what
// is stored there.
LPSTACKDATA pStackData = pCruncher->DequeueArg();
```

```
while ( pStackData != NULL ) {
    // Don't encode [out]-only arguments...
    if ( pStackData->mdType != MD_OUT ) {
        // Process the individual argument
    } // if

    // Get the next stack record...
    pStackData = pCruncher->DequeueArg();
} // while
```

Note that [out] arguments do not get SOAP encoded. There is no need to do so, although the return pointer memory must have been allocated, or there will be no place to store the returned information.

For a given method argument, you must first insert a new embedded element into the method's independent element:

```
CSOAPEmbeddedElement* pArgument = NULL;
hr = pMethodElement->InsertElement(
                    ➥std::string(pStackData->strName),
                    NULLNSCOOKIE,&pArgument);
if ( FAILED(hr) ) throw hr;
```

It's possible that the method argument was a referenced value or a string. In either case, you must add another independent element to the SOAP body and reference it from the embedded element you just created:

```
// Check for multi-ref status
if ((pStackData->nNumRefs) ||
    (pStackData->iType == TLB_BSTR)) {
    // Either a referenced value or a string, so the
    // element gets an href attribute.
    static int iCount = 1;
    TCHAR strHrefId[8] = {0};
    wsprintf(strHrefId,"#ID%03d",iCount++);
    hr = pArgument->InsertAttribute(NULLNSCOOKIE,
                    std::string("href"),
                    std::string(strHrefId));
    if ( FAILED(hr) ) throw hr;

    // The data needs to be placed in a new
    // independent element.
    CSOAPIndElement* pArgData = NULL;
    hr = pBody->InsertElement(pStackData->strName,
                            iCookie,&pArgData);
    if ( FAILED(hr) ) throw hr;
```

```
    hr = pArgData->InsertAttribute(NULLNSCOOKIE,
            std::string("id"),
            std::string(&strHrefId[1])); // skip '#'
    if ( FAILED(hr) ) throw hr;

    // The data and data type depend...
    if ( pStackData->iType == TLB_BSTR ) {
    // Is string type
    hr = pArgData->InsertAttribute(XSINSCOOKIE,
                std::string("type"),
                std::string("string"));
    if ( FAILED(hr) ) throw hr;

    pArgData->SetElementData(
        ➥std::string(W2T((BSTR)pStackData->bstrVal)),true);
} // if
```

Whether passed by value or passed by reference, the value could be `double` or `float` data and require floating point to string conversion:

```
// Is floating point type
hr = pArgData->InsertAttribute(XSINSCOOKIE,
                std::string("type"),
                std::string("number"));
if ( FAILED(hr) ) throw hr;

double dVal = pStackData->dblVal;
if ( pStackData->iType == TLB_FLT ) {
    // Adjust...value is float, not double
    dVal = (double)pStackData->fltVal;
} // if

TCHAR dblValBuf[256] = {0};
_gcvt(dVal,10,dblValBuf);
pArgData->SetElementData(std::string(dblValBuf));
```

If the data is integer by nature, it is also converted to a string using the integer conversion routines:

```
// Is integer type
hr = pArgData->InsertAttribute(XSINSCOOKIE,
                std::string("type"),
                std::string("int"));
if ( FAILED(hr) ) throw hr;

TCHAR intValBuf[64] = {0};
```

```
long iVal = (long)pStackData->lVal;
if ((pStackData->iType == TLB_I2) ||
    (pStackData->iType == TLB_UI2)) {
    // Adjust...value is short, not 32 bits
    iVal = (long)pStackData->iVal;
                ➥// handles unsigned case...
} // if

itoa(iVal,intValBuf,10);
pArgData->SetElementData(
                    ➥std::string(intValBuf));
```

The encoding you've just seen is performed only if the argument is tagged as an [in] or
[in,out] parameter. You still must save the stack information to properly return [out] values.
The stack data record in this case is removed from the original stack queue and placed onto a
special [out] data queue. If the stack data record reflected an [in]-only parameter, the stack
data is no longer required, and the record is deleted:

```
// If the data is out or in/out, save the stack data
// to later stuff the return value
if ((pStackData->mdType == MD_OUT) ||
    (pStackData->mdType == MD_INOUT)) {
    // Save the stack data
    pCruncher->EnqueueOutArg(pStackData);
} // if
else {
    // Done with this stack data, so delete the record
    delete pStackData;
} // else
```

At this point in the overall serialization scheme, you have retrieved and interpreted the call
stack and created a SOAP-encoded packet. It's now time to ship the data to the remote
server.

Transmitting the Serialized Method Information

Referring again to Listing 10.39, you find this code:

```
// Send the SOAP information to the remote server
hrFromSerialization = me.SendReceive(pTransaction);
if ( FAILED(hrFromSerialization) ) throw -1;
```

The CSOAPSerializer::SendReceive() method takes the HTTP transaction object and sub-
mits it to the remote server. Its implementation is shown in Listing 10.44.

10

IMPLEMENTING
SOAP

LISTING 10.44 CSOAPSerializer::SendReceive() Implementation

```
HRESULT CSOAPSerializer::SendReceive(CSOAPHttpTransaction*
                                    ➥pTransaction)
{
    if ( !pTransaction ) return E_POINTER;

    HRESULT hr = S_OK;
    try {
        // SendReceive by delegating to transaction object
        hr = pTransaction->SendReceive();
    } // try
    catch(HRESULT hrErr) {
        // Some COM error...
        hr = hrErr; // normalize to this error...
        TCHAR strErrMsg[256] = {0};
        wsprintf(strErrMsg,"COM error in serialization object while
                            ➥encoding SOAP packet %#08x\n",hrErr);
        OutputDebugString(strErrMsg);
    } // catch
    catch(...) {
        // Some error...
        hr = E_UNEXPECTED;
        OutputDebugString(_T("Unexpected application error in
                ➥serialization object while encoding SOAP packet\n"));
    } // catch

    return hr;
}
```

The serializer simply delegates the SendReceive() call to the HTTP transaction object:

```
// SendReceive by delegating to transaction object
hr = pTransaction->SendReceive();
```

The HTTP transaction object, in turn, creates a new thread to submit the SOAP packet, as you can see in Listing 10.45.

LISTING 10.45 CSOAPHttpTransaction::SendReceive() Implementation

```
HRESULT CSOAPHttpTransaction::SendReceive()
{
    // Platform dependent portion:
    // On each SOAP-enabled system there must be
    // a mechanism for sending/receiving HTTP
    // requests/responses. In this case, this
```

```
// implementation will break from a pure
// C++ design and rely upon the Microsoft
// free-threaded XML parser. Other systems
// will resort to using other means...
LPTHRDDATA lpThreadParm = NULL;
LPTSTR szXML = NULL;
HRESULT hr = S_OK;
try {
    // Stream the HTTP packet
    std::ostrstream ostr;
    hr = m_pHttpPacket->WriteToStream(ostr,TRUE);
    if ( FAILED(hr) ) throw hr;

    // Check for persistence of SOAP packet.  If a filename is
    // given under HKLM\MCP\SOAP\HttpRequestFile, then use the
    // string found there as a filename to store the packet text.
    CRegKey rkRoot;
    long lRes = rkRoot.Open(HKEY_LOCAL_MACHINE,
                            _T("Software\\MCP\\SOAP"));
    if ( lRes != ERROR_SUCCESS )
        throw HRESULT_FROM_WIN32(lRes);

    CRegKey rkFile;
    lRes = rkFile.Open(rkRoot,_T("HttpRequestFile"));
    if ( lRes != ERROR_SUCCESS ) throw HRESULT_FROM_WIN32(lRes);

    TCHAR szFile[_MAX_PATH+1] = {0};
    DWORD dwBytesRead = _MAX_PATH;
    lRes = rkFile.QueryValue(szFile,NULL,&dwBytesRead);
    if ( lRes == ERROR_SUCCESS ) {
        HANDLE hFile = CreateFile(szFile,
                                  GENERIC_WRITE,
                                  0,
                                  NULL,
                                  CREATE_ALWAYS,
                                  FILE_ATTRIBUTE_NORMAL,
                                  NULL);

        WriteFile(hFile,ostr.str(),ostr.pcount(),
                  &dwBytesRead,NULL);

        CloseHandle(hFile);
    } // if

    // Save the streamed XML information
    szXML = new TCHAR[ostr.pcount()+1];
```

10

IMPLEMENTING SOAP

continues

LISTING 10.45 Continued

```
        _tcsncpy(szXML,ostr.str(),ostr.pcount());
        szXML[ostr.pcount()] = '\0';
        m_bstrRequestXML = szXML;

        // Create the thread to actually send and receive the
        // SOAP data...
        lpThreadParm = new THRDDATA;
        lpThreadParm->postr = &ostr;
        lpThreadParm->pParent = this;
        lpThreadParm->hrSendReceive = S_OK;
        m_hHttpSendThread = (HANDLE)_beginthreadex(NULL,0,HttpThread,
            (void*)lpThreadParm,0,(unsigned *)&m_dwHttpSendThreadID);

        // Now block while waiting for the thread to terminate (which
        // it will do when the data is returned from the remote
        // server).
        lRes = rkRoot.Open(HKEY_LOCAL_MACHINE,
                                _T("Software\\MCP\\SOAP"));
        if ( lRes != ERROR_SUCCESS ) throw HRESULT_FROM_WIN32(lRes);

        CRegKey rkSettings;
        lRes = rkSettings.Open(rkRoot,_T("Settings"));
        if ( lRes != ERROR_SUCCESS ) throw HRESULT_FROM_WIN32(lRes);

        DWORD dwTimeout = INFINITE;
        lRes = rkSettings.QueryValue(dwTimeout,_T("ResponseTimeout"));
        if ( lRes != ERROR_SUCCESS ) {
            // Wait for INFINITE time...just make a note of it...
            OutputDebugString(_T("NOTE: SOAP response timeout period
                    ➥not specified in Registry (using INFINITE).\n"));
        } // if

        // Block while the thread completes.
        if ( WaitForSingleObject(m_hHttpSendThread,dwTimeout) ==
                                            ➥WAIT_TIMEOUT ) {
            // Timed out...
            throw CO_E_REMOTE_COMMUNICATION_FAILURE;
        } // if

        // Record response HRESULT
        hr = lpThreadParm->hrSendReceive;
        if ( FAILED(hr) ) throw hr;
    } // try
    catch(HRESULT hrErr) {
```

```
          // Some COM error...
          hr = hrErr; // normalize to this error...
          TCHAR strErrMsg[256] = {0};
          wsprintf(strErrMsg,"COM error while streaming HTTP
                         ➥packet, %#08x.\n",hrErr);
          OutputDebugString(strErrMsg);
      } // catch
      catch(...) {
          // Some error...
          hr = E_UNEXPECTED;
          OutputDebugString(_T("Unexpected application error
                              ➥while streaming HTTP packet\n"));
      } // catch

      if ( szXML != NULL ) delete[] szXML;
      if ( lpThreadParm != NULL ) delete lpThreadParm;

      return hr;
}
```

CSOAPHttpTransaction::SendReceive() begins by streaming the packet to ultimately stuff it into a BSTR. This happens after saving the packet to a file for debugging, if the HttpRequestFile Registry key exists.

```
// Stream the HTTP packet
std::ostrstream ostr;
hr = m_pHttpPacket->WriteToStream(ostr,TRUE);
if ( FAILED(hr) ) throw hr;

(save streamed SOAP packet to file)

// Save the streamed XML information
szXML = new TCHAR[ostr.pcount()+1];
_tcsncpy(szXML,ostr.str(),ostr.pcount());
szXML[ostr.pcount()] = '\0';
m_bstrRequestXML = szXML;
```

It then creates a new thread to submit the SOAP data:

```
// Create the thread to actually send and receive the
// SOAP data...
lpThreadParm = new THRDDATA;
lpThreadParm->postr = &ostr;
lpThreadParm->pParent = this;
lpThreadParm->hrSendReceive = S_OK;
m_hHttpSendThread = (HANDLE)_beginthreadex(NULL,0,HttpThread,
    (void*)lpThreadParm,0,(unsigned *)&m_dwHttpSendThreadID);
```

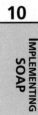

10

IMPLEMENTING
SOAP

Next, `SendReceive()` reads the Registry to see what its maximum timeout period is to be:

```
// Now block while waiting for the thread to terminate (which
// it will do when the data is returned from the remote
// server).
lRes = rkRoot.Open(HKEY_LOCAL_MACHINE,
                        _T("Software\\MCP\\SOAP"));
if ( lRes != ERROR_SUCCESS ) throw HRESULT_FROM_WIN32(lRes);

CRegKey rkSettings;
lRes = rkSettings.Open(rkRoot,_T("Settings"));
if ( lRes != ERROR_SUCCESS ) throw HRESULT_FROM_WIN32(lRes);

DWORD dwTimeout = INFINITE;
lRes = rkSettings.QueryValue(dwTimeout,_T("ResponseTimeout"));
if ( lRes != ERROR_SUCCESS ) {
    // Wait for INFINITE time...just make a note of it...
    OutputDebugString(_T("NOTE: SOAP response timeout period
        ➥not specified in Registry (using INFINITE).\n"));
} // if
```

With the timeout period in hand, the function blocks while waiting for the request thread to terminate:

```
// Block while the thread completes.
if ( WaitForSingleObject(m_hHttpSendThread,dwTimeout) ==
                                        ➥WAIT_TIMEOUT ) {
    // Timed out...
    throw CO_E_REMOTE_COMMUNICATION_FAILURE;
} // if
```

If the thread obtains a response packet from the server in time, the transaction object then records the return code from the communications process:

```
// Record response HRESULT
hr = lpThreadParm->hrSendReceive;
if ( FAILED(hr) ) throw hr;
```

The meat of the communications process is wrapped up in the thread `SendReceive()` creates. The code for this thread is shown in Listing 10.46.

LISTING 10.46   SOAPHttpThread Implementation

```
// SOAPHttpThread.cpp
//
// Kenn Scribner
// Understanding SOAP, March 2000
//
```

```
// HTTP transaction thread implementation
//
// NOTE: The HTTP request/response mechanism is in this
// separate thread because I had intended to implement
// an Abort() method on ISoapControl and provide for
// asynchronous SOAP ops. That didn't happen (it took
// long enough to write this code as it was!), but I left
// the thread in place in case you or I get to it. It
// may be this thread isn't necessary, but this code
// works as-is...rather than cut it out I just left it
// in place. My apology for not getting the added
// functionality in place...
#include <process.h>
#include "SOAPObjectSurrogate.h"
#include "SOAPHttpTransaction.h"
#include "..\SOAPObjectLib\SOAPHttpPacket.h"

unsigned __stdcall HttpThread(LPVOID lpParms)
{
    // Bring up COM runtime
    CoInitializeEx(NULL,COINIT_MULTITHREADED);

    LPTHRDDATA lpThreadParm = (LPTHRDDATA)lpParms;

    HRESULT hr = S_OK;
    try {
        // Create the HTTP request object
        CComPtr<IXMLHttpRequest> spRequest;
        hr = spRequest.CoCreateInstance(__uuidof(XMLHTTPRequest));
        if ( FAILED(hr) ) throw hr;

        // Pull the packet information
        CSOAPHttpPacket* pPacket =
                            lpThreadParm->pParent->GetPacket();
        if ( pPacket == NULL ) throw hr;

        // Open the connection to the remote host
        std::string strHost;
        pPacket->GetHostText(strHost);
        hr = spRequest->open(CComBSTR("POST"),
                        CComBSTR(strHost.c_str()),
                        CComVariant(FALSE),
                        CComVariant(VT_BSTR),
                        CComVariant(VT_BSTR));
        if ( FAILED(hr) ) throw hr;
```

10

IMPLEMENTING
SOAP

continues

LISTING 10.46   Continued

```cpp
// Set up the HTTP headers
std::string strData;
pPacket->GetPostText(strData);
hr = spRequest->setRequestHeader(CComBSTR("POST"),
                                 CComBSTR(strData.c_str()));
if ( FAILED(hr) ) throw hr;

hr = spRequest->setRequestHeader(CComBSTR("HOST"),
                                 CComBSTR(strHost.c_str()));
if ( FAILED(hr) ) throw hr;

pPacket->GetContentTypeText(strData);
hr = spRequest->setRequestHeader(CComBSTR("Content-Type"),
                                 CComBSTR(strData.c_str()));
if ( FAILED(hr) ) throw hr;

pPacket->GetSoapActionText (strData);
hr = spRequest->setRequestHeader(CComBSTR("SOAPAction"),
                                 CComBSTR(strData.c_str()));
if ( FAILED(hr) ) throw hr;

// Send the information to the remote host
CComPtr<IXMLDOMDocument> spRequestXMLDoc;
hr = spRequestXMLDoc.CoCreateInstance(
                        __uuidof(DOMFreeThreadedDocument));
if ( FAILED(hr) ) throw hr;

// Get XML (SOAP) document
CComBSTR bstrRequest;
hr = lpThreadParm->pParent->GetRequestXML(&bstrRequest);
if ( FAILED(hr) ) throw hr;

VARIANT_BOOL b = FALSE;
hr = spRequestXMLDoc->loadXML(bstrRequest,&b);
if ( FAILED(hr) ) throw hr;
if ( !b ) throw E_UNEXPECTED;

CComQIPtr<IDispatch> spXMLDisp;
spXMLDisp = spRequestXMLDoc;
hr = spRequest->send(CComVariant(spXMLDisp));
if ( FAILED(hr) ) throw hr;

// Get the status code from the response
long iStatus = 0;
hr = spRequest->get_status(&iStatus);
if ( FAILED(hr) ) throw hr;
```

```
        // Check the status code for "200"
        if ( iStatus != 200 ) {
            // An HTTP error...
            throw (SOAP_E_HTTPERROR | iStatus);
        } // if


        // Retrieve and save the response
        CComBSTR bstrResponse;
        hr = spRequest->get_responseText(&bstrResponse);
        if ( FAILED(hr) ) throw hr;


        lpThreadParm->pParent->SetResponseXML(bstrResponse);

        // Check for persistence of SOAP response.  If a filename is
        // given under HKLM\MCP\SOAP\HttpResponseFile, then use the
        // string found there as a filename to store the packet text.
        CRegKey rkRoot;
        long lRes = rkRoot.Open(HKEY_LOCAL_MACHINE,
                                _T("Software\\MCP\\SOAP"));
        if ( lRes != ERROR_SUCCESS )  throw HRESULT_FROM_WIN32(lRes);


        CRegKey rkFile;
        lRes = rkFile.Open(rkRoot,_T("HttpResponseFile"));
        if ( lRes != ERROR_SUCCESS ) throw HRESULT_FROM_WIN32(lRes);


        TCHAR szFile[_MAX_PATH+1] = {0};
        DWORD dwBytesRead = _MAX_PATH;
        lRes = rkFile.QueryValue(szFile,NULL,&dwBytesRead);
        if ( lRes == ERROR_SUCCESS ) {
            // Convert and store
            USES_CONVERSION;
            LPTSTR strResponse = W2T(bstrResponse);

            HANDLE hFile = CreateFile(szFile,
                                      GENERIC_WRITE,
                                      0,
                                      NULL,
                                      CREATE_ALWAYS,
                                      FILE_ATTRIBUTE_NORMAL,
                                      NULL);

            WriteFile(hFile,strResponse,_tcslen(strResponse),
                      &dwBytesRead,NULL);

            CloseHandle(hFile);
        } // if
    } // try
```

10

IMPLEMENTING
SOAP

continues

LISTING 10.46   Continued

```
    catch(HRESULT hrErr) {
        // Some COM error...
        hr = hrErr; // normalize to this error...
        TCHAR strErrMsg[256] = {0};
        wsprintf(strErrMsg,"COM error in HTTP send/receive
                                        ➥thread, %#08x.\n",hrErr);
        OutputDebugString(strErrMsg);
    } // catch
    catch(...) {
        // Some error...
        hr = E_UNEXPECTED;
        OutputDebugString(_T("Unexpected application error in HTTP
                                        ➥send/receive thread\n"));
    } // catch

    CoUninitialize();

    lpThreadParm->hrSendReceive = hr;
    return (unsigned)hr;
}
```

The thread begins by invoking the COM runtime in the multithreaded apartment:

```
// Bring up COM runtime
CoInitializeEx(NULL,COINIT_MULTITHREADED);
```

It then casts the incoming thread parameter pointer to the THRDDATA structure initially completed by CSOAPHttpTransaction::SendReceive():

```
LPTHRDDATA lpThreadParm = (LPTHRDDATA)lpParms;
```

The meat of the send/receive action begins when the thread creates an instance of the XMLHttpRequest COM object provided with the MSXML parser:

```
// Create the HTTP request object
CComPtr<IXMLHttpRequest> spRequest;
hr = spRequest.CoCreateInstance(__uuidof(XMLHTTPRequest));
if ( FAILED(hr) ) throw hr;
```

This object will perform the HTTP actions required to transmit the XML document to the remote server and wait for the response. With the XML HTTP Request object created, the SOAP packet is retrieved, the connection is opened, and the HTTP headers are created:

```
// Pull the packet information
CSOAPHttpPacket* pPacket = lpThreadParm->pParent->GetPacket();
if ( pPacket == NULL ) throw hr;
```

```
// Open the connection to the remote host
std::string strHost;
pPacket->GetHostText(strHost);
hr = spRequest->open(CComBSTR("POST"),
                     CComBSTR(strHost.c_str()),
                     CComVariant(FALSE),
                     CComVariant(VT_BSTR),
                     CComVariant(VT_BSTR));
if ( FAILED(hr) ) throw hr;

// Set up the HTTP headers
std::string strData;
pPacket->GetPostText(strData);
hr = spRequest->setRequestHeader(CComBSTR("POST"),
                                 CComBSTR(strData.c_str()));
if ( FAILED(hr) ) throw hr;

hr = spRequest->setRequestHeader(CComBSTR("HOST"),
                                 CComBSTR(strHost.c_str()));
if ( FAILED(hr) ) throw hr;

pPacket->GetContentTypeText(strData);
hr = spRequest->setRequestHeader(CComBSTR("Content-Type"),
                                 CComBSTR(strData.c_str()));
if ( FAILED(hr) ) throw hr;

pPacket->GetSoapActionText(strData);
hr = spRequest->setRequestHeader(CComBSTR("SOAPAction"),
                                 CComBSTR(strData.c_str()));
if ( FAILED(hr) ) throw hr;
```

If you were wondering why the connection is opened prior to completing the HTTP headers for the request, it's because the XML HTTP Request object dictates this order of operations.

At this point, the HTTP request is nearly complete. The one key piece you are missing is the actual SOAP content! For that, you must create an instance of the MSXML parser (which is compatible with the XML HTTP Request object) and pass to it the SOAP packet information you just serialized:

```
// Send the information to the remote host
CComPtr<IXMLDOMDocument> spRequestXMLDoc;
hr = spRequestXMLDoc.CoCreateInstance(
                        ➥__uuidof(DOMFreeThreadedDocument));
if ( FAILED(hr) ) throw hr;

// Get XML (SOAP) document
CComBSTR bstrRequest;
```

10

IMPLEMENTING SOAP

```
hr = lpThreadParm->pParent->GetRequestXML(&bstrRequest);
if ( FAILED(hr) ) throw hr;

VARIANT_BOOL b = FALSE;
hr = spRequestXMLDoc->loadXML(bstrRequest,&b);
if ( FAILED(hr) ) throw hr;
if ( !b ) throw E_UNEXPECTED;
```

Assuming the MSXML parser is created and that it accepts the XML document (which it should), you send the XML document using the XML HTTP Request object:

```
CComQIPtr<IDispatch> spXMLDisp;
spXMLDisp = spRequestXMLDoc;
hr = spRequest->send(CComVariant(spXMLDisp));
if ( FAILED(hr) ) throw hr;
```

The IDispatch query is merely to satisfy the IXMLHTTPRequest::send() method.

The innocent-looking send() method rolls the XML document into an HTTP packet and ships it off to the remote server. If the transmission is successful and a response is received (send() will block until the response comes back), the response's HTTP return status is checked—it must be 200 to have been successful. If it is unsuccessful, such as when the server is not found or does not respond, the send thread will terminate with an HTTP error code:

```
// Check the status code for "200"
if ( iStatus != 200 ) {
    // An HTTP error...
    throw (SOAP_E_HTTPERROR | iStatus);
} // if
```

> **NOTE**
>
> At this point a more robust implementation would check to see if the HTTP error was related to the POST header processing and respond with an MPOST request. More robust features, such as this, are left to the reader to insert into the architecture.

However, if the response was received in good shape, the response XML is retrieved and stored with the (parent) CSOAPHttpTransmission object:

```
// Retrieve and save the response
CComBSTR bstrResponse;
hr = spRequest->get_responseText(&bstrResponse);
if ( FAILED(hr) ) throw hr;

pThreadParm->pParent->SetResponseXML(bstrResponse);
```

In the next section, this response XML document will be tested for faults and method result information. The thread finishes with some code to write the XML response document to a (debug) text file, if the HttpResponseFile Registry key exists.

Interpreting (and Using) the Results Obtained from the Remote Object

Referring yet again to the serializer code in Listing 10.39, you see the SOAP packet decode mechanism initiated:

```
// Pull the return value and store any [out] data
HRESULT hrApp = hrFromSerialization = E_FAIL;
HRESULT hrDecode = me.SoapDecode(pCruncher,pTransaction,
                                 hrApp);
if ( FAILED(hrDecode) ) throw -1;

hrFromSerialization = hrApp;
if ( FAILED(hrFromSerialization) ) throw -1;
```

If the packet is successfully decoded, the method's return code will be copied to the hrFromSerialization variable to be returned as the return code for the entire serialization process.

Decoding the SOAP response begins with the call to CSOAPSerializer::SoapDecode(), which you will find listed in Listing 10.47.

LISTING 10.47   CSOAPSerializer::SoapDecode() Implementation

```
HRESULT CSOAPSerializer::SoapDecode(CStackCruncher* pCruncher,
                        CSOAPHttpTransaction* pTransaction,
                        HRESULT& hrFromSerialization)
{
    if ( !pCruncher ) return E_POINTER;
    if ( !pTransaction ) return E_POINTER;

    // Assume failure...
    hrFromSerialization = SOAP_E_UNKNOWN;

    CSOAPResponseDecoder* pDecoder = NULL;
    HRESULT hr = S_OK;
    try {
        // Retrieve the response XML document
        CComBSTR bstrResponse;
        hr = pTransaction->GetResponseXML(&bstrResponse);
        if ( FAILED(hr) ) throw hr;
```

10

IMPLEMENTING
SOAP

continues

LISTING 10.47   Continued

```
// Retrieve the packet
CSOAPHttpPacket* pPacket = pTransaction->GetPacket();
if ( !pPacket ) throw E_OUTOFMEMORY;

// Create a decoder object
std::string strMethod;
pPacket->GetMethodName(strMethod);
pDecoder = new CSOAPResponseDecoder(bstrResponse,
                        strMethod.c_str(),m_strNamespace);
if ( pDecoder == NULL ) throw E_OUTOFMEMORY;

// First check for a fault
if ( pDecoder->IsFault() ) {
    // Faulted...
    long iFaultCode =
                    CSOAPResponseDecoder::SOAP_FAULT_UNKNOWN;
    hr = pDecoder->GetFaultCode(&iFaultCode);
    if ( FAILED(hr) )  throw hr;

    // Check the fault...
    switch ( iFaultCode ) {
        case CSOAPResponseDecoder::SOAP_FAULT_VERMISMATCH:
            hrFromSerialization = SOAP_E_VERSIONMISMATCH;
            throw S_OK;

        case CSOAPResponseDecoder::SOAP_FAULT_MUSTUNDERSTAND:
            hrFromSerialization = SOAP_E_MUSTUNDERSTAND;
            throw S_OK;

        case CSOAPResponseDecoder::SOAP_FAULT_NONE:
        case CSOAPResponseDecoder::SOAP_FAULT_UNKNOWN:
            // Something very weird...
            hrFromSerialization = SOAP_E_UNKNOWN;
            throw S_OK;

        case CSOAPResponseDecoder::SOAP_FAULT_CLIENT:
        case CSOAPResponseDecoder::SOAP_FAULT_SERVER:
        default:
            break;
    } // switch

    // The fault was a client/server-specific fault, so
    // extract it and return.
    HRESULT hrApp = E_FAIL;
```

```
                hr = pDecoder->GetErrorCode(&hrApp);
                hrFromSerialization = hrApp;
                throw S_OK;
        } // if
        else {
                // Dequeue the stack [out] data and decode
                LPSTACKDATA lpStackData = pCruncher->DequeueOutArg();
                while ( lpStackData != NULL ) {
                        // Get this [out] value
                        hr = pDecoder->GetArgValue(lpStackData);
                        if ( FAILED(hr) ) {
                                hrFromSerialization = SOAP_E_UNKNOWN;
                                throw hr;
                        } // if

                        // Get the next [out] value
                        lpStackData = pCruncher->DequeueOutArg();
                } // while

                // Pull the remote object's result code
                HRESULT hrApp = S_OK;
                hr = pDecoder->GetRetVal(&hrApp);
                if ( FAILED(hr) ) {
                        hrFromSerialization = SOAP_E_UNKNOWN;
                        throw hr;
                } // if

                // Assign the code
                hrFromSerialization = hrApp;
        } // else
} // try
catch(HRESULT hrErr) {
        // Some COM error...
        hr = hrErr; // normalize to this error...
        TCHAR strErrMsg[256] = {0};
        wsprintf(strErrMsg,"COM error in serialization object
                ➥while decoding SOAP packet %#08x\n",hrErr);
        OutputDebugString(strErrMsg);
} // catch
catch(...) {
        // Some error...
        hr = E_UNEXPECTED;
        OutputDebugString(_T("Unexpected application error in
                ➥serialization object while decoding SOAP packet\n"));
} // catch
```

continues

10

LISTING 10.47   Continued

```
    // Delete the decoder
    if ( pDecoder != NULL ) {
        delete pDecoder;
        pDecoder = NULL;
    } // if

    return hr;
}
```

Decoding begins when the serializer retrieves the SOAP response packet XML information

```
// Retrieve the response XML document
CComBSTR bstrResponse;
hr = pTransaction->GetResponseXML(&bstrResponse);
if ( FAILED(hr) ) throw hr;
```

SoapDecode() then pulls the method name from the original SOAP object model and creates an instance of the CSOAPReponseDecoder object:

```
// Retrieve the packet
CSOAPHttpPacket* pPacket = pTransaction->GetPacket();
if ( !pPacket ) throw E_OUTOFMEMORY;

// Create a decoder object
std::string strMethod;
pPacket->GetMethodName(strMethod);
pDecoder = new CSOAPResponseDecoder(bstrResponse,
                        strMethod.c_str(),m_strNamespace);
if ( pDecoder == NULL ) throw E_OUTOFMEMORY;
```

The decoder object creates an instance of the MSXML parser (which is provided for the response XML document) and uses that to test for the existence (or absence) of given XML nodes. First, the serializer tests to see if there was a SOAP fault:

```
// First check for a fault
if ( pDecoder->IsFault() ) {
    (process SOAP fault)
} // if
else {
    (rocess method return information)
} // else
```

The code the decoder uses to check for a SOAP fault is shown in Listing 10.48.

LISTING 10.48   CSOAPResponseDecoder::IsFault() Implementation

```
BOOL CSOAPResponseDecoder::IsFault()
{
    if ( m_spXMLDOM.p == NULL ) return E_POINTER;

    // Check for <SOAP-ENV:Envelope>
    //              <SOAP-ENV:Body>
    //                  <SOAP-ENV:Fault>...
    //
    // Construct search string:
    //      "SOAP-ENV:Envelope/SOAP-ENV:Body/SOAP-ENV:Fault"
    CComBSTR bstrSS(L"SOAP-ENV:Envelope/SOAP-ENV:Body/SOAP-ENV:Fault");
    CComPtr<IXMLDOMNode> spFault;
    HRESULT hr = m_spXMLDOM->selectSingleNode(bstrSS,&spFault);
    if ( FAILED(hr) ) return FALSE;
    if ( spFault.p == NULL ) return FALSE;

    return TRUE;
}
```

The decoder follows the same basic pattern when probing for XML response information—it creates a search string and asks the MSXML parser if the given node exists:

```
CComBSTR bstrSS(L"SOAP-ENV:Envelope/SOAP-ENV:Body/SOAP-ENV:Fault");
CComPtr<IXMLDOMNode> spFault;
HRESULT hr = m_spXMLDOM->selectSingleNode(bstrSS,&spFault);
```

If the node does exist, the HRESULT will be S_OK and the IXMLDOMNode pointer will be filled with the appropriate node's representative COM object. If the node does not exist, the HRESULT will be S_FALSE, and the node's COM object pointer will be NULL.

SOAP Fault Response Processing

Assuming the remote method returned a SOAP fault, the serializer will execute this code (from Listing 10.47):

```
// Faulted...
long iFaultCode = CSOAPResponseDecoder::SOAP_FAULT_UNKNOWN;
hr = pDecoder->GetFaultCode(&iFaultCode);
if ( FAILED(hr) ) throw hr;

// Check the fault...
switch ( iFaultCode ) {
    case CSOAPResponseDecoder::SOAP_FAULT_VERMISMATCH:
        hrFromSerialization = SOAP_E_VERSIONMISMATCH;
        throw S_OK;
```

10

```
    case CSOAPResponseDecoder::SOAP_FAULT_MUSTUNDERSTAND:
        hrFromSerialization = SOAP_E_MUSTUNDERSTAND;
        throw S_OK;

    case CSOAPResponseDecoder::SOAP_FAULT_NONE:
    case CSOAPResponseDecoder::SOAP_FAULT_UNKNOWN:
        // Something very weird...
        hrFromSerialization = SOAP_E_UNKNOWN;
        throw S_OK;

    case CSOAPResponseDecoder::SOAP_FAULT_CLIENT:
    case CSOAPResponseDecoder::SOAP_FAULT_SERVER:
    default:
        break;
} // switch

// The fault was an application-specific fault, so
// extract it and return.
HRESULT hrApp = E_FAIL;
hr = pDecoder->GetErrorCode(&hrApp);
hrFromSerialization = hrApp;
throw S_OK;
```

The SOAP fault processing begins when the serializer requests the SOAP fault code:

```
long iFaultCode = CSOAPResponseDecoder::SOAP_FAULT_UNKNOWN;
hr = pDecoder->GetFaultCode(&iFaultCode);
if ( FAILED(hr) ) throw hr;
```

This is the meat of the decoder's fault code retrieval method:

```
CComBSTR bstrSS(L"SOAP-ENV:Envelope/SOAP-ENV:Body/SOAP-ENV:Fault/faultcode");
CComPtr<IXMLDOMNode> spFaultCode;
HRESULT hr = m_spXMLDOM->selectSingleNode(bstrSS,&spFaultCode);
if ( FAILED(hr) ) throw hr;
if ( spFaultCode.p == NULL ) throw E_POINTER;
```

There are four SOAP faults, according to the SOAP specification, and the decoder object manages the fault extraction (from CSOAPResponseDecoder::GetFaultCode() in SOAPResponseDecoder.cpp):

```
// SOAP 1.1 fault codes are enumerated values, which
// is to say they're textual rather than numerical.
// They also can potentially follow this format:
//
// fault.subfault
//
```

```
// So, we first convert the string to something we
// can use, then search for a period and take every
// character to the left of the period. We then compare
// the resulting string to the known SOAP faults
// and return a value based upon our findings...
USES_CONVERSION;
CComBSTR bstrVal(var.bstrVal);
LPTSTR pszVal = W2T(bstrVal);
_tcsupr(pszVal); // convert for comparison purposes...

// Search for the period
std::string strVal(pszVal);
int iPos = strVal.find(".",0);
if ( iPos != std::string::npos ) {
    // There was a subfault...
    //
    // TODO: A more robust implementation would
    // actually do something with the subfault
    // instead of throwing it away...
    strVal.erase(iPos);
} // if

// Now do a bunch of comparisons to see what
// fault was returned...  Note the assumption
// the fault code is namespace qualified,
// per the SOAP specification...
long iFaultCode = SOAP_FAULT_UNKNOWN;
if ( !strVal.compare("SOAP-ENV:VERSIONMISMATCH") ) {
    // SOAP VersionMismatch error...
    iFaultCode = SOAP_FAULT_VERMISMATCH;
} // if
else if ( !strVal.compare("SOAP-ENV:MUSTUNDERSTAND") ) {
    // SOAP MustUnderstand error...
    iFaultCode = SOAP_FAULT_MUSTUNDERSTAND;
} // if
else if ( !strVal.compare("SOAP-ENV:CLIENT") ) {
    // SOAP Client error...
    iFaultCode = SOAP_FAULT_CLIENT;
} // if
else if ( !strVal.compare("SOAP-ENV:SERVER") ) {
    // SOAP Server error...
    iFaultCode = SOAP_FAULT_SERVER;
} // if
```

For any SOAP fault except a client- or server-specific fault, the HRESULT from the serialization process is assigned the corresponding (custom) error HRESULT, and the serialization process

10

IMPLEMENTING SOAP

terminates (referring again to Listing 10.47). However, if the fault is client- or server-specific, then you must dig a bit deeper and extract the fault error code:

```
// The fault was a client/server-specific fault, so
// extract it and return.
HRESULT hrApp = E_FAIL;
hr = pDecoder->GetErrorCode(&hrApp);
hrFromSerialization = hrApp;
throw S_OK;
```

As with the previous decoder methods, the application fault code is retrieved from the response XML document using this code:

```
CComBSTR bstrSS
➥(L"SOAP-ENV:Envelope/SOAP-ENV:Body/SOAP-ENV:Fault/detail/errorcode");
CComPtr<IXMLDOMNode> spFaultCode;
HRESULT hr = m_spXMLDOM->selectSingleNode(bstrSS,&spFaultCode);
if ( FAILED(hr) ) throw hr;
if ( spFaultCode.p == NULL )  throw E_POINTER;
```

> **NOTE**
>
> If you're using the MSXML DOM parser to extract specific XML nodes, as shown here, you use the selectSingleNode() method. However, a better alternative may be to use a SAX (or SAX2) parser to discover XML nodes as they are parsed. At the time this was written, Microsoft had not released their SAX parser implementation, so the DOM parser was used instead. You will find all of the decoding routines implement this (DOM node search) technique, so if you modify the code to use the SAX parser when it becomes available, be sure to modify the code both for the client- and server-side SOAP components.

The next section discusses how successful SOAP response packets are processed.

SOAP Method Response Processsing

If the SOAP response indicates the method executed nominally, then you must reach into the response XML document and extract two things: the method return code and any [out] data. The SOAP specification states the following:

- The method return code is the first embedded element of the method response element, and, although the element name is not specified, this architecture assumes it is named return.

- Any [out] argument information is encoded as embedded elements of the method response element in the order they are listed in the method's signature.

The first bullet means that the method's return code is in an XML element that is hard-coded to be <return />. The second bullet means that the independent method response element is the only independent element in the SOAP body because this (sample) architecture doesn't return complex SOAP types. (There are no XPointers, and all strings will be embedded.)

As an example, suppose you have this method:

```
int iSomeValue = 0;
int SomeFunction(/*[out]*/int* &iSomeValue);
```

Assuming this method was shipped to a remote server using SOAP, the SOAP response body would look much like this:

```
<SOAP-ENV:Body>
    <m:SomeFunctionResponse>
        <return>27</return>
        <iSomeValue>49</iSomeValue>
    </m:SomeFunctionResponse>
</SOAP-ENV:Body>
```

That means the decoder must be capable of extracting both the return value and an arbitrary number of [out] parameters. Returning to Listing 10.47, the serializer executes this code to extract this information:

```
// Dequeue the stack [out] data and decode
LPSTACKDATA lpStackData = pCruncher->DequeueOutArg();
while ( lpStackData != NULL ) {
    // Get this [out] value
    hr = pDecoder->GetArgValue(lpStackData);
    if ( FAILED(hr) ) {
        hrFromSerialization = SOAP_E_UNKNOWN;
        throw hr;
    } // if

    // Get the next [out] value
    lpStackData = pCruncher->DequeueOutArg();
} // while

// Pull the remote object's result code
HRESULT hrApp = S_OK;
hr = pDecoder->GetRetVal(&hrApp);
if ( FAILED(hr) ) {
    hrFromSerialization = SOAP_E_UNKNOWN;
    throw hr;
} // if

// Assign the code
hrFromSerialization = hrApp;
```

As you might recall, the [out] argument information was placed into stack data records and queued onto a special data queue. The serializer dequeues the records and looks for each in the method response packet. After all the [out] data is processed, the method's return value is retrieved.

The decoder's [out] argument processing method GetArgValue() is shown in Listing 10.49.

LISTING 10.49   CSOAPResponseDecoder::GetArgValue() Implementation

```
HRESULT CSOAPResponseDecoder::GetArgValue(LPSTACKDATA pStackData)
{
    if ( pStackData == NULL ) return E_POINTER;
    if ( m_spXMLDOM.p == NULL ) return E_POINTER;

    HRESULT hr = S_OK;
    try {
        // Only unmarshal [out] or [in,out] data...
        if ((pStackData->mdType == MD_OUT) ||
            (pStackData->mdType == MD_INOUT)) {
            // The argument can be unmarshalled, so find the
            // corresponding DOM node.
            //
            // Check for <SOAP-ENV:Envelope>
            //               <SOAP-ENV:Body>
            //                   <m:{method}Response>
            //                       <{argname}>...
            //
            // Construct search string
            //   "SOAP-ENV:Envelope/SOAP-ENV:Body/
            //       ➥m:{method}Response/{argname}"
            std::string strSS("SOAP-ENV:Envelope/SOAP-ENV:Body/");
            strSS += m_strNamespace;
            strSS += _T(":");
            strSS += m_strMethod;
            strSS += _T("Response");
            strSS += _T("/");
            strSS += pStackData->strName;
            CComBSTR bstrSS(strSS.c_str());
            CComPtr<IXMLDOMNode> spArg;
            HRESULT hr = m_spXMLDOM->selectSingleNode(bstrSS,&spArg);
            if ( FAILED(hr) ) throw hr;
            if ( spArg.p == NULL )  throw E_POINTER;

            // Pull the node's value
            CComVariant var;
            hr = spArg->get_nodeTypedValue(&var);
            if ( FAILED(hr) ) throw hr;
```

```
// Assign the value
USES_CONVERSION;
CComBSTR bstrVal(var.bstrVal);
LPTSTR strVal = W2T(bstrVal);
switch ( pStackData->iType ) {
    case TLB_I2:
        {
            short* p = reinterpret_cast<short*>
                        ➥(pStackData->pValPtr);
            *p = (short)atoi(strVal);
        }
        break;

    case TLB_UI2:
        {
            unsigned short* p = reinterpret_cast
                ➥<unsigned short*>(pStackData->pValPtr);
            *p =  (unsigned short)atoi(strVal);
        }
        break;

    case TLB_I4:
        {
            long* p = reinterpret_cast<long*>
                        ➥(pStackData->pValPtr);
            *p = (long)atoi(strVal);
        }
        break;

    case TLB_UI4:
        {
            unsigned long* p =
                reinterpret_cast<unsigned long*>
                ➥(pStackData->pValPtr);
            *p = (unsigned long)atoi(strVal);
        }
        break;

    case TLB_INT:
        {
            int* p = reinterpret_cast<int*>
                        ➥(pStackData->pValPtr);
            *p = atoi(strVal);
        }
        break;
```

10

IMPLEMENTING
SOAP

continues

LISTING 10.49   Continued

```
case TLB_UINT:
    {
        unsigned int* p =
                    reinterpret_cast<unsigned int*>
                    ➥(pStackData->pValPtr);
        *p =  (unsigned int)atoi(strVal);
    }
    break;

case TLB_FLT:
    {
        float* p = reinterpret_cast<float*>
                    ➥(pStackData->pValPtr);
        *p = (float)atof(strVal);
    }
    break;

case TLB_DBL:
    {
        double* p = reinterpret_cast<double*>
                    ➥(pStackData->pValPtr);
        *p = atof(strVal);
    }
    break;

case TLB_BSTR:
    {
        BSTR* p = reinterpret_cast<BSTR*>
                    ➥(pStackData->pValPtr);

        // The string data could have been wrapped in
        // a CDATA section, which begins with a
        // bracket.
        CComPtr<IXMLDOMNode> spChild;
        spArg->get_firstChild(&spChild);
        if ( spChild.p == NULL ) throw E_UNEXPECTED;

        CComQIPtr<IXMLDOMCharacterData> spCData;
        spCData = spChild;
        if ( spCData.p != NULL ) {
            // Extract the string from the CDATA
            // section. The data contained within
            // the CDATA node is identical to that
            // stored in strVal, so use strVal as it
            // has been converted. The idea is to
            // parse out the stored text by locating
```

```
                    // the second '[', then by removing the
                    // trailing "]]". The test for the CDATA
                    // node was to be sure this truly was a
                    // CDATA node and not a string that began
                    // with '[' (or some other arbitrary,
                    // more simplistic test).
                    LPTSTR pszData = _tcstok(strVal,_T("["));
                    pszData = _tcstok(NULL,_T("["));
                    if ( pszData == NULL ) {
                        // Failed to find second '[', so it's
                        // not truly encoded in a CDATA
                        // section...
                        bstrVal.CopyTo(p);
                    } // if
                    else {
                        // Truly was CDATA...
                        pszData[_tcslen(pszData)-2] = '\0';
                        CComBSTR bstrData(pszData);
                        bstrData.CopyTo(p);
                    } // else
                } // if
                else {
                    // Assign the string as-is
                    bstrVal.CopyTo(p);
                } // else
            }
            break;

        case TLB_BOOL:
            {
                bool* p = reinterpret_cast<bool*>
                        ➥(pStackData->pValPtr);
                int x = atoi(strVal);
                *p = !x ? false : true;
            }
            break;

        case TLB_HRESULT:
            {
                unsigned long* p =
                 reinterpret_cast<unsigned long*>
                  ➥(pStackData->pValPtr);
                *p = (unsigned long)atoi(strVal);
            }
            break;
```

continues

LISTING 10.49 Continued

```
                    case TLB_PTR:
                    case TLB_VOID:
                    default:
                        // Not much to do here...
                        // This would be an error condition,
                        // so don't unmarshal anything...
                        break;
                } // switch
            } // if
        } // try
        catch(HRESULT hrErr) {
            // Some COM error...
            hr = hrErr; // normalize to this error...
            TCHAR strErrMsg[256] = {0};
            wsprintf(strErrMsg,"COM error in response decoding object
                    ➡while retrieving argument value %#08x\n",hrErr);
            OutputDebugString(strErrMsg);
        } // catch
        catch(...) {
            // Some error...
            hr = E_UNEXPECTED;
            OutputDebugString(_T("Unexpected application error in
            ➡response decoding object while retrieving argument value\n"));
        } // catch

        return hr;
}
```

As with the other response packet processing, the first thing to do is locate the XML node that contains the [out] data. This node is named according to the argument, so some string processing is required:

```
std::string strSS("SOAP-ENV:Envelope/SOAP-ENV:Body/");
strSS += m_strNamespace;
strSS += _T(":");
strSS += m_strMethod;
strSS += _T("Response");
strSS += _T("/");
strSS += pStackData->strName;
CComBSTR bstrSS(strSS.c_str());
CComPtr<IXMLDOMNode> spArg;
HRESULT hr = m_spXMLDOM->selectSingleNode(bstrSS,&spArg);
if ( FAILED(hr) ) throw hr;
if ( spArg.p == NULL ) throw E_POINTER;
```

Assuming the node exists, and it should—unless the object on the server and the local system were somehow out of sync—you then retrieve the node's value. The data comes in as XML, so the node's value will always be textual, which comes back to you as a BSTR:

```
// Pull the node's value
CComVariant var;
hr = spArg->get_nodeTypedValue(&var);
if ( FAILED(hr) ) throw hr;

// Assign the value
USES_CONVERSION;
CComBSTR bstrVal(var.bstrVal);
LPTSTR strVal = W2T(bstrVal);
```

Now you convert the textual representation of the result into its final form using one of several C runtime calls, depending upon the data type. A big switch() statement selects the appropriate conversion:

```
switch ( pStackData->iType ) {
    case TLB_I2:
        {
            short* p =
             reinterpret_cast<short*>(pStackData->pValPtr);
            *p = (short)atoi(strVal);
        }
        break;

    (all other data types...)

    case TLB_PTR:
    case TLB_VOID:
    default:
        // Not much to do here...
        // This would be an error condition,
        // so don't unmarshal anything...
        break;
} // switch
```

For all the data types except the string (BSTR), the value is simply placed into the local method's pre-allocated storage location. (Recall that you saved the storage location with the stack data record when the call stack was parsed. This example is for a long value.)

```
long* p = reinterpret_cast<long*>(pStackData->pValPtr);
*p = (long)atoi(strVal);
```

The BSTR is a bit different because you must allocate the memory for the returned string and place the pointer to this allocated memory in the client's variable. Also, what you get as a string value might need reinterpretation. The remote server could have placed the string within

10

IMPLEMENTING
SOAP

a CDATA block, so you will need to strip the true string from the CDATA block. (Oddly, the MSXML parser doesn't do that for you.) This code extracts the string data and creates the returned BSTR value:

```
BSTR* p = reinterpret_cast<BSTR*> (pStackData->pValPtr);

// The string data could have been wrapped in
// a CDATA section, which begins with a
// bracket.
CComPtr<IXMLDOMNode> spChild;
spArg->get_firstChild(&spChild);
if ( spChild.p == NULL ) throw E_UNEXPECTED;

CComQIPtr<IXMLDOMCharacterData> spCData;
spCData = spChild;
if ( spCData.p != NULL ) {
    // Extract the string from the CDATA
    // section. The data contained within
    // the CDATA node is identical to that
    // stored in strVal, so use strVal as it
    // has been converted. The idea is to
    // parse out the stored text by locating
    // the second '[', then by removing the
    // trailing "]]". The test for the CDATA
    // node was to be sure this truly was a
    // CDATA node and not a string that began
    // with '[' (or some other arbitrary,
    // more simplistic test).
    LPTSTR pszData = _tcstok(strVal,_T("["));
    pszData = _tcstok(NULL,_T("["));
    if ( pszData == NULL ) {
        // Failed to find second '[', so it's
        // not truly encoded in a CDATA
        // section...
        bstrVal.CopyTo(p);
    } // if
    else {
        // Truly was CDATA...
        pszData[_tcslen(pszData)-2] = '\0';
        CComBSTR bstrData(pszData);
        bstrData.CopyTo(p);
    } // else
} // if
else {
    // Assign the string as-is
    bstrVal.CopyTo(p);
} // else
```

In this case, you look for an initial bracket, '[', then a following bracket. If you find these two brackets, you can then be relatively sure the string was encoded within a CDATA block. In that case, you copy the string data you find between the enclosing brackets, [*(string)*] and return that to the client. If no brackets are found, then just return what the MSXML parser provides you. Note that the CComBSTR::CopyTo() method is used to allocate the BSTR memory. (It uses the ::SysAllocString() API call.)

With the [out] argument data parsed from the SOAP response packet, the serialization job is done, and the serialization HRESULT is returned to the client. The CSOAPSerializer::serialize() method then cleans the stack by removing the arguments and the implicit this pointer (as you saw previously) and returns control to the client. With this architecture, the client is (or can be) completely unaware that the method call was handled by a remote system.

Possible Improvements

Because this architecture was developed to show possibilities, rather than to be a commercially viable platform, there are several areas where you could add improvements and personal touches, depending upon additional requirements you might levy. Here are just a few possible improvements.

Add Support for Structures and Arrays

This language binding is like many you will find publicly available—it supports simple data types but not the more complex types like structures and arrays. You can add support for these data types, or visit http://www.endurasoft.com for updates the authors plan to incorporate over time.

Add Scripting Support

Many readers will want to make the ISoapControl interface scriptable (based upon IDispatch). This can be done rather easily. If you're interested in encoding scripted method calls, you'll have a bit more work to do because, as it stands, the IDispatch interface is not remotable by the COM language binding implemented for this chapter. (It does not encode arrays.) To make it remotable, either you must implement structures and arrays, or you can add a hook specifically to process IDispatch calls.

Additional Support for Error Notification

A related topic is richer error support, specifically to support IErrorInfo. This interface is commonly used with scripted objects. The SOAP response packet, if it contains a fault, provides more information than this architecture conveys to the client. This architecture simply returns an error code that the client must deal with. A more robust error handling system would support IErrorInfo and pass back an error object the client could use for its own purposes. This could be either to make programmatical decisions in addition to those taken by an error code, or to notify the user using the textual representation of the error that is contained in the error object.

Creation of Alternative Objects upon Failure

If a client is using an interface that is remoted using this language binding, any calls to QueryInterface() for interfaces other than ISoapControl, IUnknown, or the subsumed interface will fail, even if the original object might have supported the particular interface. As a system architect, you have to decide how you want to handle such problems, and this particular implementation simply reports an error to the caller (E_NOINTERFACE). However, you could ship all failed QueryInterface() calls to an instance of the object created locally. Whether this would be appropriate or not will depend upon the particular object, for the interface you are remoting might create stateful information upon which other interfaces will depend.

Asynchronous HTTP Send/Receive with Abort Capability

A clear improvement would be to add abort/asynchronous HTTP send/receive processing to ISoapControl. The groundwork for this has been established with CSOAPHttpTransaction and SOAPHttpThread, but the functionality is not complete with this version of the remoting architecture. The XML HTTP Request object that ships with the MSXML parser is capable of both functions, should you elect to add the code to this architecture yourself.

Respond to HTTP POST Failures with MPOST Retransmission

A related improvement would be to respond to HTTP POST failures with a subsequent MPOST transmission. This architecture makes no assumptions about the failure of the initial SOAP data transmission, so there is tremendous room for improvement with respect to error handling and retransmissions.

Other Transport Protocols

This implementation uses SOAP in the traditional sense, that is, using HTTP as the transport. It is not only possible to use SOAP with other transports—it is likely you'll see SOAP used this way, such as with SMTP or message queues. A clear enhancement would be to replace the HTTP processing in this implementation with another transport protocol, if even only to experiment with different architectures.

The chapter so far has dealt with SOAP processing on the client. It's now time to see how things are managed on the server. After all, that's where the true COM object resides!

SOAP from the Server—The Object Activator

It's hard to imagine that all the work you've witnessed thus far in this chapter only gets you halfway to the dance. The server must do the remaining work, by properly executing the object method and returning some type of response to the client. Most of this work can be done with straightforward stack manipulation and a COM method call, all wrapped up in an ISAPI extension.

The remaining portion of this chapter will be dedicated to explaining the server-side architecture. Although much of the source code is shared, neither the client implementation nor the server implementation *requires* the other. In fact, that is the entire premise behind using XML as the underlying protocol.

SOAPExtension—an ISAPI Extension DLL

Microsoft's Internet Information Server (IIS) framework provides an extensible mechanism for tapping into HTTP traffic. Microsoft calls this framework ISAPI and has provided the capability for you to construct ISAPI filters and ISAPI extensions.

In Chapter 4, "SOAP and Data: Protocol Transports," you were introduced to the ISAPI filter. Filters are simply DLLs that provide the entry points for IIS to pass information to the filter as events take place, such as during user authentication.

On the other hand, ISAPI extensions are DLLs that also provide entry points, but are designed for responding to HTTP requests, just as a Perl script or an ASP page might execute. ISAPI extensions are faster than ASP because they require minimal overhead. Building an infrastructure that was fast and efficient drove much of the design of the server architecture.

The ISAPI extension exports the `GetExtensionVersion()`, `HttpExtensionProc()`, and `TerminateExtension()` methods that IIS uses to communicate with the extension. Listing 10.50 shows the abstract base class that defines these methods.

LISTING 10.50   EXTENSIONBASE.H

```
#ifndef _ExtensionBase_h
#define _ExtensionBase_h

#include <httpext.h>

class ExtensionBase
{
public:
    ExtensionBase();
    virtual ~ExtensionBase();

    // Exported functions necessary for an ISAPI extension
    virtual DWORD HttpExtensionProc(EXTENSION_CONTROL_BLOCK *lpECB)= 0;
    virtual BOOL  GetExtensionVersion(HSE_VERSION_INFO *pVer)= 0;
    virtual BOOL  TerminateExtension(DWORD dwFlags);
};

#endif // _ExtensionBase_h
```

10

The SOAPExtension class inherits from the ExtensionBase abstract base class, and provides the SOAPExtension implementation as shown in Listing 10.51.

LISTING 10.51   SOAPExtension Implementation

```
#include "stdafx.h"
#include "SOAPExtension.h"
#include "Activator.h"
#include <msxml.h>
#include <string>

using namespace std;

SOAPExtension theExtension;

// The method header field buffer size
const int HEADER_BUF_SIZE = 1024;

// Returns the version of the ISAPI extension to the IIS server
BOOL SOAPExtension::GetExtensionVersion(HSE_VERSION_INFO* pVer)
{
    pVer->dwExtensionVersion = MAKELONG(HSE_VERSION_MINOR,
                                        HSE_VERSION_MAJOR);
    _tcscpy(pVer->lpszExtensionDesc, _T("SOAPExtension"));
    return TRUE;
}

// This method is triggered upon HTTP events within IIS
DWORD SOAPExtension::HttpExtensionProc(EXTENSION_CONTROL_BLOCK *lpECB)
{
    // Make sure this was a POST request
    string strHTTPVerb(lpECB->lpszMethod);
    if (strHTTPVerb != string("POST"))
    {
        return HSE_STATUS_ERROR;
    }

    // Initialize COM runtime
    HRESULT hr = CoInitializeEx(NULL, COINIT_MULTITHREADED);
    if (FAILED(hr))
    {
        return HSE_STATUS_ERROR;
    }

    // Try to process the request
    DWORD dwRetCode = HSE_STATUS_SUCCESS;
    try
```

```
{
    // Create the request DOM
    CComPtr<IXMLDOMDocument> pRequest;
    HRESULT hr;
    hr = CoCreateInstance(__uuidof(DOMDocument),
                          0,
                          CLSCTX_ALL,
                          __uuidof(IXMLDOMDocument),
                          reinterpret_cast<void **>(&pRequest));
    if (FAILED(hr)) throw "CoCreate";

    // Load POSTed XML into DOM
    CComBSTR bstrTemp;
    bstrTemp = (char *)lpECB->lpbData;
    VARIANT_BOOL bSuccess = false;
    pRequest->loadXML(bstrTemp, &bSuccess);

    // Retrieve the "SOAPAction:" HTTP header field
    DWORD dwMethodHeaderLen = HEADER_BUF_SIZE;
    TCHAR szMethodHeader[HEADER_BUF_SIZE];
    BOOL rc = lpECB->GetServerVariable(lpECB->ConnID,
                                       "HTTP_SOAPACTION",
                                       szMethodHeader,
                                       &dwMethodHeaderLen);
    if (rc == FALSE)
    {
        DWORD dwErr = GetLastError();
        throw "Cannot find SOAPAction";
    }

    // Find the delimeter between URI and method name
    char *s = strchr(szMethodHeader, '#');

    // Replace # with null terminator
    *s = '\0';

    // Point to the method name
    s++;

    // Create an Activator for this IID and method
    CComBSTR bstrIID(szMethodHeader);
    CComBSTR bstrMethod(s);
    CActivator act(bstrIID, bstrMethod);

    // Invoke the object's method and retrieve a response
    CComBSTR bstrXML;
```

continues

10

IMPLEMENTING
SOAP

LISTING 10.51   Continued

```
        CComPtr<IXMLDOMDocument> pResponse;
        if (act.Invoke(pRequest, &pResponse) == 0)
        {
            // Retrieve the XML response
            pResponse->get_xml(&bstrXML);
        }
        else
        {
            // SOAP Fault
            bstrXML = "<SOAP-ENV:Envelope xmlns:SOAP=
➥'http://schemas.xmlsoap.org/soap/envelope/' "
➥SOAP-ENV:encodingStyle='http://schemas.xmlsoap.org/soap/encoding/'>"
            "<SOAP-ENV:Body><SOAP-ENV:Fault><faultcode>300</faultcode>"
            "<faultstring>Invalid Request</faultstring>"
            "<runcode>1</runcode></SOAP-ENV:Fault></SOAP-ENV:Body>
➥</SOAP-ENV:Envelope>";
        }

        ULONG bufLen = bstrXML.Length();
        USES_CONVERSION;

        // Send the response to the client
        lpECB->WriteClient(lpECB->ConnID, (void*)W2A(bstrXML),
                           &bufLen, HSE_IO_SYNC);
    }
    catch (...)
    {
        // Error
        dwRetCode = HSE_STATUS_ERROR;
    }

    CoUninitialize();

    return dwRetCode;
}
```

The most important method to note is `HttpExtensionProc()`. The incoming HTTP request triggers IIS to call this method and to provide the request information in the `EXTENSION_CONTROL_BLOCK` data structure.

`HttpExtensionProc()` starts by making sure that a POST request has been issued; otherwise, it can deny the request altogether. Next, it loads the POST payload into the DOM and then checks the HTTP header for the SOAPAction field. If SOAPAction exists, it creates an Activator for the COM CLSID and interface IID, and invokes the method.

Assuming the Invoke call completes successfully, the pResponse DOM contains the appropriate XML response and is sent back to the client for processing. Sending data to the client is done via the WriteClient() method, which is an IIS callback function exposed by the EXTENSION_CONTROL_BLOCK structure.

Because the incoming XML must be parsed before activating upon its request, the DeSerializer object must get involved.

The DeSerializer

The DeSerializer object was designed to encapsulate the parsing of the SOAP request payload and make it easier for the object activation code to analyze the request contents. Listing 10.52 shows the interface to the DeSerializer class.

LISTING 10.52 CDeSerializer Class Definition

```
#ifndef _DeSerializer_h_
#define _DeSerializer_h_

#include <msxml.h>
#include <string>

#define CHECKHR(x) {if (FAILED(x)) throw "DOM Error";}
#define CHECKPTR(x) {if (!x) throw "Pointer Error";}

class CDeSerializer
{
public:
    CDeSerializer(IXMLDOMDocument *pXMLDoc);
    virtual ~CDeSerializer() {}

    bool CheckMethodAndURI(const BSTR bstrMethodName);
    bool GetCLSID(BSTR * pbstrCLSID);
    long GetParameterCount();
    bool GetParameterValue(long lParamNum, BSTR * pbstrValue);

private:
    CComPtr<IXMLDOMDocument> m_pXMLDoc;
    CComPtr<IXMLDOMNode>     m_pBodyNode;
    CComPtr<IXMLDOMNode>     m_pMethodNode;
    CComBSTR                 m_bstrMethodNSPrefix;
};

#endif // _DeSerializer_h_
```

As you can see from the object methods, the DeSerializer keeps track of various portions of the XML request payload so it can easily and quickly retrieve information as needed.

The actual implementation of the DeSerializer is fairly simple, using basic DOM navigation calls to locate the appropriate SOAP elements. Listing 10.53 shows one such method of the DeSerializer that is used to retrieve method parameters from the method element.

LISTING 10.53 GetParameterValue() Implementation

```
//
// Obtains the value of a parameter in the Request payload
//
bool CDeSerializer::GetParameterValue(long lParamNum,
                                      BSTR * pbstrValue)
{
    try
    {
        CComPtr<IXMLDOMNodeList> pNodeList;
        HRESULT hr = m_pMethodNode->get_childNodes(&pNodeList);
        CHECKHR(hr);
        CHECKPTR(pNodeList);

        // Obtain the value of a parameter
        CComPtr<IXMLDOMNode> pNode;
        hr = pNodeList->get_item(lParamNum, &pNode);
        CHECKHR(hr);
        CHECKPTR(pNode);

        // Return the parameter in a BSTR
        CComVariant var;
        hr = pNode->get_nodeTypedValue(&var);
        *pbstrValue = SysAllocString(var.bstrVal);

        CHECKHR(hr);

        return true;
    }
    catch (const char *str)
    {
        ATLTRACE(str);
    }

    return false;
}
```

The `GetParameterValue()` implementation involves some fairly straightforward MSXML DOM parser node manipulation. First, all the child (XML) nodes of the method are retrieved:

```
CComPtr<IXMLDOMNodeList> pNodeList;
HRESULT hr = m_pMethodNode->get_childNodes(&pNodeList);
```

Then, given the argument of interest, the appropriate child node is located:

```
CComPtr<IXMLDOMNode> pNode;
hr = pNodeList->get_item(lParamNum, &pNode);
```

The XML data always comes from the MSXML parser as string data, even if it represents numerical information. (It's up to you to properly convert the string representation to the corresponding numerical value, which is why you require the type data from the object's type library.) So, the argument value is extracted from the XML document and returned as a BSTR to be used to re-create the original object's call stack:

```
CComVariant var;
hr = pNode->get_nodeTypedValue(&var);
*pbstrValue = SysAllocString(var.bstrVal);
```

Now that you've seen how the DeSerializer works, let's move on to the object activation code, also known as the Activator. It's the Activator that uses the (string-formatted) argument data and builds the COM object's call stack.

The Activator

The Activator object exposes an extremely simple interface, but provides the most important aspect to the server-side implementation. By using the DeSerializer to extract the call information from the SOAP request, the Activator can construct the appropriate call stack for invoking the requested COM method. Listing 10.54 shows the Activator interface.

LISTING 10.54   `CActivator` Class Definition

```
#ifndef _Activator_h
#define _Activator_h

#include "TypeStruct.h"

class CActivator
{
public:
    CActivator(BSTR bstrURI, BSTR bstrMethod);
    virtual ~CActivator() {}
```

continues

10

IMPLEMENTING SOAP

LISTING 10.54   Continued

```
    // Invokes the appropriate COM object/interface/method
    //and returns a DOM response
    virtual int Invoke(IXMLDOMDocument *pRequest,
                       IXMLDOMDocument **ppResponse);

private:

    // Utility method
    void TypeToStringAndEnum(BYTE nRetType, LPSTR* ppstrType,
                             TypeInfo::COM_TYPETYPE *pTypeEnum);

protected:
    // Class, interface, and method of object to be activated
    CComBSTR m_bstrCLSID;
    CComBSTR m_bstrIID;
    CComBSTR m_bstrMethod;
};


#endif // _Activator_h
```

Consider the following code fragment that deserializes the SOAP request and verifies that HTTP header fields and SOAP payload match:

```
//
// Invoke the method call based on the incoming XML request
// and generate an XML response from the result.
//
int CActivator::Invoke(IXMLDOMDocument *pRequest,
                       IXMLDOMDocument **ppResponse)
{
    // Deserialize the SOAP payload
    CDeSerializer deSer(pRequest);

    // Make sure payload URI/method matches the HTTP URI/method
    if (!deSer.CheckMethodAndURI(m_bstrMethod))
    {
        ATLTRACE(">>>ERROR>>> Invalid method name\n");
        return 1;
    }
```

Not only does this provide some degree of security, but it also guarantees that any call routing that takes place will work as expected. It would be unfortunate if the call were routed to a machine that could not service the request because the HTTP headers were incorrectly formed.

The next code fragment shows how the CLSID is extracted from the SOAP request payload, verified against the valid list of remotable objects and interfaces, and used to instantiate the actual COM object:

```
// Get the CLSID from the payload
if (!deSer.GetCLSID(&m_bstrCLSID))
{
    ATLTRACE(">>>ERROR>>> No CLSID\n");
    return 1;
}

// Build GUIDs from HTTP URI (aka IID) and Method
GUID guidCLSID;
GUID guidIID;
CLSIDFromString(m_bstrCLSID, &guidCLSID);
CLSIDFromString(m_bstrIID, &guidIID);

// Use Catalog to get the TypeLib
CComPtr<ITypeLib> pITypeLib;
try
{
    CComPtr<ISOAPCatalog> spISOAPCatalog;
    HRESULT hr = spISOAPCatalog.CoCreateInstance(
                            __uuidof(SOAPCatManager));
    if (FAILED(hr)) throw hr;

    // Remotable object?
    hr = spISOAPCatalog->IsRegisteredObject(m_bstrCLSID);
    if (FAILED(hr)) throw hr;
    if (hr == S_FALSE) throw E_ACCESSDENIED;

    // Remotable interface?
    hr = spISOAPCatalog->IsRegisteredInterface(m_bstrCLSID,
                                        m_bstrIID,
                                        CComVariant(true));
    if (FAILED(hr)) throw hr;
    if (hr == S_FALSE) throw E_ACCESSDENIED;

    // Find the TLB filename
    CComBSTR bstrTLB;
    hr = spISOAPCatalog->GetTLBFile(m_bstrCLSID, &bstrTLB);
    if (FAILED(hr)) throw hr;
    if (hr == S_FALSE) throw E_ACCESSDENIED;

    hr = LoadTypeLib(bstrTLB, &pITypeLib);
    if (FAILED(hr)) throw hr;
}
```

10

```
catch(HRESULT hrErr)
{
    char strErrMsg[256];
    wsprintf(strErrMsg,">>>ERROR>>> Catalog error %#08x\n",hrErr);
    ATLTRACE(strErrMsg);
    return 1;
}

// Create COM object as specified in the SOAP header
CComPtr<IUnknown> *punk;
HRESULT hr = CoCreateInstance(guidCLSID,
                              0,
                              CLSCTX_ALL,
                              guidIID,
                              reinterpret_cast<void**>(&punk));
if (FAILED(hr)) return 1;
```

After the CLSID has been discovered, the SOAP Catalog can be consulted to see if a remote client is allowed to use this object and interface. Assuming that the object is accessible to the client, the server must load the type library information in order to understand the format of the SOAP request payload.

Finally, the COM object is created using the standard COM CoCreateInstance API. Because the Activator code can be used to instantiate any arbitrary COM object, it has no way to know what interface will be used at compile time. Therefore, a generic IUnknown interface is used to point to the object, but the client-requested interface, guidIID, has been specified.

With the type library, the TLBEncoder is able to build a stream of information about the contents of the interface. The Activator uses one piece of this information to determine the method offset into the vtbl as shown in the following fragment:

```
// Gather method information from TypeLib
long iMethodNum = -1;
long iStackSize = -1;
hr = pEncoder->EncodeMethod2(pITypeLib,
                             m_bstrCLSID,
                             m_bstrIID,
                             m_bstrMethod,
                             &iMethodNum,
                             &iStackSize,
                             lpStream);
if (hr != S_OK)
{
    ATLTRACE(">>>ERROR>>> Cannot encode TypeLib\n");
    lpStream->Release();
    return 1;
```

```
}

// Calculate method offset in vtbl
int nMethodNum = iMethodNum * sizeof(void*);
```

Recall that a COM interface is basically a pointer to a vtbl of the object (or possibly its proxy). Calling a method on an interface is the same as calling a method on an abstract base class.

Unfortunately, just knowing the method offset doesn't get you very far. You also need to understand the parameters within the method. Using similar mechanisms to the client delegation software, the type information is loaded into a BYTE stream:

```
// Extract type information from the stream
LARGE_INTEGER li = {0};
hr = lpStream->Seek(li, STREAM_SEEK_SET, NULL);
STATSTG statstg;
hr = lpStream->Stat(&statstg, STATFLAG_NONAME);
if (FAILED(hr))
{
    ATLTRACE(">>>ERROR>>> IStream::Stat failed\n");
    lpStream->Release();
    return 1;
}

// Read stream into a BYTE array
BYTE* pBuf = new BYTE[statstg.cbSize.LowPart];
hr = lpStream->Read((void*)(pBuf),
                    statstg.cbSize.LowPart,
                    NULL);
if (FAILED(hr))
{
    ATLTRACE(">>>ERROR>>> IStream::Read failed\n");
    lpStream->Release();
    delete[] pBuf;
    return 1;
}
```

Although the BYTE stream contains more information than the Activator needs, the total number of parameters and the return type can be extracted as follows:

```
// Skip unused portion of TypeLib
BYTE* p = pBuf;
p += 2*sizeof(int);          // Skip signature
p += 2;                      // Skip version
p += sizeof(int);            // Skip offset
++p;                         // Skip TLB_ITF
p += (lstrlen((LPSTR)p) + 1); // Skip interface name + TLB_NUL
```

```
++p;                              // Skip TLB_MTD token
++p;                              // Skip method number

// Next token is number of parms
int nNumParams = (int)((char)(*p));

// Skip number of parms
++p;

// Next token is return type
BYTE nRetType = (BYTE)(*p);
LPSTR strType = NULL;
TypeInfo tiTemp;
TypeToStringAndEnum(nRetType, &strType, &(tiTemp.m_type));

// Skip return type
++p;

// Method name (in ASCII), with termination
LPSTR strMtdName = (LPSTR)p;

// Skip method name
p += (lstrlen(strMtdName) + 1); // also skip trailing TLB_NUL
```

The next major effort is to discover information about the parameter types. This includes whether they are [in], [in,out], or [out] parameters. This information dictates how memory allocation should be performed. Parameter names and types are also provided through this same mechanism. The TypeInfo data structure, as shown in the following, is used to maintain the method type information for future processing:

```
#ifndef _TypeStruct_h_
#define _TypeStruct_h_

#include <string>

struct TypeInfo
{
    // Denotes the parameter attribute [in], [in,out], or [out]
    enum COM_INOUTTYPE
    {
        COM_IN = 0,
        COM_INOUT,
        COM_OUT
    };

    // Denotes the parameter type
```

```
enum COM_TYPETYPE
{
    COM_UNSUPPORTED = 0,
    COM_VOID,
    COM_SHORT,
    COM_INT,
    COM_LONG,
    COM_FLOAT,
    COM_BSTR
};

// Members
COM_INOUTTYPE m_inout;
std::string   m_strParamName;
COM_TYPETYPE  m_type;
void          *m_pMem;
};

#endif // _TypeStruct_h_
```

To construct the `TypeInfo` structure, the remaining portion of the type library BYTE stream is read and applied to the data structure as follows:

```
// Construct container for maintaining type info and
// associated memory
TypeInfo *ti = new TypeInfo[nNumParams];

// Finally, loop through params and determine [in],
// [in,out] and [out] params
int nExpectedInParams = 0;
BOOL bValidCallStack = TRUE;
int nParamNumber = 0;
while (*p != TLB_EOF)
{
        // Check for [in]
        if ((BYTE)*p == TLB_IN)
        {
            ti[nParamNumber].m_inout =
                                TypeInfo::COM_INOUTTYPE::COM_IN;
            ++nExpectedInParams;
            ++p; // skip TLB_IN
        }

    // Check for [out]
    if ((BYTE)*p == TLB_OUT)
    {
```

10

IMPLEMENTING
SOAP

```
    // Check for [in,out]
    if ((BYTE)(*(p-1))  == TLB_IN)
    {
        // Is actually [in,out]
        ti[nParamNumber].m_inout =
                        TypeInfo::COM_INOUTTYPE::COM_INOUT;
        ++nExpectedInParams;
    }
    else
    {
        // Is actually [out]
        ti[nParamNumber].m_inout =
                        TypeInfo::COM_INOUTTYPE::COM_OUT;
    }

    // skip TLB_OUT
    ++p;
}

// Get parameter type
BYTE type = (BYTE)(*p);
BOOL bIsPtr = FALSE;
if (type == TLB_PTR)
{
    bIsPtr = TRUE;

    // skip TLB_PTR
    ++p;
}

// Get string representation of type
TypeToStringAndEnum((BYTE)(*p),
                    &strType,
                    &(ti[nParamNumber].m_type));

// Any [out] or [in,out] params must be pointers
if ((ti[nParamNumber].m_inout ==
                    TypeInfo::COM_INOUTTYPE::COM_INOUT ||
    ti[nParamNumber].m_inout ==
                    TypeInfo::COM_INOUTTYPE::COM_OUT)
    && !bIsPtr)
{
    bValidCallStack = FALSE;
}

// skip type
++p;
```

```
    // Assign param name
    ti[nParamNumber].m_strParamName = (LPSTR)p;

    // Skip interface name
    p += (ti[nParamNumber].m_strParamName.size() + 1);
                              ➥// skip trailing TLB_NUL

    // Check for TLB_EOF...
    if ((BYTE)*p != TLB_EOF)
    {
        // do nothing for now, although an error
        // could be generated
    }

    ++nParamNumber;
} // while
```

With the TypeInfo structure in place, the only thing left to do is allocate the memory for the method call. Note that [in] and [in,out] parameters must be allocated and initialized by the caller—in this case, the Activator. The caller is also responsible for deleting the parameters after the call has returned. In the case of [out] parameters, they must be allocated by the COM object but deleted by the caller. The following code fragment shows a portion of the Activator that deals with short parameter types:

```
// Allocate memory for params
for (int i = nNumParams-1; i >= 0 ; --i)
{
    // Determine param type
    short sInit = 0;
    int   nInit = 0;
    long  lInit = 0;
    float fInit = 0.0;

    switch (ti[i].m_type)
    {
    case TypeInfo::COM_TYPETYPE::COM_SHORT :
        if (ti[i].m_inout != TypeInfo::COM_INOUTTYPE::COM_OUT)
        {
            // initialize [in] or [in,out] params
            CComBSTR bstrValue;
            deSer.GetParameterValue(i, &bstrValue);
            USES_CONVERSION;
            sInit = atoi(W2A(bstrValue));
        }

        ti[i].m_pMem = new short(sInit);

        break;
```

Especially note the DeSerializer `GetParameterValue()` call. This is where the initialization values are pulled from the incoming SOAP request to populate the `[in]` and `[in,out]` parameters.

The next section is wherethings start to get interesting. Now comes the time to push method parameters onto the call stack. For this type of method call order, the parameters are pushed onto the call stack, starting from the right most parameter, as follows:

```
// Push method parameters on stack, working from right to left
for (i=nNumParams-1; i >= 0 ; --i)
{
    // Shortcut pointer
    void *p = ti[i].m_pMem;

    // determine param type
    switch (ti[i].m_type)
    {
    case TypeInfo::COM_TYPETYPE::COM_INT :
    case TypeInfo::COM_TYPETYPE::COM_LONG :
    case TypeInfo::COM_TYPETYPE::COM_FLOAT :
        if (ti[i].m_inout == TypeInfo::COM_INOUTTYPE::COM_IN)
        {
            // Push the value of [in] params
            __asm
            {
                mov     ecx,[p]
                mov     edx,[ecx]
                push    edx
            }
        }
        else
        {
            // Push the address of [out] or [in,out] params
            __asm push  p
        }
        break;

    case TypeInfo::COM_TYPETYPE::COM_SHORT :
        if (ti[i].m_inout == TypeInfo::COM_INOUTTYPE::COM_IN)
        {
            // Push the value of [in] params
            __asm
            {
                mov     ecx,[p]
                mov     ax,word ptr [ecx]
                push    eax
            }
        }
```

```
        }
        else
        {
            // Push the address of [out]  or [in,out] params
            __asm push  p
        }
        break;

    case TypeInfo::COM_TYPETYPE::COM_BSTR :
        if (ti[i].m_inout == TypeInfo::COM_INOUTTYPE::COM_IN)
        {
            // Push the address of [in] BSTRs
            __asm
            {
                push  p
            }
        }
        else
        {
            // Push the address of the address of [out]
            // or [in,out] BSTRs
            BSTR *pp = (BSTR *)&ti[i].m_pMem;
            __asm
            {
                push pp
            }
        }
        break;
    }
}
```

As you would expect, all 32-bit data types are treated in the same way, and, through the use of
some inline assembler sprinkled throughout the code, you are able to simply push the parameters onto the call stack. Recall that the memory allocated for each parameter is stored in
m_pMem, a void* pointer, and you have to treat [in] parameters differently than [in,out] or
[out] parameters because the latter two require some value to be returned to the caller.

CAUTION

You must use caution when constructing a call stack. Most importantly, you cannot do
this within a method or function separate from the code that will actually make the
object method call. This is because, after you've pushed parameters onto the stack,
any call that you make to another method or function will end up adjusting the call
stack.

10

**IMPLEMENTING
SOAP**

Now that you have a valid call stack that should conform to the method's signature, you can go ahead and make the call:

```
// Build the vtbl and call the method
HRESULT hrMethod = S_OK;
__asm
{
    mov    edx,dword ptr [punk]      // Get the IUnknown ptr
    mov    eax,dword ptr [edx]       // Get the IUnknown address
    mov    edx,[nMethodNum]          // Get the method offset
    mov    ecx,dword ptr [punk]      // Get the *this* ptr
    push   ecx                       // Push the *this* ptr
    call   dword ptr [eax+edx]       // Call the IUnknown +
                                     // method offset
    mov    dword ptr [hrMethod],eax  // Get the HRESULT
}
```

All that is left to do is add the method offset to the given interface pointer to build the requested object method's address. You need to push the objects *this* pointer as the top parameter item, and call the method. At this point, control has been transferred to the COM object's method. Upon completion, the *assumed* HRESULT is extracted for use in the SOAP response.

The last step is to fully construct the SOAP response. To do this, you can use the SOAPObjectLib classes to simplify your life. The following code fragment shows how the results are pulled from the [in,out] and [out] parameters and placed in the response payload:

```
// Insert params into payload and delete associated memory
for (i=0; i < nNumParams; ++i)
{
    // Only return the [out] and [in,out] params
    if (ti[i].m_inout != TypeInfo::COM_INOUTTYPE::COM_IN)
    {
        // Build m:MethodResponse params
        CSOAPEmbeddedElement* pEmbedded = NULL;
        hr = pMethodElement->InsertElement(
                                    ti[i].m_strParamName,
                                    NULLNSCOOKIE,
                                    &pEmbedded);
        if (FAILED(hr)) return 1;

        // determine param type
        switch (ti[i].m_type)
        {
        case TypeInfo::COM_TYPETYPE::COM_SHORT :
            char strShort[64];
            sprintf(strShort, "%d", *((short *)ti[i].m_pMem));
            pEmbedded->SetElementData(string(strShort));
            delete (short *)ti[i].m_pMem;
            break;
```

After the data has been stuffed into the MSXML DOM parser, it can then be returned to the client application for final processing.

Configuring the Activation Framework

In order to set up the SOAPExtension.dll component, you only need to follow a few short steps:

1. Configure a Windows NT system with Microsoft's IIS Web server.
2. Using the Internet Service Manager, create a Virtual Directory named *soap* under a Web Site (possibly the Default Web Site).
3. Make sure the Virtual Directory has *Execute* permissions enabled.
4. Copy the SOAPExtension.dll to this directory.

Build the `SOAPCat.xml` file with the EndpointURL pointing to the IIS machine. For example, `localhost/soap/SOAPExtension.dll` would be the EndpointURL if you run IIS on your machine.

> **CAUTION**
>
> If you decide to run both the SOAP client and server on the same machine, be sure to use the delegation framework, rather than the blind interception model. Otherwise, because the registry is configured to use the Surrogate object, the server will end up creating yet another intercepted object, and the system will fail.

Now that you've seen the server implementation, here are some possible improvements you might make.

Possible Improvements

One of the most difficult tasks when writing code for a book is to provide enough meat for the reader to follow the concept, but not so much code that the reader gets lost in the details. Some of the remaining work that needs to be done to this implementation involves security, XML parsing improvements including better namespace handling, support for more types and arrays, a more robust approach to faults, and, most importantly, XML Schema support.

Security

Some effort was put forth to ensure a fairly secure environment for the SOAP application to execute in, but more work could be done to control the accessibility of objects. For instance, you could enforce that only objects exposed through DCOM configuration (DCOMCNFG.EXE) are accessible. Another security feature would be to enforce SSL connections for certain objects.

Parsing

Although the DOM is a fairly straightforward interface to use for parsing, it's not the fastest mechanism that can be used for server-side processing. A good SAX parser would probably make more sense in this case, as it would likely save time when deserializing the incoming request payload.

This language binding also handles namespaces and their prefixes rather naively, making code simpler to follow and thus a better learning experience. In this case, the method namespace is simply assumed to be "m". However, any full-fledged SOAP implementation would decode namespaces properly and return the appropriate (fault) response if the data didn't parse correctly.

Finally, the server-side implementation examines the incoming SOAP packet for specific method (and object) information only. On the other hand, the SOAP specification states the entire packet should be examined for error(s) and a fault returned if things are not encoded correctly. Full-packet parsing must also be addressed to make this implementation more commercially robust.

Support for Types and Arrays

Unfortunately, as with the client-side implementation, there was only time to provide support for the more common native types from C++/IDL. There is no structure or array support in the current implementation. Support for these may be added in a future revision to this book (or to the author's code, the updates to which you can find at `http://www.endurasoft.com`).

Enhanced Fault Processing

If a fault condition is detected, this implementation returns a hard-coded SOAP `Client` fault. A more robust approach is to better ascertain the nature of the fault and return a more accurate fault notification. The code you find here works well for illustration purposes, but you should provide much stronger error handling and fault response code in your own implementations.

XML Schema Support

The most glaring failure of this implementation is in its direct use of the type library rather than an XML Schema. This was done because type libraries exist, and their type data is relatively easy to extract. However, as schemas and parsers that incorporate schemas improve and evolve, you should consider turning away from the COM type library to instead use the type information available in the interface's schema. This might also be added to future revisions of the implementation, if publication demands merit additional printings.

Summary

This has been a somewhat lengthy, but hopefully enlightening, chapter. It isn't often you can obtain an entire remoting architecture, with source code, for the price of a book.

The goal of this chapter was to introduce an unobtrusive SOAP processing architecture (language binding) for the Component Object Model. The chapter began with a review of SOAP language bindings and presented some of the currently available language bindings. Both the Perl and Java implementations are available from the DevelopMentor Internet site at `http://www.develop.com/soap`.

Some of the elements necessary to properly intercept COM method calls were also discussed, such as the necessary Registry modifications, a persistent data store (the SOAP Catalog, in this case), and to determine the data types of the method arguments at runtime.

The chapter provided an introduction to a C++–based SOAP Object model you can use in platforms other than Intel-based, 32-bit Windows systems. You have access to the HTTP packet information as well as to the envelope, the header, and the body. Adding method support, independent and embedded elements, namespaces, and attributes to your SOAP request is easily accomplished, and streaming the SOAP packet from the object model is simplicity itself.

The chapter described the COM objects shared by both the client-side and server-side architectures—the SOAP Catalog and the type library encoder. The SOAP Catalog object manages an XML document that is used to store information regarding objects and interfaces when sending data using SOAP, such as endpoint URLs and namespaces. It's also used to determine whether or not a given interface is slated for SOAP transmission. The TLBEncoder object accepts a COM object's type library and extracts the critical type information you need to encode a method's call stack in a SOAP format. It returns to you an IStream filled with a stream of bytes that collectively represent the type information for a given interface method.

You saw the SOAP Configuration Utility, which provides a nice user interface when accessing the SOAP Catalog. It tells you which objects are registered on your system as well as which interfaces exposed by those objects are candidates for SOAP encoding with this architecture.

The SOAP Object Surrogate and its major component, the serializer, were introduced. You saw how the Surrogate manages interception and delegation, how COM call stacks are accessed and serialized, and how the SOAP packet is created (using the type information gleaned from the TLBEncoder). You learned how the resulting XML is transmitted to the remote server, and how the response is received and interpreted. You also looked at how [out] parameters were filled with data originating on the remote server.

10

IMPLEMENTING
SOAP

You were introduced to the server-side architecture in detail. The deserializer extracts the method call argument information as the Activator constructs the method's call stack. These objects, coupled with the SOAP object model library, are wrapped into an ISAPI extension DLL to facilitate HTTP packet interception.

In total, you have in your hands a complete implementation of SOAP that is compatible with the Component Object Model. This code could easily form the basis of your own SOAP processing architecture, or you can use it as a springboard for SOAP experimentation. The possibilities are boundless.

The SOAP 1.1 Specification

IN THIS APPENDIX

> **NOTE**
>
> Author's comments to the specification are shown in note form, such as this. Information in these notes should not be construed as written by the specification authors. It is for your enlightenment only.

These notes are not part of the specification and are provided to assist your understanding of specific areas. Also, the namespace schemas referred to in the specification are included at the end of the specification.

The SOAP Specification

Authors

Don Box, DevelopMentor, David Ehnebuske, IBM, Gopal Kakivaya, Microsoft, Andrew Layman, Microsoft, Noah Mendelsohn, Lotus Development Corp., Henrik Frystyk Nielsen, Microsoft, Satish Thatte, Microsoft, Dave Winer, UserLand Software, Inc.

Abstract

SOAP is a lightweight protocol for exchange of information in a decentralized, distributed environment. It is an XML based protocol that consists of three parts: an envelope that defines a framework for describing what is in a message and how to process it, a set of encoding rules for expressing instances of application-defined datatypes, and a convention for representing remote procedure calls and responses. SOAP can potentially be used in combination with a variety of other protocols; however, the only bindings defined in this document describe how to use SOAP in combination with HTTP and HTTP Extension Framework.

> **NOTE**
>
> This speaks to SOAP's roots, which lie with HTTP. The original intent was to use XML as an encoding specification to allow you to ship method argument data via HTTP. For the most part, this eliminates firewall issues and allows you to send remote method calls over the Internet (or at least over networks supporting HTTP).

Table of Contents

1. Introduction

SOAP provides a simple and lightweight mechanism for exchanging structured and typed information between peers in a decentralized, distributed environment using XML. SOAP does not itself define any application semantics such as a programming model or implementation specific semantics; rather it defines a simple mechanism for expressing application semantics by providing a modular packaging model and encoding mechanisms for encoding data within modules. This allows SOAP to be used in a large variety of systems ranging from messaging systems to RPC.

SOAP consists of three parts:

- The SOAP envelope (see section 4) construct defines an overall framework for expressing what is in a message; who should deal with it, and whether it is optional or mandatory.
- The SOAP encoding rules (see section 5) defines a serialization mechanism that can be used to exchange instances of application-defined datatypes.
- The SOAP RPC representation (see section 7) defines a convention that can be used to represent remote procedure calls and responses.

Although these parts are described together as part of SOAP, they are functionally orthogonal. In particular, the envelope and the encoding rules are defined in different namespaces in order to promote simplicity through modularity.

In addition to the SOAP envelope, the SOAP encoding rules and the SOAP RPC conventions, this specification defines two protocol bindings that describe how a SOAP message can be carried in HTTP [5] messages either with or without the HTTP Extension Framework [6].

1.1 Design Goals

A major design goal for SOAP is simplicity and extensibility. This means that there are several features from traditional messaging systems and distributed object systems that are not part of the core SOAP specification. Such features include

- Distributed garbage collection
- Boxcarring or batching of messages
- Objects-by-reference (which requires distributed garbage collection)
- Activation (which requires objects-by-reference)

1.2 Notational Conventions

The keywords "MUST", "MUST NOT", "REQUIRED", "SHALL", "SHALL NOT", "SHOULD", "SHOULD NOT", "RECOMMENDED", "MAY", and "OPTIONAL" in this document are to be interpreted as described in RFC-2119 [2].

The namespace prefixes "SOAP-ENV" and "SOAP-ENC" used in this document are associated with the SOAP namespaces "http://schemas.xmlsoap.org/soap/envelope/" and "http://schemas.xmlsoap.org/soap/encoding/" respectively.

Throughout this document, the namespace prefix "xsi" is assumed to be associated with the URI "http://www.w3.org/1999/XMLSchema-instance" which is defined in the XML Schemas specification [11]. Similarly, the namespace prefix "xsd" is assumed to be associated with the URI "http://www.w3.org/1999/XMLSchema" which is defined in [10]. The namespace prefix "tns" is used to indicate whatever is the target namespace of the current document. All other namespace prefixes are samples only.

Namespace URIs of the general form "some-URI" represent some application-dependent or context-dependent URI [4].

This specification uses the augmented Backus-Naur Form (BNF) as described in RFC-2616 [5] for certain constructs.

1.3 Examples of SOAP Messages

In this example, a GetLastTradePrice SOAP request is sent to a StockQuote service. The request takes a string parameter, ticker symbol, and returns a float in the SOAP response. The SOAP Envelope element is the top element of the XML document representing the SOAP message. XML namespaces are used to disambiguate SOAP identifiers from application specific identifiers. The example illustrates the HTTP bindings defined in section 6. It is worth noting that the rules governing XML payload format in SOAP are entirely independent of the fact that the payload is carried in HTTP.

More examples are available in Appendix A.

EXAMPLE 1.   SOAP Message Embedded in HTTP Request

```
POST /StockQuote HTTP/1.1
Host:
www.stockquoteserver.com
Content-Type: text/xml;
charset="utf-8"
Content-Length: nnnn
SOAPAction:
"Some-URI"

<SOAP-ENV:Envelope
  xmlns:SOAP-ENV="http://schemas.xmlsoap.org/soap/envelope/"
  SOAP-ENV:encodingStyle="http://schemas.xmlsoap.org/soap/encoding/">
   <SOAP-ENV:Body>
       <m:GetLastTradePrice xmlns:m="Some-URI">
           <symbol>DIS</symbol>
       </m:GetLastTradePrice>
   </SOAP-ENV:Body>
</SOAP-ENV:Envelope>
```

Following is the response message containing the HTTP message with the SOAP message as the payload:

EXAMPLE 2. SOAP Message Embedded in HTTP Response

```
HTTP/1.1 200 OK
Content-Type: text/xml;
charset="utf-8"
Content-Length:
nnnn

<SOAP-ENV:Envelope
  xmlns:SOAP-ENV="http://schemas.xmlsoap.org/soap/envelope/"
  SOAP-ENV:encodingStyle="http://schemas.xmlsoap.org/soap/encoding/"/>
  <SOAP-ENV:Body>
      <m:GetLastTradePriceResponse xmlns:m="Some-URI">
          <Price>34.5</Price>
      </m:GetLastTradePriceResponse>
  </SOAP-ENV:Body>
</SOAP-ENV:Envelope>
```

2. The SOAP Message Exchange Model

SOAP messages are fundamentally one-way transmissions from a sender to a receiver, but as illustrated above, SOAP messages are often combined to implement patterns such as request/response.

NOTE

This change was made from Version 1.0 to allow other protocols other than HTTP to be used to transport SOAP data. The specification still leans toward HTTP, with the clear intention SOAP will be used as an RPC mechanism, but the wording has been loosened to allow for other transports and uses.

SOAP implementations can be optimized to exploit the unique characteristics of particular network systems. For example, the HTTP binding described in section 6 provides for SOAP response messages to be delivered as HTTP responses, using the same connection as the inbound request.

Regardless of the protocol to which SOAP is bound, messages are routed along a so-called "message path", which allows for processing at one or more intermediate nodes in addition to the ultimate destination.

A SOAP application receiving a SOAP message MUST process that message by performing the following actions in the order listed below:

1. Identify all parts of the SOAP message intended for that application (see section 4.2.2).

2. Verify that all mandatory parts identified in step 1 are supported by the application for this message (see section 4.2.3) and process them accordingly. If this is not the case then discard the message (see section 4.4). The processor MAY ignore optional parts identified in step 1 without affecting the outcome of the processing.

3. If the SOAP application is not the ultimate destination of the message then remove all parts identified in step 1 before forwarding the message.

Processing a message or a part of a message requires that the SOAP processor understands, among other things, the exchange pattern being used (one way, request/response, multicast, etc.), the role of the recipient in that pattern, the employment (if any) of RPC mechanisms such as the one documented in section 7, the representation or encoding of data, as well as other semantics necessary for correct processing.

While attributes such as the SOAP `encodingStyle` attribute (see section 4.1.1) can be used to describe certain aspects of a message, this specification does not mandate a particular means by which the recipient makes such determinations in general. For example, certain applications will understand that a particular <getStockPrice> element signals an RPC request using the conventions of section 7, while another application may infer that all traffic directed to it is encoded as one way messages.

3. Relation to XML

All SOAP messages are encoded using XML (see [7] for more information on XML).

A SOAP application SHOULD include the proper SOAP namespace on all elements and attributes defined by SOAP in messages that it generates. A SOAP application MUST be able to process SOAP namespaces in messages that it receives. It MUST discard messages that have incorrect namespaces (see section 4.4) and it MAY process SOAP messages without SOAP namespaces as though they had the correct SOAP namespaces.

SOAP defines two namespaces (see [8] for more information on XML namespaces):

- The SOAP envelope has the namespace identifier "http://schemas.xmlsoap.org/soap/envelope/"

- The SOAP serialization has the namespace identifier "http://schemas.xmlsoap.org/soap/encoding/"

A SOAP message MUST NOT contain a Document Type Declaration. A SOAP message MUST NOT contain Processing Instructions. [7]

> **NOTE**
>
> Remember that
>
> ```
> <? xml version=1.0" ?>
> ```
>
> is a processing instruction. Therefore, you don't include this when encoding SOAP data.

SOAP uses the local, unqualified "id" attribute of type "ID" to specify the unique identifier of an encoded element. SOAP uses the local, unqualified attribute "href" of type "uri-reference" to specify a reference to that value, in a manner conforming to the XML Specification [7], XML Schema Specification [11], and XML Linking Language Specification [9].

With the exception of the SOAP mustUnderstand attribute (see section 4.2.3) and the SOAP actor attribute (see section 4.2.2), it is generally permissible to have attributes and their values appear in XML instances or alternatively in schemas, with equal effect. That is, declaration in a DTD or schema with a default or fixed value is semantically equivalent to appearance in an instance.

4. SOAP Envelope

A SOAP message is an XML document that consists of a mandatory SOAP envelope, an optional SOAP header, and a mandatory SOAP body. This XML document is referred to as a SOAP message for the rest of this specification. The namespace identifier for the elements and attributes defined in this section is "http://schemas.xmlsoap.org/soap/envelope/". A SOAP message contains the following:

- The Envelope is the top element of the XML document representing the message.
- The Header is a generic mechanism for adding features to a SOAP message in a decentralized manner without prior agreement between the communicating parties. SOAP defines a few attributes that can be used to indicate who should deal with a feature and whether it is optional or mandatory (see section 4.2).
- The Body is a container for mandatory information intended for the ultimate recipient of the message (see section 4.3). SOAP defines one element for the body, which is the Fault element used for reporting errors.

The grammar rules are as follows:

1. Envelope
    - The element name is "Envelope".
    - The element MUST be present in a SOAP message.

- The element MAY contain namespace declarations as well as additional attributes. If present, such additional attributes MUST be namespace-qualified. Similarly, the element MAY contain additional sub elements. If present these elements MUST be namespace-qualified and MUST follow the SOAP Body element.

2. Header (see section 4.2)

- The element name is "Header".

- The element MAY be present in a SOAP message. If present, the element MUST be the first immediate child element of a SOAP Envelope element.

- The element MAY contain a set of header entries each being an immediate child element of the SOAP Header element. All immediate child elements of the SOAP Header element MUST be namespace-qualified.

3. Body (see section 4.3)

- The element name is "Body".

- The element MUST be present in a SOAP message and MUST be an immediate child element of a SOAP Envelope element. It MUST directly follow the SOAP Header element if present. Otherwise it MUST be the first immediate child element of the SOAP Envelope element.

- The element MAY contain a set of body entries each being an immediate child element of the SOAP Body element. Immediate child elements of the SOAP Body element MAY be namespace-qualified. SOAP defines the SOAP Fault element, which is used to indicate error messages (see section 4.4).

4.1.1 SOAP encodingStyle Attribute

The SOAP encodingStyle global attribute can be used to indicate the serialization rules used in a SOAP message. This attribute MAY appear on any element, and is scoped to that element's contents and all child elements not themselves containing such an attribute, much as an XML namespace declaration is scoped. There is no default encoding defined for a SOAP message.

The attribute value is an ordered list of one or more URIs identifying the serialization rule or rules that can be used to deserialize the SOAP message indicated in the order of most specific to least specific. Examples of values are

"http://schemas.xmlsoap.org/soap/encoding/"

"http://my.host/encoding/restricted http://my.host/encoding/"

""

The serialization rules defined by SOAP in section 5 are identified by the URI "http://schemas.xmlsoap.org/soap/encoding/". Messages using this particular serialization SHOULD indicate this using the SOAP encodingStyle attribute. In addition, all URIs syntactically beginning with "http://schemas.xmlsoap.org/soap/encoding/" indicate conformance with the SOAP encoding rules defined in section 5 (though with potentially tighter rules added).

A value of the zero-length URI ("") explicitly indicates that no claims are made for the encoding style of contained elements. This can be used to turn off any claims from containing elements.

4.1.2 Envelope Versioning Model

SOAP does not define a traditional versioning model based on major and minor version numbers. A SOAP message MUST have an Envelope element associated with the "http://schemas.xmlsoap.org/soap/envelope/" namespace. If a message is received by a SOAP application in which the SOAP Envelope element is associated with a different namespace, the application MUST treat this as a version error and discard the message. If the message is received through a request/response protocol such as HTTP, the application MUST respond with a SOAP VersionMismatch faultcode message (see section 4.4) using the SOAP "http://schemas.xmlsoap.org/soap/envelope/" namespace.

4.2 SOAP Header

SOAP provides a flexible mechanism for extending a message in a decentralized and modular way without prior knowledge between the communicating parties. Typical examples of extensions that can be implemented as header entries are authentication, transaction management, payment etc.

The Header element is encoded as the first immediate child element of the SOAP Envelope XML element. All immediate child elements of the Header element are called header entries.

The encoding rules for header entries are as follows:

1. A header entry is identified by its fully qualified element name, which consists of the namespace URI and the local name. All immediate child elements of the SOAP Header element MUST be namespace-qualified.

2. The SOAP encodingStyle attribute MAY be used to indicate the encoding style used for the header entries (see section 4.1.1).

3. The SOAP mustUnderstand attribute (see section 4.2.3) and SOAP actor attribute (see section 4.2.2) MAY be used to indicate how to process the entry and by whom (see section 4.2.1).

4.2.1 Use of Header Attributes

The SOAP Header attributes defined in this section determine how a recipient of a SOAP message should process the message as described in section 2. A SOAP application generating a SOAP message SHOULD only use the SOAP Header attributes on immediate child elements of the SOAP Header element. The recipient of a SOAP message MUST ignore all SOAP Header attributes that are not applied to an immediate child element of the SOAP Header element.

An example is a header with an element identifier of "Transaction", a "mustUnderstand" value of "1", and a value of 5. This would be encoded as follows:

```
<SOAP-ENV:Header>
   <t:Transaction
      xmlns:t="some-URI" SOAP-ENV:mustUnderstand="1">
         5
   </t:Transaction>
</SOAP-ENV:Header>
```

4.2.2 SOAP `actor` Attribute

A SOAP message travels from the originator to the ultimate destination, potentially by passing through a set of SOAP intermediaries along the message path. A SOAP intermediary is an application that is capable of both receiving and forwarding SOAP messages. Both intermediaries as well as the ultimate destination are identified by a URI.

Not all parts of a SOAP message may be intended for the ultimate destination of the SOAP message but, instead, may be intended for one or more of the intermediaries on the message path. The role of a recipient of a header element is similar to that of accepting a contract in that it cannot be extended beyond the recipient. That is, a recipient receiving a header element MUST NOT forward that header element to the next application in the SOAP message path. The recipient MAY insert a similar header element but in that case, the contract is between that application and the recipient of that header element.

The SOAP actor global attribute can be used to indicate the recipient of a header element. The value of the SOAP `actor` attribute is a URI. The special URI "http://schemas.xmlsoap.org/soap/actor/next" indicates that the header element is intended for the very first SOAP application that processes the message. This is similar to the hop-by-hop scope model represented by the `Connection` header field in HTTP.

Omitting the SOAP `actor` attribute indicates that the recipient is the ultimate destination of the SOAP message.

This attribute MUST appear in the SOAP message instance in order to be effective (see section 3 and 4.2.1).

4.2.3 SOAP `mustUnderstand` Attribute

The SOAP `mustUnderstand` global attribute can be used to indicate whether a header entry is mandatory or optional for the recipient to process. The recipient of a header entry is defined by the SOAP `actor` attribute (see section 4.2.2). The value of the `mustUnderstand` attribute is either "1" or "0". The absence of the SOAP `mustUnderstand` attribute is semantically equivalent to its presence with the value "0".

If a header element is tagged with a SOAP `mustUnderstand` attribute with a value of "1", the recipient of that header entry either MUST obey the semantics (as conveyed by the fully qualified name of the element) and process correctly to those semantics, or MUST fail processing the message (see section 4.4).

The SOAP `mustUnderstand` attribute allows for robust evolution. Elements tagged with the SOAP `mustUnderstand` attribute with a value of "1" MUST be presumed to somehow modify the semantics of their parent or peer elements. Tagging elements in this manner assures that this change in semantics will not be silently (and, presumably, erroneously) ignored by those who may not fully understand it.

This attribute MUST appear in the instance in order to be effective (see section 3 and 4.2.1).

> **NOTE**
>
> In other words, this attribute has no effect in a schema. Rather, you use it in an actual SOAP packet, as that's where it really has meaning (the server must be capable of processing this header element or it must fail the request).

4.3 SOAP Body

The SOAP Body element provides a simple mechanism for exchanging mandatory information intended for the ultimate recipient of the message. Typical uses of the Body element include marshalling RPC calls and error reporting.

The Body element is encoded as an immediate child element of the SOAP Envelope XML element. If a Header element is present then the Body element MUST immediately follow the Header element, otherwise it MUST be the first immediate child element of the Envelope element.

All immediate child elements of the Body element are called body entries and each body entry is encoded as an independent element within the SOAP Body element.

> **NOTE**
>
> The term "body entry" is new to Version 1.1. Formerly, elements were either indepen-
> dent or embedded. (These two terms have the same meaning in both versions of the
> specification, however.)

The encoding rules for body entries are as follows:

1. A body entry is identified by its fully qualified element name, which consists of the namespace URI and the local name. Immediate child elements of the SOAP Body element MAY be namespace-qualified.

2. The SOAP encodingStyle attribute MAY be used to indicate the encoding style used for the body entries (see section 4.1.1).

SOAP defines one body entry, which is the Fault entry used for reporting errors (see section 4.4).

4.3.1 Relationship Between SOAP Header and Body

While the Header and Body are defined as independent elements, they are in fact related. The relationship between a body entry and a header entry is as follows: A body entry is semanti-cally equivalent to a header entry intended for the default actor and with a SOAP mustUnderstand attribute with a value of "1". The default actor is indicated by not using the actor attribute (see section 4.2.2).

4.4 SOAP Fault

The SOAP Fault element is used to carry error and/or status information within a SOAP mes-sage. If present, the SOAP Fault element MUST appear as a body entry and MUST NOT appear more than once within a Body element.

The SOAP Fault element defines the following four subelements:

faultcode

The faultcode element is intended for use by software to provide an algorithmic mechanism for identifying the fault. The faultcode MUST be present in a SOAP Fault element and the fault-code value MUST be a qualified name as defined in [8], section 3. SOAP defines a small set of SOAP fault codes covering basic SOAP faults (see section 4.4.1)

faultstring

The faultstring element is intended to provide a human readable explanation of the fault and is not intended for algorithmic processing. The faultstring element is similar to the 'Reason-Phrase' defined by HTTP (see [5], section 6.1). It MUST be present in a SOAP Fault element and SHOULD provide at least some information explaining the nature of the fault.

faultactor

The faultactor element is intended to provide information about who caused the fault to happen within the message path (see section 2). It is similar to the SOAP `actor` attribute (see section 4.2.2) but instead of indicating the destination of the header entry, it indicates the source of the fault. The value of the faultactor attribute is a URI identifying the source. Applications that do not act as the ultimate destination of the SOAP message MUST include the faultactor element in a SOAP Fault element. The ultimate destination of a message MAY use the faultactor element to indicate explicitly that it generated the fault (see also the detail element below).

detail

The detail element is intended for carrying application specific error information related to the Body element. It MUST be present if the contents of the Body element could not be successfully processed. It MUST NOT be used to carry information about error information belonging to header entries. Detailed error information belonging to header entries MUST be carried within header entries.

The absence of the detail element in the Fault element indicates that the fault is not related to processing of the Body element. This can be used to distinguish whether the Body element was processed or not in case of a fault situation.

All immediate child elements of the detail element are called detail entries and each detail entry is encoded as an independent element within the detail element.

The encoding rules for detail entries are as follows (see also example 10):

1. A detail entry is identified by its fully qualified element name, which consists of the namespace URI and the local name. Immediate child elements of the detail element MAY be namespace-qualified.

2. The SOAP `encodingStyle` attribute MAY be used to indicate the encoding style used for the detail entries (see section 4.1.1).

Other Fault subelements MAY be present, provided they are namespace-qualified.

4.4.1 SOAP Fault Codes

The faultcode values defined in this section MUST be used in the faultcode element when describing faults defined by this specification. The namespace identifier for these faultcode values is "http://schemas.xmlsoap.org/soap/envelope/". Use of this space is recommended (but not required) in the specification of methods defined outside of the present specification.

The default SOAP faultcode values are defined in an extensible manner that allows for new SOAP faultcode values to be defined while maintaining backwards compatibility with existing faultcode values. The mechanism used is very similar to the 1xx, 2xx, 3xx, etc. basic status classes defined in HTTP (see [5] section 10). However, instead of integers, they are defined as XML qualified names (see [8] section 3). The character "." (dot) is used as a separator of fault-code values indicating that what is to the left of the dot is a more generic fault code value than the value to the right. Example:

```
Client.Authentication
```

The set of faultcode values defined in this document is

Name	Meaning
VersionMismatch	The processing party found an invalid namespace for the SOAP Envelope element (see section 4.1.2)
MustUnderstand	An immediate child element of the SOAP Header element that was either not understood or not obeyed by the processing party contained a SOAP mustUnderstand attribute with a value of "1" (see section 4.2.3)
Client	The Client class of errors indicate that the message was incorrectly formed or did not contain the appropriate information in order to succeed. For example, the message could lack the proper authentication or payment information. It is generally an indication that the message should not be resent without change. See also section 4.4 for a description of the SOAP Fault detail sub-element.
Server	The Server class of errors indicate that the message could not be processed for reasons not directly attributable to the contents of the message itself but rather to the processing of the message. For example, processing could include communicating with an upstream processor, which didn't respond. The message may succeed at a later point in time. See also section 4.4 for a description of the SOAP Fault detail sub-element.

5. SOAP Encoding

The SOAP encoding style is based on a simple type system that is a generalization of the common features found in type systems in programming languages, databases and semi-structured data. A type either is a simple (scalar) type or is a compound type constructed as a composite of several parts, each with a type. This is described in more detail below. This section defines rules for serialization of a graph of typed objects. It operates on two levels. First, given a schema in any notation consistent with the type system described, a schema for an XML grammar may be constructed. Second, given a type-system schema and a particular graph of values conforming to that schema, an XML instance may be constructed. In reverse, given an XML instance produced in accordance with these rules, and given also the original schema, a copy of the original value graph may be constructed.

The namespace identifier for the elements and attributes defined in this section is "http://schemas.xmlsoap.org/soap/encoding/". The encoding samples shown assume all namespace declarations are at a higher element level.

Use of the data model and encoding style described in this section is encouraged but not required; other data models and encodings can be used in conjunction with SOAP (see section 4.1.1).

5.1 Rules for Encoding Types in XML

XML allows very flexible encoding of data. SOAP defines a narrower set of rules for encoding. This section defines the encoding rules at a high level, and the next section describes the encoding rules for specific types when they require more detail. The encodings described in this section can be used in conjunction with the mapping of RPC calls and responses specified in Section 7.

To describe encoding, the following terminology is used:

1. A "value" is a string, the name of a measurement (number, date, enumeration, etc.) or a composite of several such primitive values. All values are of specific types.

2. A "simple value" is one without named parts. Examples of simple values are particular strings, integers, enumerated values etc.

3. A "compound value" is an aggregate of relations to other values. Examples of Compound Values are particular purchase orders, stock reports, street addresses, etc.

4. Within a compound value, each related value is potentially distinguished by a role name, ordinal or both. This is called its "accessor." Examples of compound values include particular Purchase Orders, Stock Reports etc. Arrays are also compound values. It is possible to have compound values with several accessors each named the same, as for example, RDF does.

5. An "array" is a compound value in which ordinal position serves as the only distinction among member values.

6. A "struct" is a compound value in which accessor name is the only distinction among member values, and no accessor has the same name as any other.

7. A "simple type" is a class of simple values. Examples of simple types are the classes called "string," "integer," enumeration classes, etc.

8. A "compound type" is a class of compound values. An example of a compound type is the class of purchase order values sharing the same accessors (shipTo, totalCost, etc.) though with potentially different values (and perhaps further constrained by limits on certain values).

9. Within a compound type, if an accessor has a name that is distinct within that type but is not distinct with respect to other types, that is, the name plus the type together are needed to make a unique identification, the name is called "locally scoped." If however the name is based in part on a Uniform Resource Identifier, directly or indirectly, such that the name alone is sufficient to uniquely identify the accessor irrespective of the type within which it appears, the name is called "universally scoped."

10. Given the information in the schema relative to which a graph of values is serialized, it is possible to determine that some values can only be related by a single instance of an accessor. For others, it is not possible to make this determination. If only one accessor can reference it, a value is considered "single-reference". If referenced by more than one, actually or potentially, it is "multi-reference." Note that it is possible for a certain value to be considered "single-reference" relative to one schema and "multi-reference" relative to another.

11. Syntactically, an element may be "independent" or "embedded." An independent element is any element appearing at the top level of a serialization. All others are embedded elements.

Although it is possible to use the xsi:type attribute such that a graph of values is self-describing both in its structure and the types of its values, the serialization rules permit that the types of values MAY be determinate only by reference to a schema. Such schemas MAY be in the notation described by "XML Schema Part 1: Structures" [10] and "XML Schema Part 2: Datatypes" [11] or MAY be in any other notation. Note also that, while the serialization rules apply to compound types other than arrays and structs, many schemas will contain only struct and array types.

The rules for serialization are as follows:

1. All values are represented as element content. A multi-reference value MUST be represented as the content of an independent element. A single-reference value SHOULD not be (but MAY be).

2. For each element containing a value, the type of the value MUST be represented by at least one of the following conditions: (a) the containing element instance contains an xsi:type attribute, (b) the containing element instance is itself contained within an element containing a (possibly defaulted) SOAP-ENC:arrayType attribute or (c) or the name of the element bears a definite relation to the type, that type then determinable from a schema.

3. A simple value is represented as character data, that is, without any subelements. Every simple value must have a type that is either listed in the XML Schemas Specification, part 2 [11] or whose source type is listed therein (see also section 5.2).

4. A Compound Value is encoded as a sequence of elements, each accessor represented by an embedded element whose name corresponds to the name of the accessor. Accessors whose names are local to their containing types have unqualified element names; all others have qualified names (see also section 5.4).

5. A multi-reference simple or compound value is encoded as an independent element containing a local, unqualified attribute named "id" and of type "ID" per the XML Specification [7]. Each accessor to this value is an empty element having a local, unqualified attribute named "href" and of type "uri-reference" per the XML Schema Specification [11], with a "href" attribute value of a URI fragment identifier referencing the corresponding independent element.

6. Strings and byte arrays are represented as multi-reference simple types, but special rules allow them to be represented efficiently for common cases (see also section 5.2.1 and 5.2.3). An accessor to a string or byte-array value MAY have an attribute named "id" and of type "ID" per the XML Specification [7]. If so, all other accessors to the same value are encoded as empty elements having a local, unqualified attribute named "href" and of type "uri-reference" per the XML Schema Specification [11], with a "href" attribute value of a URI fragment identifier referencing the single element containing the value.

7. It is permissible to encode several references to a value as though these were references to several distinct values, but only when from context it is known that the meaning of the XML instance is unaltered.

8. Arrays are compound values (see also section 5.4.2). SOAP arrays are defined as having a type of "SOAP-ENC:Array" or a type derived there from.

SOAP arrays have one or more dimensions (rank) whose members are distinguished by ordinal position. An array value is represented as a series of elements reflecting the array, with members appearing in ascending ordinal sequence. For multi-dimensional arrays the dimension on the right side varies most rapidly. Each member element is named as an independent element (see rule 2).

SOAP arrays can be single-reference or multi-reference values, and consequently may be represented as the content of either an embedded or independent element.

SOAP arrays MUST contain a "SOAP-ENC:arrayType" attribute whose value specifies the type of the contained elements as well as the dimension(s) of the array. The value of the "SOAP-ENC:arrayType" attribute is defined as follows:

```
arrayTypeValue = atype asize
atype          = QName *( rank )
rank           = "[" *( "," ) "]"
asize          = "[" #length "]"
length         = 1*DIGIT
```

The "atype" construct is the type name of the contained elements expressed as a QName as would appear in the "type" attribute of an XML Schema element declaration and acts as a type constraint (meaning that all values of contained elements are asserted to conform to the indicated type; that is, the type cited in SOAP-ENC:arrayType must be the type or a supertype of every array member). In the case of arrays of arrays or "jagged arrays", the type component is encoded as the "innermost" type name followed by a rank construct for each level of nested arrays starting from 1. Multi-dimensional arrays are encoded using a comma for each dimension starting from 1.

The "asize" construct contains a comma-separated list of zero, one, or more integers indicating the lengths of each dimension of the array. A value of zero integers indicates that no particular quantity is asserted but that the size may be determined by inspection of the actual members.

For example, an array with 5 members of type array of integers would have an arrayTypeValue value of "int[][5]" of which the atype value is "int[]" and the asize value is "[5]". Likewise, an array with 3 members of type two-dimensional arrays of integers would have an arrayTypeValue value of "int[,][3]" of which the atype value is "int[,]" and the asize value is "[3]".

A SOAP array member MAY contain a "SOAP-ENC:offset" attribute indicating the offset position of that item in the enclosing array. This can be used to indicate the offset position of a partially represented array (see section 5.4.2.1). Likewise, an array member MAY contain a "SOAP-ENC:position" attribute indicating the position of that item in the enclosing array. This can be used to describe members of sparse arrays (see section 5.4.2.2). The value of the "SOAP-ENC:offset" and the "SOAP-ENC:position" attribute is defined as follows:

```
arrayPoint = "[" #length "]"
```

with offsets and positions based at 0.

A NULL value or a default value MAY be represented by omission of the accessor element. A NULL value MAY also be indicated by an accessor element containing the attribute `xsi:null` with value '1' or possibly other application-dependent attributes and values.

Note that rule 2 allows independent elements and also elements representing the members of arrays to have names that are not identical to the type of the contained value.

5.2 Simple Types

For simple types, SOAP adopts all the types found in the section "Built-in datatypes" of the "XML Schema Part 2: Datatypes" Specification [11], both the value and lexical spaces. Examples include:

Type	Example
Int	58502
Float	314159265358979E+1
NegativeInteger	-32768
String	Louis "Satchmo" Armstrong

The datatypes declared in the XML Schema specification may be used directly in element schemas. Types derived from these may also be used. An example of a schema fragment and corresponding instance data with elements of these types is:

```
<element name="age" type="int"/>
<element name="height" type="float"/>
<element name="displacement" type="negativeInteger"/>
<element name="color">
  <simpleType base="xsd:string">
    <enumeration value="Green"/>
    <enumeration value="Blue"/>
  </simpleType>
</element>

<age>45</age>
<height>5.9</height>
<displacement>-450</displacement>
<color>Blue</color>
```

All simple values MUST be encoded as the content of elements whose type is either defined in "XML Schema Part 2: Datatypes" Specification [11], or is based on a type found there by using the mechanisms provided in the XML Schema specification.

If a simple value is encoded as an independent element or member of a heterogenous array it is convenient to have an element declaration corresponding to the datatype. Because the "XML Schema Part 2: Datatypes" Specification [11] includes type definitions but does not include corresponding element declarations, the SOAP-ENC schema and namespace declares an element for every simple datatype. These MAY be used.

```
<SOAP-ENC:int id="int1">45</SOAP-ENC:int>
```

NOTE

This means you can create elements that represent simple types that are (generically) named according to their type. The SOAP encoding schema assists you with this by defining the simple types as element declarations.

5.2.1 Strings

The datatype "string" is defined in "XML Schema Part 2: Datatypes" Specification [11]. Note that this is not identical to the type called "string" in many database or programming languages, and in particular may forbid some characters those languages would permit. (Those values must be represented by using some datatype other than xsd:string.)

A string MAY be encoded as a single-reference or a multi-reference value.

The containing element of the string value MAY have an "id" attribute. Additional accessor elements MAY then have matching "href" attributes.

For example, two accessors to the same string could appear, as follows:

```
<greeting id="String-0">Hello</greeting><salutation href="#String-0"/>
```

However, if the fact that both accessors reference the same instance of the string (or subtype of string) is immaterial, they may be encoded as two single-reference values as follows:

```
<greeting>Hello</greeting>
<salutation>Hello</salutation>
```

Schema fragments for these examples could appear similar to the following:

```
<element name="greeting" type="SOAP-ENC:string"/>
<element name="salutation" type="SOAP-ENC:string"/>
```

(In this example, the type SOAP-ENC:string is used as the element's type as a convenient way to declare an element whose datatype is "xsd:string" and which also allows an "id" and "href" attribute. See the SOAP Encoding schema for the exact definition. Schemas MAY use these declarations from the SOAP Encoding schema but are not required to.)

5.2.2 Enumerations

The "XML Schema Part 2: Datatypes" Specification [11] defines a mechanism called "enumeration." The SOAP data model adopts this mechanism directly. However, because programming and other languages often define enumeration somewhat differently, we spell-out the concept in more detail here and describe how a value that is a member of an enumerated list of possible values is to be encoded. Specifically, it is encoded as the name of the value.

"Enumeration" as a concept indicates a set of distinct names. A specific enumeration is a specific list of distinct values appropriate to the base type. For example the set of color names ("Green", "Blue", "Brown") could be defined as an enumeration based on the string built-in type. The values ("1", "3", "5") are a possible enumeration based on integer, and so on. "XML Schema Part 2: Datatypes" [11] supports enumerations for all of the simple types except for Boolean. The language of "XML Schema Part 1: Structures" Specification [10] can be used to define enumeration types. If a schema is generated from another notation in which no specific base type is applicable, use "string". In the following schema example "EyeColor" is defined as a string with the possible values of "Green", "Blue", or "Brown" enumerated, and instance data is shown accordingly.

```
<element name="EyeColor" type="tns:EyeColor"/>
<simpleType name="EyeColor" base="xsd:string">
   <enumeration value="Green"/>
   <enumeration value="Blue"/>
   <enumeration value="Brown"/>
</simpleType>

<Person>
   <Name>Henry Ford</Name>
   <Age>32</Age>
   <EyeColor>Brown</EyeColor>
</Person>
```

5.2.3 Array of Bytes

An array of bytes MAY be encoded as a single-reference or a multi-reference value. The rules for an array of bytes are similar to those for a string.

In particular, the containing element of the array of bytes value MAY have an "id" attribute. Additional accessor elements MAY then have matching "href" attributes.

The recommended representation of an opaque array of bytes is the 'base64' encoding defined in XML Schemas [10][11], which uses the base64 encoding algorithm defined in 2045 [13]. However, the line length restrictions that normally apply to base64 data in MIME do not apply in SOAP. A "SOAP-ENC:base64" subtype is supplied for use with SOAP.

```
<picture xsi:type="SOAP-ENC:base64">
   aG93IG5vDyBicm73biBjb3cNCg==
</picture>
```

5.3 Polymorphic Accessor

Many languages allow accessors that can polymorphically access values of several types, each type being available at run time. A polymorphic accessor instance MUST contain an "xsi:type" attribute that describes the type of the actual value.

For example, a polymorphic accessor named "cost" with a value of type "xsd:float" would be encoded as follows:

```
<cost xsi:type="xsd:float">29.95</cost>
```

as contrasted with a cost accessor whose value's type is invariant, as follows:

```
<cost>29.95</cost>
```

5.4 Compound Types

SOAP defines types corresponding to the following structural patterns often found in programming languages:

Struct

A "struct" is a compound value in which accessor name is the only distinction among member values, and no accessor has the same name as any other.

Array

An "array" is a compound value in which ordinal position serves as the only distinction among member values.

SOAP also permits serialization of data that is neither a Struct nor an Array, for example data such as is found in a Directed-Labeled-Graph Data Model in which a single node has many distinct accessors, some of which occur more than once. SOAP serialization does not require that the underlying data model make an ordering distinction among accessors, but if such an order exists, the accessors MUST be encoded in that sequence.

5.4.1 Compound Values, Structs, and References to Values

The members of a Compound Value are encoded as accessor elements. When accessors are distinguished by their name (as for example in a struct), the accessor name is used as the element name. Accessors whose names are local to their containing types have unqualified element names; all others have qualified names.

The following is an example of a struct of type "Book":

```
<e:Book>
   <author>Henry Ford</author>
   <preface>Prefatory text</preface>
   <intro>This is a book.</intro>
</e:Book>
```

And this is a schema fragment describing the above structure:

```
<element name="Book">
<complexType>
  <element name="author" type="xsd:string"/>
```

```
    <element name="preface" type="xsd:string"/>
     <element name="intro" type="xsd:string"/>
</complexType>
</e:Book>
```

Below is an example of a type with both simple and complex members. It shows two levels of referencing. Note that the "href" attribute of the "Author" accessor element is a reference to the value whose "id" attribute matches. A similar construction appears for the "Address".

```
<e:Book>
    <title>My Life and Work</title>
    <author href="#Person-1"/>
</e:Book>
<e:Person id="Person-1">
    <name>Henry Ford</name>
    <address href="#Address-2"/>
</e:Person>
<e:Address id="Address-2">
    <email>mailto:henryford@hotmail.com</email>
    <web>http://www.henryford.com</web>
</e:Address>
```

The form above is appropriate when the "Person" value and the "Address" value are multi-reference. If these were instead both single-reference, they SHOULD be embedded, as follows:

```
<e:Book>
    <title>My Life and Work</title>
    <author>
        <name>Henry Ford</name>
        <address>
        <email>mailto:henryford@hotmail.com</email>
        <web>http://www.henryford.com</web>
        </address>
    </author>
</e:Book>
```

If instead there existed a restriction that no two persons can have the same address in a given instance and that an address can be either a Street-address or an Electronic-address, a Book with two authors would be encoded as follows:

```
<e:Book>
    <title>My Life and Work</title>
    <firstauthor href="#Person-1"/>
    <secondauthor href="#Person-2"/>
</e:Book>
<e:Person id="Person-1">
    <name>Henry Ford</name>
    <address xsi:type="m:Electronic-address">
```

```
        <email>mailto:henryford@hotmail.com</email>
        <web>http://www.henryford.com</web>
    </address>
</e:Person>
<e:Person id="Person-2">
    <name>Samuel Crowther</name>
    <address xsi:type="n:Street-address">
        <street>Martin Luther King Rd</street>
        <city>Raleigh</city>
        <state>North Carolina</state>
    </address>
</e:Person>
```

Serializations can contain references to values not in the same resource:

```
<e:Book>
    <title>Paradise Lost</title>
    <firstauthor href="http://www.dartmouth.edu/~milton/"/>
</e:Book>
```

And this is a schema fragment describing the above structures:

```
<element name="Book" type="tns:Book"/>
<complexType name="Book">
    <!-- Either the following group must occur or else the
         href attribute must appear, but not both. -->
    <sequence minOccurs="0" maxOccurs="1">
        <element name="title" type="xsd:string"/>
        <element name="firstauthor" type="tns:Person"/>
        <element name="secondauthor" type="tns:Person"/>
    </sequence>
    <attribute name="href" type="uriReference"/>
    <attribute name="id" type="ID"/>
    <anyAttribute namespace="##other"/>
</complexType>


<element name="Person" base="tns:Person"/>
<complexType name="Person">
    <!-- Either the following group must occur or else the
         href attribute must appear, but not both. -->
    <sequence minOccurs="0" maxOccurs="1">
        <element name="name" type="xsd:string"/>
        <element name="address" type="tns:Address"/>
    </sequence>
    <attribute name="href" type="uriReference"/>
    <attribute name="id" type="ID"/>
    <anyAttribute namespace="##other"/>
</complexType>
```

```
<element name="Address" base="tns:Address"/>
<complexType name="Address">
    <!-- Either the following group must occur or else the
         href attribute must appear, but not both. -->
    <sequence minOccurs="0" maxOccurs="1">
        <element name="street" type="xsd:string"/>
        <element name="city" type="xsd:string"/>
        <element name="state" type="xsd:string"/>
    </sequence>
    <attribute name="href" type="uriReference"/>
    <attribute name="id" type="ID"/>
    <anyAttribute namespace="##other"/>
</complexType>
```

5.4.2 Arrays

SOAP arrays are defined as having a type of "SOAP-ENC:Array" or a type derived there from (see also rule 8). Arrays are represented as element values, with no specific constraint on the name of the containing element (just as values generally do not constrain the name of their containing element).

Arrays can contain elements, which themselves can be of any type, including nested arrays. New types formed by restrictions of SOAP-ENC:Array can also be created to represent, for example, arrays limited to integers or arrays of some user-defined enumeration.

The representation of the value of an array is an ordered sequence of elements constituting the items of the array. Within an array value, element names are not significant for distinguishing accessors. Elements may have any name. In practice, elements will frequently be named so that their declaration in a schema suggests or determines their type. As with compound types generally, if the value of an item in the array is a single-reference value, the item contains its value. Otherwise, the item references its value via an "href" attribute.

The following example is a schema fragment and an array containing integer array members.

```
<element name="myFavoriteNumbers"
        type="SOAP-ENC:Array"/>

<myFavoriteNumbers
  SOAP-ENC:arrayType="xsd:int[2]">
    <number>3</number>
    <number>4</number>
</myFavoriteNumbers>
```

In that example, the array "myFavoriteNumbers" contains several members each of which is a value of type SOAP-ENC:int. This can be determined by inspection of the SOAP-ENC:arrayType attribute. Note that the SOAP-ENC:Array type allows unqualified element names without restriction. These convey no type information, so when used they must either have an xsi:type attribute or the containing element must have a SOAP-ENC:arrayType attribute. Naturally, types derived from SOAP-ENC:Array may declare local elements, with type information.

As previously noted, the SOAP-ENC schema contains declarations of elements with names corresponding to each simple type in the "XML Schema Part 2: Datatypes" Specification [11]. It also contains a declaration for "Array". Using these, we might write

```
<SOAP-ENC:Array SOAP-ENC:arrayType="xsd:int[2]">
    <SOAP-ENC:int>3</SOAP-ENC:int>
    <SOAP-ENC:int>4</SOAP-ENC:int>
</SOAP-ENC:Array>
```

Arrays can contain instances of any subtype of the specified arrayType. That is, the members may be of any type that is substitutable for the type specified in the arrayType attribute, according to whatever substitutability rules are expressed in the schema. So, for example, an array of integers can contain any type derived from integer (for example "int" or any user-defined derivation of integer). Similarly, an array of "address" might contain a restricted or extended type such as "internationalAddress". Because the supplied SOAP-ENC:Array type admits members of any type, arbitrary mixtures of types can be contained unless specifically limited by use of the arrayType attribute.

Types of member elements can be specified using the xsi:type attribute in the instance, or by declarations in the schema of the member elements, as the following two arrays demonstrate respectively.

```
<SOAP-ENC:Array SOAP-ENC:arrayType="SOAP-ENC:ur-type[4]">
    <thing xsi:type="xsd:int">12345</thing>
    <thing xsi:type="xsd:decimal">6.789</thing>
    <thing xsi:type="xsd:string">
        Of Mans First Disobedience, and the Fruit
        Of that Forbidden Tree, whose mortal tast
        Brought Death into the World, and all our woe,
    </thing>
    <thing xsi:type="xsd:uriReference">
        http://www.dartmouth.edu/~milton/reading_room/
    </thing>
</SOAP-ENC:Array>

<SOAP-ENC:Array SOAP-ENC:arrayType="SOAP-ENC:ur-type[4]">
    <SOAP-ENC:int>12345</SOAP-ENC:int>
    <SOAP-ENC:decimal>6.789</SOAP-ENC:decimal>
    <xsd:string>
        Of Mans First Disobedience, and the Fruit
        Of that Forbidden Tree, whose mortal tast
        Brought Death into the World, and all our woe,
    </xsd:string>
```

```
    <SOAP-ENC:uriReference>
        http://www.dartmouth.edu/~milton/reading_room/
    </SOAP-ENC:uriReference >
</SOAP-ENC:Array>
```

Array values may be structs or other compound values. For example an array of "xyz:Order" structs:

```
<SOAP-ENC:Array SOAP-ENC:arrayType="xyz:Order[2]">
    <Order>
        <Product>Apple</Product>
        <Price>1.56</Price>
    </Order>
    <Order>
        <Product>Peach</Product>
        <Price>1.48</Price>
    </Order>
</SOAP-ENC:Array>
```

Arrays may have other arrays as member values. The following is an example of an array of two arrays, each of which is an array of strings.

```
<SOAP-ENC:Array SOAP-ENC:arrayType="xsd:string[][2]">
    <item href="#array-1"/>
    <item href="#array-2"/>
</SOAP-ENC:Array>
<SOAP-ENC:Array id="array-1" SOAP-ENC:arrayType="xsd:string[2]">
    <item>r1c1</item>
    <item>r1c2</item>
    <item>r1c3</item>
</SOAP-ENC:Array>
<SOAP-ENC:Array id="array-2" SOAP-ENC:arrayType="xsd:string[2]">
    <item>r2c1</item>
    <item>r2c2</item>
</SOAP-ENC:Array>
```

The element containing an array value does not need to be named "SOAP-ENC:Array". It may have any name, provided that the type of the element is either SOAP-ENC:Array or is derived from SOAP-ENC:Array by restriction. For example, the following is a fragment of a schema and a conforming instance array.

```
<simpleType name="phoneNumber" base="string"/>

<element name="ArrayOfPhoneNumbers">
  <complexType base="SOAP-ENC:Array">
    <element name="phoneNumber" type="tns:phoneNumber" maxOccurs="unbounded"/>
  </complexType>
  <anyAttribute/>
```

```
</element>

<xyz:ArrayOfPhoneNumbers SOAP-ENC:arrayType="xyz:phoneNumber[2]">
   <phoneNumber>206-555-1212</phoneNumber>
   <phoneNumber>1-888-123-4567</phoneNumber>
</xyz:ArrayOfPhoneNumbers>
```

Arrays may be multi-dimensional. In this case, more than one size will appear within the asize part of the arrayType attribute:

```
<SOAP-ENC:Array SOAP-ENC:arrayType="xsd:string[2,3]">
   <item>r1c1</item>
   <item>r1c2</item>
   <item>r1c3</item>
   <item>r2c1</item>
   <item>r2c2</item>
   <item>r2c3</item>
</SOAP-ENC:Array>
```

While the examples above have shown arrays encoded as independent elements, array values MAY also appear embedded and SHOULD do so when they are known to be single reference.

The following is an example of a schema fragment and an array of phone numbers embedded in a struct of type "Person" and accessed through the accessor "phone-numbers":

```
<simpleType name="phoneNumber" base="string"/>

<element name="ArrayOfPhoneNumbers">
  <complexType base="SOAP-ENC:Array">
    <element name="phoneNumber" type="tns:phoneNumber" maxOccurs="unbounded"/>
  </complexType>
  <anyAttribute/>
</element>

<element name="Person">
  <complexType>
    <element name="name" type="string"/>
    <element name="phoneNumbers" type="tns:ArrayOfPhoneNumbers"/>
  </complexType>
</element>

<xyz:Person>
   <name>John Hancock</name>
   <phoneNumbers SOAP-ENC:arrayType="xyz:phoneNumber[2]">
       <phoneNumber>206-555-1212</phoneNumber>
       <phoneNumber>1-888-123-4567</phoneNumber>
   </phoneNumbers>
</xyz:Person>
```

Here is another example of a single-reference array value encoded as an embedded element whose containing element name is the accessor name:

```
<xyz:PurchaseOrder>
    <CustomerName>Henry Ford</CustomerName>
    <ShipTo>
        <Street>5th Ave</Street>
        <City>New York</City>
        <State>NY</State>
        <Zip>10010</Zip>
    </ShipTo>
    <PurchaseLineItems SOAP-ENC:arrayType="Order[2]">
        <Order>
            <Product>Apple</Product>
            <Price>1.56</Price>
        </Order>
        <Order>
            <Product>Peach</Product>
            <Price>1.48</Price>
        </Order>
    </PurchaseLineItems>
</xyz:PurchaseOrder>
```

5.4.2.1 Partially Transmitted Arrays

SOAP provides support for partially transmitted arrays, known as "varying" arrays in some contexts [12]. A partially transmitted array indicates in a "SOAP-ENC:offset" attribute the zero-origin offset of the first element transmitted. If omitted, the offset is taken as zero.

The following is an example of an array of size five that transmits only the third and fourth element counting from zero:

```
<SOAP-ENC:Array ;SOAP-ENC:arrayType="xsd:string[5]" ;SOAP-ENC:offset="[2]">
  <item>The third element</item>
  <item>The fourth element</item>
</SOAP-ENC:Array>
```

5.4.2.2 Sparse Arrays

SOAP provides support for sparse arrays. Each element representing a member value contains a "SOAP-ENC:position" attribute that indicates its position within the array. The following is an example of a sparse array of two-dimensional arrays of strings. The size is 4 but only position 2 is used:

```
<SOAP-ENC:Array SOAP-ENC:arrayType="xsd:string[,][4]">
    <SOAP-ENC:Array href="#array-1" SOAP-ENC:position="[2]"/>
</SOAP-ENC:Array>
<SOAP-ENC:Array id="array-1" SOAP-ENC:arrayType="xsd:string[10,10]">
```

```
   <item SOAP-ENC:position="[2,2]">Third row, third col</item>
   <item SOAP-ENC:position="[7,2]">Eighth row, third col</item>
</SOAP-ENC:Array>
```

If the only reference to `array-1` occurs in the enclosing array, this example could also have been encoded as follows:

```
<SOAP-ENC:Array SOAP-ENC:arrayType="xsd:string[,][4]">
  <SOAP-ENC:Array SOAP-ENC:position="[2]" SOAP-
➥ENC:arrayType="xsd:string[10,10]>
    <item SOAP-ENC:position="[2,2]">Third row, third col</item>
    <item SOAP-ENC:position="[7,2]">Eighth row, third col</item>
  </SOAP-ENC:Array>
</SOAP-ENC:Array>
```

5.4.3 Generic Compound Types

The encoding rules just cited are not limited to those cases where the accessor names are known in advance. If accessor names are known only by inspection of the immediate values to be encoded, the same rules apply, namely that the accessor is encoded as an element whose name matches the name of the accessor, and the accessor either contains or references its value. Accessors containing values whose types cannot be determined in advance MUST always contain an appropriate xsi:type attribute giving the type of the value.

Similarly, the rules cited are sufficient to allow serialization of compound types having a mixture of accessors distinguished by name and accessors distinguished by both name and ordinal position. (That is, having some accessors repeated.) This does not require that any schema actually contain such types, but rather says that if a type-model schema does have such types, a corresponding XML syntactic schema and instance may be generated.

```
<xyz:PurchaseOrder>
    <CustomerName>Henry Ford</CustomerName>
    <ShipTo>
        <Street>5th Ave</Street>
        <City>New York</City>
        <State>NY</State>
        <Zip>10010</Zip>
    </ShipTo>
    <PurchaseLineItems>
        <Order>
            <Product>Apple</Product>
            <Price>1.56</Price>
        </Order>
        <Order>
            <Product>Peach</Product>
            <Price>1.48</Price>
        </Order>
    </PurchaseLineItems>
</xyz:PurchaseOrder>
```

Similarly, it is valid to serialize a compound value that structurally resembles an array but is not of type (or subtype) SOAP-ENC:Array. For example:

```
<PurchaseLineItems>
    <Order>
        <Product>Apple</Product>
        <Price>1.56</Price>
    </Order>
    <Order>
        <Product>Peach</Product>
        <Price>1.48</Price>
    </Order>
</PurchaseLineItems>
```

5.5 Default Values

An omitted accessor element implies either a default value or that no value is known. The specifics depend on the accessor, method, and its context. For example, an omitted accessor typically implies a Null value for polymorphic accessors (with the exact meaning of Null accessor-dependent). Likewise, an omitted Boolean accessor typically implies either a False value or that no value is known, and an omitted numeric accessor typically implies either that the value is zero or that no value is known.

5.6 SOAP root Attribute

The SOAP root attribute can be used to label serialization roots that are not true roots of an object graph so that the object graph can be deserialized. The attribute can have one of two values, either "1" or "0". True roots of an object graph have the implied attribute value of "1". Serialization roots that are not true roots can be labeled as serialization roots with an attribute value of "1" An element can explicitly be labeled as not being a serialization root with a value of "0".

The SOAP root attribute MAY appear on any subelement within the SOAP Header and SOAP Body elements. The attribute does not have a default value.

6. Using SOAP in HTTP

This section describes how to use SOAP within HTTP with or without using the HTTP Extension Framework. Binding SOAP to HTTP provides the advantage of being able to use the formalism and decentralized flexibility of SOAP with the rich feature set of HTTP. Carrying SOAP in HTTP does not mean that SOAP overrides existing semantics of HTTP but rather that the semantics of SOAP over HTTP maps naturally to HTTP semantics.

SOAP naturally follows the HTTP request/response message model providing SOAP request parameters in a HTTP request and SOAP response parameters in a HTTP response. Note, however, that SOAP intermediaries are NOT the same as HTTP intermediaries. That is, an HTTP intermediary addressed with the HTTP `Connection` header field cannot be expected to inspect or process the SOAP entity body carried in the HTTP request.

HTTP applications MUST use the media type "text/xml" according to RFC 2376 [3] when including SOAP entity bodies in HTTP messages.

6.1 SOAP HTTP Request

Although SOAP might be used in combination with a variety of HTTP request methods, this binding only defines SOAP within HTTP `POST` requests (see section 7 for how to use SOAP for RPC and section 6.3 for how to use the HTTP Extension Framework).

6.1.1 The `SOAPAction` HTTP Header Field

The `SOAPAction` HTTP request header field can be used to indicate the intent of the SOAP HTTP request. The value is a URI identifying the intent. SOAP places no restrictions on the format or specificity of the URI or that it is resolvable. An HTTP client MUST use this header field when issuing a SOAP HTTP Request.

```
soapaction    = "SOAPAction" ":" [ <"> URI-reference <"> ]
URI-reference = <as defined in RFC 2396 [4]>
```

The presence and content of the `SOAPAction` header field can be used by servers such as fire-walls to appropriately filter SOAP request messages in HTTP. The header field value of empty string ("") means that the intent of the SOAP message is provided by the HTTP Request-URI. No value means that there is no indication of the intent of the message.

Examples:

```
SOAPAction: "http://electrocommerce.org/abc#MyMessage"
SOAPAction: "myapp.sdl"
SOAPAction: ""
SOAPAction:
```

6.2 SOAP HTTP Response

SOAP HTTP follows the semantics of the HTTP Status codes for communicating status information in HTTP. For example, a 2xx status code indicates that the client's request including the SOAP component was successfully received, understood, and accepted etc.

In case of a SOAP error while processing the request, the SOAP HTTP server MUST issue an HTTP 500 "Internal Server Error" response and include a SOAP message in the response containing a SOAP Fault element (see section 4.4) indicating the SOAP processing error.

6.3 The HTTP Extension Framework

A SOAP message MAY be used together with the HTTP Extension Framework [6] in order to identify the presence and intent of a SOAP HTTP request.

Whether to use the Extension Framework or plain HTTP is a question of policy and capability of the communicating parties. Clients can force the use of the HTTP Extension Framework by using a mandatory extension declaration and the "M-" HTTP method name prefix. Servers can force the use of the HTTP Extension Framework by using the 510 "Not Extended" HTTP status code. That is, using one extra round trip, either party can detect the policy of the other party and act accordingly.

The extension identifier used to identify SOAP using the Extension Framework is

```
http://schemas.xmlsoap.org/soap/envelope/
```

6.4 SOAP HTTP Examples

EXAMPLE 3. SOAP HTTP Using POST

```
POST /StockQuote HTTP/1.1
Content-Type: text/xml; charset="utf-8"
Content-Length: nnnn
SOAPAction: "http://electrocommerce.org/abc#MyMessage"

<SOAP-ENV:Envelope...

HTTP/1.1 200 OK
Content-Type: text/xml; charset="utf-8"
Content-Length: nnnn

<SOAP-ENV:Envelope...
```

EXAMPLE 4. SOAP Using HTTP Extension Framework

```
M-POST /StockQuote HTTP/1.1
Man: "http://schemas.xmlsoap.org/soap/envelope/"; ns=NNNN
Content-Type: text/xml; charset="utf-8"
Content-Length: nnnn
NNNN-SOAPAction: "http://electrocommerce.org/abc#MyMessage"

<SOAP-ENV:Envelope...

HTTP/1.1 200 OK
Ext:
Content-Type: text/xml; charset="utf-8"
Content-Length: nnnn

<SOAP-ENV:Envelope...
```

7. Using SOAP for RPC

One of the design goals of SOAP is to encapsulate and exchange RPC calls using the extensibility and flexibility of XML. This section defines a uniform representation of remote procedure calls and responses.

Although it is anticipated that this representation is likely to be used in combination with the encoding style defined in section 5 other representations are possible. The SOAP encodingStyle attribute (see section 4.3.2) can be used to indicate the encoding style of the method call and or the response using the representation described in this section.

Using SOAP for RPC is orthogonal to the SOAP protocol binding (see section 6). In the case of using HTTP as the protocol binding, an RPC call maps naturally to an HTTP request and an RPC response maps to an HTTP response. However, using SOAP for RPC is not limited to the HTTP protocol binding.

To make a method call, the following information is needed:

- The URI of the target object
- A method name
- An optional method signature
- The parameters to the method
- Optional header data

SOAP relies on the protocol binding to provide a mechanism for carrying the URI. For example, for HTTP the request URI indicates the resource that the invocation is being made against. Other than it be a valid URI, SOAP places no restriction on the form of an address (see [4] for more information on URIs).

7.1 RPC and SOAP Body

RPC method calls and responses are both carried in the SOAP Body element (see section 4.3) using the following representation:

- A method invocation is modeled as a struct.
- The method invocation is viewed as a single struct containing an accessor for each [in] or [in/out] parameter. The struct is both named and typed identically to the method name.
- Each [in] or [in/out] parameter is viewed as an accessor, with a name corresponding to the name of the parameter and type corresponding to the type of the parameter. These appear in the same order as in the method signature.
- A method response is modeled as a struct.

- The method response is viewed as a single struct containing an accessor for the return value and each [out] or [in/out] parameter. The first accessor is the return value followed by the parameters in the same order as in the method signature.

- Each parameter accessor has a name corresponding to the name of the parameter and type corresponding to the type of the parameter. The name of the return value accessor is not significant. Likewise, the name of the struct is not significant. However, a convention is to name it after the method name with the string "Response" appended.

- A method fault is encoded using the SOAP Fault element (see section 4.4). If a protocol binding adds additional rules for fault expression, those also MUST be followed.

As noted above, method and response structs can be encoded according to the rules in section 5, or other encodings can be specified using the encodingStyle attribute (see section 4.1.1).

Applications MAY process requests with missing parameters but also MAY return a fault.

Because a result indicates success and a fault indicates failure, it is an error for the method response to contain both a result and a fault.

7.2 RPC and SOAP Header

Additional information relevant to the encoding of a method request but not part of the formal method signature MAY be expressed in the RPC encoding. If so, it MUST be expressed as a subelement of the SOAP Header element.

An example of the use of the header element is the passing of a transaction ID along with a message. Since the transaction ID is not part of the signature and is typically held in an infrastructure component rather than application code, there is no direct way to pass the necessary information with the call. By adding an entry to the headers and giving it a fixed name, the transaction manager on the receiving side can extract the transaction ID and use it without affecting the coding of remote procedure calls.

8. Security Considerations

Not described in this document are methods for integrity and privacy protection. Such issues will be addressed more fully in a future version(s) of this document.

9. References

[1] S. Bradner, "The Internet Standards Process—Revision 3", RFC2026, Harvard University, October 1996

[2] S. Bradner, "Key words for use in RFCs to Indicate Requirement Levels", RFC 2119, Harvard University, March 1997

[3] E. Whitehead, M. Murata, "XML Media Types", RFC2376, UC Irvine, Fuji Xerox Info. Systems, July 1998

[4] T. Berners-Lee, R. Fielding, L. Masinter, "Uniform Resource Identifiers (URI): Generic Syntax", RFC 2396, MIT/LCS, U.C. Irvine, Xerox Corporation, August 1998.

[5] R. Fielding, J. Gettys, J. C. Mogul, H. Frystyk, T. Berners-Lee, "Hypertext Transfer Protocol—HTTP/1.1", RFC 2616, U.C. Irvine, DEC W3C/MIT, DEC, W3C/MIT, W3C/MIT, January 1997

[6] H. Nielsen, P. Leach, S. Lawrence, "An HTTP Extension Framework", RFC 2774, Microsoft, Microsoft, Agranat Systems

[7] W3C Recommendation "The XML Specification"

[8] W3C Recommendation "Namespaces in XML"

[9] W3C Working Draft "XML Linking Language". This is work in progress.

[10] W3C Working Draft "XML Schema Part 1: Structures". This is work in progress.

[11] W3C Working Draft "XML Schema Part 2: Datatypes". This is work in progress.

[12] Transfer Syntax NDR, in "DCE 1.1: Remote Procedure Call"

[13] N. Freed, N. Borenstein, "Multipurpose Internet Mail Extensions (MIME) Part One: Format of Internet Message Bodies", RFC2045, Innosoft, First Virtual, November 1996

A. SOAP Envelope Examples

A.1 Sample Encoding of Call Requests

EXAMPLE 5.   Similar to Example 1 but with a Mandatory Header

```
POST /StockQuote HTTP/1.1
Host: www.stockquoteserver.com
Content-Type: text/xml; charset="utf-8"
Content-Length: nnnn
SOAPAction: "Some-URI"

<SOAP-ENV:Envelope
  xmlns:SOAP-ENV="http://schemas.xmlsoap.org/soap/envelope/"
  SOAP-ENV:encodingStyle="http://schemas.xmlsoap.org/soap/encoding/"/>
  <SOAP-ENV:Header>
      <t:Transaction
          xmlns:t="some-URI"
          SOAP-ENV:mustUnderstand="1">
             5
      </t:Transaction>
  </SOAP-ENV:Header>
  <SOAP-ENV:Body>
      <m:GetLastTradePrice xmlns:m="Some-URI">
          <symbol>DEF</symbol>
      </m:GetLastTradePrice>
  </SOAP-ENV:Body>
</SOAP-ENV:Envelope>
```

EXAMPLE 6. Similar to Example 1 but with Multiple Request Parameters

```
POST /StockQuote HTTP/1.1
Host: www.stockquoteserver.com
Content-Type: text/xml; charset="utf-8"
Content-Length: nnnn
SOAPAction: "Some-URI"

<SOAP-ENV:Envelope
  xmlns:SOAP-ENV="http://schemas.xmlsoap.org/soap/envelope/"
  SOAP-ENV:encodingStyle="http://schemas.xmlsoap.org/soap/encoding/"/>
  <SOAP-ENV:Body>
      <m:GetLastTradePriceDetailed
        xmlns:m="Some-URI">
          <Symbol>DEF</Symbol>
          <Company>DEF Corp</Company>
          <Price>34.1</Price>
      </m:GetLastTradePriceDetailed>
  </SOAP-ENV:Body>
</SOAP-ENV:Envelope>
```

A.2 Sample Encoding of Response

EXAMPLE 7. Similar to Example 2 but with a Mandatory Header

```
HTTP/1.1 200 OK
Content-Type: text/xml; charset="utf-8"
Content-Length: nnnn

<SOAP-ENV:Envelope
  xmlns:SOAP-ENV="http://schemas.xmlsoap.org/soap/envelope/"
  SOAP-ENV:encodingStyle="http://schemas.xmlsoap.org/soap/encoding/"/>
  <SOAP-ENV:Header>
      <t:Transaction
        xmlns:t="some-URI"
        xsi:type="xsd:int" mustUnderstand="1">
          5
      </t:Transaction>
  </SOAP-ENV:Header>
  <SOAP-ENV:Body>
      <m:GetLastTradePriceResponse
        xmlns:m="Some-URI">
          <Price>34.5</Price>
      </m:GetLastTradePriceResponse>
  </SOAP-ENV:Body>
</SOAP-ENV:Envelope>
```

EXAMPLE 8. Similar to Example 2 but with a Struct

```
HTTP/1.1 200 OK
Content-Type: text/xml; charset="utf-8"
Content-Length: nnnn

<SOAP-ENV:Envelope
  xmlns:SOAP-ENV="http://schemas.xmlsoap.org/soap/envelope/"
  SOAP-ENV:encodingStyle="http://schemas.xmlsoap.org/soap/encoding/"/>
   <SOAP-ENV:Body>
      <m:GetLastTradePriceResponse
        xmlns:m="Some-URI">
          <PriceAndVolume>
              <LastTradePrice>
                  34.5
              </LastTradePrice>
              <DayVolume>
                  10000
              </DayVolume>
          </PriceAndVolume>
      </m:GetLastTradePriceResponse>
   </SOAP-ENV:Body>
</SOAP-ENV:Envelope>
```

EXAMPLE 9. Similar to Example 2 but Failing to Honor Mandatory Header

```
HTTP/1.1 500 Internal Server Error
Content-Type: text/xml; charset="utf-8"
Content-Length: nnnn

<SOAP-ENV:Envelope
  xmlns:SOAP-ENV="http://schemas.xmlsoap.org/soap/envelope/">
   <SOAP-ENV:Body>
      <SOAP-ENV:Fault>
          <faultcode>SOAP-ENV:MustUnderstand</faultcode>
          <faultstring>SOAP Must Understand Error</faultstring>
      </SOAP-ENV:Fault>
   </SOAP-ENV:Body>
</SOAP-ENV:Envelope>
```

EXAMPLE 10. Similar to Example 2 but Failing to Handle Body

```
HTTP/1.1 500 Internal Server Error
Content-Type: text/xml; charset="utf-8"
Content-Length: nnnn

<SOAP-ENV:Envelope
```

```
 xmlns:SOAP-ENV="http://schemas.xmlsoap.org/soap/envelope/">
  <SOAP-ENV:Body>
      <SOAP-ENV:Fault>
          <faultcode>SOAP-ENV:Server</faultcode>
          <faultstring>Server Error</faultstring>
          <detail>
              <e:myfaultdetails xmlns:e="Some-URI">
                <message>
                  My application didn't work
                </message>
                <errorcode>
                  1001
                </errorcode>
              </e:myfaultdetails>
          </detail>
      </SOAP-ENV:Fault>
  </SOAP-ENV:Body>
</SOAP-ENV:Envelope>
```

The SOAP Envelope Namespace Schema

```
<?xml version="1.0" ?>
<!-- XML Schema for SOAP v 1.1 Envelope
  -->
<!--
 Copyright 2000 DevelopMentor, International Business Machines
➥Corporation,
     Lotus Development Corporation, Microsoft, UserLand Software


  -->
<schema xmlns="http://www.w3.org/1999/XMLSchema"
  xmlns:tns="http://schemas.xmlsoap.org/soap/envelope/"
  targetNamespace="http://schemas.xmlsoap.org/soap/envelope/">
<!-- SOAP envelope, header and body
  -->
<element name="Envelope" type="tns:Envelope" />
<complexType name="Envelope">
  <element ref="tns:Header" minOccurs="0" />
  <element ref="tns:Body" minOccurs="1" />
  <any minOccurs="0" maxOccurs="*" />
  <anyAttribute />
</complexType>
<element name="Header" type="tns:Header" />
<complexType name="Header">
  <any minOccurs="0" maxOccurs="*" />
  <anyAttribute />
```

```
</complexType>
<element name="Body" type="tns:Body" />
<complexType name="Body">
  <any minOccurs="0" maxOccurs="*" />
  <anyAttribute />
</complexType>
<!--
 Global Attributes.  The following attributes are intended
        to be usable via qualified attribute names on any complex type
        referencing them.

  -->
<attribute name="mustUnderstand" default="0">
  <simpleType base="boolean">
    <pattern value="0|1" />
  </simpleType>
</attribute>
<attribute name="actor" type="uri-reference" />
<!--
 'encodingStyle' indicates any canonicalization conventions followed
        in the contents of the containing element.  For example, the
        value 'http://schemas.xmlsoap.org/soap/encoding/' indicates
        the pattern described in SOAP specification.

  -->
<simpleType name="encodingStyle" base="uri-reference"
 ➥derivedBy="list" />
<attributeGroup name="encodingStyle">
  <attribute name="encodingStyle" type="tns:encodingStyle" />
</attributeGroup>
<!-- SOAP fault reporting structure
  -->
<complexType name="Fault" final="extension">
  <element name="faultcode" type="qname" />
  <element name="faultstring" type="string" />
  <element name="faultactor" type="uri-reference" minOccurs="0" />
  <element name="detail" type="tns:detail" minOccurs="0" />
</complexType>
<complexType name="detail">
  <any minOccurs="0" maxOccurs="*" />
  <anyAttribute />
  </complexType>
</schema>
```

The SOAP Encoding Namespace Schema

```xml
<?xml version="1.0" ?>
<!-- XML Schema for SOAP v 1.1 Encoding
  -->
<!--
 Copyright 2000 DevelopMentor, International Business Machines
 ➡Corporation,
     Lotus Development Corporation, Microsoft, UserLand Software


 -->
<schema xmlns="http://www.w3.org/1999/XMLSchema"
  xmlns:tns="http://schemas.xmlsoap.org/soap/encoding/"
  targetNamespace="http://schemas.xmlsoap.org/soap/encoding/">
<!--
 'root' can be used to distinguish serialization roots from other
        elements that are present in a serialization but are not roots
        of a serialized value graph.


 -->
<attribute name="root" default="0">
  <simpleType base="boolean">
    <pattern value="0|1" />
  </simpleType>
</attribute>
<!--
 Attributes common to all elements that function as accessors or
        represent independent (multi-ref) values.  The href attribute
        is intended to be used in a manner like CONREF.  That is, the
        element content should be empty if the href attribute appears.


 -->
<attributeGroup name="commonAttributes">
  <attribute name="id" type="ID" />
  <attribute name="href" type="uriReference" />
  <anyAttribute namespace="##other" />
</attributeGroup>
<!--
 Global Attributes.  The following attributes are intended
        to be usable via qualified attribute names on any complex type
        referencing them.


 -->
<!--
 Array attributes. Needed to give the type and dimensions of an array's
        contents, and the offset for partially-transmitted arrays.
```

```
  -->
<simpleType name="arrayCoordinate" base="string" />
<attribute name="arrayType" type="string" />
<attribute name="offset" type="tns:arrayCoordinate" />
<attributeGroup name="arrayAttributes">
  <attribute ref="tns:arrayType" minOccurs="1" />
  <attribute ref="tns:offset" />
</attributeGroup>
<attribute name="position" type="tns:arrayCoordinate" />
<attributeGroup name="arrayMemberAttributes">
  <attribute ref="tns:position" />
</attributeGroup>
<!--
  'Array' is a complex type for accessors identified by position.


  -->
<element name="Array" type="tns:Array" />
<group name="Array">
  <any minOccurs="0" maxOccurs="*" />
</group>
<complexType name="Array" content="elementOnly">
  <group ref="Array" minOccurs="0" maxOccurs="1" />
  <attributeGroup ref="tns:arrayAttributes" />
  <attributeGroup ref="tns:commonAttributes" />
</complexType>
<!--
  'Struct' is a complex type for accessors identified by name.
        Constraint: No element may be have the same name as any other,
        nor may any element have a maxOccurs > 1.

  -->
<element name="Struct" type="tns:Struct" />
<group name="Struct">
  <any minOccurs="0" maxOccurs="*" />
</group>
<complexType name="Struct">
  <group ref="Struct" minOccurs="0" maxOccurs="1" />
  <attributeGroup ref="tns:commonAttributes" />
</complexType>
<!--
  'Base64' can be used to serialize binary data using base64 encoding
        as defined in RFC2045 but without the MIME line length
        limitation.

  -->
```

```
<simpleType name="base64" base="binary">
  <encoding value="base64" />
</simpleType>
<!--
Element declarations corresponding to each of the simple types in
     the XML Schemas Specification.

  -->
<element name="string" type="tns:string" />
<complexType name="string" base="string" content="textOnly">
  <attributeGroup ref="tns:commonAttributes" />
</complexType>
<element name="boolean" type="tns:boolean" />
<complexType name="boolean" base="boolean" content="textOnly">
  <attributeGroup ref="tns:commonAttributes" />
</complexType>
<element name="float" type="tns:float" />
<complexType name="float" base="float" content="textOnly">
  <attributeGroup ref="tns:commonAttributes" />
</complexType>
<element name="double" type="tns:double" />
<complexType name="double" base="double" content="textOnly">
  <attributeGroup ref="tns:commonAttributes" />
</complexType>
<element name="decimal" type="tns:decimal" />
<complexType name="decimal" base="decimal" content="textOnly">
  <attributeGroup ref="tns:commonAttributes" />
</complexType>
<element name="timeDuration" type="tns:timeDuration" />
<complexType name="timeDuration" base="timeDuration"
➥content="textOnly">
  <attributeGroup ref="tns:commonAttributes" />
</complexType>
<element name="recurringDuration" type="tns:recurringDuration" />
<complexType name="recurringDuration" base="recurringDuration"
➥content="textOnly">
  <attributeGroup ref="tns:commonAttributes" />
</complexType>
<element name="binary" type="tns:binary" />
<complexType name="binary" base="binary" content="textOnly">
  <attributeGroup ref="tns:commonAttributes" />
</complexType>
<element name="uriReference" type="tns:uriReference" />
<complexType name="uriReference" base="uriReference"
➥content="textOnly">
  <attributeGroup ref="tns:commonAttributes" />
```

```
    </complexType>
    <element name="ID" type="tns:ID" />
    <complexType name="ID" base="ID" content="textOnly">
      <attributeGroup ref="tns:commonAttributes" />
    </complexType>
    <element name="IDREF" type="tns:IDREF" />
    <complexType name="IDREF" base="IDREF" content="textOnly">
      <attributeGroup ref="tns:commonAttributes" />
    </complexType>
    <element name="ENTITY" type="tns:ENTITY" />
    <complexType name="ENTITY" base="ENTITY" content="textOnly">
      <attributeGroup ref="tns:commonAttributes" />
    </complexType>
    <element name="NOTATION" type="tns:NOTATION" />
    <complexType name="NOTATION" base="NOTATION" content="textOnly">
      <attributeGroup ref="tns:commonAttributes" />
    </complexType>
    <element name="QName" type="tns:QName" />
    <complexType name="QName" base="QName" content="textOnly">
      <attributeGroup ref="tns:commonAttributes" />
    </complexType>
    <element name="language" type="tns:language" />
    <complexType name="language" base="language" content="textOnly">
      <attributeGroup ref="tns:commonAttributes" />
    </complexType>
    <element name="IDREFS" type="tns:IDREFS" />
    <complexType name="IDREFS" base="IDREFS" content="textOnly">
      <attributeGroup ref="tns:commonAttributes" />
    </complexType>
    <element name="ENTITIES" type="tns:ENTITIES" />
    <complexType name="ENTITIES" base="ENTITIES" content="textOnly">
      <attributeGroup ref="tns:commonAttributes" />
    </complexType>
    <element name="NMTOKEN" type="tns:NMTOKEN" />
    <complexType name="NMTOKEN" base="NMTOKEN" content="textOnly">
      <attributeGroup ref="tns:commonAttributes" />
    </complexType>
    <element name="NMTOKENS" type="tns:NMTOKENS" />
    <complexType name="NMTOKENS" base="NMTOKENS" content="textOnly">
      <attributeGroup ref="tns:commonAttributes" />
    </complexType>
    <element name="Name" type="tns:Name" />
    <complexType name="Name" base="Name" content="textOnly">
      <attributeGroup ref="tns:commonAttributes" />
    </complexType>
    <element name="NCName" type="tns:NCName" />
```

```xml
<complexType name="NCName" base="NCName" content="textOnly">
  <attributeGroup ref="tns:commonAttributes" />
</complexType>
<element name="integer" type="tns:integer" />
<complexType name="integer" base="integer" content="textOnly">
  <attributeGroup ref="tns:commonAttributes" />
</complexType>
<element name="nonPositiveInteger" type="tns:nonPositiveInteger" />
<complexType name="nonPositiveInteger" base="nonPositiveInteger"
➥content="textOnly">
  <attributeGroup ref="tns:commonAttributes" />
</complexType>
<element name="negativeInteger" type="tns:negativeInteger" />
<complexType name="negativeInteger" base="negativeInteger"
➥content="textOnly">
  <attributeGroup ref="tns:commonAttributes" />
</complexType>
<element name="long" type="tns:long" />
<complexType name="long" base="long" content="textOnly">
  <attributeGroup ref="tns:commonAttributes" />
</complexType>
<element name="int" type="tns:int" />
<complexType name="int" base="int" content="textOnly">
  <attributeGroup ref="tns:commonAttributes" />
</complexType>
<element name="short" type="tns:short" />
<complexType name="short" base="short" content="textOnly">
  <attributeGroup ref="tns:commonAttributes" />
</complexType>
<element name="byte" type="tns:byte" />
<complexType name="byte" base="byte" content="textOnly">
  <attributeGroup ref="tns:commonAttributes" />
</complexType>
<element name="nonNegativeInteger" type="tns:nonNegativeInteger" />
<complexType name="nonNegativeInteger" base="nonNegativeInteger"
➥content="textOnly">
  <attributeGroup ref="tns:commonAttributes" />
</complexType>
<element name="unsignedLong" type="tns:unsignedLong" />
<complexType name="unsignedLong" base="unsignedLong"
➥content="textOnly">
  <attributeGroup ref="tns:commonAttributes" />
</complexType>
<element name="unsignedInt" type="tns:unsignedInt" />
<complexType name="unsignedInt" base="unsignedInt" content="textOnly">
  <attributeGroup ref="tns:commonAttributes" />
```

```
  </complexType>
  <element name="unsignedShort" type="tns:unsignedShort" />
  <complexType name="unsignedShort" base="unsignedShort"
➥content="textOnly">
    <attributeGroup ref="tns:commonAttributes" />
  </complexType>
  <element name="unsignedByte" type="tns:unsignedByte" />
  <complexType name="unsignedByte" base="unsignedByte"
➥content="textOnly">
    <attributeGroup ref="tns:commonAttributes" />
  </complexType>
  <element name="positiveInteger" type="tns:positiveInteger" />
  <complexType name="positiveInteger" base="positiveInteger"
➥content="textOnly">
    <attributeGroup ref="tns:commonAttributes" />
  </complexType>
  <element name="timeInstant" type="tns:timeInstant" />
  <complexType name="timeInstant" base="timeInstant" content="textOnly">
    <attributeGroup ref="tns:commonAttributes" />
  </complexType>
  <element name="time" type="tns:time" />
  <complexType name="time" base="time" content="textOnly">
    <attributeGroup ref="tns:commonAttributes" />
  </complexType>
  <element name="timePeriod" type="tns:timePeriod" />
  <complexType name="timePeriod" base="timePeriod" content="textOnly">
    <attributeGroup ref="tns:commonAttributes" />
  </complexType>
  <element name="date" type="tns:date" />
  <complexType name="date" base="date" content="textOnly">
    <attributeGroup ref="tns:commonAttributes" />
  </complexType>
  <element name="month" type="tns:month" />
  <complexType name="month" base="month" content="textOnly">
    <attributeGroup ref="tns:commonAttributes" />
  </complexType>
  <element name="year" type="tns:year" />
  <complexType name="year" base="year" content="textOnly">
    <attributeGroup ref="tns:commonAttributes" />
  </complexType>
  <element name="century" type="tns:century" />
  <complexType name="century" base="century" content="textOnly">
    <attributeGroup ref="tns:commonAttributes" />
  </complexType>
  <element name="recurringDate" type="tns:recurringDate" />
  <complexType name="recurringDate" base="recurringDate"
```

```
➥content="textOnly">
  <attributeGroup ref="tns:commonAttributes" />
</complexType>
<element name="recurringDay" type="tns:recurringDay" />
<complexType name="recurringDay" base="recurringDay"
➥content="textOnly">
  <attributeGroup ref="tns:commonAttributes" />
</complexType>
  <!--
Element declarations and types corresponding to the ur-type in the
    W3C XML Schemas Specification. This is the soap
    representation for the type described as the ur-Type in the W3C
    schema specification.  This type will be dropped from the SOAP
    specification or modified appropriately if the W3C schema's
    workgroup can give us a proper xsd:ur-Type name soon enough
    for us to use, or else deprecated.

  -->
  <element name="ur-type" />
<complexType name="ur-type" />
</schema>
```

Resources

IN THIS APPENDIX

XML-Related

Specifications and General XML-Related Information

W3: http://www.w3.org

IETF: http://www.ietf.org

XML.COM: http://www.xml.com

OASIS: http://www.oasis-open.org/

XML-RPC: http://www.xmlrpc.com/

HP's E-speak: http://www.e-speak.net

XML Introduction: http://www.xml101.com

XML Parsers

The Apache XML Project: http://xml.apache.org

IBM: http://www2.software.ibm.com/developer/tools.nsf/xml-parsing-byname

Microsoft: http://msdn.microsoft.com/xml/default.asp

Oracle: http://technet.oracle.com/tech/xml

A more detailed list of available parsers can be found at
http://www.xml.com/pub/Guide/XML_Parsers

XML Resource Kit

Microsoft: http://msdn.microsoft.com/vstudio/xml/default.asp

XML and PHP

PHP with XML support: http://www.php.net/version4/

Periodicals

XML Developer's Journal: http://www.xmlmag.com

Books

Morrison, Michael. *XML Unleashed*. Sams Publishing (0-672-31514-9), 2000.

Pardi, William J. *XML in Action*. Microsoft Press (0-7356-0562-9), 1999.

SOAP-Related

DevelopMentor: `http://www.develop.com/soap`

SOAP Discussion Group: `http://discuss.develop.com`

A Look into Late-Breaking Technologies That Support SOAP

IN THIS APPENDIX

As this book was going to press, SOAP's popularity continues to increase. Naturally, some big players are incorporating SOAP into their systems and architectures, to the benefit of the computing public at large. This appendix, not originally planned to be included in the book, presents a brief overview of some technologies IBM, IONA, and Microsoft are releasing. This appendix is meant to whet your appetite for SOAP-related Windows services you can download and try.

IBM

If you're into Java and SOAP, you'll be excited about IBM's new Java language binding (see `http://www.alphaworks.ibm.com/aw.nsf/files?searchview&Query=DOWNSOAP+for+ JavaDOWN` to download). This implementation encodes your remote data in SOAP 1.1 format or according to IBM's XML Toolkit, which shares information between Java applications using XML and DTDs. But probably more exciting is the fact that IBM's implementation ships SOAP data via either HTTP or SMTP. If you'd like more information, visit IBM's AlphaWorks Internet site (`http://www.alphaworks.ibm.com`) or see the AlphaWorks SOAP discussion group at `http://www.alphaworks.ibm.com/aw.nsf/discussion?ReadForm&/forum/ soap4j.nsf/discussion?createdocument`.

IONA

You know IONA best as the creator of the first commercial CORBA ORB, but you'll also now know it as the company that brought SOAP to CORBA. IONA demonstrated its systems work with SOAP packets created by Microsoft's SOAP Toolkit at the 2000 TechEd conference (see `http://www.iona.com/pressroom/2000/20000605.htm` for more details). You can also send SOAP data to IONA yourself at `http://www.iona.com`.

Microsoft

As this book neared its completion, Keith Ballinger, a Microsoft program manager, heard of the book and offered to introduce you to some of the SOAP-related technology that is planned for Visual Studio 7.0. The authors would like to extend their sincere gratitude and appreciation to Keith, as well as to Rob Howard and Mike Culver of the Microsoft Corporation for their assistance and support. There is little doubt that if you develop software for Microsoft platforms you'll be seeing SOAP-enabled systems in the very near future. The information discussed below is based on a technology preview. This information may change. Microsoft will solidify this with the release of the next version of Visual Studio.

Web Services

The architectural model that Microsoft proposes will enhance the traditional client/server relationship you're used to seeing with distributed applications by introducing Web Services. Normally, a client (such as a browser, but it could be a thick client of any variety) connects to an HTTP server and accesses information internal to the server. The server may implement all manner of n-tier code, access a variety of back office data stores, and apply a vast number of business rules to the client's request. Typically, though, the server presents data internal to that site (see Figure C.1).

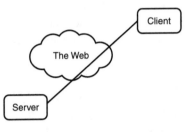

FIGURE C.1

Traditional distributed client/server architecture.

A Web Service allows you to provide capabilities, via the Internet, designed to enhance such traditional servers. That is, the client can now connect to a given server, which is then free to easily access information remote from that server, process it in some fashion, and then present the sum of that information to the client. This is shown in Figure C.2.

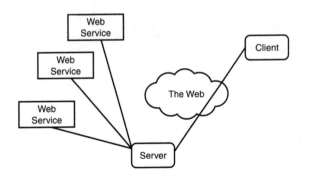

FIGURE C.2

Distributed client/server architecture using Web Services.

A Web Service is a programmable URI that makes accessing a Web site—or exposing information to be returned from a Web site—as easy as creating and using an object. In a sense, you program your distributed application using resources accessible to you without concern (or with little concern) as to whether those resources are local to your system. Your application's view of the Internet is that the Internet provides a smorgasbord of objects you can interact with to get your job done.

Naturally, the way Web Services deal with each other and with remote clients is by using SOAP, or by employing other, simpler protocols, depending upon their individual natures. This allows you to seamlessly share information with business partners (much like BizTalk) while providing a powerful and easy programming model.

Web Services are created using ASP+ and SDL, which you may remember from Chapter 8, "SOAP: BizTalk and the SOAP Toolkit." They're accessed using the NGWS SDK, which introduces the C# language (pronounced "C-Sharp," as in the musical notation). Let's look at each of these in turn.

ASP+

An enhanced version of Microsoft's Active Server Pages, ASP+ offers a new mechanism for exposing Web-oriented information. In addition to extended services through a new file type (.asmx) and the ability to compile your ASP+ pages into DLLs (versus simple script execution), ASP+ offers you attribute-based programming services. These enable you to easily call into play supported services and capabilities by simply adding an attribute to a method call (much like IDL).

For example, consider Listing C.1, which exposes a C#–based object designed to return two strings, depending upon the method invoked.

LISTING C.1 ASP+ Code to Be Exposed as a Web Service

```
<%@ WebService Language="C#" %>
using System;
using System.Web.Services;

public class HelloWorld {

    [ WebMethod ]
    public String SayHelloWorld() {
        return "Hello World";
    }

    [ WebMethod ]
    public String SayHelloName(String name) {
        return "Hello " + name;
    }
}
```

In this case, if a remote client is invoked during the SayHelloWorld() method, the ASP+ server would return the string "Hello World". If you were to look at the network bits and bytes, you would find that SOAP was used to make the remote method call and return the string data.

SDL

For simple remote method access, you may find it's enough to request a string or an integer and leave it at that. Many of the demonstration language bindings take this approach. But if you're interested in more complex interactions, you'll soon find you want to validate the SOAP-based XML using a schema. It would be even better if the schema conveyed some information regarding the intent of the remote method call. That is, if the remote method adds two integers and returns the result of that addition, you can make use of that information when checking the result or placing reasonable constraints on the input arguments.

This latter intent is the purpose of the Service Description Language, or SDL. SDL actually defines an XML grammar your Web Services use to express their capabilities, allowing them to expose the services they offer so you can better match the service you need.

Returning to the previous example, Listing C.2 shows you the corresponding SDL that the ASP+ server would use to export the two strings returnable through the HelloWorld class.

LISTING C.2   SDL Description of the HelloWorld ASP+ Class

```
<?xml version="1.0"?>
<serviceDescription xmlns:s0="http://tempuri.org/main.xsd"
  xmlns:s1="" name="HelloWorld" targetNamespace=""
  xmlns="urn:schemas-xmlsoap-org:sdl.2000-01-25">
  <soap xmlns="urn:schemas-xmlsoap-org:soap-sdl-2000-01-25">
    <service>
      <addresses>
        <address
          uri="http://comnet/services/HelloWorld/HelloWorld.asmx"/>
      </addresses>
      <requestResponse name="SayHelloWorld"
        soapAction="http://tempuri.org/SayHelloWorld">
        <request ref="s0:SayHelloWorld"/>
        <response ref="s0:SayHelloWorldResult"/>
      </requestResponse>
      <requestResponse name="SayHelloName"
        soapAction="http://tempuri.org/SayHelloName">
        <request ref="s0:SayHelloName"/>
        <response ref="s0:SayHelloNameResult"/>
      </requestResponse>
    </service>
```

continues

C

TECHNOLOGIES
THAT SUPPORT
SOAP

LISTING C.2 Continued

```
</soap>
  <httppost xmlns="urn:schemas-xmlsoap-org:post-sdl-2000-01-25">
    <service>
      <requestResponse name="SayHelloWorld"
➥href="http://comnet/services/HelloWorld/HelloWorld.asmx/SayHelloWorld">
        <request>
          <form/>
        </request>
        <response>
          <mimeXml ref="s1:string"/>
        </response>
      </requestResponse>
      <requestResponse name="SayHelloName"
➥href="http://comnet/services/HelloWorld/HelloWorld.asmx/SayHelloName">
        <request>
          <form>
            <input name="name"/>
          </form>
        </request>
        <response>
          <mimeXml ref="s1:string"/>
        </response>
      </requestResponse>
    </service>
  </httppost>
  <httpget xmlns="urn:schemas-xmlsoap-org:get-sdl-2000-01-25">
    <service>
      <requestResponse name="SayHelloWorld"
➥href="http://comnet/services/HelloWorld/HelloWorld.asmx/SayHelloWorld">
        <request/>
        <response>
          <mimeXml ref="s1:string"/>
        </response>
      </requestResponse>
      <requestResponse name="SayHelloName"
➥href="http://comnet/services/HelloWorld/HelloWorld.asmx/SayHelloName">
        <request>
          <param name="name"/>
        </request>
        <response>
          <mimeXml ref="s1:string"/>
        </response>
      </requestResponse>
    </service>
  </httpget>
  <schema targetNamespace="http://tempuri.org/main.xsd"
```

```
      xmlns="http://www.w3.org/1999/XMLSchema">
      <element name="SayHelloWorld">
        <complexType/>
      </element>
      <element name="SayHelloWorldResult">
        <complexType>
          <element name="result" type="string" nullable="true"/>
        </complexType>
      </element>
      <element name="SayHelloName">
        <complexType>
          <element name="name" type="string" nullable="true"/>
        </complexType>
      </element>
      <element name="SayHelloNameResult">
        <complexType>
          <element name="result" type="string" nullable="true"/>
        </complexType>
      </element>
    </schema>
    <schema targetNamespace=""
      xmlns="http://www.w3.org/1999/XMLSchema">
      <element name="string" type="string" nullable="true"/>
    </schema>
</serviceDescription>
```

As you can see from Listing C.2, the HelloWorld class's description is contained in an XML document bound by the serviceDescription tag. The serviceDescription tag contains several other tags:

- soap—Describes the SOAP packet itself
- schema—XML schemas associated with the SOAP data

Essentially, you are scripting the layout of the SOAP packets and telling external clients that you export certain methods composed of certain input and output argument data types.

C#

If there is a new technology around that helps you expose services over the Internet, there needs to be a way to easily access those services from the client. And, in fact, there is. Visual Studio 7 introduces the attribute-based COM programming model Mary Kirtland originally wrote about in the November and December 1997 editions of *Microsoft Systems Journal*. You saw C# used in the ASP+ code from Listing C.1. But you can also use C#, which resembles a combination of IDL and Java, to access a Web Service from a client (which may itself be a server to an third client).

To finish the HelloWorld class example, Listing C.3 shows you the C# code you'd use to access the remote methods HelloWorld exposes.

LISTING C.3 C# Code to Access the HelloWorld ASP+ Class

```csharp
using System.Xml.Serialization;
using System.Web.Services.Protocols;
using System.Web.Services;

public class HelloWorld : SoapClientProtocol {
    public HelloWorld() {
        this.Path =
            "http://comnet/services/HelloWorld/HelloWorld.asmx";
    }
    [SoapMethod("http://tempuri.org/SayHelloWorld")]
    public string SayHelloWorld() {
        object[] results = Invoke("SayHelloWorld", new object[] {});
        return (string)results[0];
    }
    public System.IasyncResult
    ➥BeginSayHelloWorld(System.AsyncCallback callback,
    ➥object asyncState) {
        return BeginInvoke("SayHelloWorld",
                            new object[] {},
                            callback,
                            asyncState);
    }
    public string EndSayHelloWorld(System.IAsyncResult asyncResult) {
        object[] results = EndInvoke(asyncResult);
        return (string)results[0];
    }
    [SoapMethod("http://tempuri.org/SayHelloName")]
    public string SayHelloName(string name) {
        object[] results =
                    Invoke("SayHelloName", new object[] {name});
        return (string)results[0];
    }
    public System.IasyncResult
    ➥BeginSayHelloName(string name,
    ➥System.AsyncCallback callback,
    ➥object asyncState) {
        return BeginInvoke("SayHelloName",
                            new object[] {name},
                            callback, asyncState);
    }
```

```
public string EndSayHelloName(System.IAsyncResult asyncResult) {
    object[] results = EndInvoke(asyncResult);
    return (string)results[0];
}
}
```

Keep in mind that the preceding code is auto-generated and you as the developer will never need to see it. The code developers will write is

```
HelloWorld h=new HelloWorld();
```

and then

```
h.SayHelloWorld
```

This is literally all a developer needs to do in order to use the HelloWorld service.

If you're used to looking at either IDL or Java, the syntax should look familiar. But look at this particularly interesting line of code:

```
[SoapMethod("http://tempuri.org/SayHelloWorld")]
```

The SoapMethod keyword is an attribute. (You can tell this because the entire line is enclosed in square brackets, [ ]). What makes this line of code so interesting is the power it packs behind the scenes. Given the URI you supply (http://tempuri.org/SayHelloWorld in this case), the underlying Microsoft SOAP infrastructure makes the remote call for you when you use the Invoke() method (imported from System.Web.Services):

```
Invoke("SayHelloWorld", new object[] {});
```

In this case, the SayHelloWorld() method of the HelloWorld ASP+ class is invoked at http://tempuri.org/SayHelloWorld. The entire method call, from a network perspective, is all SOAP.

INDEX

A

X-Z